WILLIAM ST

LECTURES ON EARLY
ENGLISH HISTORY

Elibron Classics
www.elibron.com

LECTURES

ON

EARLY ENGLISH HISTORY

LECTURES ON EARLY ENGLISH HISTORY.

By WILLIAM STUBBS, D.D., FORMERLY
BISHOP OF OXFORD AND REGIUS PROFESSOR
OF MODERN HISTORY IN THE UNIVERSITY
OF OXFORD

EDITED BY

ARTHUR HASSALL, M.A.

STUDENT OF CHRIST CHURCH, OXFORD

LONGMANS, GREEN, AND CO.
39 PATERNOSTER ROW, LONDON
NEW YORK AND BOMBAY
1906

PREFATORY NOTE

THIS collection of Lectures, delivered at various times by Bishop Stubbs, will prove a valuable addition to our authorities for Early English History.

The Constitution under the Early English and Norman Kings is described very clearly, and the full explanations given of the technical terms which are used in the Laws and Charters of the Norman Kings are a very noticeable feature in many of the Lectures.

All students of Stubbs's ' Select Charters ' will find in many of these Lectures elucidations of passages which have hitherto presented great difficulty. It is not too much to say that for the first time historians have been presented with a full commentary upon the most difficult portions of the ' Select Charters.'

The later Lectures are upon general subjects connected with Early English History. An account and comparison of Early European Constitutions, and discussions upon the character of the Early Ecclesiastical Systems in Europe, of the origins of the European Land System, and of European Law, represent but a few of the interesting and important topics treated of by the learned writer. The volume closes with an admirable Lecture upon the Beginnings of English Foreign Policy.

In preparing this invaluable collection of treatises for the press, very great difficulty has been experienced in deciphering the manuscript of the Lectures upon ' The Laws and Legislation of the Norman Kings.' In view of the extreme value of these Lectures, it was, however, thought advisable to publish them, even though some still further revision may be required in a future edition. As they stand these Lectures will be of enormous assistance to students of the Norman period, who will profit greatly from a careful perusal of

the weighty remarks of Bishop Stubbs on the administration of the
Norman Kings.

Though much new light has been thrown on many points in
the period covered by these Lectures by the works of Professors
Vinogradoff, Pollock, and Maitland, and of Mr. Round, it will be found
that in the main the conclusions arrived at by Bishop Stubbs are
still accepted by the best authorities, and that in many respects the
results achieved by the labours of the above-named distinguished
historians not only corroborate the views expressed in this volume,
but increase our admiration of the learning which it contains.

A. H.

CONTENTS

Errata et Corrigenda

I

THE ANGLO-SAXON CONSTITUTION

THE history of our country is in one way of looking at it the history of ourselves ; it is the history of our mind and body—of our soul and spirit also—for it tells how our fathers before us became what they were, and how our ways depart from or resemble theirs—how they won the liberties in which we have grown to be what we are—how they received and modified and handed down to us the inheritance of the old times before them—how the true history of a people is the history of its laws and institutions, more especially of its manners : and manners, as we know, maketh man.

The knowledge of our own history is our memory, and so the recorded history of a nation is the memory of the nation : woe to the country and people that forget it; an infant people has no history, as a child has a short and transient memory : the strong man and the strong nation feel the pulsation of the past in the life of the present: their memory is vital, long and strong. Neglect of historical study and knowledge is to a nation what the loss of memory is to a man—a sign of old age and decrepitude, or the effect of some terrible disease in an individual; it is in a nation a sign of lost independence in manners and ways of thought—a moral decrepitude waxed old and ready to vanish away ; or perhaps in this case also the result of some terrible convulsion—a wave of revolution rolling over the land, overthrowing laws and institutions, and washing away old landmarks, as you may see in the France of this day. The lives and memories of no two men are alike : the true life of any one man is fuller of inconsistencies and anomalies than any fictitious or imaginary tale. While we speak time flies, and we cease at the end of a word to be physically the same beings that we were at the beginning. So also history is full of anomalies and single events giving colouring to periods and making things to be what they are ; and as there are anomalies in every history, so there is a history for every anomaly. Our constitution is full of such, so are our time-honoured customs, our laws and liturgy, our terri- torial divisions, our language written and spoken. Each of these is a growth of a thousand years, and every irregularity in each has a history, if we could get at it, more or less precious, and certainly interesting to one who will take the trouble of exploring it.

The tendency of the present day is to destroy these historical specialities : the Ecclesiastical Commission has done for our ecclesiastical fabric what phonetic science was to have done for our language and what certain persons want to do for our Prayer Book. Much may be said for simplification and equalisation in such things ; but gold itself may be bought too dear, and every improvement based on such principles has a heavy counterbalance in the destruction of historical associations, in the disidentifying ourselves with our forefathers and with what helped to make our country great. We hear of the dead past and the living present : we are bid (and we do well to remember that it is an American poet who so adapts the words) to let the dead past bury its dead. But surely the past lives in the present, the process by which we became what we are is a part of our living being ; if we are cut off from what we were, we only half live.

The old map of France is full of memories—recollections of Gaul and Rome, the empire of the Cæsars, Burgundians and Aquitanians, Franks and Armoricans—Clovis, Charles the Great, and St. Louis—knights, troubadours, saints, and heroes. The history of the land was written on its face. The map of modern France is a catalogue of hills and rivers, a record of centralisation, codification, universal suffrage, government by policemen. Probably the work of simplification will never be carried so far in England, but there is a tendency towards it, which is a sign of the decline of independent thought and character, as I said before.

Look at an old church, any old church you like ; you will find in every peculiarity of its structure and decoration something that has a history and a bearing on the general history of the place and country it stands in. The tracery of its windows, the moulding of its cornices, tell of different epochs of architecture, each of which has a definite relation to a period of history : the rude work called Saxon work, or even—as in some churches you find—the still earlier remains of Roman brickwork, the round massive columns and arches of Norman art, the elegant Early English lancet, the beautiful Decorated work of the Edwardian period, the square-headed Tudor work, the Elizabethan, the Jacobæan work of the chancels so common in Essex, and last and least the cheap and dirty work of the reign of George III. The very names of these styles connect the building with the history of the nation. Not to speak of the direct materials for history that may be found in the sepulchral monuments on the walls, there are in every church signs and tokens of changes in religious thought and ritual—disused furniture, such as holy-water stoups and sacring-bell cots, remains of broken windows of stained glass, that could tell, if they might speak, a touching tale of three periods at least of change. Like an old soldier who has a story for every scar that marks him from his brothers, every old building, church or not, has a history for every broken stone.

How do our parishes come to be bounded with the boundaries that do bound them? Why are they so different in size and shape and population and endowments? Why is one part in this manor and another in that? Why is one in this county and another in Hertfordshire? Why are we at all in the diocese of Rochester or the hundred of Chafford? Why and how is Brentwood a hamlet, and South Weald a mother church? Who burned the original and 'not ignoble' wood that gave name to this place? Here are a lot of questions that now admit perhaps of very dim and scanty answers, but which tell of the certain existence of causes by the existence of the effects. To explore the minutiæ of such things is the province of antiquarian research. Antiquarian topography and genealogy are most interesting studies, and supply the matter in great measure from which history, written history, is obliged to borrow in order to construct and correct itself. It is not my province now and here to go into anything that concerns them. History deals more with generalities, and a short view of history such as can be embraced in a lecture must deal with very wide generalities. I am not, for instance, to tell you why a man is in the county of Essex, or the diocese of Rochester, or the hundred of Chafford, or the parish of Weald; but I may tell you something as to how it comes to pass that you are here at all—what is a county, a diocese, a hundred, a parish, or a township. When I come to the feudal system we can talk about manors and freeholds and copyholds; and if you like to follow the stream further down than I intend to take you, you may come in time to unravel for yourselves the equally mysterious arrangements of poor law unions and postal districts and sanitary jurisdictions and boards of works.

It is to Ancient Germany that we must look for the earliest traces of our forefathers, for the best part of almost all of us is originally German: though we call ourselves Britons, the name has only a geographical significance. The blood that is in our veins comes from German ancestors. Our language, diversified as it is, is at the bottom a German language; our institutions have grown into what they are from the common basis of the ancient institutions of Germany. The Jutes, Angles, and Saxons were but different tribes of the great Teutonic household; the Danes and Norwegians, who subdued them in the north and east, were of the same origin ; so were the Normans : the feudal system itself was of Frank, i.e. also German origin. Even if there is still in our blood a little mixture of Celtic ingredient derived from the captive wives of the first conquerors, there is no leaven of Celticism in our institutions. The rights of women were not much respected, one would fear, in such connections. The question whether it is so or not might be interesting, but there is next to no evidence either way.

It is a very fortunate thing for the German races that we have from the pens of two such writers as Cæsar and Tacitus a sketch of the institutions of their fathers as they were flourishing 1800 years since : a sketch indeed fragmentary, meagre, and obscure, but all the better for that ; those very faults are a proof of genuineness. They do not guarantee the accuracy, but they do guarantee the good faith of the writers : a man evolving history (as our German cousins are fond of doing) out of his own consciousness would have drawn a much more complete and consistent and clear picture. I am not going now to trouble you with the details of those sketches, we have not time to do so; and those who know enough Latin to understand them can easily search them out for themselves, while to those who do not it would be unintelligible to enter into them : I must confine myself to the conclusions that the laborious students of those and suchlike sources have arrived at.

It is a very common thing to speak of Anglo-Saxon laws and institutions as if they were something definite and invariable for the time during which the race was independent and supreme. Just as foolish would it be to consider the Anglo-Saxon language to be as definite and fixed as classical Latin, or Anglo-Saxon architecture as regular and uniform as that of the most formal period of Italian or Greek art. I have heard it observed that history has been written on the assumption that all the Anglo-Saxons were alive at the same time : Hengist and Horsa, Ina and Offa, Edward and Harold are all clubbed together as kites and crows; for as such John Milton, a great poet but an execrable historian, is pleased to designate the heroes of the Heptarchy. We will guard ourselves at the outset from this silly blunder, remembering that as to time the authentic history of Anglo-Saxon law reaches from Ethelbert to Harold, a space of 460 years : that as to origin, it is indeed all radically German, and the germs of much of it may be discovered in the German customs of the age of Cæsar and Tacitus, but that these germs had by the commencement of the historical period developed in different ways among different tribes : so that the laws of the different nations who conquered Britain might, if we possessed them, be found to possess only a family resemblance, as those of successors certainly do :

further, that the conquerors came from different parts of Germany and at different periods, and brought some full-grown institutions with them, of which not even the germs can be traced in the earlier settlers. So far from being an age of uniform stagnation, it was a period of ever varying growth and development, scarcely a century passing that did not bring some new influence to bear on it, scarcely two divisions moving on at the same rate or in the same direction. It would require a long series of volumes to trace these differences as to their historical causes and effects; and such an investigation would probably interest only legal antiquaries. It is to those most conspicuous developments and most lasting institutions that have left their marks on the map of the land or on the manners and customs of the nation, that we must devote the short time allotted to a lecture like this.

The earliest form of community of which we can find a trace is that described by Tacitus : a body of men living together in separate district dwellings with no several ownership in land, but cultivating the common estate in portions which were changed and redistributed every year. Cæsar describes the Suevi as having no several or private estates, and as not inhabiting the same lands for more than a year. This seems to be a sign of earlier customs than Tacitus found existing. Cæsar does indeed represent the Suevi as nomads. Tacitus says of the German agricultural races generally : ' The lands are held by the collective community, according to the number of cultivators, turn by turn : afterwards they divide them according to their estimation among themselves—the wide extent of the plains makes these constant partitions a matter of no difficulty—they change their cultivated lands every year, and there is land over.' I have translated the passage literally, and you see how involved it is. I will not lead you into the mazes which contradicting critics have woven round it. It seems to hint, however, at two descriptions of property—the actually divided and allotted property on the one hand, and that held in common by the community—private and public lands. Indeed, it seems almost impossible that a settled community could exist, inhabiting houses such as Tacitus describes, 'not,' he says, ' as in our fashion with buildings joined to and communicating with one another, but each house surrounded by an open space, either for the prevention of fires or owing to their ignorance in building ;' it seems impossible that a community could exist in this way without private estate in land. Each cottage would demand a garden, a cornfield, a stableyard, an orchard. The race was no longer a nomad race that could dispense with such—settled habitations involve privacy, and every man's house is his castle. Imagine, then, a tract of land as extensive as a large English parish ; surround it with a belt of wood a mile or two in breadth ; dot little cottages or farms about it at consistent distances, each with its hide of land attached to it ; mark out these hides or private properties from the rest of the land. This rest continues to be the property of the community—it will be divided into allotments as the increase of population requires it, or some one who requires rewarding for great services will have a slice cut from it for himself, or, perhaps, in the end, a king or duke may rise up and get it all. Now, however, in the state of primitive equality, some portion of it is arable and let out to the richer and larger families in consideration of bearing certain burdens and payments to the community ; some remains in pasture, and each man has common pasture rights upon it. The woodland round the settlement is not divided nor divisible, but is sacred to the gods ; it is called the mark, and the inhabitants of the settlement have a sort of right to turn out their swine to eat the mast and acorns it produces. The inhabitants of the settlement are probably all akin to one another : in this point of view they are called the *mægth* or kindred. Their land, as well as the boundary round it, is called the *mark*, and the name is applied to the community itself as a settled occupier of land. Several marks constitute a gau or ga, analogous in some measure to the hundreds of later times ; several ga's make up a scyr ; several scyrs in process of time make up a kingdom or county, governed by an ealdorman, earl, or count. Each of these divisions—the mark proper, the gau, the shire, the kingdom—has its proper belt of uninhabited land around it. Cæsar tells us that the Suevi in particular held it the highest public glory for the mark to be as wide as possible, as a token that for their prowess no other nation dare come near them. In one place the march on the borders of the Suevi extended 600 miles. These larger marks, or marches, were kept in memory for many ages. The lords president of the marches of Wales were officers of state all through the middle ages. The title of marquis, marchio, markgrave, margrave is still existent. There is still an earl of a march whose ancestors guarded the march between England and Scotland. This wider use of the word is worth remark, but must not cause confusion.

Whenever I have occasion to speak of a mark in this lecture, I shall mean the first or primary community, the village, the vicus. Well, Britain was a conquered country, and the conquerors as soon as they were settled divided the lands in the way I have described. Every free household had a hide of land of its own, an alod, an ethel : there was besides this the public land held in common now and to be divided in time. On this common land possibly the old British proprietors were suffered to remain as tenants, or possibly it was cultivated by slaves, or still more probably the cultivation devolved on landless freemen, sons of allodial proprietors who had not yet got an alod for themselves. Of a state of things exactly like this we have, I believe, no direct record : it is not likely that we should, for the use of direct records was primarily to fix the ownership and tenure of lands ; and as soon as direct records begin to exist, the division of land is not simply into allodial and public land, but into bocland and folcland, that is land held by title deeds as freehold of inheritance and land held of the community in consideration of certain services.   But the division into bocland and folcland is not an exhaustive one.   There were many allodial estates which had existed long before title deeds were invented ; others that were conveyed by the gift of a horn or a clod of grass or some other token, and of these especially were grants for religious endowments.   There were therefore three kinds of estates, allodial, and secondly the bocland, and in the third place the folcland.   The allodial proprietor held his land of no one : he was bound of no homage : he was free, he owned no lord or king over his estate ; but he was subject to what is called the *trinoda necessitas*, the duty of contributing to the building of bridges and castles, and of serving as a soldier in defence of the community, *pontis et arcis edificatio, et expeditio*.   The tenants of folcland had, on the other hand, besides these duties, a liability to have strangers, messengers, horses, hawks, and hounds quartered on them by government ; the duty of entertaining and sustaining the king and his officers and servants on their journeys, and of providing them with carriages and horses ; and several others.

Proceeding from this meagre sketch of the land to the description of the persons who hold it and cultivate it, we find of course our first division into free and unfree.   The unfree, slaves, theows or eones, were either the remains of the Ancient Britons, called also Wealas or Welshmen, or they were prisoners of war, or criminals condemned to penal servitude, or persons who had sold themselves into captivity for the purpose of raising a sum of money, or as the result of gambling transactions, which were not uncommon.

The free are divided exhaustively into *eorl* and *ceorl*, noble by birth and non-noble, but all originally possessed of land as the basis of freedom and citizenship.   This simple and primary distinction is, however, early in historic times replaced by others ; the churl, indeed, retains his title, but sinks in position into the villain of later times.   The eorl, the noble by birth, ceases to be conspicuous in that dignity, and reappears as the ealdorman, or is revived as the Danish jarl or the Norman earl, or as the gesith, companion, comes or count, or thane and servant of the semi-feudalised court.   This calls for an explanation at greater length, and we must look at the development of an aristocracy of blood into one of power, wealth, and preponderating influence in government.

We have seen the mark inhabited by its free settlers, friends and kinsmen. Among friends and kinsmen even in the patriarchal stage quarrels arise, and much more so when the lapse of a few generations has loosened the tie of kindred, and spread an increased population over a confined space. Every community had a judge—perhaps at first the eldest or wisest member of the kin, the ealdorman in its primary signification, later the elected magistrate, the reeve, graf, or graphio, the origin of whose name is unknown. The mark reeve presided in the courts of the mark; the gau-reeve, if there was such a person, in the courts of the gau; the shire-reeve or sheriff in the scyrmote or county court. These were originally all elective officers. In time of war each mark and scyr contributed its quota to the army—the command of the national army was entrusted to a heretoga, herzog, duke or leader, who would probable choose his own officers. In this heretogaship or elective commandership originated the royalty of the German races. The kings were the elected generals in war, chosen from the nobles, mostly of the race of Woden. I need not describe the stages by which such an office becomes first perpetual, then hereditary in one family, then subject to the ordinary laws of succession by primogeniture or otherwise. The Anglo-Saxons had arrived at the hereditary stage when they came to Britain.[1] They had kings—cyn-ing—the son or child of the kin or race. Although in a manner hereditary, the crown was not strictly so in our acceptation of the term. When the king died, his successor was chosen from his family, sometimes the eldest, sometimes the wisest or the richest or most able, not until later times necessarily the nearest in blood. The royal domain consisted, of course, of the original alod of the leader elected, of such portions of the folcland as were allotted to him in consideration of his services, and latterly at least the folcland itself, the duties and services payable by the tenants of it, such as sustenance &c., but it does not appear that the folcland was ever so vested in the king that he could alienate it or turn it into bocland without the consent of the community in the witenagemot or scyrgemot, parliament or county court.

Given a king, a new order of nobility was sure to arise—nobility by service. The ancient leaders of the Germans surrounded themselves with a court of brave men, the heroes and wise men of the nation. These are called the king's gesiths or companions, his servants or thanes; his comites or counts; his principes or princes.[2]

---

[1] Lappenberg thinks not, and makes Ælle of Sussex the first (ii. 308).

[2] King's followers, geferscipo, folgarth. Lapp. ii. 311; Tacitus, *Germ.* 81.

Of course many of these were noble by birth, but it was by no means necessary : they were enriched by the king with estates cut out of the folcland, they were the king's men, and so far forth were unfree.[1] They were not feudal vassals, for the essence of that relation was in the tenure of land : there was no such in the character of the gesith—he was personally, and not by reason of his tenure, the king's man and creature. The king furnished him with a horse and armour to go to war in ; and when he died the gift was returned to the king under the name of the heriot : his lands did not descend hereditarily unless under special deed.

Of the gesiths or thanes themselves there were two classes, the ealdorman, who owned forty hides of land, and the smaller thane, who owned five ; but these distinctions seem to come in after the nobility by service had become hereditary and the gesithship to have been lost sight of. The thaneship was now even within reach of the churl who could scrape together the five hides of land, the merchant who had made three voyages on his own account, or the British unfree tenant who had acquired the requisite territory. Next in dignity to the king were the æthelings, his sons or near relations, then the ealdormen, then the simple thanes ; next to them the churls. Of course the offices of the court were at first personal, not hereditary : there was the staller, that is the marshal or high constable ; the discthegn, dapifer or high steward ; the pincerna or cupbearer ; the chamberlain or bower thane, who was also the high treasurer ; the hrægelthegn or keeper of the robes ; traces of these offices subsist to this day. This was the court. But besides this there were numerous inferior officers, reeves of the king : for the king had his town reeve, and village reeve, and sheriffs to look after his interests, as the elective reeves represented the communities.

Before we proceed to take a view of the way in which the government was conducted, we must first give a glance at the church. The conversion of the Anglo-Saxons to Christianity followed immediately upon the establishment of their supremacy in Britain : placing their arrival about 450, 150 years may be allowed for the conquest. In 597 the conversion began, and the ecclesiastical organisation was completed by Theodore before 690. A comparison of these dates will show that as soon as the admitted supremacy of the invaders gave scope for their national institutions to work orderly, they are pervaded and modified by a new influence which had not been present in the land of their origin. The most ancient Anglo-Saxon laws that we possess are the laws of Ethelberht, the first Christian

---

[1] King Stephen made comites on this principle, and endowed them out of the demesne. W. Malmesb. *Hist. Nov.* c. ult.

king. Another very important result of the introduction of Christianity and the organisation of the church by Archbishop Theodore in the south and Archbishop Egberht in the north, was this. There was no English state—no commonwealth, no kingdom of England as yet : there were the eight great kingdoms of the Heptarchy, there were the subkingships as of the East and West Kentings, the North and South Gyrvii, the Hwiccas, the Magasætas, and many others. Each of these was independent of his neighbour : they came from different parts of Germany, spoke different dialects, used different laws. There was occasionally a bretwalda, a sort of emperor over the whole, from time to time ; but of his functions, if he had any, nothing at all is known. Every district was independent of every other. Mercia had no rights in Wessex, or Wessex in East Anglia : there was no bond, no unity in the land.

On the other hand, the church was one, well organised and regulated and closely united by every possible bond. There were eight kingdoms, but there were only two ecclesiastical provinces, York and Canterbury : the tribes that owned the political sway of six kings all obeyed spiritually the see of Canterbury. Every bishop had as a basis of his authority not the mere nomination or acceptance of the king within whose dominion his diocese lay, but the unity and fellowship of fifteen or sixteen other bishops under the archbishop, each precisely in the same circumstances, a unity and fellowship over which the royal power had no control. Now we might suppose that such a state of things was likely to lead to quarrels between church and state. But it was not so : whether it was that the kings were so pious as always to choose good bishops, or that the bishops were so strong that it was no use for the king to contest with them, or that the actual power and efficiency of the church machinery was less prolific of effects than we should expect, I cannot say ; but it is clear that there were very few quarrels between the two powers before the Conquest, hardly any before the time of Egberht and the union of the Heptarchy, except the great one that exalted Lichfield for a few years into an archbishop's see, in the reign of Offa.

The result of this peaceable working of church and state side by side was twofold. In the first place, it promoted the gradual uniting of the kingdoms. The people were in all spiritual matters one nation already. When one king fell in battle, or one royal family became extinct, and Mercia or Wessex annexed the vacant dominion, there was no repulsion on the part of the people ; it was easy for them to become one politically as they had long been religiously. The other result was this : that the bishops were not only ecclesiastical but civil functionaries. Every bishop sat with the king and his gesiths in the witenagemot or great council of the kingdoms; and in the shiremotes the bishop sat and judged with the ealdorman, or, in his absence, the king's shire-reeve or sheriff. Nor was their dignity in any respect less than that of their civil compeers. The life of an archbishop was estimated at the same rate of compensation with that of a prince of the blood ; that of a bishop with that of an ealdorman ; that of a priest who had an endowment of five hides, with that of a thane.[1] But of this we shall have to speak by-and-by.

The legislative functions of government were discharged by the witenagemot—the meeting of the wise men—the king and his bishops and abbots, the ealdormen of the shires, and such other councillors as they or the king summoned for the purpose. In these meetings laws were proposed and sanctioned, grants of folcland made and ratified, appeals heard in the last resort, and general measures consulted on and taken for the welfare of the kingdom. It was in a witenagemot of Northumbria that Christianity was nationally adopted ; in a witenagemot of all England that Edward the Confessor was elected. Probably the elections of bishops and ealdormen were settled at these meetings, if not formally transacted through them. From the witenagemot we must carefully distinguish the ecclesiastical council, although constituted very much of the same persons and held at the same time and place. These assemblies were strictly confined to spiritual matters. Before the consolidation of the Heptarchy there were occasionally national or provincial councils, at which two or three kings were present ; but these were purely religious assemblies, and could not interfere authoritatively in politics.

In a state of society so simple as that of the Anglo-Saxons a very remote court of appeal was hardly needed ; and probably only a very small proportion of causes reached the appellate jurisdiction of the witenagemot. In general, they went no further than the county court. This, the shiremote or county court, was the great judicial resort of the people. We have seen how the mark was constituted, how a certain number of marks constituted a gau or a hundred, and how a number of gaus or hundreds made up the shire. We must now look at them in the reverse order, and describe the shire as divided into hundreds, and the hundreds into tithings. I do not mean to say that these divisions exactly correspond, for I believe the mark to have been the original unit of community, whereas the tithing does not appear before the age of Canute ; but for most practical purposes they must have nearly coincided. A tithing contained probably ten free families ; and a hundred, ten tithings, i.e. originally a hundred free families. You must know that there

[1] *Select Charters*, p. 65.

is a never-ending dispute among antiquaries as to the origin of hundreds ; for they are of all sorts and sizes, and no theory will apply to account for all ; some of the small shires having the largest number, and the largest counties the smallest. It appears to me probable that each hundred contained in the first instance ten tithings, or a hundred free families ; and that as soon as the enumeration was made, the shire was divided into hundreds with local names and boundaries. In a few generations, the number of free families increasing, new tithings would be formed ; but instead of forming new hundreds to take them in, and so necessitating a redivision of the whole shire, the most natural course would be to affiliate the new tithings to the hundred in which they locally were. So the institution of tithing remaining, the name of hundred would lose its original applicability, as we know it did in other cases, in the Roman civil centuriæ and military centuries especially. Now, each of these divisions had its court : the tithing court was probably little more than a modern vestry meeting—the tithing man, so far as his judicial functions went, was about on a par with a petty constable ; and the court of the hundred and the shiremote were the real administrators of justice.

In the shiremote the ealdorman, or in his absence the sheriff, with the bishop presided ; but all the thanes sat as assessors, and the inferior freemen also were summoned to attend. In it the civil and criminal causes of the county were investigated and decided. In its criminal jurisdiction it must be looked on as parallel to our courts of quarter session, and in its civil administration to the operation of the newly restored county courts. It moreover decided causes connected with land which come under neither of these tribunals. The part that the churls had in this jurisdiction was but small, for they did not constitute juries : trial by jury was not yet. Still they had duties : oaths of allegiance to take, frankpledges to enter into, and possibly arbitrations to decide among themselves. The judges were the bishop and ealdorman, with the thanes as assessors.

The hundredmote, or court of the hundred, was held under the writ of the sheriff, presided over by its hundred-man, and its power was restricted to its own hundred. It punished small offences and exercised view of frankpledge. The mention of frankpledge takes us down again to the tithing.

Every tithing contained ten freemen : every freeman must belong to a tithing ; every ten freemen constituted a distinct tithing. The members of each tithing were responsible for each other's good behaviour : in this relation the tithing was called a frith-borh, or security for peace, and in later times frankpledge, which seems to be a corruption of the term.[1] The members of the frith-borh were bound to produce in the court of justice any one of their number who was summoned. They were a sort of perpetual bail for one another. If one of them was accused and failed to appear, they might purge themselves by oath of being accessary to his flight; if they could not do so, they were obliged to make good the penalty of the offence of which he was accused. This institution is, as I said, of late growth: it was not until the time of Canute that it was made obligatory on every freeman. The obligation was examined into in the sheriff's hundred court. This examination or seeing into the frankpledges was called *visus franciplegii*, view of frankpledge. One of the ten was called a tithing-man, headborough, or constable, who represented his tithing in the courts and acted as a petty constable. In another point of view the tithing would often be coextensive with the township; and as a township sent a reeve and four freemen to represent it in the shiremote and hundred court, a tithing was in the north of England called a ten-man's-tale.

Besides the security of frankpledges every man was bound to have a lord or patron in whose protection or mund he was. As the frith-borh secured his responsibility to justice, the protection of the mund was intended to secure justice for him. If he was slain or injured, the mund was said to be broken, and the culprit had to make a compensation to the lord as well as to the relations of the injured person. We shall see presently how the custom of the mund was one of the most efficient preparations for the reception of feudalism.

I have now glanced at most of the remarkable institutions of the Anglo-Saxon races: it remains to say a few words, at the risk of seeming tedious, on the leading Anglo-Saxon laws and customs. The most cursory view of the subject would be very incomplete without them.

The first of these is the wergild, the compensation that the criminal was bound to make to the family and protectors of the injured, especially of the slain. Capital punishment was inflicted only in cases of foul murder,[2] arson, and theft: the exaction of the penalty was left to the will and execution of the injured party. But besides the capital penalty, and in cases where it was not exacted, there was a wergild to be paid. This differed according to a regular table of values. The life of a king was esteemed at 7,200 shillings,[3] that of the ætheling or the archbishop at 3,600, that of a bishop or an ealdorman at 1,200 shillings, that of an inferior thane at 600, that of a simple ceorl at 200. There were other valuations for Britons and slaves

---

[1] Frith-borh, corr. fri-borh, tr. frankpledge.
[2] Conspiracy against the king's life. L. Alfr. Lapp. iii. 310.
[3] Wergild for king peculiar to Anglo-Saxons.

Besides the wergild, there were the following money penalties in case of murder : the king's mund, or fine for breach of his protection ; healsfang, or commutation for the pillory ; manbot, compensation to the lord or patron for the loss of his man ; and frith-wite, a fine due to the crown for breach of peace. Besides capital punishment, there were banishment, outlawry, and mutilation for theft. Wergilds or *bots* were not payable only for murder ; there was a regular tariff of wounds to be compensated by money payments. The piercing of the nose was estimated at 9 shillings, other wounds in it at 6 shillings apiece, 3 shillings a nostril ; 50 shillings an eye ; 12 for an ear— if one ear be deaf, 25 ; a thumb nail, 3 ; the thumb itself, 20 ; the shooting or forefinger, 8 ; the middle finger, 4 ; the gold or ring finger, 6 ; the little finger, 11. Even when the wergild was paid, the manslayer was not safe until he had paid a further bot, by which he redeemed himself from feud or enmity on the part of the relations of the slain.

The second point I have to remark on is process of trial. It used to be a favourite theory that trial by jury was a legacy of our early Anglo-Saxon forefathers. Modern lawyers have decided that the institution in its true character is not of so early a date. The error arose from a confusion between such trial and that which really took place. The real judges were the bishop and ealdorman or sheriff with the thanes as assessors. The number of twelve thanes was convenient and probably usual: it is fixed by a law of Ethelred II. Obviously it is a very different thing for a ceorl to be tried by twelve thanes and for every man to be tried as now by a jury of his equals.

There is another point that has lent assistance to the old theory. If a man denied that he was guilty of the act he was charged with, he was allowed to clear himself by producing twelve of his equals who were to swear with him that he was innocent. If he was under a lord, the lord or his reeve might come forward and swear that he had not failed in oath or ordeal since the last court day, after which the accused might clear himself by ordeal, or by his own oath and that of his companions. If the lord could not so swear, thrice the number of compurgators must be forthcoming. Each man's oath had a value proportioned to his rank, and if an accused thane could not find twelve thanes to swear for him, he might make up the number by supplying six ceorls for each. The accuser was obliged also to support his charge by the oaths of compurgators, but a smaller number was sufficient. The germ of the present system may possibly be traced in the number twelve, and in the assumed equality of the compurgators ; it is difficult to find any nearer approach to the custom.

The system of ordeal is probably sufficiently known to you all. Neither trial by combat nor ordeal by the corsnæd, hot water, hot iron, or otherwise, was in common use except in cases where the accused had forfeited his credit by some previous crime or was unable to produce compurgators.

Almost all the foregoing remarks, although primarily applicable to a country population, are true of the inhabitants of towns and cities : we ought further to notice the origin of municipal institutions during the same period. As, however, this subject will come largely into the next two lectures, in its relation to the feudal system and to the growth of our parliamentary constitution, I will not dwell upon it now at length. The principal influences to be noticed are the ecclesiastical ones, the protection afforded by a great monastery to the town growing up under its walls, and the commercial ones. The latter, which are of course most apparent in maritime towns, are traceable in the frith-gilds, voluntary associations of trade, for mutual security, each governed by an ealdorman, the lineal predecessors of the aldermen of the present day. These gilds—and they were religious as well as commercial—acquired first a legal recognition and status, then endowments, subsequently a municipal unity, in consideration of which they were allowed to acquire the franchises of the city, soc and sac &c. on paying a rent or farm to the lord of it, who in most instances was the king. We shall see another day how these franchises ripened into boroughs and cities. The city of London is the best known and most eminent of course among them.

These, then, are the laws under which our fathers grew for 450 years, and which have left their marks so conspicuous upon our map and statute book. Those of us who live in Essex live not in a department of the Chelmer and Thames, but in the ancient kingdom of Essex, the realm of the East Saxons ; we have at the head of our magistracy not a prefect, but a lord lieutenant much in the same position as the ealdorman of old ; the courts are held by the shire-reeve in the shire hall. Our thanes are represented by county magistrates, the shiremoot by the quarter sessions, the hundred motes by the petty sessions and sheriffs' court of tourn and leet. The old names of hundreds and deaneries retain something of their meaning still. Our bishops and thanes represent us in the witena-gemote ; and our ruler is the cyn-ing, the child of the nation.

In other respects all is changed. We have a proper system of jurisprudence instead of partial and local statutes ; trial by jury instead of compurgation and ordeal ; local self-government is becoming less and less the rule among us. Still there is much unchanged and much unchangeable.

A slight knowledge of history is enough to show that these laws and customs grew up under difficulties, that nearly all the Anglo-Saxon period was a time of war, sometimes internal, more generally against foreign invaders. These invaders were of the same original stock with the invaded. They conquered full half of England, the north and east; but owing to the system begun by Alfred and perfected by Canute they amalgamated with the Anglo-Saxons so entirely that before the Conquest they were one people. Some of the institutions that I have mentioned were perhaps Danish rather than Anglo-Saxon: they gave as well as received. Notwithstanding all this, the race was great in arms and art; the Anglo-Saxon merchants were found in all marts, the Anglo-Saxon manuscript painting is of the most refined and elegant description, their gold work was the astonishment of continental artificers. It was by Anglo-Saxon missionaries from the seventh to the eleventh centuries that Germany, Sweden, Denmark, Norway, and Iceland were converted to the gospel. The age of flourishing literature was over long before the Conquest; but there were still poets and prose writers in the monasteries who kept up the fame of the island of Bede and Alcuin.

I have left to the last the most interesting inquiry of all. What virtues were these institutions the most likely to foster, and which to neglect? No doubt their general tendency was to produce independence of character: local self-government was especially the discipline of self-reliance: the Anglo-Saxon was always a brave man. But the discipline of self-reliance is not the same as that of self-restraint, and we are hardly surprised to learn that our fathers, brave as they were, were temperate neither in appetite nor passion. Then, again, too great independence is incompatible with obedience, and the Anglo-Saxons had but a very poor talent for obeying—for putting their own immediate views, likings, and interests out of sight for the common good. If they had been more disciplined they would have been more united—the battle of Hastings would not have decided the fate of the kingdom. That Harold, who possessed all the qualities needed for a great national leader, was unable to unite the nation, is a proof that something more was wanted to make them great: that discipline they got in the grinding despotism of the Norman kings and under the machinery of the feudal system. Happily the despotism did not grind their independence out of them; more happily still, the feudal system taught them loyalty and obedience. The admixture of the two is needed to make a great people. Poland was once an independent republic, so independent as to be almost anarchical: it was the standing nuisance of Europe; its crown was bought and sold; its princes were Arabs, every man's hand against his neighbour. So when it had made all the world its enemies, it was found too weak to stand, and has now for about a hundred years been learning obedience by subjection to Russia, Austria, and Prussia. When it has learned it, learned to submit private interests and parties to the general good, to be honourable, open, manly in proceeding and loyal to truth and justice, Poland also may become great. But a mere sense of injustice and tyranny on the part of others is not enough to do this; the Poles must learn to see their own faults as well as their enemies'.

Well, that discipline England passed through, as grinding a despotism as ever depressed a nation; but in two hundred years from the Conquest it had arisen in might and liberty, strengthened by adversity, and begun that glorious course of self-reliance and self-restraint which is the true nobility of any land, and which we pray may be for ever the true character of our own.

[NOTE.—*Recent research has in some respects modified and developed certain statements in the above lecture. See Vinogradoff, ' The Growth of the Manor ' ; Seebohm, ' The English Village Community ' ; Maitland, ' Township and Manor ' ; Stubbs, ' Constitutional History,' vol. i.*]

II

FEUDALISM

'I HAVE remarked,' says Mr. Carlyle, 'that of all things a nation needs first to be drilled, and no nation that has not been first governed by so-called tyrants and held tight to the curb till it became perfect in its paces and thoroughly amenable to rule and law, and heartily respectful of the same, and totally abhorrent of the want of the same, ever came to much in this world. England itself, in foolish quarters of England, still howls and execrates lamentably over its William Conqueror and vigorous line of Normans and Plantagenets; but without them, if you consider well, what had it ever been? A gluttonous race of Jutes and Angles, capable of no grand combinations, lumbering about in pot-bellied equanimity, not dreaming of heroic toil and silence and endurance, such as leads to the high places of this universe and the golden mountain tops where dwell the spirits of the dawn. Their very ballot boxes and suffrages, what they call their liberty, if these mean ，liberty and are such a road to heaven, Anglo-Saxon high road thither, could never have been possible for them on such terms. How could they? Nothing but collision, intolerable interpressure, as of men not perpendicular, and consequent battle often supervening, could have been appointed these undrilled Anglo-Saxons, their pot-belled equanimity itself continuing liable to perpetual interruptions, as in the Heptarchy time.'

I have read this long extract as pertinent to the remarks with which I concluded my last lecture and as containing the key to the history of the times that succeed the Conquest. I think that it describes very well the need of the fresh discipline that was to bring out the better points of the Anglo-Saxon character. But it does not convey the whole truth. For the merely tyrannical rule of the Norman and Plantagenet kings was not enough to bring out of the nature of the people the self-restraint which, added to their already acquired self-reliance, was to help them on to and make them worthy of greatness. Tyrannical government might force them to unity and drill them to obedience, but could never make them orderly, loyal, or patriotic. The feudal system, with all its tyranny and all its faults and shortcomings, was based upon the requirements of mutual help and service, and was maintained by the obligations of honour and fealty. Regular subordination, mutual obligation, social unity, were the pillars of the fabric. The whole state was one : the king representing the unity of the nation. The great barons held their estates of him, the minor nobles of the great barons, the gentry of these vassals, the poorer freemen of the gentry, the serfs themselves were not without rights and protectors as well as duties and service. Each gradation, and every man in each, owed service, fixed definite service, to the next above him, and expected and received protection and security in return. Each was bound by fealty to his immediate superior, and the oath of the one implies the pledged honour and troth of the other. Doubtless there were many hardships, more in theory perhaps than in reality. It would seem hard to the allodial landowner who until now had held his land of no earthly lord, as free as heart might wish or eye might see, to be obliged to own a superior of whom he should hold his land, subject to exactions, fines, reliefs, escheats, forfeitures, without whose consent he could not part with an inch of ground, or raise a sum of money, or even leave his children as he wished at his death. Doubtless it seems a hard thing for necessary military service to be taken and exercised under the command of a foreign nobleman, instead of the leisurely and desultory exercise of the old militia, in which every man was very much like his own master—to exchange the theoretical equality of all freemen for the theoretical bondage of feudal subjection. But if, as we saw partially the other day, the reality of Saxon equality was fast disappearing, and the security of allodial possession coming already to require the maintenance of the superior lord, as the military service was becoming a perpetual grievance instead of an occasional duty, and the protection of law universally required almost as much as its restraints, we may not be far from the truth if we conclude that a well-administered feudalism was better for the people than a continuance in their old state. As to the look of the thing, a theoretic feudalism was better than the practical wretchedness men were sinking into : the mischief was that the feudalism they got was in its way as far degenerate from the ideal as their old liberty had been, and, to add to the mischief, was administered for a century and a half at least by as strong and as cruel a race of tyrants as ever vexed man's heart.

I mentioned at the beginning of the first lecture that the origin of feudalism must be sought for among the German nations, and that the germs of it might already be traced in the nobility by service of the gesiths or thanes, and in the distribution of folclands with their additional burdens. Indeed, if we like to refine upon our theory, we might say that the feudal system bears to the warlike occupations of the German families the same relation that the allodial system bears to their peaceful ones. The one was based on the cultivation of land, the other on its conquest; the one was a system for countrymen, the other for soldiers; the one grew up naturally out of their ancient quiet homes in the forests, the other was forced up by the exigencies of continual war and conquest. The Frank kings, like the rest of the German princes, were surrounded by a court of nobles, in Germany and England called, as we said, gesiths, in the Frank countries on the Rhine and Meuse called antrustiones or leudes. To these were committed the great offices of state, the governorships of provinces, duchies, and counties; and they were provided for by benefices out of the lands at the disposal of the crown. These benefices were not at first hereditary, and did not involve any fixed service as due in consideration of their possession, but it is obvious that such a state of things could not continue long: the tendency of all such endowments is to become hereditary, and the tendency of all such services to become fixed matters of obligation. I cannot say whether things had actually reached this point in the time of the Emperor Charles the Great; but they certainly did in the century that succeeded his death. He, as you know, embraced within his empire France, Italy, Germany, and the greatest part of Spain; and those are exactly the regions in which feudalism grew up and maintained itself the longest. The necessity for protection and military subordination which began during his conquests became universal and perpetual during the insecure and troublous times that followed. The wars and complicated relations of the Karolings are among those passages of history which are most difficult to retain in memory. Fortunately we have no occasion at this moment to enter into them. Sufficient it is to lay down that this system, into whose peculiar details we shall examine by-and-by, grew up in the ninth century in its perfection in the kingdom of France. It was still German—the race that conquered France was a German race, although the conquered population formed the bulk of the people, and was mixed Celtic and Roman. And here one of the curious facts of history meets us. We say William the Conqueror was not a Frank, neither he nor the Franks, his feudal superiors, were Celtic or Latins, and yet both he and they spoke a Roman dialect, not a German one. Might not their feudal system as well as their language have come from the Roman empire? It is sufficient answer to say, whatever it might have done, it did not, for, with the single exception of the practice of clientship or commendation (that is, the custom for every freeman to be in the mund or protection of a lord), there is no resemblance between them. But it is a strange thing that the strong and hardy Franks should have exchanged their German tongues for the language of the conquered Gauls and Romans; and it is stranger still that the haughty Northman should exchange his for the French language of the people he conquered; but most strange of all is it that this powerful and insidious Roman-Gallic tongue, which had supplanted the German in the mouths of the Franks, and the Norse in those of the Normans, should, when brought face to face with the old Anglo-Saxon, vanish and fly before it. It is not always that the language of the conqueror gives place to that of the conquered, it is not always that the reverse is the case; but here the twice victorious French has to yield to the oppressed and discouraged English. It is true there are very many words of Latin and French origin in English, but the basis of the language is, and ever will be, Teutonic; and these importations into the vocabulary are not traceable to the Norman Conquest, but rather to the increased use of Latin in the services of the church, and of Norman French in the courts of law,[1] than either to the use of Latin as the language of the learned world, or to the fact that the English always have been the greatest travellers in Europe. This is a digression, but, I trust, a pardonable one.

Well, as the Franks had come in their strength and conquered Gaul, so the Norsemen came in their strength on the degenerate Franks and conquered Normandy: with the tongue of the conquered race they learned the feudal system and organised Normandy upon it, and when William the Bastard came to England he brought the full-grown system with him. I have said that things were verging towards feudalism already; the perpetual unrest and disquietude of war was evolving it in England and had done two centuries ago across the Channel; but it was not so to come, it was not as an indigenous growth that it was to prevail, it was forcibly introduced by quite other means.

Now we will consider first what the feudal system was; secondly, how and with what modifications it was introduced. In doing this we shall see how it differed from and entirely superseded the allodial system, and what particular details it took from it and absorbed by an assimilating process into itself; and so we may find out, as we did in the former case, how it acted on the life of the nation (a thought we have anticipated already), and what parts of its machinery and outer working yet remain to us.

A feodum or fee or fief is an estate held of a superior lord on

[1] No laws or deeds in Norman French are extant earlier than Henry III., and the courts of the hundreds &c. were administered in English during the Norman period (Hallam, *Mid. Ages*, ii. 306). Norman French lasted in the courts till the time of Edward III.

condition of the performance of certain services and with the right
of security and protection. The introduction of the feudal system
was the redistribution of all the lands in the kingdom on this principle. England was a conquered country ; all the land was vested in
the king, *par excellence*, the conqueror, the acquirer, or, as lawyers say,
the purchaser ; all was to be held of him by military tenure. ' The
essential principle of a fief,' says Hallam, ' was a mutual contract of
support and fidelity. Whatever obligations it laid upon the vassal
of service to his lord, corresponding duties of protection were imposed by it on the lord towards his vassal. If these were trans-
gressed on either side, the one forfeited his land, the other his
seigniory or rights over it.' We have seen that this feudal
arrangement was different from the old German freedom ; it was
a very different thing also from the highland clanship, in which the
bond is not one of spontaneous compact of vassalage, but of imagined
kindred and respect for birth. Still less is it like the Russian or
Polish system, in which each nobleman is independent and all equal,
all less than noble left in servitude ; it was one of slow and endless
gradation. We have mentioned two circumstances in the old system
that may have led the way to it : the grants of folcland, and the custom
of commendation. But they were not of it, and are to be carefully
distinguished from it ; commendation had nothing to do with the
tenure of land, and grants of folcland had nothing to do necessarily
with military service ; both these are of the essence of feudalism.

Rome was not built in a day, and it took the Conqueror twenty
years to accomplish the work. During these years the repeated
rebellions of the nobles placed vast estates at his disposal, and pre-
texts were never wanting to get rid of Anglo-Saxon proprietors
to make way for Normans. Besides forfeitures, marriages were
arranged with the same result. Still, it is a mistake to suppose that
all the land in England changed hands. We have in Domesday
Book an exact account of every acre of land in the kingdom in 1085 ;
and it appears from it that very many estates—nearly half of 8,000, the
total of mesne tenants—large and small, were in the same hands that
had held them in the time of the Confessor. But all new grants
were made on the feudal principle—weak and isolated free allodialists
came pouring in ready to exchange their freedom for safe protection
—and in 1085 William received at Salisbury the fealty of all landholders in England, both those who held immediately of him and
their tenants. Before this time, all the lands had been subjected to
the feudal superiority of Norman lords. In taking the fealty of all
the landholders William at once and from the first infringed on the
great principle of feudalism. According to it, he ought to have
required it only at the hands of his own tenants in capite ; that is,

those who held immediately of him ; for the principle of fealty was between every tenant and his next lord, not the superior of that lord. The tenants in capite owed it to the king and required it of their vassals ; those vassals owed it to them, not to the king, and required it in turn from their tenants ; these owed it to the vavassor alone, and required it from their villeins ; and so on, the tie being always to the next superior and to the king only through him, so that if he rebelled the vassal was in strict right bound to follow his lord even against the king. William at once set aside this ; he had seen how the great vassals in France—himself, for instance—had in reliance upon it made themselves independent of the crown. He would not have it so in England, and it was not. The introduction of the system was not then an expedient of tyranny, for it was the system that he was himself subject to for his continental dominions, and was that by which he managed his best friends and most favoured subjects ; nor was it so much a scheme of deep policy, as the reduction of all his dominions alike to the same method, and that the best and wisest that he knew. It is only when viewed in conjunction with his other acts for the systematic depression and degradation of the English race, that it becomes to our eyes a portion of the bitter discipline of conquest. When we find how it was administered, that it was made as heavy and aggravating (purposely) as it could be made, when we see how little dependence the English vassal could place on his lord and how little protection he got from him, when we remember that for a hundred years no Englishman attained the least promotion in either church or state, that bishops were dispossessed and their sees sold, that the heroes of the nation were driven to death and exile on a mockery of law and justice, that the very name of Englishman was a reproach, then we look into it and see how vast a machinery was made available for purposes of oppression and exaction.

The feudal relation was entered on with three distinct processes or ceremonies—homage, fealty, and investiture. The act of homage, by which the vassal put himself in the hand of his lord as his man, homo, consisted in his placing his hands between the hands of his lord with the words, 'Devenio vester homo.' He knelt down, unarmed, belt ungirt, sword and spurs removed, and placing his hands so, promised to become his man henceforward, to serve him with life and limb and worldly honour, faithfully and loyally, in consideration of the lands he held of him. The act of homage concluded with a kiss. It could be paid only to the lord in person. The act of fealty consisted in an oath of fidelity to the lord : it might be done by proxy. The act of investiture was of two kinds, proper or improper : in proper investiture the lord actually put the vassal into possession of the land by livery of seisin; in the improper it was done in some symbolical way, as the presenting of a clod of turf or a branch or a stone.

The service which the vassal by these ceremonies was bound to perform was in the first and most honourable tenure, military service. This was incumbent on all tenants in chief, in capite, that is those who held immediately of the king. It is defined by Thorpe to be the obligation to furnish a certain number of knights completely armed for the king's service and to maintain them in the field for forty days. Every estate of 20*l.* annual value was bound to provide one knight: hence it is called a knight's fee. The greater barons of course had estates to the value of hundreds of these fees, and each was bound to furnish his exact number accordingly. If the estate was worth half the money the knight was bound only to half the length of service. If the estate failed to furnish its quotum it in strict law was forfeit, but in practice the forfeiture was remitted and a fine called escuage was imposed.[1] Later on, when money was more needed than knights, the knight service was generally commuted for escuage, which is still paid by all the lands in the kingdom under the name of land tax. The obligation was limited by various usages or customs: in some fiefs the vassal was not bound to go beyond his lord's territories, and in some he must follow his lord on all his expeditions. The actual service was not, however, the only obligation of fealty. The vassal was not to divulge his lord's counsel, to conceal from him the machinations of others, to injure his person or fortune, or to violate the sanctity of his roof or the honour of his family.

Besides the duty of military service, the vassal had duties of peace: he was bound to do suit to the lord, that is to attend his courts: the great barons attended the king's court, and there heard causes under the presidency of the grand justiciary of the realm (this is the origin of the appellate jurisdiction of the House of Lords): the minor tenants attended the courts of their mesne lord— courts baron as they were called—and there answered complaints brought against them or formed a homage or jury for hearing complaints against others; they were called pares curtis or pares curiæ—peers—hence not only the name of the peers in the king's court, but the origin of the right of every man to his trial by peers, trial by jury. The vassal could not dispose of his fief, or bequeath it by will except by the permission of his lord; and, on the other hand, the lord could not dispose of his seigniory without the permission of his tenants. Besides all these advantages which the

---

[1] In lands not held by knight's service, towns &c. this was called tallage, and was very arbitrarily fixed.

superior lord had from the services of his tenants, Hallam enumerates six others called feudal incidents. 1. Reliefs, a sum of money—a succession duty—paid by everyone succeeding by descent to the possession of a fief. You will remember how in the old Saxon law the representatives of every deceased gesith or noble by service had to return to the king the heriot, the horse, and armour with which he had originally equipped him. The relief due by incoming feudal tenants took the place of the ancient heriot; but as the amount of it was not fixed, it was a ready method of extortion and was so used. Henry I. promised to fix a proportional amount, but it was not done until the Magna Carta, by which it was settled at about a fourth of the annual value.

The second class of feudal incidents were fines on alienation—sums paid to the lord by the tenant for leave to alienate his lands. As we saw just now, the bond between lord and tenant could not be dissolved without the consent of both : if the lord alienated the estate, the tenants signified their assent to the act and accepted their new lord, by what was called attornment. When the tenant wished to alienate, he had to pay a fine for leave to do so. Such payments being found oppressive, a custom of subinfeudation crept in, by which the new purchaser became the vassal of the old tenant and held the land of him : thus—A is the superior lord, B the selling tenant, C the new purchaser : if C is to buy all the estate of B, he must become a vassal of A, as his predecessor has been, and B must pay a round sum to get A the lord to consent to the arrangement; but if B can accept C as his vassal, then the lord need not be consulted about it nor any money paid. This is the custom of subinfeudation, a very decided infringement of the rights of the lord, and as such checked by Magna Carta and forbidden by a statute 18 Edward I. called Quia Emptores, which gave the tenant power to alienate his lands so as to be holden of his own superior lord.

The third feudal incident was escheat and forfeiture : escheat when the line of the original tenant having died out, the fief reverted to the lord ; forfeiture when it became forfeit to him through the failure of the tenant to perform his feudal duties, or through crime against the state.[1]

The fourth class were aids—which were at first numerous and oppressive, but were restricted by Magna Carta to three occasions on which the lord had a right to call on his vassal for assistance : 1. to make his eldest son a knight; 2. to marry his eldest daughter; 3. to redeem his person out of captivity.

In the fifth place comes the right of wardship, by which the lord had the custody and guardianship of all orphans of his tenants in

[1] The most usual in England was to enable the lord to pay his own relief.

military fiefs, both in estate and person. This might be alienated, and the king might assign the ward lands and person to the guardianship of a stranger, whose only object would be to make the most profit out of the transaction.

The sixth and last was the right of marriage, that is of tendering to the female wards while under age a husband of his choosing : in case of a refusal the ward forfeited as much money as the intending spouse would have paid to the lord for his goodwill.

So far I have spoken of the principal feudal tenure, that by military service ; there are two others akin to it, grand and petty serjeanty. In grand serjeanty the tenant held his fief under an obligation to do some special honorary service to the king, as e.g. to carry his banner or sword, or to be his butler or chamberlain at the coronation ; in petty serjeanty the tenure was by a meaner service, as that of forester, cook, goldsmith, &c., in connection with which was the custom by which some estates were held, of presenting the king with a bow and arrow, or a pair of spurs, and suchlike. Both these tenures as well as the proper military tenures were subject to relief, wardship, and marriages. The tenure by which the under-tenants mostly held, and which we may look upon as the most general, was socage. Blackstone thus divides tenures in general, according to the freedom and certainty of the service involved : 1. Military tenure, or tenure by chivalry, in which the service is, as we have seen, free but uncertain ; 2. Free and common socage, in which the service is free and certain ; 3. Villein socage, where it is base but certain ; 4. Pure villenage, in which it is base and uncertain. We have considered military tenure ; there remain three : 1. Free and common socage ; 2. Pure villenage; 3. Villein socage; and we can dismiss them in a few words, as they may be described by exceptions or negations as contrasted with military service.[1]

Free and common socage (the word seems to be derived from the obligation to suit at the lord's courts or soken) depended on a fixed and determinate service ; such as the payment of annual rent or the ploughing a certain field in a certain time. Socage tenure was not subject to homage, or to the feudal incidents of wardship, marriage, or relief, at least not in their most oppressive forms, and in socage tenures of the king in capite. It is obvious that this tenure is the one under which the Anglo-Saxon proprietors would be most likely to retain their lands, and under it the lawyers class the Anglo-Saxon custom of gavelkind prevalent in Kent, under which the children succeed in equal shares to the estates of their father ; and borough English, in which the youngest, not the eldest, succeeds

[1] I ought not to omit without notice the tenure by frankalmoign or free alms, by which church lands were and are still held.

to a burgage tenement. Burgage tenure is socage in a corporate town. Petty serjeanty is sometimes counted as a socage tenure. Thus much we may say with Blackstone of the two grand species of tenure under which almost all the free lands in the kingdom were held till the Restoration in 1660, when all free tenures were absorbed in free and common socage—military service and the servile duties of serjeanty were commuted for this.

The two base or villein tenures cannot be understood without reference to the nature of a manor. When a great vassal was put into possession of an estate he organised it in this way : first, a portion was kept in hand for the use of the family and household—this was the demesne ; secondly, portions were granted to tenants in free and common socage ; a third part was distributed among the labouring inhabitants as tenants at will of the lord ; another part was waste. It is the third part that was held in villenage. These villeins were serfs, not freemen as their Anglo-Saxon forefathers the churls had been, and are said to have been divided into two classes, villeins *regardant*, that is villeins belonging to a particular manor ; and villeins *en gross*, belonging wholly to their lord and transferable at his will. There is, however, a good deal of doubt about this, and it seems probable that villeins *en gross* were never used in England at least. A villein, however, in his worst estate was only villein to his lord, and had the rights of a freeman as regarded other people. Well, this old villein tenure or tenancy on sufferance had a natural tendency towards tenant right, and by-and-by the villeins got a hold on the land that was not to be taken from them ; and the right was further secured to them by the custom of court rolls : they had held their lands so long that the common law gave them a prescriptive right to them ; this claim was enrolled in the court of the manor, and the copy of this court roll became the title deed of the villein tenant, the origin of copyhold tenures. Such tenures as they became fixed were assimilated with the higher feudal ones—there were reliefs, heriots, escheats, fealty and services according to the original theory of villenage, wardships, and fines : most of these remain to the present day. The differences between villein socage and pure villenage are not very clear or distinct. The former, according to Blackstone, the same as ancient demesne, is an exalted kind of copyhold in which the tenants were bound only to certain determinate services. Such is the outline of the feudal tenure of land on which the feudal system was based. You will see that the notion of self-government was now entirely dropped. Justice had to be obtained from the lord, not from the court of the shire or the hundred. The king's council was no longer the wise and great men of the native race, but his tenants in capite, his own creatures most of them, ready to applaud any decision just or unjust, and back up any tyranny, accountable only to him at whose beck they acted. Perhaps, however, the best way of exhibiting the system in its oppressive character will be for us to take a short historical sketch of the reigns of the Norman kings.

William the Bastard claimed the crown of England as heir of Edward the Confessor, and as soon as the alarm and confusion that followed the battle of Hastings had in a measure subsided, the English nation acquiesced in the claim. It was found impossible to rally a party to the boy Edgar, and the ancient custom of the realm did not prescribe direct hereditary succession to the crown. Sixty years before, Canute had been accepted as king of England ; and now, repulsive as the thought must have been to a pure Anglo-Saxon that the throne of Alfred should be filled by the spurious child of the Norman devil, the precedent of the illustrious reign of Canute was suffered to rule the present case, and on Christmas Day 1066 William was elected and crowned king of the English at Westminster by Archbishop Ealdred of York : he then gave the archbishop a pledge upon Christ's book, and also swore before he would set the crown upon his head, that he would govern this nation as well as any king before him had done if they would be faithful to him. At Lent the king went over to Normandy, leaving England under the government of Odo and William Fitzosbern. Hardly had the king departed when the confusion began again. Eustace of Boulogne, brother-in-law of the Confessor, invaded Kent ; Eadric the Wild with the Welsh broke into Herefordshire ; the Northumberland people rose up and slew their newly appointed earl; the people of Exeter massacred the king's sailors, and Edgar Ætheling escaped from custody and fled to Scotland, where his supporters began to prepare for war. The cruel measures of Odo and Earl William had produced all this in a very few weeks : they built castles wide throughout the land and oppressed the people, and ever after it greatly grew in evil. Then King William came back, seized the land of the revolted nobles and distributed it among his followers, and laid heavy taxes upon the people. The next year the rebellion was renewed. North and south were both in arms; the sons of Harold in Somersetshire, Edgar Ætheling and Gospatric in Yorkshire. In 1069 the Danes sailed into the Humber ; and then the patience of the king was exhausted. He laid waste the whole of Yorkshire, that immense district was utterly desolated ; towns and fields alike laid waste, fruit and grain destroyed by fire and water, and for seventy years after that great county remained desolate and depopulated. This strong and cruel measure following after a series of victories on the king's part produced order and peace. No more organised rebellion was attempted, although the nobles held out long in the Isle of Ely, until 1071, when the king forced them to surrender. From this time the obligation of the oath that he had sworn at his coronation appears to have vanished from his mind, and England was treated as a conquered country. The monasteries and churches were given over to pillage: the patriotic archbishop of Canterbury and several of his brethren were deposed and imprisoned for life. Norman abbots were appointed far more faithless and cruel than their master. The name of Lanfranc, archbishop of Canterbury, shines almost alone among the Norman chiefs: by his advice William governed church matters of the kingdom, and his influence was always used for good. Still, this period was a reign of terror, such as at no other time except during the Commonwealth and reign of Cromwell has ever prevailed in England. But a show of legality was still maintained, and this very year the laws of Edward the Confessor, as they were called, were promulgated in London, and there are several charters extant in which the king promises justice and freedom as fairly as any of his successors were obliged in after years to do.

We have already seen how the feudal system was organised: all will remember the history of the desolation of the New Forest and the introduction of the Norman forest law. Forty-eight great castles were built in this reign: the king's income was raised to 1,060*l.* a day, that is nearly 1,200,000*l.* a year (in value of silver, or, calculating the difference in price, about 20,000*l.* a day). He left 60,000*l.*—180,000*l.* silver=equal to 3,600,000*l.*—treasure at his death.

The whole annual revenue of the Confessor was 60,000 silver marks, absolute value 40,000*l.* or relative value 800,000*l.* The population of the country in 1085 was not more than two millions. The amount of revenue seems incredible.[1] The revenue, however, was not raised from the demesne lands only, heavy tallages were imposed on the towns; the danegelt, which had been abolished by Edward the Confessor, was reimposed, varying from two to six shillings for every hide of land; the charters of the monasteries were forfeited, even those which were of the king's own granting, and redeemed with large sums wrung from the land; every mode of extortion was practised by the king and his officers. The spirit of the country was dead apparently, for this poverty was accompanied by peace and order. The Norman police was perfect and effective; a girl loaded with gold might, as we read, travel from one end of England to the other without hindrance. But all that was good and noble was eliminated: some of the English nobility emigrated

---

[1] William had 1,290 manors; Edward had 165; Harold, 118.

with Edgar Ætheling to Apulia ; many took service at Constantinople, where they were known as the emperor's Varangian guards.

I need not tell the story of the rebellion of the king's sons and of his awful burial, the details of which are sickening and appalling.

Terrible as the tyranny of the Conqueror was, it was gentle compared with that of his sons. He was a great man, though covetous and unscrupulous : they were monsters of rapine, cruelty, and lust. As long as Lanfranc lived he exercised a salutary power over the mind of William Rufus, who had been his pupil, but on his death he gave rein to his ambition and avarice.

Yet William Rufus could make fair promises ; but it was indeed only one of his ways of exacting money, in which he was more ingenious and unscrupulous than his father had been. As the Anglo-Saxons had rebelled against the Conqueror, the Norman nobles, his uncle Odo among them, rebelled against him. Their lands were a nice addition to his own. The bishops began to die off, and as the king (who seems to have been a freethinker if not an infidel) did not see the need of having bishops at all, the sees were kept vacant and he enjoyed the revenues in the vacancy. Then he bought or took a mortgage of Normandy of his brother Robert, who wanted to go on the Crusade ; and the treasure needful for this was raised by extortion, the very monasteries being plundered of their plate and jewels. In 1093 the king had a severe attack of illness, in which, with the fear of death before his eyes, he repented, promised an amendment of laws and government, and appointed S. Anselm archbishop of Canterbury, but hardly was he recovered than he began the old system over again and took the first opportunity of quarrelling with his new monitor. He died in 1100.

The reign of Henry I. lasted thirty-five years ; these were comparatively speaking years of peace to the English ; his only wars were foreign wars. His absences from England were long and frequent, and the tendency of his cruel and unscrupulous nature was checked by the influences of his queen, the Anglo-Saxon princess Matilda, whom the grateful people remembered for many years as the good Queen Molde. He also began his reign with good promises—he made a promise to God [1] and all the people before the altar at Westminster that he would abolish the injustice that prevailed in his brother's time, and observe the most equitable of the laws established in the days of any of the kings before him ; and the charter in which he embodied his promises is the basis of English liberties and the foundation stone of the structure on which was raised the noble fabric of the Magna Carta. Its provisions are as follows, and I will read them as significant of the future rather

[1] *Anglo-Saxon Chronicle*, 1100.

than as for the present amending the condition of the people, for the reign of Henry I. does not seem to have witnessed any positive improvement in this, but rather a rest under present oppression and security from increase of misery. Through the mercy of God and with the common advice and consent of the barons of England (who are here first mentioned in the place of the old witan) being crowned king, he will, as the realm was oppressed by lawless exactions, before all things free God's church, so that he will not sell or farm, nor on the death of an archbishop, bishop, or abbot accept anything from the possessions of the church or its tenants until the entrance of a successor ; and will abolish all oppressive imposts, so that if any of his barons, earls, or other persons die who holds immediately of him, his heir shall not redeem his land as in the time of his brother, but with a lawful and just relief. In like manner the tenants of his barons shall redeem their lands from their lords. And if any one of his barons or vassals shall wish to give his daughter, niece &c. in marriage, he shall speak with the king, who shall accept nothing for the permission nor forbid the marriage unless he proposes to bestow her on the king's enemy ; and on the death of a baron or vassal of the king, if he leaves an heiress, the king will give her in marriage together with her land by the advice of his barons. If a widow is left childless, she shall possess her dowry and marriage, and not be given in marriage except by her consent. If she is left with children, she shall possess the dowry and marriage as long as she leads a spotless life, and shall not be given in marriage but with her own consent. And the wife or relation of upright character shall be guardian of the children and land. And the king's barons shall act in like manner towards the sons or daughters or wives of their tenants. False coining is prohibited. The debts due to the late king are remitted. The barons shall have the power of bequeathing their money by will. If one dies intestate his representatives shall distribute his effects to the benefit of his soul. The system of amercement of penalties used in Anglo-Saxon law, for the minutiæ of which one comprehensive system of forfeiture had prevailed under the last two reigns, is restored. An amnesty up to the day of coronation is proclaimed. The forests are to remain as they were. Tenants holding by knight service are exempted from payments and works ; and he restores finally the laws of King Edward with those emendations they received from his father with the consent of the barons. If the terms of this engagement had been kept, obviously the worst evils of the feudal system in its pressure on all but the very lowest classes of society would have been remedied. We have no warrant in believing that they were. The iron hand pressed as heavily, although

perhaps more evenly, as it had done during the reigns of the father
and brother of Henry.

The exactions were as heavy as ever : the year 1103 was a year
of much distress from manifold taxes ; in 1104 we read, 'It is
not easy to describe the misery of this land which it suffered at this
time through the various and manifold oppressions and taxes that
never ceased nor slackened ; moreover, wherever the king went his
train fell to plundering the wretched people, and withal there was
much burning and manslaughter. By all this was the anger of God
provoked and this unhappy nation harassed.' The next year, 1105,
this was a year of great distress from the failure of the fruits, and
from the manifold taxes which never ceased, either before the king
went abroad, while he was there, or after his return. 1110 was
a year of much distress from the taxes which the king raised for
his daughter's dowry ; in 1115 the nation was many times sorely
oppressed by the taxes which the king raised both within the towns
and out of them.

In all these years there were also bad harvests and high prices.
In 1124 ' Our Lord God Almighty, who seeth all things, seeth that
the miserable people are oppressed with all unrighteousness ; first
men are bereaved of their property, then they are slain. Full heavy
a year was this ; he who had any property was bereaved of it by
heavy taxes and assessments, and he who had none starved with
hunger.' These are the notes of the contemporary chronicler, and
yet these days were better than those that were to come, for, as he
says himself, King Henry was a good man and great was the awe of
him, for no man durst ill treat another in his time ; he made good
peace for men and deer. The sum of his goodness seems to have
been that he oppressed Norman and Saxon alike, a system that was
not incompatible with the administration of strict justice between
them or with a considerable measure of personal security.

Stephen, as his uncle had done before him, purchased the adhesion of the people by the grant of liberties : the church lands seized
by William Rufus and Henry are restored; the forests made by Henry
are disforested ; ecclesiastics are allowed to make wills, and the other
engagements made by Henry are enlarged and confirmed. But if
Stephen had the will, he had not the power to keep his promises,
and his reign was one continuous civil war ; we cannot enter into
the details. The following is the judgment of the chronicler. ' The
nobles on both sides cruelly oppressed the wretched men with castle
work, and when the castles were built they filled them with devils
and evil men. Then they took those whom they suspected to have
any goods, by night and by day, seizing both men and women,
and they put them in prison for their gold and silver, and tortured

them with pains unspeakable, for never were any martyrs tortured as they were. They hung up some by the feet and smoked them with foul smoke, some by their thumbs or by the head, and they hung burning things on their feet. They put a knotted string about their heads and twisted it until it went into the brain. They put them into dungeons wherein were adders and toads and snakes, and thus wore them out. Some they put into a crucet house, that is into a chest that was short and narrow and not deep, and they put sharp stones within it and crushed the man therein so that they brake all his limbs. There were hateful and grim things called rachenteges in many of the castles, and which two or three men had enough to do to carry. The rachentege was made thus: it was fastened to a beam, having a sharp iron to go round a man's throat and neck so that he might noways sit nor lie nor sleep but that he must bear all the iron. Many thousands were exhausted with hunger. I cannot and I may not tell of all the wounds and all the tortures that they inflicted upon the wretched men of this land, and this state of things lasted all the nineteen years that Stephen was king, and ever grew worse. They were continually levying an exaction from the towns which they called tenserie; and when the wretched inhabitants had no more to give, they then plundered and burned all the towns, so that thou mightest well walk a whole day's journey nor ever wouldest thou find a man seated in a town or its lands tilled. Then was corn dear, and flesh and cheese and butter, for there was none in the land: wretched men starved with hunger; some lived on alms who had been erewhile rich, some fled the country. Never was there more misery, and never acted heathens worse than these. At length they spared neither church nor churchyard, but they took all that was valuable therein, and then burned the church and all together. Neither did they spare the lands of bishops nor abbots nor priests, but they robbed the monks and the clergy, and every man plundered his neighbour as much as he could. If two or three men came riding to a town, all the township fled before them and thought that they were robbers. The bishops and clergy were for ever cursing them, but this to them was nothing, for they were all accursed and forsworn and reprobate. The earth bare no corn; you might as well have tilled the sea, for the land was all ruined by such deeds, and men said openly that Christ and His saints slept.' Of course these evils are not to be charged on the feudal system; still that system did put men at the mercy of such oppressors, and this was really the discipline by which Englishmen were taught endurance and prepared for united effort. The worst period ended with the reign of Stephen

D

Henry II., who was hailed as the restorer of the native line of kings, began by breaking the power of the great vassals : he ordered the destruction of the castles, and sent justices round to the counties to hold assizes. In these measures we trace the English hand of his chancellor, the great Thomas of London, Thomas Becket, to whom, whether or not you esteem him as a saint and martyr, English liberty as asserted against the king and the barons owes an eternal debt of gratitude. As chancellor for the first eight years of Henry's reign he was prime minister, and organised the ameliorating measures by which that king gained his popularity. When he became arch-bishop of Canterbury he went at once into opposition in defence of what he esteemed to be the necessary liberties of the church, and continued in that attitude until he was murdered. Even if, as many of you will think, he was wrong in his estimate of church liberties, and still more wrong in the temper in which he supported them, he was the first Englishman who broke through the hard deaden-ing crust of misery which had burst from the flaming volcano of Norman tyranny, and for that deserves to be counted a hero. We shall not have occasion to pursue his history, for the course of our lectures does not carry us into the transactions between the crown and the papacy ; but I will take advantage of the mention of his name to say a few words respecting the position of the church at this time in relation to the people. The church was not Normanised by the Norman kings ; they forced bishops and abbots of their own into the rich places, and some of these were oppressors, but they were in many cases non-resident, and the conduct of the priests and monas-teries was much as it had been before : they were plundered and per-haps persecuted, but that only made what light they had burn clearer ; in some measure the shield of their oppressors was a defence to them as well—when as much as possible was extorted, the rulers took care that none else should try it. Now these priests and monks were Englishmen, and relations generally of the English families who lived near the monasteries ; they had sympathy of race and blood to keep up the charity that they were bound by their vows to show to those that needed. Hence they were centres of security and civilisa-tion, and the only centres of civilisation during the Norman reigns. Their liberties were looked on by the people as their own ; their sym-pathies were always on the side of liberty, and their freedom was won with the freedom of the people. As we shall see, it was men like Archbishops Langton and Winchelsey who really won liberty both in church and state.

The day was the darkest just before the dawn : the misery of Stephen's reign was the preparation for the little instalment of freedom that was gained in Henry II.'s. No sooner was the administration of the kingdom in strong hands than law and justice were restored. The old Saxon courts of the shire and hundred had been retained under the feudal system, with the substitution of Norman for English judges. The Conqueror had separated the civil from the ecclesiastical courts; the bishop no longer sat in the sheriff's court as co-ordinate judge, and justices *in itinere* had begun to go circuits in the latter end of Henry I.'s reign. But the system of regular assizes was begun in the reign of his grandson, and the system of trial by jury dates probably from this time. Money was becoming more necessary than the services of turbulent and unmanageable vassals; so escuage was levied instead of personal attendance, and the king fought his foreign wars with mercenary soldiers. There was as yet no word of constitutional government, but the system of the two Williams, personal and despotic, gave way to the restored witenagemot, the great council of the vassals of the crown, the bishops and judges. And yet the following is the picture drawn of the administration of justice during the early Plantagenet reigns by Hallam. 'It was not a sanguinary despotism. Henry II. was a prince of remarkable clemency, and none of the Conqueror's successors were as grossly tyrannical as himself; but the system of rapacious extortion from their subjects prevailed to a degree which we should rather expect to find among Eastern slaves than that high-spirited race of Normandy whose renown filled Europe and Asia. The right of wardship was abused by selling the heir and his land to the highest bidder; that of marriage was carried to a still grosser extent—women and men, not as wards, simply as tenants in chief, paid fines to the crown for leave to marry whom they would, or not to be compelled to marry one another. Towns not only fined for original grants of franchises, but for repeated confirmations. The Jews paid exorbitant sums of money for every common right of mankind—for protection, for justice: in return, they were sustained against their Christian debtors in demands of usury which superstition and tyranny rendered enormous. Men paid fines for the king's good will, or that he would remit his anger, or to have his mediation with their adversaries.' Many fines seem, as it were, imposed in sport, if we look to the cause, though their extent and the solemnity with which they were recorded prove the humour to have been indifferently relished by the two parties. Thus, the bishop of Winchester paid a tun of good wine for not reminding King John to give a girdle to the countess of Albemarle, and Robert de Vaux five best palfreys that the king might hold his peace about Henry Pinel's wife. Another paid four marks for licence to eat. But of all the abuses which deformed the Anglo-Norman government, none was so flagitious as the sale of judicial redress. The king, we are told, is the fountain of justice, but in those ages it was one which only gold could unseal.

I have tried to present to you, I feel very imperfectly, a description of what the feudal system was in theory and of its real pressure on the English nation. We are not to look on it as done away with by Magna Carta, nor by the statute of Charles II. which abolished most of the remaining evils of it: much of its nomenclature and customs still lives among us. We have seen what it was at its worst, in its most oppressive form, administered by the most unscrupulous and cruel of men. It taught the English race endurance —it taught them a common sympathy—it blended them together in one community of misery, that, having suffered together, they might, when the time for liberty came, be freed together. It served to amalgamate Norman and Anglo-Saxon, churchman and layman, in common interests. The liberty they were to win was not a class liberty like that of Poland and Hungary; it was freedom for all from the highest to the lowest. This was the Egyptian bondage of our fathers. Loyalty and patriotism were other lessons of these dark days. Not all lords were cruel oppressors; those who were faithful to their feudal obligations suffered with their people and won their affection and service. Justice became very precious. Laws were looked on as treasures to be vindicated in spite of tyranny and anarchy. The stubborn independence of the ancient race, leavened with fellow-feeling and sympathy, loyalty, justice, and the love of peace, was forming a character worthy to win and hold fast freedom. We shall see, if you please, in another lecture, how that liberty was won and maintained and handed down to us. *Esto perpetua.*

[*See Stubbs, ' Constitutional History,' vol. i.; Pollock and Maitland, ' The History of the English Law before the time of Edward I.' ; Maitland, ' Domesday Book and Beyond ' ; Round, ' Feudal England.'*]

III

THE LAWS AND LEGISLATION OF THE NORMAN KINGS

No one I hope will suspect me, in offering an informal course of
lectures on the Laws and Legislation of the Norman Kings, of any
intention of intruding on the ground already fully occupied by our
guides, philosophers, and friends of the sister faculty. That is by
no means the case. The ways of examining the subject are so
different, as they offer themselves to the student of law and the
student of history, that there is little chance of collision. Like a
certain set of mathematical lines, however closely we may approxi-
mate, it is in our nature never to meet. The difference between the
historical study of law and the legal study of history is one not of
method only, but emanates in the point of view from which the
student works. It is not that the one is analytical and the other
synthetical; that is perhaps in the main true, but it is not all the
truth. It is that the essence of the historical study is in the working
out the continuity of the subject, while the essence of the legal
study is in the reducing of it all to certain theoretic principles.
You may think perhaps that this is much the same as the difference
between synthetic and analytic treatment; but it really is more; for
the historian has an analytic method as well as the lawyer, and the
difference may easily be seen between them. But the student of
history has wider sympathies and a somewhat wider grasp. Of
course I speak as a student of history, so you will take my account
of myself with some grain of allowance. We are both of us set
down, we will say, in a garden of facts: it is my business to investigate in the case of each fact, where it comes from and what becomes
of it; it is my friend's business to cultivate one particular set of
facts until he gets it into the most scientific form and the most
sound and effective condition. I have to deal with a good deal that
turns out to be weeds, rubbish in fact, only I do not know it to be
rubbish until I have worked it out. My friend's purpose is to produce
a perfect cabbage, we will say; mine is to find out all that is worth

finding out about the whole plot. Of course there are merits in both schemes : the historian is, in the judgment of the world, a much less useful person than the lawyer ; but educationally he has his uses still, and one of them is to train the mind to careful habits of investigation and to sound judgment on the points that have been investigated. Our friend has the advantage in the point of concentration and of professional utility. There is likewise much more competition and both larger profits and, I venture to think, when there are any at all, quicker returns.

But my object now is not to insult the student of law, nor to puff the constitutional history of England. It is rather to impress upon you the importance, from our point of view, of the method of study which, beginning at the beginning of history, takes especial pains in finding out the causes and consequences of things, where they come from and what becomes of them. And if we want a better example than the cabbage we shall find it in the subject that I have chosen for the course. The history of Norman law is a subject which very well illustrates what I have been saying. It is a phenomenon, not very large, not very clear ; a piece of history lying in a debatable land between Anglo-Saxon law, which is to a great extent matter of antiquarianism and archæology, and the common law of England, which dates its historical shaping from the reign of Henry II. How much of the Norman law is rooted in antiquity corresponding with that of the Anglo-Saxon law, and how much of it goes on living and incorporating itself in the continuous life of the English common law—where it comes from and whither it goes—this may be regarded as the chief point to be kept in view in the course that lies before us, but it is not by any means the only point on which we shall have to dwell, for there is something in the literary history and more in the constitutional aspect of the thing that will demand continual digression for investigation. And even putting the point as I have put it, I may be laying myself open to be misunderstood. We shall come on examination to find that about much that is called Norman law there is no question, but that it is Anglo-Saxon law pure and simple ; and that instead of ceasing in a mysterious manner to exist at all, it does continue to exist under the comprehensive shadow of the later common law. There is an historical doctrine of the conservation of energy, and it is very strong in these regions of history ; nothing that has once been can be so unmade as to leave everything that follows it to continue as if it had not been :

> μόνου γὰρ αὐτοῦ καὶ θεὸς στερίσκεται
> ἀγένητα ποιεῖν ἄσσ᾽ ἂν ᾖ πεπραγμένα.

(Arist. *Eth.* 6. 3.)

Well, I have no doubt you think the moral of all this is that he is going, where he knows anything about the legal side of things, to tell us about it, and where he does not to say that belongs to the lawyers. I am not at all sure that that may not be the result ; but I may say that that is not the intention with which I set out. I propose to begin with a somewhat detailed examination of the text of the documents that we are going to deal with, so that if possible we may understand what they mean. By doing this I shall have, no doubt, to invite you into a region that is dull and to a certain extent laborious ; the frightful Norman French of one form of the code of the Conqueror's laws is repelling in the extreme, and there are difficulties about the authenticity of even that ; the Latin of the other laws is scarcely more attractive, although it is not quite so unintelligible. We may find some reason to inquire why should this French be so barbarous, and this Latin so extremely bad ? We will leave our speculation on the answer until we come to the question. Then again, there are points of chronology which I know beforehand will never get a firm footing in your notes. A good deal of light may be thrown on the importance of a piece of law by making out the exact date at which it was promulgated ; but alas, alas, as you probably know, the Norman kings did not date their edicts at all ; and the men who transcribed them for our learning, in nine cases out of ten, omitted to transcribe the names of the witnesses, by comparison of which the date of the document might have been approximately ascertained. This is an unfortunate drawback to the interest of our study ; for it is almost impossible to infuse an element of human or national sympathy into the examination of texts that cannot be referred to a distinct place in history : unfortunately we see that every day exemplified in Egyptian and Assyrian antiquities ; and to me it is a very melancholy thing to go to the British Museum and walk up those avenues of alabaster figures, man-headed lions and others, and to think that of the generations that carved them out and walked about among them first, I have no idea, defined by chronology to within one or two thousand years, of who they were, or what they did, or why they set up these wonderful things, or how they made them ; where they came from, or whither they have gone. Well, it is not quite so bad with these Norman laws ; in reading them we are not, as our Assyrian friends used to be, nonplussed by the difficulty of determining whether the cylinder before us is a list of drugs or a royal pedigree, a Christmas bill or a fine and recovery. We know that they all fall within the space of one century, between 1066 and 1166 ; you may say between the battle of Hastings and the assize of Clarendon, and we know that they are laws—although, by the bye, what are laws ? for that

also is a preliminary point—and that they come midway between two
systems, with neither of which they are identical. One cannot be
expected to know all about them ; if it were so, what would be the
use of historical training ? I can only reply that I wish we did.

An introductory lecture is always a desultory one. I dare say
you will think that some of mine are desultory without being introductory. It may be so. But the first lecture is always desultory,
because the professor has to come prepared to say something, and
without any notion of what sort of class he will have to say it to,
and therefore how he should put it ; with the easy conviviality of
sine ulla sollennitate, or with the dignified and attractive air of the
man who is quite at home in his subject, or with the majesty,
undefined, something like the royal supremacy in ecclesiastical
causes, the full undefined majesty of the professorial chair. I
cannot get over this. I do not feel convivial, or quite at home, and
certainly not majestic. I should very much like a class that would
be content to work with me through these documents without finding it necessary to tell me that as it is of no use for the schools they
do not much care about taking notes ; and I do not much care about
the man who comes ready armed with questions from a coach which
all the wise men in the world cannot answer. It is obvious that if I
were to prepare a lecture for such a class as I want, and find myself
when I come here face to face with such a one as I do not want, I should
begin by feeling as much at home as if I were at a popular concert.
I must, however, during the course lecture on the subject I have
set myself, but there must be all the difference in the world in the
way in which I shall treat it. Still, there are certain preliminaries
which may be as well taken at once. And we may as well lose no
more time, but go into these.

There is a certain number of well-defined pieces of Norman
legislation into which we must go first ; there is a certain number of
undefined measures of policy, matters, that is, which we know either
as recorded facts of history or as the necessary inferences from a
comparison of preceding and succeeding history, which is not
recorded documentarily ; and there is a region of more minute
technical interest, the details of legal procedure and minutiæ of
archæological detail. Into these last it is, of course, to-day quite
problematical whether we shall have time during the course to
adventure ourselves : if we cannot within the compass of our
eighteen lectures do this, I can give those of you who wish for them
the names of the books on which a more careful reading should be
bestowed. But into the first and second of these classes of matters
we may, I think, go with profit and at our ease. The actual laws
we may read and explain, so far as we can ; the constitutional

tendencies that are not to be found in the text of laws we can likewise examine, either as they meet us from time to time, or when we have read through the laws.

There are about a dozen documents of the reigns of William the Conqueror, Henry I., and Stephen that will have to be first read or reviewed. Some of these—all except three or four—are printed in my ' Select Charters,' which will be our most convenient text-book. The others were too long and of interest so far from constitutional that I could not well introduce them into that book, and indeed they are only to be found in books too cumbrous for me to expect you to bring them. I will give you the names of the books, so that if you can, or wish to do so, you may procure them ; but I intend, if I can do it, to give you in the course of the lectures as m ch of the text as I shall feel myself qualified to dilate upon, and not to puzzle you with too many references. The laws which I am going to work upon, and which are not in the ' Select Charters,' will be found in these books ; and in all of them, for they are simply recensions of texts of the same documents. I may take them in chronological order, although it is quite unlikely that you may wish to have the earlier ones ; and I shall not mention more obscure editions.

Lambarde's ' Archaionomia,' a small folio of the seventeenth century, contains all that we shall want ; or Wilkins' ' Leges Anglo-Saxonicæ,' of the eighteenth ; or Thorpe's ' Laws and Institutes of the Anglo-Saxons,' of the nineteenth. The handiest form is a German edition, Schmid's ' Gesetze der Angelsachsen,' which contains, beside all that the rest contain, a good index and glossary and some valuable notes, not always to be followed, but always interesting and curious. Any one of these costs from a pound to thirty shillings, but I do not think it necessary that you should bring one ; I hope to do all that we need do without them.

The list of documents which we shall, if all is well, explore is this : for the reign of William the Conqueror, three texts will be found in the ' Select Charters ; ' the edict on appeal of battle ; the edict on the separation of the courts, and the ten articles of emendation of the laws of England. The edict on appeals of battle, a code of fifty-two articles, will probably be the first thing we take. For the reign of William Rufus there are no documents, but there are some historical details of tendency and inference in the excerpts in the ' Select Charters,' to which I shall call your attention as we find time allows. For the reign of Henry I. there are again three documents in the ' Select Charters,' the coronation charter, the charter of the city of London, and the writ for the holding of the shiremoot ; but besides these there is a somewhat bulky compilation, called the ' Leges Henrici primi,' which is only contained in the larger collections which I have mentioned, but which will probably supply us with a good deal of matter that to me, at least, seems interesting. Besides these, there are some canons and other writs of Henry I., which may be brought in from other books. For the reign of Stephen, all that we want may, I think, be found in the 'Select Charters;' and for the reign of Henry II., so far as we shall find it possible to enter on the legal history of it, all, I think, will be found there.

There are some other introductory considerations which, although perhaps needless, ought not to be taken for granted. We ought, I think, to begin with getting some idea of what we mean by laws and legislation, and of what material the Norman jurists had to begin with and work upon. That is a wide subject for exploration, and one on which I should not venture to set an unnecessary step; but as I shall have to speak of law, and of the civil law, the canon law, the laws of the barbarians, and the capitularies of the Frank emperors, it is necessary to define at first what I mean. The first chapter of Justinian's Institutes might form the text of a whole lecture, but I shall not do more than cull from it what I want to set me right with you; and it will not take a long time for us to see in it how much applies and how much does not apply to a period and a system so far removed in date and so much farther removed in spirit and conformation as that of the Conquest is from Justinian and Tribonian.

The favourite definition of law in the middle ages was one derived from a saying of Aristotle, which was not intended for a definition, ὁ δὲ νόμος ἀναγκαστικὴν ἔχει δύναμιν, λόγος ὢν ἀπό τινος φρονήσεως καὶ νοῦ, which was inverted in Latin into the form, 'lex coactiva habet potentiam sermonis ab aliqua prudentia et intellectu.' The phrase contains the material for a fair description. Of course you all have many definitions of law at your fingers' ends, but this we may regard as the combination of coercive force with the enunciation of sound reason and practical wisdom, or the enunciation with coercive force of the rules of reason and practical prudence. Justinian's definition of lex as jus scriptum stands on a different point, and involves further the inquiry of what is jus, an idea perhaps, on the whole, too simple to admit of definition. What, however, we have now to do is connected rather with Justinian than with Aristotle. The Roman jus may not have become lex until it was written; but the barbarian lex was in its very nature customary, and comes thus under the subsidiary definition of the Institutes, 'diuturni mores, consensu utentium comprobati, legem imitantur.' All our ancient laws, whether written or unwritten, are of this character; they are the customs of the nations, preserved in the memory of the judge, and, if recorded in writing, not claiming for the record greater authority than resides in the viva vox of the community and its recognised judges. It is curious how long the idea that the English law is primarily an unwritten and customary law lasts. It lasts long after kings and parliaments had begun to pass acts ; the barons in the reign of Edward II. insisted that England was not governed by written law. This saying was perhaps an intentional perversion of an old tradition, but it bears witness to the fact of such tradition; and another evidence of the reality of the idea may be found in the ways in which our kings, when propounding edicts, choose to give them names less imposing and conveying less distinct sanctions than the name of law implies. They are establishments, assizes, charters, constitutions, edicts, or statutes ; law underlies them, not as genus to species, but rather as spirit to matter; they contain law rather than constitute law, they are records or tentative expressions, or some other function, but not the sovereign ideal of LAW. Well, on this matter I am perhaps fanciful, but, if I am under a delusion, I have no doubt you see through it. Anyhow you will see that lex being the expression of jus, and jus being the abstract of φρόνησις and νοῦς employed in social relations, our ancient institutes, if they did not claim the full force of lex, were still records of jus—the peculiar sort of jus that our ancestors cultivated by custom, stored in memory, cited *viva voce*, and in so doing imitated, as Justinian says, the laws of their betters.

That being so, we may again turn to Justinian and see how he divides the oracles of the jus scriptum ; by so doing we shall see how our own laws, as they develop historically, may be arranged under his headings. He makes five sorts of laws—that is, of Roman laws : *plebiscita, senatus consulta, principis placita, magistratuum edicta,* and *responsa prudentum.* At first sight it would seem that this division does not contain any heading under which the primitive law of any state could come ; that none of the headings would include, for instance, the law of the Twelve Tables, which was, I suppose, a record of the previously existing customary law of Rome, the primary, fundamental, prehistoric law without the presumption of which we cannot expect society to have existed. I do not think that this matters much, for the author of the Institutes obviously is not analysing all written law, but simply the laws that he had before him codified or edited in the Pandects, the principles of which he was going to enunciate in the Institutes, and he probably considered that under the *jus naturale, jus gentium,* and *jus civile* he had accounted for all that it was necessary to account for. Still by a sort of analogy the description may be made sufficient.

The *plebiscita* of the Romans were the enactments which were made by the plebs, on the proposition of a plebeian magistrate. These decrees by the effect of the Lex Valeria and the Lex Hortensia were made equal to *leges*, and bound the patricians as well as the plebeians. What processes they went through before they acquired this force, whether they required the confirmation of the senate or of the other sorts of *comitia*, is beyond my purpose to inquire now ; but it is clear that in their origin they were resolutions of the plebs or commons as we should call it, modifying or enforcing more ancient customary institutions. They were the sort of law that begins from below and rises into the rank of statute ; that is, they were analogous to the customary, innate, inherent laws that proceed from the nation and not from the king. In mediæval law Latin, the word *plebiscitum* means a by-law, and a by-law means the custom of a manor or township—the word by being equivalent to the term villata, and having in the north English and Scottish townships an equivalent, bur ; not akin to the same syllable in our word borough, but derived from a root akin to that in the word boor, or cultivator. The bylawmen or *plebiscitarii* of manorial law were those charged with the enforcement of the customary regulations of the courts ; the remnant and survival of a great system of popular judicature which has become now so attenuated as to be scarcely visible to the eye of anyone who has no interest in the local profits. Thus inter-preted the *plebiscitum* would represent customary or popular laws.

The second heading, *senatus consultum—quod senatus jubet atque constituit*—would represent formal recensions or enactments by superior but still not royal or personal supremacy ; such as were the canons of ecclesiastical councils and the doms of the Anglo-Saxon witenagemots ; in which the king legislated with the advice and assent of his principes, whether bishops or ealdormen or thanes, and which after promulgation in the county courts were incorporated in the treasury of the customary law.

The third class of laws—*principis placita*—we may make analogous to the charters of the Norman kings—analogous, not identical—emendations as they are called by the Conqueror and Henry I. of the laws of Edward the Confessor—expressed, however, not in enacting words strictly so called, but rather as favours granted to their subjects. These laws rest on a basis very distinct from that of either of the earlier forms. This is worth your attention. The *principis placita* of Justinian were the laws which the Roman emperor made by virtue of that devolution of legislative authority which, as a part of imperium, the Roman people conferred by the lex regia. This was the basis of legislative authority in the hands of modern kings. The king who by hook or by crook managed to possess himself of it was an imperator in his own domains. But the kings of the Germanic races, much as they liked to avail themselves of their imperiality, were shy of enunciating it absolutely; even William and Henry I., therefore, exercise the power of legislating 'with advice and consent of their court.' You may, I think, say that this is a fanciful parallel. We shall see as we proceed how far it holds good; of course there may be intermediate stages, documents in which transition is obvious, but compare the documents issued by Henry II. with counsel and consent, with those which Alfred, Ethelred, and Canute issued, and you will see at once what is presumed to be the source of authority. The laws of the Anglo-Saxons, like those of constitutional England, are those *quas vulgus elegerit*; the charters of Henry I. are condescensions of a royal inexhaustibility of authority, however alike may be the words in which the concession is clothed.

The *magistratuum edicta* of the Institutes, the jus honorarium of the elder law, are the rules of justice promulgated by the executive officers of the law. The corresponding enactment in English law to these is the assizes of the early Plantagenet sovereigns, especially Henry II., rules issued for the administration of justice, which in their form perhaps claim to be little more than rules of procedure, but in their substance are material alterations, amendments, or developments or adaptations of the law that is presumed to underlie them. The king, such as Henry II., issues his prætorian edict as the supreme prætor or enforcer of justice, not as the emperor or fountain of legislation. As we may see some day, jurisdiction in the hands of a judge is a very elastic thing, and it is a maxim of the faculty 'boni judicis est ampliare suam jurisdictionem.' No doubt he is so convinced of the divinity and beneficence of his own function that he is warranted in applying his powers even in regions to which they were not originally intended to apply. The assizes of Henry II., and, as we shall see, one of the legal acts of the Conqueror, under the form of a rule of procedure, introduced radical changes. The whole of the mediæval and modern jury system grew out of assizes, and indeed I am not quite sure whether they may not claim a large share in the paternity or maternity of the mediæval common law which certainly was the offspring of some sort of union between the ancient popular law and the royal authority in executive justice.

The last head of Justinian's classification is the *responsa prudentum*; that is, not the scientific elucidation of legal points by self-appointed jurists, but the replies by the authorised judges of the state to questions placed before them officially. That at least is the definition which the author of the Institutes gives; and if we apply it in its simplicity to our own law books, then our *responsa prudentum* would be the year books or registers of judicial sentence in the high courts of justice of England. But we may enlarge it further and comprehend in it the writings of our literary or scientific jurists, most of whom were either at the head of the legal administration or were commissioned by the king to write on the subject. Glanville's work on the laws may be put in this class, if it is thus widened; if not, it must fall into the class of collections of formulæ. Bracton and Britten and Fleta also may either be counted among the *prudentes*, or be supposed to have worked on the model of the Institutes themselves. Coke himself in his Institutes comprised very much of a code as well as Institutes, and in his reports gave the world the *responsa prudentum* of his own time. So long as the law was in the mouth of the judge, the *responsa prudentum* once admitted as precedent were *ipso facto* law. These were collected by Justinian in the Pandects—the other four classes form the collection called the Code, from which and its sister Code of Theodosius all bodies of collective enactments have since been called codes. Thus understood, the name belongs to some of the early Anglo-Saxon collections, and in a mixed sense to the fifty-two articles of the Conqueror's laws which will be the subject of our next lecture.

Our object in this course is to treat the subject-matter historically—the laws and legislation of the Norman kings, with an investigation of where they came from and what becomes of them. This involves some recurrence to earlier history and earlier precedents. Not to follow the example of the Oxford tutor who, undertaking to lecture on the French Revolution, had at the end of the first term got only so far as the building of the pyramids, still we must be prepared to run back into considerable antiquity. And especially with this first document, on which I proposed to begin our course to-day—the fifty-two articles of the code or record of laws purporting to be granted or confirmed by William the Conqueror. The text of these fifty-two articles rests upon authority which is by no means trustworthy; it is found in two forms, two languages, an early Norman French form and an early Latin form, but not in manuscripts whose antiquity at all approaches the date of the Conquest. Unfortunately, one of the forms in which it is best known to the world is that in which it is preserved in the so-called Ingulf, the fabricated history of the Abbey of Crowland: a work which, pretending to be of the eleventh or early twelfth century, is certainly of the fourteenth century at the earliest, and which is so palpable an imposture that it infects with doubts even the more authentic documents that are embedded in it; but happily the text does not rest on Ingulf alone, it is found also in what is called the Holkham MS., an ancient collection of the thirteenth century which once belonged to Sir Edward Coke, and which anyhow is a century older than the Ingulfine version. The thirteenth century, it is true, is a good way off the eleventh, but as the matter of the text contains nothing that might not be William's, and as it is difficult to say what good it would do to anybody to forge such a document, we accept it as *prima facie* valid. It does not follow, however, that by accepting it as *prima facie* valid, we accept its present form as genuine. It is very improbable that the Conqueror would legislate in Norman French for the English people. The use of Norman French for English legal documents is not common until two centuries after the Conquest, i.e. until about the date at which the earliest extant manuscript of these laws was written ; and the earliest French document in our records is of the time of Archbishop Langton, a century and a half after the Conquest. I am inclined, therefore, to think that the French version is a translation from an earlier form made for the use of the lawyers of the latter part of Henry III.'s reign or of that of Edward I. What, then, about the Latin form, the manuscripts of which are of nearly the same date? Dr. Schmid is inclined to trace in the Latin form as well as in the French vestiges of translation ; and, indeed, if we accept the articles as they stand as a direct expression of the Conqueror's will or legislative confirmation, we must suppose that they would be a translation from some lost Anglo-Saxon document. In default of that lost document, we will suppose them to be a collection, made by some Latin-writing collector or historian, of the laws of the elder kings which William was said to have confirmed, and which, as we shall see, he did confirm, but whether in detail or not it is hard to say.

You see what my conclusion is, that, although there is nothing in the substance of these laws that may not have come from under the Conqueror's hand, there is much in the form of the text and in the character of the sources that have transmitted them that prevents us from accepting them as unquestionably authoritative.

Let us now turn to the circumstances under which we may suppose the articles (if authentic) to have been formulated. William the Conqueror maintained that he claimed the throne of England as the heir of Edward the Confessor, and, as he received the crown in the legal form from the Anglo-Saxon witan and clergy, we cannot question the fact that he undertook to govern them by their national law—by the law, in fact, which a little later, and possibly as early as his coronation, was known as the laws of the good King Edward. That at an early period of his reign he did undertake so to govern, we know on the evidence of an irrefragable document, which we shall take in an early lecture—the ten articles of emendation, as I call them. But it is known that the good King Edward was not a legislator ; he simply followed the laws that Canute before him had accepted as the national customs, and that without making any addition to them. What, then, would be the laws that the Conqueror bound himself to follow ? The authorities of the time fail us altogether ; but a hundred years later Hoveden, under the eye of the great justice Glanville, recorded a story which may have been traditional, and on which, a century later, other chroniclers added a superstructure which is apparently imaginary. According to Hoveden, the Conqueror, in the fourth year of his reign, caused an assembly to be held, out of all the counties of the realm, of the men instructed in the national laws, twelve from each county, who put on record a body, or custumary, of 39 articles, which are henceforth received as the laws of Edward the Confessor. Into these articles I do not propose to examine, because they are really known to us only as edited 120 years after the death of Edward the Confessor, because they do not pretend to any higher authority than that which, on their own showing, they had under the Conqueror's manipulation. It appears from two of these, however, that there had been in William's mind a question whether he should conform to the English, the Danish, or the Anglo-Saxon laws, and that he himself preferred the Danish, but was prevailed upon by the prayers of the *compatriotæ* whom he had brought together to confirm the laws of the Anglo-Saxons, which they then put on record as the laws of Edward and his grandfather, King Edgar the Peaceable.

Now, if we attempt to rationalise upon this story, what do we come to ? William has promised to observe the national laws ? What are the national laws ? The most recent edition of them that could be laid before him was the law of Canute, the Danish or Norse law, as it would be called, although really little more than a recension of the laws of Ethelred and his predecessors. Suppose, then, the king to have said, ' Shall I confirm the laws of Canute ? ' We may imagine some dissent ; not Canute's laws, but Edward's. But where are Edward's ? Only in the loving memory of the *compatriotæ*. Let them be recorded, and let the king confirm in them what he will. This I offer you only as a rationalisation of the fable or tradition preserved in Hoveden.

But what have the 39 articles of the Edwardian tradition to do with the 52 articles of William the Conqueror ? We must not be impartial ; but we have not yet got back to the pyramids of Egypt. It is worth while pointing out that traditions like this are not uncommon prefaces to the recensions of early laws. As I have already said, the national laws existed really in the memories and mouths of the people ; and the written codes are simply records

of the unwritten customs, called forth and recorded on particular
emergencies : *compatriotæ* do not like emergencies, and it is natural
enough to find these records, which circumstances necessitated,
prefaced by fabulous accounts of the legislation in its origin.   Thus
the most ancient of all the codes of the Germanic nations, the law
of the Salian Franks, is said in its preface to be the result of the
deliberations of four elected rulers, Wisogast, Bodogast, Salogast,
and Windogast, who lived at Bodoheim, Saloheim, and Windoheim,
who assembled in three *malli* and issued the laws, which Clovis
afterwards confirmed.   Whether these names are imaginary or have
local belongings, we need hardly inquire ; all sorts of interpretations
re given them, but the story is in parallel with ours.   Similar
stories are connected with other codes.   What historically underlies
them seems to be not that any historical data can be alleged for the
original legislation, but that for the formal recording some historical
crisis may be conjecturally alleged.   There is no doubt that the
laws, for instance, of Alfred and Guthrum, and of Edward and
Guthrum, were an actual concordat and record of the common
terms on which the Danish and Anglo-Saxon neighbours were to
live side by side.   Alfred's own code, containing also as appendix the
laws of his ancestor Ine, and possibly also the laws of Offa, was
probably the first act of his government restored after the conquest
of the Danes, and when he was really, if not by title, lord of the
whole of Southern England.   Certainly Canute's code is the body
of laws to which he was compelled to swear when at Oxford he
received the adhesion of all England ; the codes were rewritten and
amended and perhaps altered, but they were (1) really the sum of
the customs of the nation preserved in memory, and (2) recorded on
the particular occasion, frequently an occasion of pacification or
change of dynasty.

Further on we shall see, as the idea of the king as chief and
original legislator becomes accepted, more frequent confirmations
exacted and vouchsafed, as if, in the newly developed theory of
autocracy, it was uncertain whether the new sovereign would be
content to act upon laws which it was in his power to set aside
until by a solemn promise he had confirmed them.   As the king's
peace was thought to die with him and not to revive until his
successor was crowned, so the laws of the late king seem, if not to
expire, at least to require a new infusion of life in the coronation
oath or coronation charter of the incoming sovereign.   This being
so, and being obliged to refer the laws so-called of Edward the
Confessor to a later date, we may provisionally and conjecturally
suppose the 52 articles of the Conqueror's code to be the redaction,
possibly by a lawyer of the court, possibly by an historian, of

E

those parts of the earlier law on which the king notified himself
willing to act; whether those were collected by the evidence of the
compatriotæ or embodied in a royal manifesto which may possibly
have existed in Anglo-Saxon and is certainly now not forthcoming.
The reason why I have gone into so much detail on this is, of
course, the doubt which I have as to the authenticity of the present
form.

We will now turn to the matter of these laws. They begin thus:
'These are the laws and customs which King William after the
conquest of the land granted to the whole people of the English to
hold; the same to wit as those which Edward King, his cousin and
predecessor, observed.' This preamble shows, I think, that even if
the code is a later redaction of a document of William's, it is older
than the compilation known as Edward's laws, which are much
fuller, and to which it does not refer. Then follow the 52 clauses.
Of these 52, 7 clauses, I think, contain new matter not contained
in the laws of Canute, or easy to be found in the codes of the earlier
kings. We may then first dismiss the 45 re-enacted clauses, and
then say a word or two about the new ones. The whole collection
partakes of the character of the earlier codes in being extremely
confused. There is no attempt at arrangement such as scientific
law-books adopt of distinction of things, persons, and actions, or
between criminal and civil enactments; nor is there the orderly
arrangement of offences and penalties that are found in some of the
earlier codes. The 1st article, however, as usual both now and
long after in codes, charters, and even parliamentary petitions,
provides for the peace and immunity of the church; the 2nd for
the king's peace, with its variety of penalties in the West Saxon
law, the Dane law, and the Mercian law; the 3rd is on the law
administered to persons who having been put under pledge have fled
from justice, with similar distinctions of the local customs in regard
to payment of penalties. Not to be too circumstantial, however,
clauses 5 and 6 relate to theft or detention of lost or stolen cattle;
7 to 11 to homicide and mutilation, and 12 to adultery; 13 is on false
judgment; 14, 15, 16 on theft and sacrilege; 17 on Peter pence
or Romescot; 18, 19 rape and injury to the eyes; 20 on reliefs or
heriots; 21 on warranty; 22 on murdrum; 23, 24 on proceedings in courts of justice; 25 on frankpledge; 26 on the king's
highways; 27 on the thief caught with his plunder; 28 on watch
and ward; 29, 30, 31, 32 on the villein cultivators of the land;
33 forbids a pregnant woman to be put to death; 34 on intestacy;
35, 36 on fornication and poisoning; 37 on *jactura in periculo
mortis*; 38 on allowing one co-partner to suffer by the failure of the
other in litigation; 39 on judges; 40, 41 on capital punishment

and selling into slavery ; 42 on refusal to submit to just judgment ;
43 forbids application to the king until hundred and shire moot
have failed ; 44 is on distraint; 45 on buying before witnesses;
46 on cases in which witnesses are to be required ; 47 on disobedience
to summons; 48 on the reception of strangers ; 49 on allowing a
thief to escape; 50 on refusing to join the hue and cry ; 51 on purgation in the hundred court; and 52 on the lord's duty to have all
his servants in frankpledge.

You will observe, then, with reference to these : (1) that the
provincial distinction of Dane law, West Saxon, and Mercian law
still subsists in its fullness, with variations of penalties, and of the
value of men's lives or weregeld.   (2) That the graduated system
of payments for various injuries, the botes or compensations for
mutilations, &c., still subsist; such injuries are not so much
breaches of the peace as wrongs compensable between individuals.
(3) That in the case of intestates no provision is yet made for the
ecclesiastical jurisdiction to determine the administration of the
goods ; they are to be divided by the children equally. (4) That
the payment of Peter pence to Rome, which in Wessex was traditionally ascribed to Ine, in Mercia was historically referred to Offa,
in united South England was confirmed by Ethelwulf, and newly
arranged and settled by Canute, was recognised as a permanent
institution, as indeed it remained until the reign of Henry VIII.
(5) That ancient customs, the usages of the hundred court and
shire court, of hue and cry, of compurgation, and compurgatory
oaths [of primitive watch and ward]; the prohibition against the
sale of Christians into captivity, which had been forbidden by
Canute, but was still alleged to be practised occasionally ; the
restraint of appeal to the king until justice has failed in the
inferior courts, the requiring witnesses for sales in market, and the
requisition of frankpledge or free pledge in a form to which we
shall have to recur by-and-by, are all re-enacted, confirmed, or
recorded as valid in the words of the more ancient laws. I may
have something more to say in a general way about these ; but we
will now turn to the enactments which are not discoverable in the
older codes.

The first is No. 4, concerning a thief taken without hue and
cry : it seems to refer to the concealment, or not bringing before
the courts, of a person known to be guilty of theft, but not captured
by the hue and cry. In matter it differs little from No. 49, which
deals with the case in which the thief is allowed to escape from
arrest, and the material points in it are common enough, although
the wording is peculiar ; it contains two words which are new to
the English law : the word *divise*, for a court day, and the word

justice for the presiding magistrate; in the Latin, *divisæ* and *justitiarius*. These words come into regular forms in the reign of Henry I.: of the word justice there is no question; of the meaning of *divisæ* the most probable explanation is that it was the court held on the boundaries of the estate or district to which the suit belonged. Of course, in intertribal disputes we can understand that a neutral territory was the fit place for decision; it is less clear in the sense of an ordinary court of justice; hence another meaning has been sought for it, and it is explained to mean a device, that is a solution or decision of a knotty question—an arbitration, in fact. I think myself that it merely means cross-roads, or the point at which several territorial divisions centre, and which would be, as for meetings of foxhounds, so also for hundredmoots and the like, the fittest place. The use of the words, however, is chiefly important here as indicating a possible anachronism, that would be fatal to the authenticity of the text if it were not capable of explanation. But its importance increases when we come to the next article of novelty, No. 22; if anyone kills a Frenchman, and the men of the neighbourhood do not within a week take the slayer and bring him before the justices (a la justise) to show why he did it, they, that is the men of the hundred, are to pay for murdrum 46 marks. Here you see the neglect to help the carrying into effect of the law is made punishable. But this law has a much more important bearing. For in the first place it is distinctly a new law; the Frenchman murdered and the concealment of the murderer are new phenomena. It is possible that Canute may have enacted a similar law to protect the Danes; and indeed, in the laws of Edward the Confessor, the composition of which I have just described, Nos. 14 and 15, such a law is ascribed to Canute. The extant laws, however, of that king contain no such provision, and as in the short and unquestionably genuine record of ten articles which we shall take in a future lecture, this enactment occurs as one of the emendations of the English law introduced by the Conqueror, I am inclined to believe that it really was an innovation, and that in it we have the germ of that *collective responsibility of the hundred* about which there have been so many disputes and on which we have a large controversial literature.

The whole subject of the *frith-borh* and system of *surety* is full of difficulties, and I think it will be better if we examine it, as far as can be done in a lecture like this, when we come to the ten articles; I may just say now that this is, of course, the regulation on which the doctrine of *presentment of Englishry* depends, the usage which directed that if the slain man could not be proved to be a native Englishman, the hundred in which the body was found was responsible for the murder fine: he was, on the fact of being murdered, supposed to be a Frenchman: the burden of the proof lay on the hundred. You will find the current account of the regulation in the 'Dialogus de Scaccario,' lib. i. c. 10; we may say more about it when we come to it again. Anyhow, we may set this down as a piece of new legislation. Art. 23 is new:—if anyone wishes to covenant regarding land tenure with his lord, he shall do so by his peers, whom he shall call to witness, for he cannot do it by strangers. I suppose there need be no question that this enactment belongs to the same class as those of the Francman emperor Conrad the Salic, especially in the passage which I have cited from the Libri Feudorum in the 'Const. Hist.' i. 604, to which I shall have to call your attention again: no knight, miles, greater or smaller, shall lose his benefice except according to the custom of his ancestors and the judgment of his peers. So also the Emperor Lothar in the century following this, and the laws of Henry I. also. Of the fact of judgment by peers—that is, the equals or neighbours of the litigant—there can be, I think, no doubt that it was of the very essence of Anglo-Saxon and Teutonic usage; but this is an early instance of the use of the form *per pares*, and may be regarded as anachronistic, although only by a very few years. No. 24 is also new. In every court, save in the king's presence, if it is charged on anyone that he has said in plea something that he says he has not said, unless he can prove by trustworthy witness of eye and ear that he has not said it, his first statement must hold good. There is something in this that accords with the regulation 13 of the assize of Clarendon, and with the law on courts of record as explained by Glanville in the ninth chapter of Book VIII., where it is stated that except the court of the king, no court has record generally, for in other courts if a man has said anything and repented of it, he may against the whole court deny that he has said it, on the assertion of two other witnesses and his own oath; but the practice in Glanville's own time was changing, and in some cases minor courts had record, by assize of the realm made thereon. The assize of Clarendon, if that be the assize referred to, makes the law more stringent, and the assize of Northampton makes it more stringent still, article 3. Article 28, providing for watch and ward, streetward as it is called, is in this form new, and so new that one feels rather inclined to question its authenticity: four men of every hide in the hundred are to be found to act as streetwards, from Michaelmas to Martinmas, the chief of the guards to have thirty hides quit of tax for his labour. This is very puzzling, for why the streetward should be limited to the weeks between September 29 and November 11 it is difficult to imagine; and it seems better to give up the passage as corrupt than to waste

time upon it. That there was such an office as streetward, *custos
viarum*, surveyor of highways, person responsible for the disposal
of waifs and strays, we know from other sources ; but unless the
particular provision has something to do with watching the roads
after or during the later harvest, or providing for the clearing of
them when the fences were thrown down and the common lands
opened for the cattle, I give it up.

We go on to article 81. If the lords of the lands cannot procure
fit and sufficient cultivators to cultivate their lands, the justices
shall do it. This, again, is a very curious provision, to which, so
far as I know, we have nothing analogous in earlier or later law ; and
I can find no commentator who has touched it. It is an inviting
text for a long speculation, and might be used by the agitators of
the present day, if they knew of it, with a good deal of the courage
that arises from the certainty of not being contradicted. The French
of this law is scarcely concordant with the Latin : ' Si les seignurages
ne facent altri gainurs venir a lour tere la justice le facet ; ' if the
lordships do not make other cultivators come to their lands the
justice may do so. Does it mean that the crown, or the law, or
the national authority still retained such hold on the land that rather
than let it fall out of cultivation, the magistrate was to enter on it
and to compel the lords to have it cultivated ; or does it mean that
land was to be so free that if the lord refused to admit a strange
tenant to unoccupied ground the justices might compel him ? Or
does it mean nothing at all, or something quite different that the
insertion of a new word or discovery of a new text might explain ?
We know from the statute of Merton that the rights of the lord to
inclose were limited by the requirements of his tenants for common
land ; is it possible that there is some restriction here on the right
of the lord to inclose hunting grounds as William inclosed the New
Forest ? I cannot decide.

No. 36 is new. If anyone kills another by poison, he shall either
be put to death or perpetually exiled. Happily this is new—
poisoning was not an English crime, and in the legend of Queen
Eadburga, who poisoned her husband Brihtric, is handed down
traditionally for detestation. Did the Normans introduce poisoning ?
Certainly they introduced the treatment of it as a legal offence.
Some of our pessimist friends will perhaps tell us that among the
Anglo-Saxons it was no crime ; or others that, like parricide in the
old Greek story, it was so unheard-of an offence that the law could
prescribe no punishment for it. Here it stands as the subject of a
new law. We know from Ordericus Vitalis that poisoning was a
charge alleged against the Conqueror by his enemies ; putting two
and two together, we conclude that it was a crime on the increase,

more commonly imputed, more clearly requiring preventive and punitive treatment.

The next two articles which I shall mention owe their interest to the fact that they relate to matters treated of in the Roman law but as yet new to English law: art. 37, de jactura metu mortis facta; if a shipmaster to save his ship throws into the sea lading that belongs to another, he shall purge himself by oath of any other motive than the fear of death, and the salvage shall be divided among the other owners according to their respective shares in the original lading. Now this regulation throws us back on the ancient lex Rhodia de jactu, Digest 14. 2 (where the law is ' ut si levandæ navis gratia jactus mercium factus est, omnium contributione sarciatur quod pro omnibus datum est '); there is not much correspondence in the words, and the principle is scarcely the same. The English law divides the salvage, the lex Rhodia divides the damage but leaves the salvage to its owners. Now how can this bit of ancient legislation have got into William's code? The Digest, you are aware, was very little indeed known in the West until forty years after this; the legislation of the Theodosian Code, which was to some extent known in France, leaves the decision of all such matters in the hands of the judges, but does not, so far as I can find, prescribe the same rule (lib. xiii. pt. 9). It is an older law far than the Theodosian, and occurs among the *sententiæ* of Paulus the legist, who lived soon after Adrian. In all these matters you will find a great deal of illustration in each of the four volumes of Twiss's Black-book of the Admiralty. Of the question how it got here I can only say that it appears in one shape or another in all the legal systems of the maritime nations which Dr. Twiss has collected in various parts of his work, and may very well be indigenous. The relation to the law of the Pandects is not fatal to its genuineness here, but I question whether any more ancient regulation than this of William can be found in black and white in any of the Western codes. The laws of Oleron, the assizes of Jerusalem, and the French sea laws are all later in date, and this Act, if it be genuine, may be regarded as our first Act of admiralty law.

The question which arises on art. 39 is of a kindred character. ' If two or more divide an inheritance, and one without the other or others, being called to law, out of folly or other cause loses his suit, the partners ought not to undergo loss therefrom, because res inter alios judicata does not prejudice, especially if they were not present.' This is new and has a certain relation to Roman law, i.e. to book 8 of the Code, c. 45, and 3 Code 36, l. 8, and indeed must have been suggested by a state of things in which some shadow of the Roman law was operative as it was in the South of

France, and in some respects in the customary law of the North. I can only guess that it crept in with the other from some early law book. Certainly it does not imply any acquaintance with the text of the Code, but with the principle of the Roman law, præjudicari non debet alii per alium, it does seem to agree more perfectly than the text of the laws to which at first sight it might be referred.

The other points of interest in this Code of 52 articles I shall take in an examination of the 10 short articles of emendation, which we will examine in the next lecture. I will only add now that of all the documents which I propose to investigate in this course, this is the only one about the authenticity and purity of which there can be any question ; many of the details that I have noticed lose all force and bearing when the authority of the document is questioned, and I have been obliged to speak conjecturally and tentatively where I would gladly have worked the matter more deeply had I been sure of my ground.

WILLIAM I.

1. De pace ecclesiæ, 63.
2. De pace regia, 12–15.
3. De plegiatis fugientibus.
4. De latrone capto sine uhtesio.
5. De averiis quos prepositus hundredi restari fecerit.
6. De averio errante.
7. De homicidiis.
8. De were diversorum.
9. Quid fiat de were.
10. De vulnerante alium.
11. De membrorum mutilatione.
12. Si quis violat uxorem proximi, 50.
13. De judicio falso, 15.
14. De appellatis ex furto, 22.
15. Si appellatur quis de violatione ecclesiæ vel cameræ, 63, 65.
16. De forisfacturis.
17. De denariis S. Petri, 1. 9.
18. De vi opprimentibus, 53.
19. De oculo eruto.
20. De releviis, 71.
21. De waranto producendo.
22. De murdre.
23. Si quis contra dominum suum terram petat.
24. Si quis negat in curia se dixisse quod ei imponitur.
25. De francoplegio, 20.
26. De tribus stratis regiis.
27. Si furtum cum fure reperitur.
28. De stretwarde.
29. De colonis terræ.

30. De nativis, 28.
31. De terra colenda.
32. Ne quis justum servitium domino subtrahat.
33. Ne fœmina prægnans judicium mortis subeat.
34. De sine testamento morientibus, 71.
35. Si pater filiam, etc.
36. De veneficio.
37. De jactura metu mortis facta, Digest 14. 2.
38. Ne quis ex judicio alterius præjudicium patiatur, See Code 3. 36–8. 45.
39. De judiciis et judicibus, 2–2. 15.
40. Ne quis pro parvo delicto morti adjudicetur, 2.
41. Ne Christiani extra terram vel paganis vendantur, 3.
42. De hiis qui justum judicium repellant.
43. Ne quis regi conqueratur, 17.
44. Ne quis temere namium capiat, 19.
45. Ne quis sine testibus aliquid emat, 24.
46. Ne probatio fiat super testes, 24.
47. De rectato qui vocatus non comperit, 25, 26.
48. Ne quis hospitem, 28.
49. Ne quis furem, 29.
50. De non insequentibus, 29.
51. De culpato in hundredo, 30.
52. Ut dominus in francoplegio, c. 31.

The document on which I am going to lecture to-day is the 10 articles of amendment or emendation by which William the Conqueror altered or added to the laws of Edward the Confessor, as the ancient customs of the nation recorded and confirmed by Canute had now come to be called. The Code which we have already criticised was, as we concluded, a record, or translation of a record, of a similar confirmation by the Conqueror; but we saw reason, both in the sources from which we derived the text and from the intrusion of some strange articles into the material texture of the record, to recognise its authenticity only with some distinct reservations and with some misgivings. The document which we take to-day will lead me to recapitulate some similar misgivings. We have it in two forms. One is that printed in the ' Select Charters,' which is not in the form of a distinct legislative act, whether as a law, a charter, or an assize; but in the form rather of a memorandum, a sort of historical appendix to a previously recognised code or historical memoir. The other shape in which we have it is in the form of a charter, in which form the matter of the 10 articles, together with some additional articles to which we shall have to give detailed attention, appears as a sort of letters patent or grant made by William, king of the English and duke of the Normans, to all his homines, French and English; and in this form contains 17 articles; assuming moreover to be attested like a proper charter, ' Testibus &c.,'

but the names not being given. This document, which in this shape is headed 'Carta Regis Willelmi Conquæstoris de quibusdam statutis,' is found in its oldest authority among the materials inserted in the reign of Edward I. in the Red-book of the Exchequer, that very important treasury from which the 'Dialogus de Scaccario' and several other invaluable illustrations of constitutional history are derived. The document is in fact the first of a series of additions made to the Liber Ruber after folio 162, where the original hand, of about 1230, ceases. I shall point out to you the features which, in my mind, impress upon it a date of about sixty years later; but I will here anticipate so far as to say that I think it is a forgery, a fabrication based on the earlier and genuine record of the 10 articles which we have in manuscripts of the early years of the twelfth century, especially in the famous Textus Roffensis, the Codex Diplomaticus of the ancient church of Rochester, of the authenticity of which there cannot be a shadow of a doubt.

Before entering on the analysis I should like to follow up some of the remarks which I have made on Ingulf, with an observation or two on the nature of mediæval historical forgeries which I think will interest you ; for they are very numerous, and are not to be judged exactly by the same rule by which you would gauge the impostures of Chatterton or of Ireland in more recent times. Mediæval forgeries are of several kinds : there are forged Anglo-Saxon and Norman charters, forged royal confirmations and papal bulls, forged and interpolated civic documents, forged and fabricated histories like that of Ingulf, forged writings of tendency like the *Modus tenendi parliamentum* which is printed at the end of the 'Select Charters,' and forged state documents such as those which were procured or constructed by the historian Harding in the fifteenth century to support the claim of the English crown to the overlordship of Scotland. Of the forged Anglo-Saxon charters this is the most probable account. All the earliest gifts of land to churches or individuals were made by what was later called livery of seisin before witnesses : if offered to a church, by presenting a sod or something else, a horn or a cup, or suchlike, on the altar ; and if bestowed on an individual, possibly, as in later manorial proceedings, by delivery of a wand : there may be some doubts as to the method of conveyance, but there can be no doubt that it was formal and oral, and in very few cases by the composition of a written grant. But as the settlement of England under the Anglo-Saxon dynasties gained firmness and permanence, and as the nation increased in knowledge of letters, and conformed to Catholic and continental civilisation, as the churches began to collect their documents and examine the title deeds or titles by which they held their lands, when the possession of a book or libellus became a common if not universally required evidence of title, and it was found that many estates were held without such title, a strong temptation was put before men to construct *ex post facto* title deeds. That I believe to be the secret of all the early monastic forgeries they were attempts, not to get hold of estates which did not really belong to the churches, but to substitute a written title for the immemorial prescriptive title that rested on oral witness and a succession of traditions.

The importance of having a clear view on this head is so great that I must dwell on it in more detail. The idea having been once broached that an antedated title deed would be valid, the occasions for the construction of such title deeds multiplied. The flood of Danish invasion swept over the land, many whole tribes were extinguished, and many local sanctuaries were left desolate. But when peace returned, as it did under Alfred and Edward, and when the royal authority was re-established universally by Edgar and Dunstan, when settled society in church and state revived, there arose questions about property which were insoluble without written evidence. The churches which were reinstated, reinhabited, and restored looked about for their estates, and a great accumulation of new charters was constructed to vindicate claims to lands which were imperfectly identified : some monastic bodies that were powerful enough to do it, recovered and held fast more than their predecessors had lost, and got valid new charters ; some, I grieve to say, unquestionably fabricated grants for themselves, copying the genuine title deeds of their neighbours and inserting names and boundaries to suit themselves. The moral guilt involved in this proceeding is certainly considerable, but it is not complicated with aggressive wrong doing. That no doubt was occasionally to be found : men forged title deeds to get the property of others secured to themselves ; as a rule these early forgeries were simple fabrications to secure by an additional sanction property that already belonged to the fabricators. The great stock of fabricated charters belong to the age of Edgar, the era, as it was supposed, of monastic revival; but many much later records are detected, and the foundation charters of Westminster among them.

When, after a generation or two, these very questionable evidences had gained repute for antiquity, the monastic houses began to look out for an historian, and the historian in more or less perfect good faith began to construct a history out of what was known to be the true history of his house, and what inferences he could draw from the evidences. Such was William of Malmesbury in his relation to the history of his own abbey and that of Glastonbury, a writer of perfect soundness and honesty, but obliged to work on material the authenticity of which he could scarcely help suspecting. As the centuries passed on and the early history became in memory still more obscured, the growing monasteries, like rising families at the present day, grew more and more anxious about their pedigrees. The process of fabrication, once begun, required ever new fabrications to sustain the old ones, and this necessity produces such a wanton forgery as that of the Ingulfine history of Crowland : a composition partly based on forged charters, partly concocted to give a rational and probable explanation of those forgeries, and partly the result of simple wanton mischief. Ingulf is the greatest example of this sort of wickedness, which is quite different from the half-honest, half-dishonest conduct of the early cartularists ; but the pseudo-Ingulf does not stand quite alone ; and there are in the early chronicles of Peterborough and some other abbeys phenomena scarcely less repulsive ; but let us not get back to the pyramids.

Another class of forgeries is of even more importance, the class to which belong the forged decretals of the pseudo-Isidore, the collection of fabricated bulls and privileges of the popes, which appeared in the time of Charles the Bald, and, although always suspected, exercised a fatal influence on the policy of the church of Rome until the Reformation. The fabrication of new religious laws was even more abhorrent to our ideas of justice than the forging of title deeds ; and although I would not put the pseudo-Isidorian decretals on the level of the Book of Mormon, for they, like the fabricated title deeds, were probably meant originally to sustain existing but unproven rights, still they sapped the moral sense of legists and set a very bad example. It was found soon as easy to forge papal privileges as to concoct grants of land ; and although, whenever it was discovered, it leads to condign punishment, it was not always discovered, and the fountains of history were, until critical diplomatic power was set to work on them, to some extent corrupted. There was a further and very ancient line of forgery, to entitle a new work by the name of an old writer, and so produce a set of apocryphal books, such as those which are collected in the appendices to Augustine and Jerome ; or even without intentional supposititious fathering, to publish recensions and expansions as the work of original authors of note. Archbishop Theodore was a great authority on penance, and composed a small tract on it. Two centuries later a large and heavy compilation on the subject was current under his name ; also the received works of Archbishop Egbert of York and some of the other penitentialists have only a small substratum of original matter. Now this form of fabrication was easily applicable to books of law, the authority of which depended in a great degree on the name of the legist. Many

capitularies were very early in circulation ascribed to Charles the
Great and Charles the Bald, the authenticity of which is more than
questionable, but which possibly contain a germ of authentic enactment. Why men should have cared to forge such things is a
problem inscrutable, unless we suppose it to have been done in order
to establish some small right in the law courts, and to wrap up the
point to be gained in a cloud of obscure probabilities : to produce in
support of a false claim a charter or record that contains so much
that is probable and respectable that the little but all-important
point at issue shall not be seen to have been foisted in inten-
tionally.

This brings us to the last class of forgeries, which is that of
state documents ; the adapting a genuine document by garbling or
important apparently casual interpolation, to the obtaining of some
further point ; and this brings us to the fabrication of the documents
before us. I very much fear that the lawyers of Edward I.'s court
were not above the trick of introducing into older records little
expressions that helped the theories, political or otherwise, that prevailed in their own days. In the copies of the laws of Edward the
Confessor, which we talked about in the last lecture, preserved
among the records of the city of London, there is a distinct inter
polation bearing on the right of the counties to elect their own
sheriffs, which, if it were necessary, would prove that particular
recension to have been written out at a time when the election of
sheriffs was a moot point between the crown and the counties ; and
in the document we are now to examine we shall find similar points.

As I have spent so much of our time on these fabrications,
I propose that we take the fabricated form of the 10 articles first,
and reserve the genuine form for consideration when we have
rejected the forged clauses. With the copy of the ' Select Charters '
before you, you will easily follow the text, and recognise the interpolations in the supposititious document. The so-called charter
begins with the salutation ; it is in itself peculiar ; if you look at
the genuine charter on the division of the courts, p. 85 of the
' Select Charters,' you will see that it begins with a salutation to
definite persons of a definite county and in the first person. The
genuine letter is to all my faithful ; the fabricated charter is to all
his *homines*. The form addressed to *sui* comes in so soon, certainly
under Henry I., that not much can be inferred from this, but more
from what follows ; there is no preamble, no motive clause, no such
order as is always apparent in letters patent, as know ye, or whereas,
but simply *statuimus* super omnia ; the king begins to speak in
the first person plural, *statuimus, volumus, interdicimus, pro-
hibemus*. Now, whatever **may have** been the usage in informal

writing, in formal letters no king of England before Richard I. ever writes in the first person plural; from that date it is common. I think that this sign is fatal to the supposition that this is a genuine Act; but you will tell me, Ah, but look at the form which you assume to be genuine, the 10 articles printed in the 'Select Charters;' there you have *statuimus* in the 1st article and *interdicimus* in the 5th. That is true; but if you look at the heading of the document you will see that it purports not to be an edict drawn up by the king himself, but an intimation of what was done by him with his chief counsellors. Of the clauses that begin with the plural form, we may very well suppose them to be either the constitutions of a witenagemot or the redaction of a compiler, but they cannot be regarded as the form of an authentic legislative Act. The record of the 10 articles is simply a record of articles; it is not the imperative and formal precept by which the enactment is made.

We will now take the garbled and inserted articles of the charter form; just premising that while we are quite clear as to the validity of the objections taken on the ground of the wording and on some of the interpolated articles, as against the genuineness of the form, it is not necessary to reject entirely all the matter that is not found in the Textus Roffensis. But I will distinguish as we proceed. The first clause stands thus in what for shortness I shall call the genuine copy as distinct from the Exchequer Charter. In the first place he would that above all things one God should be worshipped through the whole of his kingdom, one faith of Christ be always kept inviolate, peace and concord be preserved between English and Normans. The Exchequer Charter reads: 'We ordain that, using the same words, but adding to the English and Normans, French and Britons of Wales and Cornwall, Picts and Scots of Albany, likewise between the French and the islanders, provinces and countries which belong to the crown and dignity; defence and observance and honour of our realm and among all our subjects through the universal monarchy of the realm of Britain, be firmly and inviolably observed, so that none injure another in anything upon our full forfeiture.' This very extraordinary amplification, the talk about the Scots and Picts of Albany, and the universal monarchy of Britain, is not indeed impossible in the age of the Conqueror, who certainly at what we must suppose to have been a later period of his reign obtained from Malcolm Canmore the acknowledgment of his feudal superiority over Scotland, and who likewise, as his predecessors had done, kept the Welsh princes under nominal subjection; but the tone and language of this clause, the distinction between French and Normans, *Picts and Scots*, and so

on, is out of all real harmony either with the history or the diplomacy
of the time. I can hardly doubt that the concoction of the article
belongs to the reign of Edward I., and possibly to a period as late
as the parliament of Lincoln in 1301, when that king drew up in
answer to the papal claims his statement of the rights of the
English crown over Scotland. Read thus, it is natural enough to
speak of the monarchy of the island, for Edward was really king
over all Britain, Balliol having incurred forfeiture, and Bruce
having not yet been crowned ; for ten years, 1296–1306, there was no
titular king of Scots ; Edward I. did not, so far as I am aware,
incorporate the title in his legal documents, but he was in his own
idea the king as well as the overlord of the escheated fief. If this
document had been in existence or known in 1292, I think it must
have been adduced in support of the historical claim. I do not for
a moment suspect Edward I. of forging it, but that it was done in
the interest of some political party among his ministers I have no
doubt. If you provisionally agree to this you will find that it
explains the use of the words Normans as well as French. I
believe that William in genuine documents always uses the form
Franci for his own followers ; but in the genuine articles of the
Textus Roffensis *Normannos* is used ; those genuine articles not
purporting to be a legal edict would not be confined to legal language, but the use of *Normanni* in the genuine form of course
accounts for the use of it in the garbled form. But if that is
granted, who are the *Franci* who come afterwards ? Edward had
other French subjects, the Gascons and people of Ponthieu ; but
William's French subjects were all Normans, or Norman lords of
outlying dependencies. And who are the *insulani* ? In William's
reign the Channel islanders were a part of the Norman people, but
in Edward's the Norman people were lost, and the men of Jersey
and Guernsey were the only Normans left. *The Picts and Scots of
Albany*, that is a pedantic expression, very foreign to the reign of
the Conqueror, but not strange to the pen of an antiquary who had
been hunting through Bede and Geoffrey of Monmouth and
William of Malmesbury to find arguments for the monarchia. The
Picts of Galloway and the Scots of Dalnada and the Albans of
Central and Eastern Scotland had been forgotten by the time of
the Conqueror, who if he wanted to distinguish the various populations would have spoken of the Galwegians and Cumbrians and
Scots, possibly throwing in the Picts to make weight ; but between
his days and those of the Exchequer Charter, William of Malmesbury, Geoffrey of Monmouth, and Henry of Huntingdon had
written, and made the more ancient names familiar.

I do not wish to dwell at an unnecessary length upon this point;
but if any of you would like to pursue it farther, I may add that by
comparing the form of the laws of Edward the Confessor as given
by Hoveden with the form in which they appear in Lambarde's
Archaionomia and in the record books of the city of London,
printed in the N.R. Series, and put in their present form *early in
the fourteenth century*, you will have no doubt whatever as to the
spirit and possibly the hand that formulated this article. I leave
the authentic matter of this clause for future comment, and go on
to the next, which stands thus in the Textus Roffensis : ' We ordain
that every freeman affirm by covenant and oath, that within and
without England they will be faithful to King William, will preserve
his lands and honour in all fealty with him and before him to
defend them against all enemies.' This is a very important article,
but I notice now only the point that in the Exchequer Charter
the simple word *Angliam* is expanded into 'universum regnum
Angliæ quod olim vocabatur regnum Britanniæ,' *Willelmo regi* is
supplemented with the words *domino suo,* and to the word *inimicos*
is added *et alienigenas.* The universal monarchy of Britain is the
idea, of course, that we have stigmatised in the former clause ; the
words *domino suo* seem to substitute the doctrine of feudal obligation
for the one of simple allegiance expressed in *regi* ; but I do not
know that, except as a straw showing the way of the wind, that is of
any importance, and indeed the word *domino* is in some earlier
copies, but the *alienigenæ*, the aliens, the dreaded enemies of the
reigns of Henry III. and Edward II., were people who had no political
existence in the reign of the Conqueror, and may be regarded as an
amplification in this place quite proving by themselves a later date.

The 3rd article, except for the use of the plural number, and
the foisting in the *universum regnum*, is the same in both documents ; the 4th also, but this in the genuine form closes with the
note that it was granted in *civitate claudia* in the city of Gloucester,
which, with the change of London for Gloucester, appears as a note
to the 9th article of the Exchequer Charter. Articles 5, 6, 7, 8,
and 9 of the Exchequer Charter are not among the genuine articles.
Take them one by one. ' We will also and firmly enjoin and grant
that all free men of the whole monarchy of our realm aforesaid have
and hold their lands and possessions well and in peace, free from
all unjust exaction and from all tallage, so that nothing be exacted
or taken from them except their free service which they owe
and are bound to make to us of right, and as has been appointed
to them, and given them by us and granted by hereditary right for
ever, by the common counsel of all our kingdom aforesaid.' Ah,
what a wonderful thing is this ! A charter that forbids tallage and

unjust exaction, and which in all the contests of the thirteenth
and fourteenth centuries was never once appealed to, that forbids
tallage long before the word tallage came into use for an English
tax, that alleges the *commune consilium* of the kingdom as a joint
authority with the king in establishing hereditary right. I take it
there can be no doubt that this clause belongs to the age in which
the so-called statute de tallagio non concedendo was framed, and in
which it had begun to be believed that as the king was the supreme
lord of the land, all land was mediately or immediately held by
statutory gift made by him at the Conquest.

Article 6.—'We order and firmly enjoin that all cities and
boroughs, castles, hundreds and wapentakes, of our whole kingdom
be watched and guarded every night all round, for evil doers and
enemies, as the sheriffs, *aldermen*, and reeves and others our bailiffs
and servants shall best provide by common counsel for the interest
of the kingdom.' Really and truly, all that ever was practicable in
this enactment was the watch and ward, in reference to which
I noted the difficulty about streetward in a former lecture, which
was provided for between Michaelmas and Martinmas by clause 28
in the French laws, but which was made a general and legal police
regulation only by the statute of Winchester in the year 1285. The
use of the word *alderman* for an inferior officer to the sheriff is itself
a proof of late fabrication, and the final clause, leaving these inferior
officers to determine how for the interest of the kingdom they
should arrange the discharge of their duties, is one that could not
have come from a hand experienced in the ordinary forms of
governmental administration.

The 7th is an unimportant point: that they have through
the whole kingdom most faithful and signed measures and most
faithful and signed weights as our good predecessors have ordained.
William I.'s good predecessors had not regulated weights and
measures; they had accepted the customary weights and measures
of the several districts just as they and he accepted the variations of
fines and moneys in the Dane law, the West-Saxon law, and the
Mercian law. But Edward I.'s predecessors, every one of them since
Richard I., had been striving in vain to secure uniformity; Magna
Carta had had a clause, but a feeble one; Edward I. even fixed his
own arm as the standard of measure, at least so the story goes.
This is not an enactment of the Conqueror's age, and it is one
which is scarcely observed now; after so long a series of laws as we
have on the subject, local weights and measures are not yet extinct
in many parts of the universal realm of England.

The 8th article is one on which a great deal of history would
hang if it were genuine. 'We ordain and firmly enjoin that all

earls, barons, knights, and servientes, and all free men of our whole
realm aforesaid, have and hold themselves always well in arms and
horses as becomes and behoves them, and that they be always
prompt and well prepared to fulfil and perform for us their entire
service whenever the need shall arise, according to what they ought
to do to us for their fiefs and holdings of right and as we ordained
to them by the common counsel of our whole realm aforesaid, and
gave them and granted in fee by hereditary right.   Let neither
precept be violated in any manner on our full forfeiture.'   This last
threat is borrowed from another and genuine clause.

The 8th clause itself is a fairly well drawn exposition of the
feudal doctrine as it was held in the reign of Edward I., but not as
it was either formulated or executed under the Conqueror; the
wording of the article is in the language of the writs of Edward I.,
as may be easily seen ; and the reference to a parliamentary security
for the grant of the fiefs is redolent of the belief of the same period.
The idea that the Conqueror did formally grant or regrant the
lands of the country with some novel obligation of service, is older
than the reign of Edward I., and may be traced in the Dialogus de
Scaccario ; and it was very potent in the fifteenth century, when
Henry IV. was implored not to base his title on conquest lest it
should unsettle the ownership of land throughout the country ; but
there is no historical ground for believing that the Conqueror, however large and numerous the grants he made, or however novel the
terms may have been on which he granted them, ever by any general
enactment ordained a general *hereditary tenure*, or introduced any
change whatever into the national rules of succession.   The clause
as it stands has, however, like that on the tallage, bearings far wider
than we can take in a lecture like this, which is mainly on textual
criticism ; and for those material bearings if we cannot take them
in another lecture, I must refer you to what I have said in the
Constitutional History on the relation of William's Acts, especially in the Great Council of Salisbury, to the true history of the
growth of feudalism.

The 9th clause runs as follows : ' We ordain and firmly
enjoin that all free men of the whole of our realm aforesaid be
sworn brethren, sworn to defend to the utmost of their power, and
to preserve with their might against our enemies, our monarchy
and our kingdom according to their power and means, and to
maintain the peace and dignity of our crown, and to do right ·judg-
ment and justice by all means after their power, without dole and
without delay.'   This decree was established in the city of London.
It is a very pretty sentiment we say, and charmingly in concert with
the Edwardian view of the duty of the subject.   England was to be

a sort of sworn guild, a fraternity of goodwill. This is not like the language of the Conqueror, even in his best frame. Poor John in 1205, when he expected a French invasion, directed that his subjects should form themselves into a *communitas or guild for national defence,* and his grandson was quite sufficient of an idealist to conceive the same idea in a higher and nobler form; but neither the guild nor the oath, nor the supposed solidarity of king and people which is traceable in this article as it stands, *would have been intelligible in the age of the Conqueror.*

The 10th clause of the Exchequer record is the 5th clause of the genuine articles. The 11th is new, but not important as matter of criticism; it is against the continuance of markets except in cities and walled towns, and contains a clause stating that castles, burghs, and cities are founded for the defence of the people and of the realm. I am not at all sure that this clause may not preserve some relic of real legislation; but if it does we may discuss it when we come to consider the bearing of the genuine clauses. The 12th, 13th, 14th, and part of the 15th article are genuine, and answer to articles 6, 7, 8, and 9 of the true record. The 15th is this : ' We forbid that any shall sell a man out of his country.' To this the Exchequer record adds : ' If any one wishes to make his servant free, let him deliver him to the sheriff in full county court by the right hand; and quit-claim him from the yoke of slavery by manumission, and show him free ways and gates ; and deliver to him free arms, that is to say lance and sword ; then he is made a free man.' In connection with this take the 16th article, which is likewise new : ' Also if slaves remain without being claimed for a year and a day in our cities or in burghs and walled towns, or in our castles, from that day let them be made free, let them be free for ever from the yoke of their slavery.' Here we have two plans laid down apparently by royal edict to enable the serf to obtain his liberty. Of these, the second, the emancipating power of the 'year and day's' abiding in a free town, is a well-known fact of the twelfth-century law; and if it stood alone would not prove an anachronism in this place. The other, the form of manumission, is curious, and not improbably as old as the Conqueror's time; it is at all events among the Leges Henrici I., No. 78, and there is a case in the History of Ramsey where the bestower of an estate in the monastery manumits 30 men 'quemadmodum eum sors docuit, ut in quadrivio positi pergerent quocunque vellent.' This, then, whether a part of William's legislation or not, is of pretty nearly the same date.

The last article is in substance the same in both codes, but with an amplification in the Exchequer article which is doubtful. We may consider them both together in the next lecture, which I shall give to the historical bearing of the genuine clauses.

My objections to the Exchequer version are firstly formal, based on the inconsistency of the language of the articles with the language of the Conqueror's times; and secondly material, based on the anachronistic character of the legislation conveyed in them. But it must not be forgotten that while the objections to the language arise from the employment of forms that warrant the Edwardian assumptions of a monarchy of the whole of Britain, some of the material anachronisms relate to the antedating of Acts which seem to limit the royal power as asserted by that great king; while others illustrate a feudal theory that all his contemporaries would hold. But, on the other hand, the 10 articles which we shall next examine can scarcely claim to be either the full text or an exhaustive résumé of the Conqueror's legislation; little pieces of despotic legislation may very well have escaped the eye even of the compiler of the Textus; the mere fact of these articles of the Exchequer record not being in the Rochester record is not fatal to them; some of the minor ones may be real relics; if there are any such we may expect to meet with them again among the laws of Henry I.

I now proceed to take really at last in order the several clauses of the record of 10 articles lying before you in the 'Select Charters.' The first of these is one the importance of which cannot be over-rated, and yet which requires little comment. It is the clause which recognises the duty towards God as the first of all obligations and as the basis of all duties towards men. In the majority of the ancient English codes the first article is a religious regulation. The laws of Ethelbert begin with recognising the rights of the church, and those of Alfred by a recapitulation of most of the bases of moral and religious law that he and his wise men wished to impress on the minds of Englishmen. The direct pedigree, however, of this article begins with the laws agreed upon by Edward the Elder and Guthrum, the Danish king, when they made their great peace. Possibly the form is one that Alfred and Guthrum had used, for it is entitled with Alfred's name, and it was under his auspices that the elder Guthrum received Christianity. The first article is, 'Imprimis est ut unum Deum diligere velint et omni paganismo renuntiare.' Similar words appear at the head of the laws recorded by Ethelred II. in 1008, and in some of the other rescripts issued during his reign by the witenagemot at seasons when, believing that the visitations of the Danes were a judgment of Divine indignation upon them, they strove by recognitions of the authority of the Almighty to set the duty of repentance and good life more strongly before the people.

In the laws of Canute, whose father had been a pagan, and who was himself, one might almost say, a neophyte, the words read almost like a concordat with a Christian people. They appear at the head of his laws ecclesiastical, the establishment or confirmation which he makes of the joint working of spiritual and temporal government. 'Imprimis est ut Deum et Dominum nostrum tota mente diligamus et unam Christianitatis sanctæ fidem Catholicam orthodoxe teneamus.' It is due to Canute to say that the spirit which runs through the whole of his laws is a really religious spirit, quite as much so as that which appears in the legislation of the earlier kings; but there can be little doubt that there was great significance in his thus putting at the head of his laws the determination to maintain the worship of the Christian's God. Many of his followers were doubtless still pagans, and did not accept the law which their master had accepted with his whole heart; them he sent back to Denmark when in the third or fourth year of his reign he determined to accept the English laws and to rule England as a national king.

In the laws of the Conqueror the words have perhaps a less significant force. There was no paganism here, or indeed among the Norman followers of William; the words are not a renunciation of heathenism or polytheism, nor expressive of a determination to abolish false worship. They read rather as a general assertion of Christian belief, a fit preliminary to a code intended to secure under Divine as well as human sanctions good government, peace, justice, and equity. The corresponding clause in the 52 articles which we reviewed in a previous lecture is a direction to respect the immunities of the church. In the present collocation this clause probably was considered to have an equivalent force, but it does not appear in the words.

The 1st clause of the 52 is analogous to corresponding legislation in the laws of Edmund and Edgar; here, as we have seen, the very language is that of Canute, followed by a declaration of the unity of the faith and the peace and security of English and Normans under one sceptre. I do not want to make too much of the wording of this article, but it is to me rather impressive as the declaration of one who, with all his tyrannical and selfish instincts, was desirous to set himself before the nation and the world outside as a true national king. I believe that besides their relation to older laws the words express the meaning and may even reproduce the language of the promises made at the coronation, when the new king undertook to observe three precepts—to keep the peace of the church and people, to put down all iniquities and rapacities, and ordain in all judgments equity and mercy.

The 2nd clause prescribes a duty on the part of the nation corresponding with the promise of good government made by the king in the first clause; just as at the coronation the royal promise of good government is followed by the homages of the lords and people, so here the declaration of religion and peace on the one side is supplemented by the undertaking of fealty on the other. 'We ordain that every freeman shall affirm by covenant and oath, that within England and without they will be faithful to King William, to conserve his lands and honour in all fealty with him, and before him to defend him against his enemies.' This oath of fealty to the king may be very ancient indeed; it appears in the English laws in the form of an oath first in the laws of Edmund, which you have in 'Select Charters,' p. 67, in a form corresponding to the prescribed oath of allegiance among the forms of oath, Schmid, p. 405. This oath of William's, however, seems to be a little more than the mere oath of allegiance, without amounting to the later oath of fealty that was bound up with the ceremony of homage. It may be a transitional form, or it may be not a form at all, but simply the description of a form; and that being so, I am not sure whether we ought to say distinctly that the oath prescribed here is exactly analogous to the oath taken by all landowners at Salisbury in 1086 ('Select Charters,' p. 82), by which, whosesoever men they were (and whatsoever their tenure, for we must suppose that to be included in the generalisation), they swore that they would be faithful to the king against all other men. But there is no doubt that substantially it is the same oath—the oath of faithful allegiance to the king intended to supersede all minor obligations subsisting by virtue of feudal relations between the vassal and his immediate lord. This is not exactly the place, and it would moreover take us too far from the present subject of study, to go in any detail into the difference between the obligations of allegiance and homage and fealty, or to trace how the one principle, that of allegiance, was, as regards the nation, worked into all administrative action by the kings from the Conquest to the reign of Edward I., while the other, that of homage and fealty, service for land, and feudalism properly so called, was the leading principle and most powerful instrument in the land of the great lords of the Conquest and the almost independent earls of the twelfth century as against the king. It would be a very good thesis for an essay, but for anything like complete treatment would require as large a book as indeed I have given to it in devoting the first volume of the Constitutional History mainly to its illustration.

We will therefore go on now to the 3rd clause, which is one the matter of which we touched upon in a preceding lecture.

' I will that all the men whom I brought with me or who have come after me be in my peace and quiet; and if any of them has been killed, his lord shall have the homicide within five days if he can, but if not he shall begin to pay me 46 marks of silver as long as the substance of that lord shall hold out, and when his substance fails the whole hundred in which the murder has been done shall pay in common what remains.' There are two or three points of interest here : first, the contention that these Norman followers of the king are in the king's peace ; the admission, that seems to be, that there was other peace and protection besides the king's, that is in itself a relic of an idea that was wellnigh obsolete that the peace of the nation, the peace of the shire, the peace of the ealdorman and sheriff were real protections, without the peace of the king.   This article places, however, the Norman followers of the Conqueror under a special guarantee ; injuries committed on them were injuries to the crown, and properly speaking their death or damage would have to be accounted for by a fine not to the shire but to the king, for whatever was the doctrine of the king's peace that was the practical result of the doctrine—if any man injures another, if an Englishman injures another Englishman, it is a matter of ordinary procedure : the wronged person may accept compensation, or the penalty may go to the magistrate, the ealdorman, or whoever else has an interest in the wite or penitential fine ; but in this case the account has to be made with the king, it is his peace that is broken, and the fine for breach of his peace is a royal perquisite, and the man lies at the king's mercy ; going on, you will observe a difference between the wording of this article and that of the corresponding article 22 of the French articles, where the men of the venue or visnetum, that is of the hundred, are made primarily and immediately responsible for producing the homicide within a week ; here the onus for five days lies upon the lord of the slain man, if he is not taken then he has to pay the fine, if he cannot pay it the hundred must.   It would seem from this that the Anglo-Saxon doctrine that every man (not having land of his own) must have a lord was in working at the time that this article was put in its present shape, and that the fact of the man being in the king's peace did not entirely dispense with the lord's duty of protecting and avenging him.   But I cannot say that the clause is very clear, and this portion of it scarcely seems to have been acted upon ; not only is the lord's duty not mentioned in the French articles, but in the laws of Henry I., in which very minute regulations are given about the murdrum, the hundred is the body immediately responsible, and in the early pipe rolls, in which instances of murder fines abound, there is no mention of the lord, only of the hundred.   Either then the lord here is the lord of a franchise, in which case he has hundredal jurisdiction and responsibility, or, as I said, he is the lord of the murdered man and has an intermediate duty of revenge and right of fine before the king's mercy comes in. It does not much matter, as we know the actual practice. If, then, the lord within five days or the hundred within a week cannot produce the homicide, a fine is to be levied, which is here 46 marks; the fines actually recorded as murder fines in the pipe rolls are of different amounts even in the same hundreds, and we must conclude from that that as the matter was really one of the king's *misericordia*, where an arbitrary fine was leviable at discretion, sometimes the amount was fixed at the discretion of the sheriff, or the sums noted in the pipe rolls may have been properly only instalments of the whole fine, or possibly a share may have gone to the kindred of the slain man, or possibly the sum is the residue paid by the hundred when the means of the person primarily accountable had failed.

Observe next that there is in this article no provision for the securing that this penalty shall be exacted only in the case in which the slain man is a Frenchman or Norman ; but the wording is directly addressed only to such a point, and the necessary proof must be taken for granted. That is, the custom of 'presentment of Englishry' must have come on at the same time as the murder fine ; if the hundred could prove that the slain man was an Englishman then the fine could not be enacted. Now this 'presentment of Englishry' is, if not the one institution, at least the most specific and definite legal institution by which the Conqueror showed his mind of dealing with his Norman subjects in a way different from his dealings with the native English : we may be sure that it was a necessary regulation, ugly as the colour of it is. And as it really is so important in this way, we will look at the later practice on it, as it is found in the laws or custumal of Henry I., 13 § 2, 75 § 6, 91 § 1, 92 §§ 6, 9, 59 : the first passage merely records 46 marks as the proper murder fine ; the second records the same fine, but allows to the discoverer of the murder the wergild of the slain Frenchman if he has no relations, but adds that if the discovered murderer can prove the victim to be an Englishman he may go to the ordeal of hot iron, or be otherwise punished by the customary common law. The third regulation supplies that element of uncertainty as to the fine which I have noted in the pipe rolls. It repeats the former injunctions, but adds that the ealdorman of the hundred who has to give pledge for the fine is to be dealt with discreetly, according to the case ; it also seems to make the responsibility in the first instance lie on the person on whose land the body is found, in which case the *dominus* of the text before us may mean that. And a

further regulation looks still more that way : if the murder be found
in the open fields, the fine shall be paid not only *ab eo cujus terra est*,
but by the whole hundred ; *si in divisis*, that is on the crossways,
both sides, that is both hundreds, shall pay ; if on the king's highway, the lords of the adjacent lands. Thus the collective responsibility of the hundred, as it is called, comes in only after the
alderman has failed to exact the fine from the parties more directly
liable, which seems fair enough.

There is, however, another rule (92 § 6) which defines murdrum
more clearly. ' Anciently the man was *murdritus* whose slayer was
unknown, wherever or however he was found slain ; but now, even
if the slayer is known, if he is not caught within seven days, it is a
case of murdrum ' (that is, for the exaction of the murder fine).
The rest of the law is very unintelligible, but it seems to mean that
this right of exacting the murder fine is to be relaxed only when the
murdered person can be proved to be English ; if he is not so proved
he is to be accounted French. Even if the murderer obtains the
pardon of life and limb from the king, the fine is still to be paid.
Then the procedure in the case is briefly sketched. ' If a murdrum
be found anywhere, let the hundred be called together with the
reeve and the neighbours, and whether it be recognised or not, let
it be kept seven days raised on a hurdle, with a wood fire burning
round it at night, and rewards are to be promised and given to the
helpers. If between the term the malefactor can be caught and
delivered to the justice let the hundred be quit ; if he is not and
there be no one who can prove him an Englishman on his father's
side, the law must take effect. It is held to be murdrum if an alien
be slain, and the slayer be unknown or not arrested before the day
fixed. If anyone accused deny the charge, let him purge himself
with a threefold purgation or judgment of 60 shillings. If the
hundred wants to prove that the man was not a Frenchman, it may
be done by oath of the twelve best men of the hundred. The person
who has been convicted or confessed is to be handed over to the
kinsfolk of the murdered man to be at their mercy. If he has no
relations the king is to exercise his right.' (That seems to be a relic
of antiquity or of the universal vendetta, it can scarcely be a piece
of law.) There are a few other regulations which are difficult in the
present state of the text to understand, and which do not much
illustrate, if they can be guessed at, the subject in hand. It is a very
curious question altogether, for the practice in its integrity can only
have prevailed for a few years, and yet the enactments or customs
that belong to it remain in force for nearly three centuries.

When the ' Dialogus de Scaccario ' was written, about 1188, the
difference between English and Norman extraction was so far

obliterated that except where it was clear that the slain man was a villein he was held to be a Frenchman and the fine was exacted. The 'presentment of Englishry' was abolished by the Act 14 Edward III. c. 4, which, in consequence of the tyrannical amercements laid on the hundred by over-severe justices, abolishes the whole thing with all its circumstances and appurtenances, and blots out for ever thus much of the oppressive doctrine of the Conquest. The great interest of this point must be my excuse for saying so much upon the matter.

Article 4: 'Every Frenchman who in the time of my kinsman King Edward was in England partaker of the customs of the English, let him pay, or let be paid, what they call scot and lot according to the law of the English.' This decree was established in the city of Gloucester. Gloucester, by the bye, was not a city in the ordinary sense in the reign of William I., and the word is simply a translation of the Gleaweceaster, or Gloucester, which must have been in the Anglo-Saxon document which was first issued. Now the actual force of this article is obscure; it is possible that it may be somehow connected with the preceding article, and that it means to restrict the operation of the murder law so as not to include the Normans settled in England before the Conquest. Article 3 refers, you remember, to the men who came with the king or came after him; this refers to those who came before him—the difference turns on the word *persolvat* or *persolvatur*. If you read *persolvatur*, it may mean, I do not say that it does, let him be paid for. According to the custom of the English, that is let the murder fine to the king not be exacted for him. Then *quod ipsi dicunt* on lot and on scot is simply an amplification of *consuetudinem*; but if you read *persolvat*, it must mean that these first comers are, so far as regards the payment of taxes, to rank as Englishmen; let him pay what the English call scot and lot. That is perhaps a more reasonable interpretation, but it does not connect itself so directly with the former article or the distinction between first, second, and third classes of immigrants.

What is 'scot and lot'? It means the due proportion of local taxation, whether it be by way of amercement, as the murder fine would be, or for the *trinoda necessitas*, the threefold obligation of the castle-building, bridge-mending, and militia service. The law was made at Gloucester, where, as we are told, the Conqueror used to celebrate his Christmas festival. I am not sure whether this date does not belong to the whole of the preceding articles or especially to articles 3 and 4. In either case we are at a loss to determine which of his Christmases is in question here. Mr. Freeman, I see, gives it a wide limit, 1076–1087; one would prefer

the earliest possible date, but it is possible that the better known
assembly of 1081 or 1086 may be the occasion. It is not, indeed,
necessary to fix it to the Christmas meeting. There was a great
gathering at Gloucester in 1072, at which Archbishop Lanfranc
consecrated the bishop of Lichfield. I should, for William's sake,
prefer that, as showing a less grudging spirit of recognition of his
people's rights. However, if we restrict the date to the articles 3
and 4, it makes no great difference where we place it.

The 5th article is the same as the 45th of the French
articles : ' We forbid that any live stock be sold or bought except
within towns, and that before three faithful witnesses ; nor any res
vetusta without a surety and warrant. If anyone does this let him
pay, and pay forfeiture too.' Here the text is difficult ; *viva pecunia*
must mean live stock—cattle, in fact—which should always be
bought and sold where there is a concourse and stolen animals
may be identified and claimed. That seems fair enough ; but *res
vetusta* is in the Government editions *res retita* on fair manuscript authority, and seems to correspond with the mortuum
of the article 45. *Vetitam* makes nonsense, for how could the
presence of a surety legalise the sale of things which were forbidden to be sold ? It must be an antithesis to live stock, and mean
something, furniture or other chattel, which had a previous owner
under the title of theam. In the form *toll and theam* the Anglo-
Saxon law gave to certain jurisdictions the right of inquiry into
the ownership of any property which was suspected to be dis-
honestly obtained, or the right of which was disputed. By this
provision the purchaser, although he might not bar the right of a
previous owner, was enabled to clear himself from complicity in
theft or other questionable method of acquisition. He was able to
call to witness the persons who had seen the sale and transfer in
either case, and in the case of the res vetusta he had a warrant on
the part of the seller that he had a right to sell. There is nothing
in this law which is not given equally circumstantially in the laws
of Æthelstan and Canute, and I do not see why the Conqueror
thought it necessary to re-enact it unless it was to restrict the
buying and selling altogether to the civitates, for Canute's law left
it open, ' sit in civitate, sit extra civitatem.'

In connection with this, it may be as well to note what the laws
of Edward the Confessor (that is, as you remember, the compilation
of a century after the Confessor's time) say about this : for *rem
vetustam* they read *pannum usatum*, secondhand cloth, which
certainly confirms my reading, *vetustam*. A careful arrangement
is described by which the security of the buyers is provided for in
case of buying gold and silver work : the witnesses are to be the

goldsmiths or silversmiths who would be likely to identify the work supposing it to have been stolen. As to the *viva pecunia*, they leave no doubt as to what it means, for they tell us that the butchers strongly objected to this form of law, urging that in the fresh meat season they would have to kill daily and so to buy daily, and if they bought daily they could not submit to so stringent a rule. Not only the butchers took alarm, but the townsmen generally complained that it was an interference with their freedom to buy beasts at Martinmas to be fattened for their Christmas dinners. The king, it is then said, did not wish to proceed so cruelly as to deprive them of their discretion. It is a curious bit of tradition if it be tradition, or fabrication if it be fabrication.

The next clause on appeals, and the use of ordeal or trial by battle, is of so wide interest and ranges over so much ground that it will demand a lecture pretty nearly to itself. But in connection with this law we will recur for a moment to the 11th of the Exchequer articles, which I passed over summarily in the last lecture. It seems to have been fabricated as an amplification or explanation of the genuine enactment. 'No market or forum shall be or shall be permitted to be except in the civitates and cities of our realm, and in burghs closed and walled and in castles and in the safest places, where the customs of our realm and our common right and the dignities of our crown which were settled by our good predecessors cannot be lost or defrauded or violated, but all things ought to be done duly and in the open, and by judgment and justice. And therefore castles and burghs and cities were placed, founded, and built, to the protection of the nations and peoples of the realm and to the defence of the realm, and therefore ought to be observed with all liberty, integrity, and honour.' If this additional article has any meaning or any germ of authentic authority, it means that transactions such as are noted in the genuine article are restricted to the town markets, which are under the greatest security of publicity. The right to forbid a market held without royal authority was hereby made or confirmed as a matter of law; and whatever may have been the rule previously, the granting of a licence to hold a market became a part of the royal right of protecting or interfering with trade.

The issue of letters allowing markets and fairs, thus constituting the class of towns called market towns, becomes frequent on the rolls of John, and would no doubt be found in the shape of licences in the as yet unprinted pipe rolls of his predecessors; Madox mentions one in the reign of Richard I., in which a fine of 10 marks is paid for the grant of a market. I must not stay now, but it would be very interesting to work out what were the real restrictions

of trade internal, as the operations with the foreign merchants were
on the trade external at this early period. By restriction on or
licensing guilds, by forbidding or licensing markets, by exactions
at the ports and tolls on internal traffic, bridge dues, &c., we
gradually see our way towards the more elaborate institutions of
the customs duties, the staple system, and the rigorous enforcement
of market dues farmed by particular officers or bestowed by way of
endowment on individuals, lords of manors, or even on churches.
The mention of churches, to which not unfrequently the grants of
markets are made, reminds me that in the early times, the Anglo-
Saxon and Anglo-Norman, there was a very common tendency to
hold markets and conduct sales in churchyards, which were thus
profaned frequently by quarrels and frays, which occasionally intruded within the limits of the churches themselves. There are
many ecclesiastical canons against this profanation, running down
into the thirteenth century, when the constitutions of the legate
Othobon in 1268 entirely forbade the holding of them in the churches.
The practice of holding them in churchyards, however, was too
convenient to be given up, and the fact that the fairs were frequently
held coincidently with the dedication feast of the churches—as, in
fact, the two great fairs here at Oxford are still held—no doubt led
to the continued use of the churchyards for the purpose. Possibly
this statute may have been intended to restrict the number of these
rural adulterine fairs ; but if so, it was practically overridden by the
royal right to license the holding of them.

Article 6 of the genuine form stands thus : 'It is also
decreed there, possibly still at Gloucester, that if a Frenchman has
appealed an Englishman of perjury, murder, theft, homicide, ran,
which is in English open rapine which cannot be denied, the
Englishman may defend himself as he best can either by ordeal
of iron or by duel, but if the Englishman be infirm he may find
another to do it for him. The one who is conquered shall pay
40s. to the king. If an Englishman has appealed a Frenchman
and is unable to prove it by ordeal or duel, I will that the Frenchman shall purge himself with an unbroken oath.' The suggestion
which I made to you in the last lecture, that the several clauses of
this short code may be abstracts of some longer enactments put
forth severally by the king in the native language, gains probably
from the fact that for this particular enactment we have the full
text in both Anglo-Saxon and Latin in the form of letters patent
preserved in the Textus Roffensis. It will be the simplest plan to
ground our exposition on the full text. 'William, by the grace of
God king of the English, to all to whom this writing shall come,
safety and friendship.' This is the Latin form ; the English is :

'William king greets all those to whom this writ comes over all England friendly, and bids and gives notice to all men over all Anglecynn to hold.' You must see that he retains the old Anglo-Saxon form of giving notice of a public act, but it is needless to dwell further on the verbal variations. '(1) If an Englishman appeal a Frenchman to battle for theft, homicide, or anything for which battle ought to be held, or judgment betwixt two men, he may have full licence to do so; and if the Englishman does not wish for the battle, the Frenchman appealed may purge himself by oath against him by witnesses according to the Norman law. (2) If a Frenchman appeal an Englishman to battle for the same things, the Englishman may with full licence defend himself by battle or by judgment of ordeal of iron, if he prefer it; and if he be unable or unfit for battle, and will not or cannot undertake it, he may seek for himself a lawful champion. If the Frenchman is beaten he shall pay the king 60 shillings; and if the Englishman will not defend himself by battle or by witnesses, he shall purge himself by judgment of God, i.e. by ordeal of iron. (3) As to all matters of outlawry the king ordains that the Englishman may purge himself by ordeal of iron. And if the Englishman appeal a Frenchman of outlawry, and is willing to prove it upon him, the Frenchman shall defend himself by battle; and if the Englishman does not prove him by battle, the Frenchman shall defend himself by a full oath, not in observances of words.'

There are here some things very hard to be understood, but we had better take the straightforward points first. Trial by battle is, I need hardly say, a deeply rooted institution of fallen humanity. It is unnecessary, perhaps, to carry it back as a judicial expedient to the time of Cain and Abel, whom the mediæval jurists looked upon as the first instance of a formal appeal to the judgment of God in this shape; but the custom clearly runs back to the early stages of society in which a man had to right his own wrongs, and had no other appeal than to that might which constituted right. The custom is so ancient and so general that there need be no hesitation in referring it to the simplest of all origins. The first restriction upon the exercise of violence, against the simple club law of primitive savage society, would be the placing of the appeal to violence under such conditions as would make it if not just yet an orderly tribunal; and when religion—Christianity—began to leaven the practice of the nations, that proceeding would be developed, where the unreasonable custom itself could not be entirely abolished, by making it as difficult and solemn as it could be made; making it, in fact, like the ordeal, a direct appeal to God, who would help the weak man to his right, possibly by a miracle, if a miracle were needed. Although some of the churches of the barbarian nations were unable altogether to get rid of it, the whole spirit of Christianity was against it; but so it was against the ordeal. So deeply rooted were both that it was found practicable only to surround them with such guarantees as would prevent oppression so far as it could be prevented, even at the occasional cost or risk of a pious fraud.

It is a curious point to note that the trial by battle, although practised by all the Germanic races outside of England, cannot be proved to have been a practice in England at all before the Conquest; and has generally been held to have been first introduced here by this law of the Conqueror. I have heard of some recent speculations which rather set this traditional view on one side, and of arguments that so general a practice could not have helped being known and used here; but I believe no case really anterior to the Conquest has ever been adduced; although we have a complete system of ordeal and compurgatory procedure in the laws, we have no order for the *ornest*, nor any illustration in contemporary chronicles; that the idea was not, as an idea, unknown is, of course, proved by the fact that this name *ornest* is found for it; unfortunately I am not able to tell you how soon this word appears in this signification in Anglo-Saxon literature; this is its first appearance in the laws. It is found in the form *orrest* in the Chronicle 1097, describing a case of trial by battle, when Mr. Earle explains that it is a Danish word, not likely to be unknown in the Dane law. If I am right in supposing that *ornest* and *orrest* are akin in origin if not identical words, then I presume we may agree that the word may have come in through the Danes, to whom, as to all the Norsemen, the custom on their own soil was probably familiar enough. It seems thus on our present information to be a foreign custom; ordeal was deeply rooted in England, so was compurgation, that by battle was not, and in the early charters of the towns, granted at a time when the procedure was in its fullest operation, freedom from liability to the custom was granted by the king as a special favour. So you find it in the charter of London granted by Henry I., 'Select Charters,' p. 108, 'nullus eorum faciat bellum,' a clause which was imitated in the charters of other towns.

I must add that the trial by battle was not restricted to cases of appeal of accusation of crime; it was likewise from the Conquest to the reign of Henry II. the ultima ratio in civil suits in which by conflict of evidence or appeal against a simple decision all other means of proof had been found unsatisfactory. The institution of the Grand Assize by Henry II. had the effect of substituting in the most important lawsuits a recognition by jury for this rough and ready method in civil matters; but in criminal appeals, where not restricted by local privilege or legal reforms providing an easier remedy, or by the good sense of mankind, it still retained its legality and was only abolished with criminal appeals generally by an Act passed within the nineteenth century, 59 George III. c. 46.

In the document before us the application is only to criminal appeals, and I need not, as not being a lawyer, go beyond the record. The document which I have just read to you proceeds in an orderly way through the alternative cases in the reverse order to that in the 10 articles. It seems to assume that compurgation and ordeal are the English *ultima ratio*, while *duellum* or trial by battle is the French; still, in both cases, it is as a proof of the truth of an assertion primarily, and only secondarily as a proof of the justice of a claim. In the first case the Englishman is the accuser: if he chooses to accuse the Norman of an offence or anything else on which proof is customarily taken by trial by battle, he may do so; if he will not fight on his claim, the Frenchman may repel the charge by compurgation; he is not to be made to undergo the ordeal. In the second case, if the Frenchman appeal the Englishman, the Englishman has his choice between the ordeal and the battle, and if he be unfit for battle may employ a legal champion. If he cannot or will not defend himself by battle or by testimony, he must go to the ordeal, judgment of God. The Englishman, i.e., may have his choice, but he is not to force the Frenchman to the ordeal. The 3rd clause confines itself to matters of outlawry, and seems to be the one on which the abstract in clause 6 of the 10 articles is chiefly framed. In this case if the Englishman appeal the Frenchman, the Frenchman may defend himself by battle; if the Englishman dare not fight, the Frenchman may defend himself by a compurgation. If the case be reversed, in all cases the Englishman must purge himself by the ordeal. On the whole the law seems quite as much directed towards saving the Frenchman from the ordeal as towards saving the Englishman from trial by battle. It is a curious reversal of our modern creed that one Englishman is worth five Frenchmen, the case of the Frenchman being *untrum* not apparently being provided for at all.

The oath by which the Frenchman is to purge himself is spoken of in our short text as *sacramento non fracto*, for which the manuscripts of Roger Hoveden reproducing the passage read *non ferro* the interpretation coming to the same thing really, that the purgation was to be by oath, not by ordeal; but it is clear from the Anglo-Saxon form and Latin translation of the royal edict that *non fracto* is the right reading, ' plano juramento non in verborum observantiis.'

What the unbroken oath is, is a question of deep controversy, so deep and, as I believe, as yet so unsettled that it would be of very little use for me to attempt to penetrate the mystery in a lecture. I will state the explanation given by Mr. Bigelow in his book on Norman procedure, although I confess it seems to me to be only a tentative explanation. He thinks that the *sacramentum frangens* or *fractum* was a triple compurgation, three several compurgatory oaths ; while the *sacramentum infractum* was a simple compurgation ; the *non fractum* was then a simpler and less solemn act of purgation than the *fractum*, and it was moreover evidently less formal, being *non in verborum observantiis*. This likewise is capable of two explanations ; for the *verborum observantia* may have been of two sorts : (1) the formulæ of oaths were exceedingly minute, and the least failure of a word or syllable was construed as an insufficient fulfilment of the law ; but also (2) the thing which was contested was also reduced to a form of the utmost strictness ; the point being, A struck B so many blows on the head ; B swears to a distinct assertion. A if he denies it must swear an exact categorical negative—the least change in the language involved a variatio loquelæ, a miskenning apparently, as it is called in the charters, that disabled the litigant, and subjected him to fines if he wished to reform his deposition and make it more distinct.

We must suppose that one or both of these requisites were necessary for the fullest form of oath, the *sacramentum fractum et observatum* ; and the simpler, looser, more general assertion and denial sufficed for the *sacramentum infractum non in verborum observantiis*. But, as I have said, none of the books, not even the latest, that I have been able to consult, explain the whole thing very confidently, and perhaps all that is needed for our present purpose is to note that the *non fractum* oath was one which was simpler and left less room for flaws and stumbling-blocks than the other. That is the opinion of the editors of the laws, both Schmid and Thorpe. It makes good sense here, where the purpose obviously is to make matters comfortable for the Frenchman and not to lay him open to technical difficulties arising on formulæ which he would not understand. In all this I am presupposing, in you at all events, a knowledge of what is meant by compurgation, ordeal, and the other technical proceedings, such as may be gathered from our usual textbooks. I do not propose, therefore, at this stage to work into further detail. Perhaps when we come to the more minute regulations of the laws of Henry I. it will be as well to get some general idea of the outlines of the subject of procedure, the forms of oath and ordeal. Now I think we must pass on.

The 7th clause is that in which the king undertakes to main-

G

tain the national laws. ' This also I enjoin and will that all have
and hold the law of King Edward in lands and in all things augmented by those enactments which I have appointed for the benefit
of the people of the English.' I have explained what is meant by
the law of Edward ; generally merely the customary law of the
nation, more particularly the legislative code or record which had
been last recorded by Canute, and prospectively the laws which, as
traditionally gathered by report of a body of representatives of the
shiremoots, appear in the following century under the title of the
Laws of Edward the Confessor. I am inclined to give the words
here the first and widest meaning ; for we know from later history
how watchwords like this have only had the loosest meaning in the
mouths of people. Magna Carta was a watchword for centuries to
people who knew nothing of what it contained ; nay, we have Magna
Carta associations at the present day. So the cry for the provisions
of Oxford, in the barons' wars, really meant the liberties which the
provisions were supposed to secure, not at all the provisions themselves ; the laws of Henry I. were a rallying point to the barons of
1215, before Stephen Langton unearthed the charter itself from the
record room at St. Paul's : so were the avitæ consuetudines to
Henry II. long before he had them drawn up and recorded by the
recognitors at the council of Clarendon. The 'laga regis Edwardi'
is mentioned several times in the great or coronation charter of
Henry I. as regulating monetage and murdrum, as well as in general
terms ; although it is most improbable that the murdrum at any
rate was in existence in Edward's time. We have lately taken it for
granted (p. 72) that the custom was introduced by the Normans,
but I mentioned that it might have been in some shape or other
known under Canute ; and the reference to it in Henry's charter
would show either that there was such a belief current in the year
1100, or that the Leges Edwardi, which I have always relegated to
a later part of the century, had been drawn up before the death of
the Conqueror, possibly in the year 1070, as the tradition alleged.
However, here we need not regard it as more than the watchword of
national traditional freedom.

The 8th clause contains two distinct enactments; united,
however, by the fact that they both relate to procedure in the law
courts : ' Every man who would wish himself to be held as a freeman
must be in pledge, that his pledge shall have him and hold him to
justice, if he shall have committed an offence ; and if any such has
escaped, let the pledges see that they simply pay what is claimed,
and purge themselves of complicity, that they know no fraud in
the escaped.' That is the first part. It corresponds with clause 25
of the 52 articles. This clause lands us again in the midst of a

country full to overflowing of debatable points—the law of frankpledge, or of frith-borh, or collective responsibility, as it has been
called.

I need perhaps hardly tell you that in the old books on Anglo-
Saxon and Norman constitutional matter, the frankpledge occupies
a very important position, and, while in some authorities it is treated
like the mark, or village community idea, in others it is made a
fundamental law, and the fundamental law of Anglo-Saxon society.
This has come about by the process of throwing back the mediæval
law of frankpledge to too early a date, and giving it an importance
and extension that it cannot be shown historically ever to have
possessed. On the extreme view of this side all society was bound
together in little associations of ten men, who were responsible for
each other's good conduct ; for payment of wergild, for co-operation
in compurgation, for appearance in courts of justice, and general
good behaviour. The frankpledges again were bound together in
hundreds, and the hundred was collectively responsible for the good
behaviour of the frankpledges, so all men were under a double
bond for obedience to the law.

I believe that some theorists have gone farther than this, and
have regarded the law of collective responsibility as pervading the
institutions of the whole German race, in some shape or other ; but,
as a matter of fact, the frankpledge or association of tens in its
mediæval form belongs only to England ; the decaniæ and con-
tubernia of the foreign systems which have been connected with
it requiring different explanation. Nor does it appear in England
until after the Conquest, according to the best authorities ; possibly
not very long after the Conquest, for all identifications of it with
local tithings or associations of tens as subdivisions of hundreds, and
all frithgilds, voluntary associations for mutual protection, and the
like, which have been confused with it, fail to answer the test of
criticism such as Dr. Waitz, the great ruling authority on the point,
has applied to them. What, then, was the frankpledge ? It was an
association of ten men answerable for the production of one another
in the court of justice—the *visus franciplegii*, the examination into
the observance of the rule, the securing that every man of the township, who had not material guarantees in the shape of land of his
own, and perhaps including such cases also, was a part of the business
of the hundred court, and of the sheriff's tourn in the county court ;
often also in the manorial courts themselves, where they were
exempted from superior jurisdiction. And this seems to be all that
the hundred court had to do with the frankpledges, for its own
responsibility for the murdrum was quite independent of the frankpledge responsibility, and all its other collective acts belong to

ordinary jurisdiction, or executive energy, that belong by nature to law courts, not to any doctrine of so peculiar a colour as this.

That the compulsory association of ten men collectively responsible succeeded to some earlier form of pledges is very probable, nay it is almost certain; for although the Anglo-Saxon laws say nothing about the ten men in the frankpledge (they do recognise a frithgild or police defence association in the judicia civitatis Londoniensis). In that document they say a great deal about frith pledges and the duty of some one or other to produce everybody in the courts when needed. The lord was the borh, or surety for the production of his vassal, or sometimes the kinsfolk were collective surety for the kinsman, as they were the sharers in his wergild, and the men of the guild may have been sureties for the members of the guild. The clergy might have the bishop as their protector, but they also were under pledge; by the laws of the Northumbrian priests, every priest had to find twelve borhs or bondsmen, as sureties that he would keep the law; and even an archbishop had bondsmen, although whether that was a matter of course, or only a particular expedient in particular suits, I cannot presume to say; certainly as the oath of a bishop was irrefragable one cannot see what, if his character were unimpugned, he could want with a body of sixty bailsmen. So, however, the north country law directed, and if it was an anomaly, it was only one of many. The accepted theory is that the man who had not in land such a stake in the country as was practical security that he would not fly from justice, should have such sureties as would secure the same end. That being the principle under which a good deal of the Teutonic laws work, serves to explain the passages in the earlier laws, where reference is made to the frithborough, or security for the peace ; the word frankpledge is a bad translation of the word free-borough, which is a corruption of frithborough—frith means peace, franc means free, the other half of the word is right.

The historical question turns on the point of the compulsory association of ten men ; that institution is not found in the Anglo-Saxon laws before the Conquest, it is found in the laws of Edward the Confessor, drawn up probably, as we have several times held, in the first half of the following century. Was it introduced as a police measure by William the Conqueror, or by William Rufus ? In the 52 articles, No. 25, it occurs only in the simplest form, ' omnis qui sibi vult justitiam exhiberi, vel se pro legali et justitiabili haberi sit in francoplegio ; ' here is the frankpledge, not the ten men. In the French version it is art. 20, and applied only to the villani, ' e puis seient tuz les vilains en franc plege.' (1) You may conclude either that as the association of ten men in frankpledge is not mentioned by the Conqueror and is mentioned in the pseudo-Edwardian laws, and certainly was a part of the common law in the twelfth century, that therefore it was introduced by the Conqueror; or (2) you may argue that as the Conqueror mentions frankpledge, and as that is the name by which in the following century the ten men were known, that therefore we may understand the word to have the same meaning in his laws. If that is the case, then the institution may have been much older, or it may have been a thing of his institution; but if it was much older than the Conqueror, still it is a mistake to extend it too far, either to suppose that it was connected with the hundredal responsibility or that it was a universal institution among the Germans.

I do not wish to influence your opinions, if you will take the pains to form opinions. Many good books have been written on the assumption of the primitive antiquity of the institution, as for instance Schmid's notes on the subject show; later investigators are inclined to throw it over. My own opinion is that way; but even if we should be proved right, the particular history of this regulation would remain a curious illustration, and a curiously permanent part of our popular customs. For to the present day view of frankpledge, that is the ascertaining that the men of the manors are in the associations of ten men, is held to be a part of the work of manorial courts, where they continue to go through the form of business. It is but a name and a shadow, but I believe it still exists, or did a very few years ago.

Taking it for granted that I have said enough about this, let us take the remaining half of the clause : ' Let recourse be had to the hundred and county court as our predecessors appointed ; and let those who ought to come and will not, be summoned once ; and if at the second summons they will not come, let an ox be taken, and let them be summoned the third time ; and if the third time they will not come, let another ox be taken ; and if they do not come on the fourth summons, let what is called ceapgeld, the sum in dispute, be taken of the goods of the man who will not come, and besides that the foris factura regis, the king's forfeiture.' The enactment may possibly connect itself with the foregoing clause ; and if so, it would seem to intimate that the view of the frankpledge was already a part of the duties of the hundred and shiremoot. But I should prefer to take it independently as an order, that judicial proceedings shall continue as they had been of immemorial time, in the two moots of the hundred and the shire ; recourse being had first to the hundred, then, if justice was delayed, or refused, or impeded by forms that could not be got over, the shiremoot being resorted to. It would be for debt or dispute about money matters that these courts would be most frequently employed, and the illustration in the text is taken from a suit of money-claim. If the accused or debtor does not obey the summons to the court, or if, it being his duty to attend without summons, he fails to do so, he is after the second citation to be fined, after the third to be fined again, and after the fourth not only to pay the sum in dispute but an additional fine to the king for having contemned the order of a court which, although not the king's court, is under the king's protection as defender of the law and the peace. Ceapgeld is the worth of the chattel in dispute. The *foris factura* is the fine for oferhyrnesse or disobedience to the lawful summons. As to the general importance of the clause : it is a valuable proof that William the Conqueror maintained the ancient English courts in something like their integrity, and that the decay into which they had fallen in or about the year 1108, when Henry I. issued his writ for the regular holding of them, must have been the result of the tyrannical measures of the intervening reign, and the ubiquitous energy of Ranulf Flambard, who, ' driving ' the king's courts over all the realm, most probably weakened as much as he could all such relics of local independent administration.

There is nothing in the clause that makes it necessary to suppose that the Conqueror introduced any change into these customary courts ; but if he had, he could not have materially interfered with their history, for they certainly continued for a century and a half very slightly modified. I may, perhaps, as well note for you in this lecture the principal heads under which the history of these courts should be worked out. According to the generally received opinion of German constitutionalists, the hundred court was the sole and single court of customary popular justice ; there might be township moots in which the business was prepared for the hundred court, but these were not courts of what we should call contentious jurisdiction ; they could allot lands, receive new inhabitants, witness sales and probably prove wills, or whatever form of devise preceded the use of written wills, but except in occasional cases, where the hundredal jurisdiction was granted to the lord of a township, they were not what we should call courts of justice.

On the Continent I believe the hundredal jurisdiction continued to be the only popular jurisdiction during the whole of the ages the history of which is in analogy with English constitutional history, and possibly longer, but we need not examine that now ; the Karolingian *missi* and the growth of feudal magistracies create a number of analogies which would only puzzle us if we tried to work them out. But although we may grant that in English history there was no lower court of jurisdiction than the hundred, there was a higher court in the shiremoot or folkmoot, an institution which did not apparently exist in the old Germanic institutions and which probably originated in the fact that many of the English shires were ancient tribal or even monarchical aggregates.

In England, therefore, before the Conquest, there were hundred courts assembling; the hundred court met according to the law of Edward the Elder every four weeks, and according to the law of Edgar the shiremoot was held twice a year. Both assemblies were attended by the same persons: all the landowners, lay and clerical, in the hundred, and the men of the townships, the villani represented by the reeve and four best men; the bishop and ealdorman in person or by deputy attending to explain the law, secular and divine. As the litigation would not always arise between litigants within a single hundred, it was necessary that provision should be made for a tribunal that could enforce its decisions in more than one such area, and this was done, sometimes by collecting three or more hundreds in a central place, cross roads, or open ground in the centre of the territory, but I imagine most frequently in the shiremoot or half-yearly court of the whole county. And thus constituted, the shiremoot was also a court of resort by what we may call appeal from the hundred court.

You will remember that I told you in a previous lecture that there was no proper appeal in the Germanic courts originally except by challenging the judges; and as that was not usual in Anglo-Saxon England, we must suppose that the want was met by having, if it were possible, recourse to a higher court to remedy delay or refusal of justice in the lower. The Law of Canute certainly implies that there was such a graduation of appeal. No man might distrain another until he had three times applied to the hundred for leave. If at the fourth time he fail, he may go to the shiremoot; but what to do there? not to reverse the judgment of the hundred, but to insist on another hearing, a fifth term; if he could not then get authority to distrain, he might proceed on his own responsibility with the leave of the county court. Well, that being the relation between these two gemots, this is the condition in which we find them at the Conquest, a half-yearly shiremoot and a monthly hundred court. As litigation increased, and as the interference of royal justice diminished the powers of these courts, they seem to have been held more frequently; at least under Henry II. the hundreds are said to have met every fortnight, and under Henry III. they were ordered to meet every three weeks; the 42nd regulation of the Great Charter of 1217 must be understood as having this meaning; the term comitatus, which was to be held every month, probably referring to the hundred court, and the

sheriff's tourn in the hundred, twice a year, with view of frankpledge in the Michaelmas tourn representing the old proper county
court.   Already large sections of business were being transferred
from the old judicatures to the king's judges, and the process went
on by the use of itinerant justices, justices of assize, justices of
the peace, and the like, and by excusing the attendance of more
important members by the statutes of Merton and Marlborough,
until merely the shadow of jurisdiction remained, and the chief
function of the hundredmoot was to enable the litigants to recover
small debts, the main action of the counties to despatch other
business, elections, assays and collection of taxes, affording, however,
the basis still of the assembly in which the royal judges in eyre and
assize had their constitutional position.   Of course you will find all
this in my 'Constitutional History' and much of it in the 'Select
Charters,' but sometimes it is as well to make up our accounts.

   Clause 9: 'I forbid that any should sell a man out of his
country on penalty of my full forfeiture.'   It is clear from the
enactments of the former kings, Ethelred and Canute, that there
was among the Anglo-Saxons a sort of contraband slave trade;
this was very largely maintained at Bristol, as is known from
the life of S. Wulfstan, and Ireland was the centre to which the
English kidnappers took their slaves to market.   Lanfranc and
Wulfstan have the credit of compelling the abolition of this
abominable usage.   You will find a good deal about it in Mr.
Freeman's fourth volume on the Norman Conquest, where, however,
possibly we ought to distinguish between the kidnapping at Bristol
and the legal sale of persons who, either as condemned criminals or
as lawful slaves, were sold with a profit due to the king on the
transaction.   The king had 4d. for every man sold in the borough
of Lewes, and doubtless in other boroughs likewise; this he did not
like to forgo, but Lanfranc and Wulfstan put it before him in such
strong terms that it was renounced.   The contraband trade from
Bristol must have always been illegal, although we are told of
Gytha, the wife of Earl Godwin and mother of Harold, making
herself rich by it.   We will hope that it was a libel.

   We now come to our last clause, the curious regulation which
forbids hanging and legalises blinding and mutilation, and in the
Exchequer form ordains a graduated system of mutilations for
graduated offences.   I think that in the Latin of this law *pro
aliqua culpa* can scarcely mean to prohibit hanging altogether, but
simply that it is not to be the only punishment inflicted for every
crime.   The Exchequer version adds to the sufficiently cruel details
the cutting off of the hand and foot.   This was not uncommon
later; common enough, as also was hanging, under Henry I., and

still lawful under Henry II., being authorised by the assize of Northampton, which probably reproduces the penalty which in its predecessor, the assize of Clarendon, was omitted as a mere detail of common law practice. The forest assize of Henry II. likewise refers to Henry I.'s penalties, which were of the most savage and abominable tyranny conceivable. The brutality of the Conqueror was bad enough, but the mutilation of hand and foot, which meant really lingering death, were refinements of savagery.

This completes our survey of this very important little set of articles, the three most significant and controverted of which are those to which we have given most time—I trust not in vain—the murdrum, the trial by battle, and the law of frankpledge.

We have now come to the edict, not by any means the least important and interesting of the Conqueror's laws, by which he separated the work of the ecclesiastical litigation from the secular business of the shiremoot and hundredmoot, with which it had become to some extent and in some peculiar ways entangled. In order to see more exactly what was the purport of the Act, I will at once take you into the far more ancient and straightforward region of early Anglo-Saxon history, and ask you to look for a moment at the origin of ecclesiastical jurisdiction. The creation of an ecclesiastical jurisdiction, or, I should rather say, the historical process by which it is developed, is divisible into three elements or processes. We must accept as our first element the Christian religion in that condition and self-contained constitution at which it has arrived when it is first brought into the land over which it is ultimately to gain jurisdiction; a second process is the acceptance by the body of the people, either by authority of its rulers or by the slow process of missionary enterprise, of the system imported; and a third stage is attained when to the system thus imported and accepted, powers of enforcing its own legal sentences are given or allowed to be exercised by the national will. First, it is a missionary church; secondly, it is a voluntary society; thirdly, it is a national establishment, with laws, tribunals, and an executive authority of its own. It is only in the second stage that it begins to have jurisdiction even consensual, that is binding on the conscience of the members who have joined it, and who, in accepting its rules, bind themselves to obey its sentences on penalty of expulsion. In this voluntary stage its authority is simply moral and spiritual, its sentence of excommunication from divine offices is valid only by the consent of those who share in those offices and by the acquiescence of the delinquent; it involves no secular penalties, and is executed by no secular arm. The body which exercises it is a recognised body, capable of managing its own affairs, and of holding such property as it can hold subject to the common obligations of temporal property, but if it demands tithe or offerings it demands them as a matter of religious or moral, not of legal, obligation ; and where its demand is resisted, it strives to enforce it not by legal but by spiritual sentences.   In the third stage, in which it has fully achieved the position of a national church, not only are its estates secured to it by the common law of society, but it is enabled by legal machinery to enforce its claims, to pass and enforce its sentences, or to call upon the secular power to do so for it.

So, you see, on the historical theory of ecclesiastical establishment the national church is not merely the nation in its religious aspect, but the nation in a religious aspect as a part of a catholic universal church, other branches or nations of which live, or assume to live, by the same law, and to work together in the world for the same spiritual interests.   It is in no sense the creature of the state or the creature of the nation ; but its constitution, its powers of self-government and of self-defence, are varied by the circumstances of the nation which it has gathered in to the general body, and by the decrees by which its hold upon the governmental system of that particular nation is originated, strengthened, or weakened.

Every historical church in Christendom has of course begun with the missionary stage ; it comes with the Bible and the liturgy, and the rules of church government that are accepted at the moment by the mother church that sends forth the mission.   Then it lays hold on the people as a voluntary profession with a voluntary organisation, or rather with its original and inherent organisation voluntarily accepted or rejected.   At last it arrives, as a national church, at the power of enforcing its rules and claims by material means.   The second stage in the early history of England and most of the Western nations was a very short one ; that is, only a short period elapsed between the acceptance of Christianity by the nations and the bestowal of coercive authority on the tribunals which were in their first aspect consensual ; but there was such a period, and it was in all cases long enough to contradict the possible assumption that the company of voluntary believers created for themselves a new and original constitution.   They accepted what came to them : afterwards they increased, and to some extent materialised, its power, but they did not create it.   It came with a spiritual law, with a consensual jurisdiction, and an organisation in common with the churches outside.

In England, as we are constantly told, the church had kings for its nursing fathers and queens for its nursing mothers in a very especial way ; the governing classes, apparently, in most of the Anglo-Saxon kingdoms were the first to receive Christianity, and the heathenism that preceded was so thoroughly worn out that the great body of the peoples without delay accepted the faith, and from the earliest days of it with brilliant examples of sanctity, and great intellectual expansion as well as moral improvement. But the fact that England at the time of the conversion was divided into seven kingdoms had the effect of prolonging the voluntary period of church development, especially in the higher regions of the organisation. By an alliance which was close, vital, and spiritually extremely strong, by a thorough spiritual and moral incorporation, so to speak, the Anglo-Saxon church was one and indivisible in all the seven states, but the union was still in its nature voluntary or consensual; the same law might be recognised in all the states, but it was not by a common act of the states; if there was a common act, it was the common act of the churches, the canon of a council or the constitution of an archbishop. The assistance given by the secular arm to the spiritual arm in the several kingdoms might and did vary, no doubt. There is no reason to suppose, when one kingdom gave its bishops the right to enforce Romescot, or tithe even, that the same rule was adopted in every other. For the main spiritual purpose the church was a united spiritual consensual body; before, its rights had been, on exactly the same lines, recognised and formulated in all the states of the Heptarchy.

From the time of the union of the kingdoms, which you will fix in the tenth century, in the period of Edward the Elder and his sons and grandsons, the English church in its integrity entered on the full possession, the equalised and universally recognised exercise of the powers which in the several kingdoms it had already enjoyed, but in its central administration had possessed by voluntary or religious cohesion only; and from that date to the Conquest, partly from the fact that its kings were weak and its prelates strong, it acquired and held such great power, both spiritual and temporal, as has been regarded as the most complete possible union of church and state, the powers of either being almost merged in, confused with, and exercised through the powers of the other. The prelates, bishops, and abbots were the statesmen of the period; they held great estates, and even provincial governorships, it is said; certainly they were the chief members of the witenagemots, they declared the spiritual law in the folkmotes, they commanded armies, they constrained kings to obedience, and it is by no means clear that they themselves or the nation they ruled distinguished very clearly between the religious and the coercive machinery by which they enforced the observance of their rule.

But when we come to the eleventh century, of which in our own history the Norman Conquest is the great central event, we come to a period full of new life and revived intellectual as well as moral energy. The church of Rome, that is the catholic church of Western Christendom, arises in great force under the influence of Hildebrand to purge away its own sins and enforce what it conceives to be righteousness upon the nations; it insists on the liberation of spiritual machinery from secular control; nay, it goes farther, and in its extremest pretensions insists on the subordination of the temporal to the spiritual sword; and the strength of the revival is augmented by the miserable condition of the church within the empire under the Franconian dynasty. With the revived sense of spiritual corporeity, there is a great development of ecclesiastical constitutionalism, church law begins to be studied and codified, and the canonical systems of different countries to be brought into uniformity; the free and easy union between church and state in countries like Spain and England has to be examined and set right, and the general administration in things spiritual to be brought up to a fair standard, although the full attainment of the Hildebrandine ideal is impossible. Such, speaking generally, was the idea of the period of the Conquest; what was there in the condition of England to meet that idea; and what bearing has it on the measure before us?

Let us keep before our minds now three points to be observed: first, the existence of a church law, common to all the churches; secondly, the existence of a church jurisdiction, common as to its framework to all the churches of the West, but modified as to its powers and in details by the particular circumstances of the nations; and thirdly, an ecclesiastical procedure, in its first elements uniform, but in all its executive details and in the amount of power with which it could exercise its authority differing largely in different countries. Fix these in your minds by an illustration: (1) The same ecclesiastical law governed the whole of the Western Church, that was the Holy Scripture and the canons of the general councils; (2) the same system of jurisdiction by archbishops and bishops covered as by a network the whole area, and in its essence the authority of these officers was the same, but in its details there were variations, as for example the modifications introduced by provincial and even diocesan canons, the different share of authority exercised in different provinces by archbishops over bishops or by bishops through archdeacons and archpriests; in one country the whole hierarchical jurisdiction might be fully elaborated, while in another it was simple and unentangled; in one country it might be exercised with, and in another without, a concordat with the secular power; it is easy to imagine modifications; (3) in the separate states, there being no universal law of ecclesiastical procedure, the proceedings of the courts must vary and did vary very largely, the procedure in one being according to the Roman law, the Theodosian Code or even the Code of Justinian, while in another it might still be of the consensual sort, or even closely assimilated to the common popular law of the realm which accepted it. As to executive, too, one state might allow to the bishops the direct right of enforcing their own sentences by their own officers, their own provisions, and so on; another might agree to enforce all spiritual sentences by the secular arm; another might insist on examining the spiritual sentences before it executed them itself, or allowed the bishops to exercise them. We have thus drawn the lines on which to frame our answer to the question, what was the state of things in England on which this edict of the Conqueror came?

First as to the law: you will see from the words of the edict itself that there was a recognised ecclesiastical law and a recognition of a general system of canons. The episcopal laws, he says, up to my time have not been well kept, nor according to the precepts of the canons. What were the episcopal laws and what the precepts of the canons? The latter first, the body of canons accepted in the Western Church; these canons were the basis and germs of all ecclesiastical law; the canons of the general councils, and more especially the collections of authoritative enactments born of general councils and of provincial councils which by the adherence of particular churches had acquired pretty nearly the same force and universality. The most ancient collection of these was made by Dionysius Gaignus, a Roman monk, who lived early in the sixth century, and may therefore have been in the hands of Augustine when he came to England. There were many similar collections founded on that of Dionysius and in use in different churches; we have the forged decretals of Isidore in the ninth century, which has a separate and special history of its own, but I mean local collections of received canons such as that which belonged to Dunstan and is now in the Bodleian Library. Besides canons there were penitentials, that is the handbooks of confessional discipline prescribing the punishments for the several sins confessed by the penitents, and there were other authoritative writings of the fathers and the great jurists which possessed great religious authority. Early in the eleventh century Burchard of Worms codified these, and very soon after the reign of the Conqueror, Ivo of Chartres, who was able to use the Corpus Juris of Justinian, while Burchard had only that of Theodosius, drew up a new collection called the Panormia, which was generally received as sufficient until Gratian about the year 1151 issued the renowned Decretum on the same principles. None of the books that I have mentioned was in itself an authoritative code, but each contained the letter of the canons which were authoritative, much of the law now, as ever, residing in the mouth or breast of the judge. But when the Conqueror contrasts the *episcopales leges* with the *præcepta canonum,* what does he mean? Surely simply that the practice of the English ecclesiastical law had not been kept close to the letter of the canons in particular causes that affected the government of souls, had been brought to the judgment of secular men and laymen, and had been allowed to interfere with the laws that belonged to the government of the bishops.

This leads to another point. What was the jurisdiction of the bishops under the Anglo-Saxons, which William undertook to reform? There is no doubt that throughout the Anglo-Saxon period the bishops had a clear spiritual judicature; how it was worked is a matter that admits of question, but it is clear they had it, from the penitentials, from the canons of councils, from their participation in the general features of church organisation in other countries. It was very extensive, it covered all questions of morals; it comprehended the protection of the clergy, who were all under the mund of the bishop, the vindication of ecclesiastical rights as to persons and things, and extended to the moral conduct of the laity as well as to questions of marriage and legitimacy. Besides this authority exercised by purely spiritual sanction and enforced by purely spiritual censures, the bishops had a place in all the secular tribunals of the country, in the witenagemot, in the shiremoot, and in the hundredmoot, where they sat both to declare the spiritual law, while the ealdorman declared the temporal law, and to secure justice, possibly to administer it also, over clerks accused of criminal offences, and in the case of disputed possessions. In days in which the prelates were all-powerful, we should not be surprised to learn that their functions in these two capacities were sometimes confounded, and that the bishop sitting in the shiremoot sometimes decided causes by the popular method which more properly belonged to his tribunal of spiritual discipline, and sometimes in his spiritual tribunal prejudged questions that belonged to the secular forum. But that there was confusion between the spiritual authority and the secular authority in relation to its source, objects, and proper limits, I for one should deny.

I have accounted, then, for the law, the ancient canons, for the jurisdiction, in the bishops and archbishops; how about the procedure? I conclude from what I have read in the laws and councils of the Anglo-Saxons, that so far as spiritual jurisdiction in its limited sense was concerned—that is, the moral and ceremonial discipline of the clergy and the penitential discipline of the laity— that was exercised by the bishops, either publicly in synods, which

were very numerous, or in private and informal sessions in their
own churches, chapter-houses, or palaces, where they could act more
freely as arbitrators, confessors, or directors, as the particular case
before them required.   And in those sessions they acted on the letter
of the canons or on their own knowledge and responsibility,
possibly in accordance with the rules of foreign law procedure, as in
the Gallican and Roman Churches, possibly, as the common idea has
been, in an informal and paternal way, possibly in ways analogous
to the proceedings of the popular courts.   But when we look at the
edict before us we find that it was intended to correct abuses which
arose from the trial of certain ecclesiastical causes before the county
court, according to the law of the hundred, and in the laws of
Ethelred and Canute it is directed that the bishop and ealdorman
should attend in the county court to declare the spiritual and the
secular law.   It is clear from this that certain ecclesiastical causes
did come before the popular courts.

I will not dwell upon the point that has been by extreme partisans maintained, that in the declaring of the law the ealdorman
had an equal right with the bishop to declare the ecclesiastical law ;
that contention, although it has some great names to support it, is
really untenable, and I must not obscure what I have to say by
dwelling upon it; our question is what were these ecclesiastical
causes touching the government of souls which were despatched,
according to the Conqueror's words, by the judgment of secular men.

Well, first, you may be quite sure all questions touching the lands
of the churches came before the secular courts ; and with them
must have come suits that touch the right of appointing to churches,
suits of patronage.   Secondly, you may be sure that the bishops'
synods would frequently coincide with the sessions of the courts ;
at a little later time we know that it was so, that the three-week
courts of the rural deaneries and the annual visitations of the archdeacons were framed on the analogy of the three-week courts of the
hundred, and the annual tourn and view of frankpledge held by the
sheriff ; and as the bishop was a leading member of the hundred
court, of course he found it convenient enough to take his ecclesiastical causes at the same meeting of the people at which he took
his secular business.   I conclude thus that directly large numbers
of church property cases, and indirectly some more distinctly
spiritual cases of litigation, would come before the county court.
And these causes would most probably be decided on the same
principles as the simply secular causes ; if a priest was accused of
an offence he would have to bring his compurgators and to go to the
ordeal just like a layman, the bishop seeing that he had fair play,
but the judicial procedure of the court being popular, that is what

William calls here *secundum legem hundret*. What, then, is the force of the edict primarily? William, with his experience of French litigation, and to some extent under the influence of the Hildebrandine idea, acting on the advice and counsel of the bishops, archbishops, abbots, and other princes, all or nearly all French and Hildebrandine too, orders that the confusion introduced by these practices shall cease. No bishop or archdeacon shall henceforth hold pleas of episcopal laws in the hundred; amplius—clearly the suits that have been heard in the popular courts have been held there wrongly, but still it has been the bishop and archdeacon, not the ealdorman or sheriff, that has held them—that is to cease; nor shall they bring a cause which concerns the government of souls to the judgment of secular men; that they must have done by using the popular methods of compurgation and witness in the customary modes—that also is to cease. And thirdly, as to criminal charges: whoever, according to the episcopal laws, shall be accused of any cause or fault whatsoever, shall come to the place which the bishop shall choose or name, i.e. not to the county court, but to the bishop's court, and shall there do right to God and his bishops, not according to the hundred, but according to the canons and episcopal laws— not, that is, according to the popular form of fines and penalties, but under the dread of the spiritual sentence of excommunication or suspension. Fourthly, if anyone so summoned refuse to come, in exact analogy with contempt of the summons to the hundred court, he shall be excommunicated after the third disobedience; and if he still be obstinate, the force and justice of the king or sheriff shall be applied; while for each act of contempt to the first, second, or third summons he shall be subject to the spiritual censure as the bishop may order it, and be obliged to make amends. Fifthly, no sheriff or reeve, or king's minister, nor any layman, is to interfere with the administration of the laws which belong to the bishop; the abuse that is corrected, the hearing church suits in the lay courts, had afforded too great opportunity for this confusion; the direction that it should cease is supplementary to the direction to the bishop to withdraw his suits. And sixthly, the ordeal is only to be administered in the bishop's see, or in the place appointed by the bishop. Here, then, are six points; all worth remembering.

Observe, however, two or three more points. First, the bishop and archdeacon are not deprived of their place in the shiremoot and hundredmoot: there are no words to that effect, and as we know from later laws and later writs, the bishops, archbishops, and all clergy who had lands included within the area of the shiremoot were summoned to it and were components of the full assembly.

Secondly, although the suits that are proper to be tried by

episcopal law and the canons are removed from the area of the
shiremoot and hundred, not all ecclesiastical causes are so removed.
We find in the laws of Henry I. in the directions for the arrangement
of business in the shiremoot, that the first place is given to the suits
which have a bearing on ecclesiastical matters. 'Agantur primo
debita veræ Christianitatis jura;' an extract from a capitulary of
Charles the Great, but represented here as a part of the English
practice in the early years of the twelfth century. I have mentioned
causes of patronage as likely to be the suits pertaining to the
regimen animarum which came before the shiremoot; if it were so,
it was sure to lead to difficulties, for rights of patronage are rights
of property and cannot be disassociated from them. But it is
probable that from 1066 onwards until the Constitutions of
Clarendon, it was uncertain to which forum these suits belonged;
Henry II. revindicated them for the lay courts, and appealed to the
avitæ consuetudines as his warrant; but it is certain from the letters
of John of Salisbury, who acted as secretary or chancellor to Archbishop Theobald from 1140 or to 1161, that such suits during the
whole of Stephen's reign were tried in spiritual courts and very
frequently with appeal to Rome. I infer from this that so far as
suits of church property are concerned the Act of the Conqueror
did not draw a certain permanent and conclusive line.

Thirdly, look at the three heads that we marked out for
particular comment, Law, Jurisdiction, Procedure. The edict
instituted no new laws, but recognised the episcopales leges and
jura canonum. The want of authoritative books of these laws and
canons was supplied first by Burchard, whose book was well known
in England, as is evident from the large quotations from it in the
so-called laws of Henry I., then by Ivo of Chartres, who was at work
on his Panormia at this very time: then by Graham and the later
decretalists. But this canon law was never regarded as a binding
statutory law in England; the study of it was regarded as a
scientific preparation for office, but not as an absolute code to be
followed, and to the present day only such parts of it as are
received by the English church and nation and are not opposed to
the statute law are regarded as influencing the judgment of the
courts.

Then as to jurisdiction; this edict recognises the jurisdiction of
the bishops and the executive if not judicial functions of archdeacons: it does not result in the foundation of a new system of
courts; but as it certainly had one effect in multiplying ecclesiastical
suits and putting the spiritual judges on their mettle, it had the
effect of increasing the number of archdeacons. Hitherto one archdeacon had been enough for one bishop. The Norman bishops with

H

the increase of their work increased their administrative staff and broke up their dioceses into numerous archdeaconries and also deaneries; both subdivisions acquiring by custom either jurisdiction or judicial functions of an executive kind.

And lastly as to procedure. There can be little doubt that to this period we should refer the introduction of such parts of the Roman civil law procedure as were at work in the continental churches; based just now on the Theodosian Code and customary methods of the courts, but shortly after the rediscovery of the Pandects and the revived study of the Corpus Juris of Justinian to be reformed according to stricter and more developed uniform usage which constitutes the Catholic ecclesiastical procedure throughout the middle ages.

The importance of the reign of the Conqueror in its bearing on the church history of England is so very great that I shall not apologise for inflicting upon you another lecture on the subject. Not that I need defend myself under the circumstances at all; for during the age on which we are at work, though the church law may not be the whole of the national law, the church history is nine-tenths of the national history. Witness the action of Anselm in the reign of Henry I., and of Becket in the reign of Henry II. Much of the constitutional history is new, as we understand it, a great superinduction of new elements that have to be forced into union with the old; the reigning classes are new and alien, and much of their political programme is new also. In the church history there is likewise some considerable infusion of new elements, but there is a much greater preponderance of the old; the ecclesiastical fabric is not nearly so much modified as the civil, and the ecclesiastical population, so to speak, is more permanently and continuously English than the baronial or the landowning classes of the twelfth century in England. We have not to go far to look for a text for another discourse. In my last lecture we confined ourselves entirely to the domestic exercise of ecclesiastical jurisdiction: we have in the political relations of church and king a subject more interesting perhaps and better illustrated; and we find a very good summary of the points that define it in the words of Eadmer at p. 82 of the 'Select Charters.' I propose to make them the basis of a short examination of the more general relations of church and state at this time; adding in other points of kindred interest under each head.

The first of the new principles which, according to this very trustworthy writer, William imported into the English system was this: *he would not suffer anyone settled in the whole of his dominions to receive as apostolic pope the bishop of Rome unless at his command, or to receive letters of the pope on any account if they had not been previously shown to him.* In this first head you see you have two points : first, the right of the king of England to refuse recognition to a claimant of the papacy ; secondly, his right to forbid the reception of letters from the apostolic see. Take them in that order. As you probably are aware, England had before the Conquest troubled herself very little about the pope ; the nation professed itself truly catholic and faithful to the mother see, paid its Romescot and sent its archbishops to receive their palls from the pope, but certainly did not inquire much into the rights or wrongs of disputed elections to the chair of St. Peter ; probably any Englishman who went to Rome would have been content to recognise as pope anyone who had told him that he was so. There had been more intercourse since the days of Edgar, but the relation was not one of supreme authority and abject dependence, but of very devout profession and very slight practical interest. Dunstan had refused to allow the marriage of a nobleman who had obtained leave at Rome to marry within the prohibited degrees ; Elfric had in his homilies enunciated a doctrinal statement on the Holy Eucharist that was a good way behind the fully developed view of the Roman theologians ; Canute had patronised the pope rather than been patronised by him, and Edward the Confessor's relations with him had been rather those of a devout recluse than of the king of a great nation. In truth in Edward's time the less England saw of the papacy the better it was for the papacy and the national belief in its authority, for matters at Rome were at a very low ebb ; and those who went there came back as a rule well shorn.

During Edward's reign of twenty-four years there were seven popes and certainly not less than three antipopes ; the pope who was reigning at the beginning of his reign was Benedict IX., who, after three times reaching the dignity and three times losing it, died in 1048. The pope who was reigning at the end of it was Alexander II., who took a lively interest in the acquisition of England by the Conqueror, and who acted, as his predecessor had done, very greatly on the advice of Hildebrand, who succeeded him as Gregory VII., to have a long and fatal struggle with Clement III. as antipope. Edward had not been much troubled about the state of the holy city ; but Stigand, his archbishop, had, most unfortunately for himself, accepted his pall from Rome at a time when the see was occupied by the antipope Benedict, and by doing so, and not readjusting his position when a more constitutional pope was appointed, had incurred a stain of schism or schismatic irregularity of which the Norman party in 1070, strengthened by the presence of a legate of Alexander II., made use to procure his deposition. It was probably with relation to the events of 1080, when as Clement III. Guibert of Ravenna usurped the papal throne under the influence of Henry IV., that William found it advisable to lay down this principle, for this was the only occasion on which an antipope arose during his reign; but he seems to have foreseen the importance of the point, which was perhaps more prominent in the reign of his sons, unless the fact be that Eadmer, who wrote under the impression made by the investiture controversy, has antedated a claim which more properly belongs to William Rufus or Henry I. However that may have been, you will observe the importance of the point, not merely as affecting the royal prerogative, but the political position within and without England of the king himself.

In the first place we have to consider that by accepting the pall from the popes the archbishops of Canterbury and York recognised a dependence on the apostolic see of the closest kind. Whatever may have been the original meaning of the gift, a complimentary offering or an act of honorary recognition, it had long before the Conquest become the type of metropolitan authority, and the reception of it by the archbishops a sort of spiritual investiture with the plenitude of metropolitical jurisdiction. Down to the time of the Reformation no archbishop before he received his pall ventured to perform acts of metropolitical authority such as the consecration of bishops and the like: and there were, besides the customary meaning of the emblem, oaths and promises of obedience to the giver which, although they varied from time to time, were very stringent, binding the archbishop to fealty and other obligations that might not improbably run counter to his obligations to the king.

Next you have to consider that the archbishops, especially the archbishop of Canterbury, were the first subjects of the realm, the first peers of parliament as they have been the first members of the witenagemot, and the most eminent members of the royal council. If, then, the king were to allow the archbishops to enter into the close relation that I have described with a pope who was linked with his enemies, or who was supported by the powers that were antagonistic if not overtly hostile to England, he would have an enemy in the very inmost circle of his court, council, and parliament. Nor would his difficulties be confined to internal administration. The whole network of European politics was closely interwoven with papal and ecclesiastical administration; the ambassadors, the international lawyers, were mostly bishops or clerks, and the court of Rome was the tribunal of international arbitration.

It is worth while to run briefly through the several cases of disputed elections and schisms at Rome in order to see what effect they really had on the policy of the kings. I have mentioned the schism of Guibert of Ravenna, which began with his election in 1080 and lasted more or less until his death in 1100. Guibert was never recognised as pope by France or England; but when, during the vacancy in the orthodox papacy on the death of Victor III., the antipope held possession of Rome or great part of it, and Urban II., who was elected in 1088, was, through a great part of his reign, in a very dubious position of authority, the question became practical. There was nothing in William Rufus's character to make him prefer a good pope to a bad one, but there was something that made him very angry when Anselm on his promotion to Canterbury took upon himself to take it for granted that Urban II. was the true pope. In that case—and it is the first—you see not so much the importance of the matter itself as the use which would be made of it.

Well, going on, the next important schism is that of 1130, when Anacletus II. and Innocent II. were the rival popes. Henry I. was then king, and he no more than William Rufus was likely to allow the English church to be committed to a party in Europe that might play into the hands of a rival politician. He was, however, early persuaded by S. Bernard to recognise Innocent II., and the recognition of Anacletus was never within measurable distance in England; but in Scotland it was not only possible but probable, although not perhaps so long as Henry I. lived and directed more or less the policy of his brother-in-law, King David. But when in 1138 England and Scotland were at war, Richard of Hexham, the historian of the battle of the Standard, distinctly accuses the Scots of favouring the antipope, and even if this is not true it is singularly curious as a forecast of what really happened in the later schisms when England recognised one pope and Scotland with France the other.

Next we come to the schism of 1159, when Alexander III. was opposed by antipopes in succession lasting until 1176, when by the peace of Venice he reconciled himself with Frederick Barbarossa and his other opponents, and brought about a most important, almost universal European peace. Coincident with that schism was the great struggle in England between Henry II. and Becket. During this struggle, Lewis VII., the most earnest supporter of Alexander III., was also the most zealous supporter of Becket, and Henry II. was more or less in alliance with Frederick Barbarossa. There were many of Henry's advisers who would gladly have brought him over to the side of the antipope; and indeed, in 1165, in the council of Würzburg, it was confidently asserted by Becket's supporters that the king's agents had committed him to the cause of the antipope. But if he then advanced a single step towards it, he must instantly have drawn back. He was too great a politician not to see how the struggle between the pope and the emperor must end; his son-in-law, Henry of Saxony, was hereditarily the champion of the orthodox papacy, and Alexander III., by his lukewarmness in support of Becket, did his best to avert the possibility of a rupture. But the crisis is a curious one ; any real support given by Henry to the emperor must have decided the quarrel for the time against the pope, and Henry would have won the victory over Becket and all his supporters ; but he looked further and saw that it would not do. Neither, we must remember, were France and Germany just then, although on different sides of the papal contest, hostile on other grounds ; so far the Hohenstaufen interest had not come, as it did later, into competition with that of the French dynasty.

Well, we pass on over a long time before we come to another real schism ; and when we do, it affects England only slightly. I mean the crisis on the election of Lewis of Bavaria to the empire and the setting up of Peter of Corvara as antipope to John XXII. If that quarrel had fallen a few years earlier or a few years later, it might have drawn in England. Either Edward I. or Edward III. might have been committed. But it really fell within the reign of Edward II. and that part of Edward III.'s reign in which he was on the best terms with France. If it had happened that Lewis of Bavaria had had his great struggle with John XXII. when England was at war with France, we might have antedated the Reformation of the sixteenth century by 200 years. Among Lewis's supporters were not only the great English schoolman, Ockham, but Marsilius of Padua, the philosophic constitutionalist whose conclusions as to the relations between church and state were largely taken up by Cromwell and other reforming ministers of Henry VIII.; Edward was, moreover, brother-in-law to Lewis, and in the beginning of his long war with France was commissioned by him as vicar of the empire on this side of the Rhine. But, whether fortunately or not, the religious storm was over before the Hundred Years' War began. Still we find Charles IV. the pope's Cæsar at the battle of Crecy, where his father fell, and the echoes of his earlier controversy are again and again heard in following years.

In the year 1378 the great schism of the West began under Urban VI. and Robert of Geneva or Clement VII., the popes at Rome and at Avignon. This is a good illustration of the Conqueror's doctrine becoming practical. Richard II. was then king, and he was a child ; but the parliament of England took on itself to recognise Urban VI., and not only to recognise him but to arm a crusade on his behalf under Henry le Despenser, the warlike bishop of Norwich. Urban was recognised by England, Spain, Germany, and Italy ; Clement by France and her allied and dependent states. Scotland and France were, as usual, thorns in the side of England,

and the religious element added no small colour to the rivalry. The popes were made to earn the support of the factions that sustained them, often one would imagine with some diminution of their self-respect. In 1388 Urban VI., at the application of the lords appellant, translated Archbishop Neville of York, one of the deposed ministers of Richard II., to the see of S. Andrews, which, being within the kingdom of Scotland and recognising the rival pope, was pretty much on the level of a bishopric *in partibus infidelium*. Ten years later Pope Boniface IX. in the same way, on the request of the king, translated Archbishop Arundel to S. Andrews in the same summary fashion.

The later history of the schism, although interesting, does not very much affect the point before us, but it is worth while noting the share taken by England at the council of Constance by Henry V. and the Emperor Sigismund in the election of Pope Martin V., and the labours of Henry VI. in connection with the council of Basel, into all of which, in a more or less remote degree, the royal right to recognise the legitimate successor of S. Peter enters. I need not pursue the subject further. We all know that practically the importance historically of the right came to an end when in 1534 the church, at the king's solicitation, declared that the pope has by the word of God no greater authority in the realm of England than any other foreign bishop.

We will now proceed to the second clause. '*The king did not permit the primate of his kingdom, that is to say the archbishop of Canterbury, if he assembled and presided over a council general of bishops, to enact or forbid anything, except what was agreeable to his will and had been previously ordained by him.*' In connection with this point the same question arises as we mentioned in regard to the first clause. It does seem possible that the writer antedated a difficulty which really arose in the reign of William Rufus and Henry I.; for we have no information which makes it even probable that the Conqueror had any such understanding or misunderstanding with his great friend and minister Lanfranc, while we know that this, like the last, was a point at issue between William Rufus and Anselm. The explanation would of course be that when William Rufus or Anselm asserted the right to stay or control ecclesiastical legislation, he would most likely refer for a precedent or authority to the practice of his father, and that which the father might have done became historically ascribed to him by this citation on the part of his son. Of course it is possible that there were episodes in the Conqueror's ecclesiastical régime of which we have no record. Well, the right of the archbishop to legislate in council, and the claim of the king to restrict the exercise of it, or to deprive it of all effect, were two conflicting elements which certainly affected English history for two centuries from this time; and then, after two centuries and a half of slumber, woke into importance again in the days of the Reformation. And this is a second point on which the Reformation lawyers may have looked back for a precedent to the days of Eadmer.

Well, the rule thus formulated was not only enforced but exceeded by William Rufus, who never allowed the holding of a council once during the thirteen years of his reign. Henry I. acted with more moderation: in 1102 Anselm was allowed to hold an ecclesiastical council coincidently with the king's council or witenagemot; and again in 1107, although a stormy period had intervened, the assembly of prelates, in which the question of episcopal homage was settled, was held in the king's palace and presence, as was that of 1108, in which reform was instituted as to the manners and character of the clergy. The best instance, however, of Henry's policy on the subject is that of the year 1127 or 1128, in relation to which the king issued a straightforward edict of confirmation: 'Know ye that by my royal authority and power I concede and confirm the statutes of the council celebrated by William, archbishop of Canterbury, and legate of the Holy Roman Church at Westminster, and what was there forbidden I forbid. So if any shall have been a violator or contemner of these decrees, if he shall not have humbly satisfied ecclesiastical discipline, let him know that he must be heavily coerced by the royal power because he has presumed to resist the Divine disposition.' In this the king, I think, duly recognises the proper principle on which alone a free church can exist in a free state; or an independent church in an independent state. The initiative comes from the church, the executive is regulated by the crown. The crown has a veto on ecclesiastical legislation, but does not originate it. However, on that hangs a whole world of controverted questions.

Under Stephen the hold which the king had on the church was weakened; there were two parties within the ecclesiastical body, with both of which he managed to quarrel, so that practically he was unable on the one side and unwilling on the other to interfere much with church councils. It was a church council, held by his brother Henry during his imprisonment, which elected the Empress Matilda lady of the English, and a church council which refused to recognise his son Eustace as heir apparent to the crown. But both these councils were mixed in their actual ingredients, and really acted rather as parliaments than as congregations. Stephen, in the latter part of his reign, acting on a similar right, forbade Archbishop Theobald to attend the council held by Eugenius III. at

Rheims, but Theobald went in spite of him, and, although there were threats of outlawry and actual sentences of interdict, neither party was strong enough to claim a distinct victory, and the quarrel was settled as between equals and by reconciliation, not by legal sentence. I will not connect this particular point with the vexed questions of state at issue between Henry II. and Becket, for it did not directly enter into them. Becket did not attempt to hold a formal council of bishops during the short period of his authority, except for the most formal business, certainly not to enact canons. After Becket's death his successors held their assemblies with the king's co-operation, and in some cases in his presence. Under Richard, whose ministers were great ecclesiastics, no question arose as in the early days of John, although on one occasion we find Archbishop Hubert Walter forbidden by the justiciar to hold a general council; but as soon as John's troubles begin this point emerges, and from the year 1207, when we find him issuing a prohibition to the council at S. Albans, forbidding the bishops to venture on any unauthorised proceeding, there is a string of similar interferences reaching down until the end, or near the end, of the reign of Edward I. These inhibitions were not uncalled for; for some of the archbishops had set themselves determinately the task of increasing the area and pressure of ecclesiastical jurisdiction and of resisting interference from the royal courts, even in matters of the most secular character; for example, they not only extended their claims to jurisdiction about tithes and advowsons, but directed the issue of sentences against the king's officers whenever they interfered with ecclesiastical procedure, and attempted in every way to defeat the prohibitions issued by the temporal courts to keep the courts Christian within the lines of their own jurisdiction. Some of them went further, Archbishop Peckham even so far as to order the republication of Magna Carta on church doors without leave of the king, and so attempted to get up a constitutional outcry against Edward I. during the most important legislative portion of his reign. In this the king got the better, for he not only persisted in issuing orders to the prelates not to make statutes or constitutions in disparagement of national law and royal right, but he compelled the enterprising primate to retract and annul some of the constitutions which he had made. However, after the close of this struggle, and especially after the king had yielded to the clergy the right of voting their taxes in their own convocations, an occasional expression of discontent in parliament is all that we hear of the matter.

The parliaments of Edward III. once or twice petition that the ordinances of the clergy in convocation may not be allowed to prejudice the rights of the laity, but no peremptory inhibition is

issued, nor does any conflict occur. In the prospect of such a conflict it was that in 1532 Henry VIII. obtained from the clergy in
their act of submission the undertaking that the convocations
should never henceforth make or attempt to enforce canons without
royal licence : a principle which has been acted upon, under circumstances sufficiently altered, and with various degrees of fairness, to
the present day, when some such power of ecclesiastical legislation
seems, under the conditions of a parliament largely consisting of
men opposed to the discipline of the historic church, to be loudly
called for.

The third clause of this latter formula requires no lengthy
exposition : *William I. did not permit leave to be given to any of the
bishops to compel and prevent, to excommunicate or subject to
the punishment of ecclesiastical discipline any of his barons or his
servants, even if he were defamed for adultery, incest, or any
capital crime, unless by his injunction.* This seems a hard saying,
but if you look at it closely you will see that it was almost a
necessity of the times: in Germany and France, by the excommunication of the kings, the realm had been thrown into extreme
confusion, and although the Conqueror was not himself a man
likely to be excommunicated, he knew that the penalties of
excommunication extended not only to the inculpated person but to
all who held converse with him, while among his courtiers, unless
there was a very sudden outbreak of vice under William Rufus, we
must needs suppose that there were many who must have deserved
the extreme sentence. However this may have been, you will
observe how great a danger a king might stand in of becoming
excommunicated and losing some part of his claim on the allegiance
of his people, especially after the acceptance of the Hildebrandine
theory of church and state, almost by accident.

Well, the practical importance of this point comes into stronger
relief later, for one of the Constitutions of Clarendon, the 7th,
formally enacts and extends the operation of the principle, which
is made to apply there to the lands as well as to the persons of the
tenants in chief and ministers of the king. Becket, it is true,
contemned it, and attempted by excommunicating from his French
place of refuge the chief members of the curia of Henry II. to reduce
his master, by a side blow, to the position of an excommunicated
person ; later on you may remember how carefully Archbishop
Winchelsey, by excommunicating Piers Gaveston in the event of
his return from exile, tried to shut out the possibility of the king
receiving him, and how Edward II. had to fortify himself with bulls
of absolution before he ventured to welcome his friend on his
return. The solemn excommunications *in genere*, that is without

naming the persons to whom the sentence was intended immediately
to apply, which were issued against all persons who should infringe
the charters, under the provisions of the council of Oxford held by
Langton and at other dates in the reign of Henry, show how, even
when wrapped, so to speak, in olive branches, the sword of the
spiritual sentence was brandished against a king and a court that
could not be trusted.

There are some other points of ecclesiastical administration,
besides those of which I have already spoken, which have great
prospective importance ; in particular the check on the reception of
Roman legations and bulls or other letters from Rome, and the check-
ing of appeals, or refusing permission to would-be appellants to leave
the country ; but these, I think, may be better connected with a
later period of our legal history, and I may have more to say of them
when we come to the reign of Henry I. I may, however, add that
although Lanfranc had letters from the pope in which he was
empowered to exercise the *vices meas*, the impassible papal powers,
he is not therefore styled legate ; while Anselm had to resist the
mission of the archbishop of Vienne as an infringement of his
privileges. Under the next primate, Ralph, the crown interfered to
prevent the right of the primate from being infringed ; and his
successor, William of Corbeuil, himself, by way of closing the
difficulty, sought and obtained for himself the commission of legate.
This measure, which, with some few intermissions, from that date to
the Reformation united the ordinary powers of the primate with the
extraordinary powers of a legate, confused the view of the ecclesiastical constitution in a very unfortunate way, and indeed made
comparatively easy the breakdown of the spiritual authority of the
archbishop at the Reformation. But on this point it is scarcely
necessary now to enlarge.

I have said and written so much about Henry I. that I shall not
on this occasion spend your time in repeating general remarks
on the history of his reign ; and as the first document of the
reign is the charter which we generally know as his coronation
charter, a document which, owing to its relation to Magna Carta,
may be looked upon as one of the most elementary parts
of our constitutional study, I shall not go into the minute
detail upon it which I have given to the examination of the
less well known legislation of William the Conqueror. It is
the first of our charters of liberties, not a recognition of existing
rights, but a grant or bestowal of rights on the motive of regard to
God and love of all his faithful people. Yet this high and mighty
beneficence is mainly an acknowledgment that England had been
wrongly and unjustly treated by William Rufus, and an undertaking

that it should be so no more. The church had been enslaved, it was to be made free ; the customs had been bad, they were to be put away ; the exactions had been unjust and the kingdom oppressed, the exactions were to be regulated and adjusted, and the kingdom was to be relieved and kept in peace. It was to be done by the solemn will of the king, now by the mercy of God and the common council of the barons of the whole realm crowned king in his brother's place. . Although it is a confession of wrongs and a concession of rights, it has a very sovereign tone about it, as if it were a mere matter of the king's grace and favour to do the rights and undo the wrongs : *I make the church free*, although on every principle of religion of the time the church had a full right to freedom ; *I restore the law of King Edward*, although the law of King Edward had never been withdrawn or suspended. It all reads as the outcome of a royal omnipotence which was free to give or withhold ; the counsel and consent of the barons had been given to the coronation, and are alleged as countenancing or warranting certain clauses of the charter, but they do not, as both before and later, enter into the motive clause or take their place between the respect for God and the love of the people which induce the despot to make these welcome alleviations.

But while we wonder that Henry, who at the moment of his coronation certainly needed all the help that he could get from all classes of the nation, and who might, we think, and would most naturally have availed himself of every opportunity of posing as the national king and countryman of the English people, did not use the old form to which even his father had condescended, and seem to legislate with the advice and consent of his wisemen, it is of little use to pry too critically into the reasons of an omission which, after all, may be accidental. It may have been thought needless, after stating that it was by common consent that he was crowned, to repeat that by common consent he was going to legislate ; and perhaps the mention of the regard for Almighty God and of the king's love towards his people has the effect of making the charter more of a personal act, more individually stringent and binding on the royal conscience ; as if he would say, ' I am making no new law ; I could if I would with the advice of my wisemen, but I am undoing wrong, I am emancipating myself without law from the unrighteous ways with which my brother encompassed his royalty ; of love of God and man I by myself put away the injustice.' You may remember in relation with this how Henry III. makes a personal matter in the same way of his confirmation of the Great Charter in 1225, when he substitutes *spontanea et bona voluntate mea* for the *consilio* of the earlier issues, as if willing either to assert a more distinctly sovereign right or to put himself under a more distinctly personal obligation.

However, we will let that be, and run through the text, and note the less obvious peculiarities of the document before us. The first clause concerns the liberties of the church, which, as you may remember, in the several collections of the Conqueror's articles of legislation, as well as in the elder Anglo-Saxon laws and the later petitions of parliament, has the prerogative place : it is instructive to note, however, what the king does not give, as well as what he gives. ' In the first place I make God's holy church free,' as free as it was in King Edward's time, when the churches, at least in theory, chose their own bishops. No ; the time has not come for that concession, if it ever is to come. Nor is anything said about the church's own courts or immunities from taxation or freedom to legislate. Much may be implied, but the specified relief given is the one that has been felt to be the burning question between king and bishops in the last reign : ' I make the church free, that is that I will neither sell nor let to farm ; nor when an archbishop, bishop, or abbot is dead will I take anything of the demesne of the church or of its vassals until the successor shall enter upon it.' Here is a renunciation of simony, I suppose, ' I will not sell,' and of the royal right to delay the election of a prelate in order to lay hands on the profits of the see during vacancy, ' nor will I let to farm ; ' and a renunciation of the right of seizing the property of the church and demanding extraordinary services from its vassals during the vacancy : until the successor is appointed nothing shall be taken.

Well, we may say, so much the worse for the successor, for however he comes in, the king has not bound himself to show any mercy to him—not less than William Rufus will Henry expect a handsome douceur from a newly appointed prelate, or it will be worse for him. The importance of the boon, if we consider that the investiture controversy was not yet fought out, does not appear very great ; at all events it requires to be supplemented with some substantial additions. We know, looking on, that as a part of the reconciliation scheme of 1107 a show of canonical election was restored to the churches ; that the elections were made by the chapters in the king's chapel before the king or the justiciar as his representative ; that the canonical right of election was in a way recognised by Stephen in his charter of 1136 ; but that the old system of compromise between nomination and election was really maintained as the rule until in 1214 John, in order to detach the bishops from the barons, granted in full the claim of free election, which, whatever it was worth, continued to be the law of the church until, first by the popes and after them by the reforming kings, it was snatched out of the hands that were too weak to hold it independently and fairly.

There are some other points touching ecclesiastical liberties which are more fully stated in Stephen's charter, and which throw light on the scantiness of the interpretation of the present grant, especially the corresponding clause: 'I promise that I will do or permit nothing simoniacal in the church or things ecclesiastical;' that, I think, would prove that *vendam* in this article does not mean alienation, but simoniacal sale. But this and the other points will recur when we come to the Act of Stephen, and we may pass on now. 'All the evil customs with which the kingdom of England was unjustly oppressed I take away from it, which evil customs I here in part rehearse.' Then follow 13 articles, some of which are descriptive of evil customs and some not. For instance, clauses 12, 13, and 14 have no direct relation to the misgovernment of the late reign, although the boons which they convey may and probably were suspended by William Rufus. Clauses 6 and 9 are acts of amnesty, the remission of the debts due to William Rufus, and the murder fines still due at the king's accession; clause 10 is not a boon, but the announcement that such a boon is not to be given, unless we are to suppose, what we are not expressly told, that the king renounced forest encroachments which William Rufus had added to the inclosures made by his father; and clause 11 is put as a new and spontaneous gift of the king himself to the tenants by knight service, which has no relation to anything granted or withheld by the tyrant whose evil customs are abolished. This reduces the express renunciation of evil customs to those clauses which have the negative form, *non redimet, defendo, non dabo, defendo, non dabit*, that is articles 2, 3, 4, 5, 8, to which we may add clause 7 as by implication abolishing a persistent abuse.

Now let us construe 2: 'If any of my barons, earls, or others who hold of me, die, his heir shall not redeem his land as he did in the time of my brother, but he shall relieve it by a just and lawful relief; and likewise the vassals of my barons shall relieve their lands of their lords, by a just and lawful relief.' No doubt the substitution of a just and lawful relief for a vexatious and exorbitant ransom was a great boon; but who was to be the judge of what the just and lawful relief should be, the payer or the crown? It would have been a much greater and more trustworthy amendment of evil practice if the king would have established an exact tariff. But it was not yet the time for that; rather we must be thankful for the appended clause, that the *arrière* vassals should have at the hands of their lords exactly the same sort of benefit that their lords now took by the gift of the king. What the evil custom was we see: William

Rufus and his precious minister had exacted from the heir of the
dead baron such a great payment for permission to enter on his inheritance as really amounted to a *redemptio*, a repurchase of the
estate.   Henceforth the payment required should be just and proportionate.   Where did this doctrine of relief come from ?   We saw in
the laws of the Conqueror a *relevatio* answering to the Anglo-Saxon
heriot, and in Anglo-Saxon form.   The relief of the baron is four
horses, two saddled and bridled, and two suits of arms ; the relief
of the earl was double the relief of the vavassor, either a simple
heriot or 100 shillings composition ; and the relief of the villein
his best ox or horse.   Whence, then, comes this new sort of relief,
which may amount to a full ransom ?   I think from William Rufus
and Flambard.   And what becomes of it ?   Well, we know from the
'Dialogus de Scaccario' that in the reign of Henry II. the relief of the
baron remained a matter of composition between the crown and
the payer, but the relief of the inferior vassal was 100 shillings on the
knight's fee (' Select Charters,' p. 243).   Still, *in regis bene placito est*,
in the case of barony, *quæ debeat esse summa relevii*.   Nor was it
altered until by the second clause of the Great Charter of 1215 a relief
of £100 was fixed as the sum due on this account from earls and barons.
A subsequent reading of the time of Edward I. placed earl, baron,
and knight in this particular in the relation of pound, mark, and
shilling.

The next evil custom renounced in clause 3 concerns the right
of *maritagium*, also new, or at all events non-apparent among the
articles of the Conqueror's legislation.   'If any of my barons or
other of my vassals wish to give his daughter in marriage, or his
sister or niece or kinswoman, he may speak with me thereon ; but
I will neither take anything of his for this licence, nor will I forbid
him to give her to whom he pleases except to an enemy of mine.
And if on the death of a baron or other my vassal his heir be a
daughter, I will give her with her land by the advice of my barons.
And if, the husband being dead, his wife survives and be without
children, she shall have her dower and marriage, and I will not give
her to a husband except according to her will.'   This again is new—
the Conqueror had not left behind him a word on the subject ; nay,
I believe a good deal of it is almost peculiar to England.   It came
from William Rufus, and we infer from the words in what shape.
He must have taken fines for licence for his great lords to give their
daughters in marriage ; he must have forbidden them to marry them
to whom they would ; just as the lord of the manor long after this
took a fine on the marriage of a daughter of a villein, so the king has
been used to treat his great lords as villeins, and so much the worse
for their dependants.

But the 4th clause concerns the same point : 'But if the wife survives with children she shall have indeed her dower and her marriage so long as she keeps chaste, and I will not give her to a husband except according to her will. And of the lands and children the guardian shall be either the wife or another of the relations who has greater right to be. And I enjoin that my barons shall behave with like moderation towards the sons and daughters and wives of their dependants.' There again you have the noble redeeming feature of the whole of this royal grant, that the poorer men shall enjoy every right at the hands of their lords that their lords enjoy at the hands of the king. I need hardly remind you to compare these clauses with clauses 6, 7, 8 of the Great Charter of John. This royal right of interfering with and making profit by the marriage and wardship of tenants in chief was a very tiresome and a very long-lived piece of prerogative, and its historical importance is very great. The disparagement of heiresses by unequal marriages, that is the use of them to enrich a new rising man or favourite minister at court, or the delay of their marriage in order to gather in the profits of minority, was a great subject of complaint under Henry II., whose enemies accused him of giving away noble ladies to the grooms of the court. I do not suppose that Henry literally did anything of the kind ; every unpopular *novus homo* was spoken of as a groom or a lackey, just as Carlyle would have spoken of a flunkey or Thackeray of a snob ; and it takes a great deal of sympathetic flunkeyism or snobbery to distinguish those disagreeable characteristics in the majority of mankind. But there is little doubt that it was a dangerous policy. The marriage of Piers Gaveston with one of the Gloucester heiresses was a great cause of his misfortunes, although she was not what we should call an heiress until after his death, her brother surviving him for two years. The marriage of Hugh le Despenser was likewise regarded as a disparagement, and the cry was no doubt a convenient one for a malcontent aristocracy, as the practice was a convenient one for a king who dared not take the lands of the heiress to himself, and did not wish that it should fall into the hands of a foe or a possible foe. Well, the Court of Wards and Liveries, as we know, lived a long life, not becoming extinct until Charles II. at the Restoration surrendered the remnants of the feudal income and feudal exactions of his predecessors.

The next article introduces us to some comparatively new matter. '5. The *monetagium commune*, the common mintage which was taken through the cities and counties, which was not in the time of King Edward, that I forbid to be taken from henceforth. If anyone be taken with false money, be he moneyer or other, right justice shall be done upon him.' The early history of the coinage is, comparatively speaking, obscured rather by the great unlikeness to our present system than by any difficulty existing on the subject. In the Anglo-Saxon reigns we know that the right of coining silver was a royal right shared by the two archbishops and some of the bishops who had ancient privilege or prescription. But it was exercised by a class of persons called moneyers, who received their stamps, punches, or wedges from London, and having paid handsomely for them made as much profit as they could on the metal which they impressed with the king's mark. The towns in which these moneyers were allowed to exercise their functions were fixed by list in the time of Athelstan. Each king exercised the power of altering the coinage, *monetam mutare*, the calling in of the worn-out silver, and on proportionate payment impressing it with the new stamp. All this seems clear, but it is not quite so clear what is the meaning of *monetagium* in the text of the law. The explanation is that a heavy sum was charged by the crown through or by the moneyers when the coinage was altered; that may have been very likely done, and the explanation would accord well enough with the rest of the article, which seems to be dealing with the technicalities of the coinage, and especially with the offence of falsifying the coin.

It so happens that among the few other relics of Henry's legislation which are extant we have a complete edict on the subject of the coinage, preserved in the Liber Ruber of the Exchequer, and like the edict for the holding of the county courts addressed to the sheriff and thanes of Worcestershire. That it was a very important Act in the view of the time is clear from the mention made of it by both Eadmer and Florence of Worcester, who enable us to date the document itself in 1108, seven years, that is, later than the charter before us. I will translate the document. ' Henry, king of the English, to Sampson the bishop and Urso d'Abitot, and all barons, French and English, of Worcestershire, greeting: Know ye that I will and enjoin that all burgesses and all those who dwell in burghs, as well French as English, swear to keep and preserve my money in England, and not to consent to the falsification of my money. And if anyone has been found with false money, if he can vouch a warrantor for it, let it be taken to him, and if he can prove it my justice shall be done on the warrantor himself; but if he cannot prove it my justice shall be done upon the falsifier, that is he shall lose his right fist and be otherwise mutilated. And if he can vouch no warrantor for it, he may go to the ordeal therefore to prove that he knows not how to name or recognise the person from whom he has received it. Moreover I forbid that any moneyer shall change the money except in his own county, and that before two lawful witnesses

ɪ

of the crown by itself; and if he shall have been caught changing money, that is altering the coin, in any other county, he shall be treated as a falsifier, *falsonarius*. And let no one dare to change . . . money except a moneyer. Dated at Westminster at Christmas.' It is clear from this that the falsifying of money was a prevalent evil at the time ; and it was probably falsified not only by clipping, but by the introduction of base alloys into the metal itself. This we know was the case in Stephen's reign, for he is accused of conniving at the debasement of the coin. Henry II. also by his ill-wishers is accused of making undue profits out of the new coinage, and of sacrificing the moneyers whom he had made his tools to the indignation of the people. To him, as you will remember, probably is due the credit of restoring the royal coinage to metallic purity, which it retained to the days of Henry VIII. ; the abuses of the coinage in the meanwhile being connected mainly with the introduction of foreign coin, Flemish in particular, which gave Edward I. a good deal of trouble, and also with clipping, which so long as the Jews were in England was generally laid to their charge and visited upon them, even by the justest of our kings, with great severity. Some hundreds of Jews were put to death between 1280 and 1290 for clipping.

The first parliament of Edward II. treated of the coinage as then an important question, and it was there agreed that the coin current under the father should remain current under the son, as if there were some risk even then of an arbitrary calling in of the old coin and some exaction on the ground of a new mintage. That brings us round to the text again; and accepting the explanation that I gave in the first instance, we understand it to mean simply that on the occasion of recoinage of old silver no exorbitant charge shall be made by the moneyers, but the work shall be done honestly as in the time of the Confessor. There is, however, a further explanation of the monetagium, which may be the true one here, and although derived from the former not entirely identical with it. According to this view the monetagium was not so much the payment made to the moneyers when the coin was restamped to enable them to bring it up to the standard value, but an *ad valorem* increase on all payments of rents, ferms, and other taxes paid to the king, to compensate him for the depreciation of the coinage. For example, if your rent to the king was 100 pence, and the depreciation of the coinage at the time owing to wear and tear and clipping was as much as 5 per cent., you would be charged 105 pence ; and sometimes, instead of doing it in the single case, a regular impost would be collected on this ground in the form of a general tax. This was done in Normandy under the name of *focagium*, or hearth tax, which is supposed to answer to a monetagium or mint tax in England. This explanation is very ingenious, and may be the correct interpretation of this article, for, as you will see by reading the ' Dialogus de Scaccario,' the whitening, *dealbatio*, of the ferm, that is the melting down and weighing of the coin paid in, and the payment of an additional charge to bring it up to the real value, was a very important part of the exchequer business, and so full of occasions of oppression that a substitution of a charge of 6*d*. in the pound was imposed.   You will find a great deal of curious detail on this subject in the ' Dialogus de Scaccario,' and of explanation in Mr. Stapleton's preface to the ' Rotuli Scaccarii Normanniæ.'   Perhaps, considering the importance of the subject, I have said enough about it now.

The 6th article need not detain us ; it is simple enough: ' All pleas and all debts which were due to my brother I condone, except my right ferms and except those sums which were agreed to be paid for the inheritances of others, or for those things which justly pertained to them.   And if anyone has made any bargain for his own inheritance, that I forgive him, and all reliefs which had been agreed upon for right inheritances.'   The first part is simple : Henry will not enact the debts due to William Rufus ; but payments due to the crown for certain things he will enforce ; bargains made by heirs for the entry on property directly heritable, and the relief due on the occasion, he will remit, but not the payments for the inheritances of others ; that must be, I suppose, the bargains made by grantees who enter on the inheritance of persons who have incurred forfeiture, as so many did under William Rufus ; and possibly where heirs were instituted or adopted in default of *sui heredes*.

Clause 7 : ' And if any of my barons or vassals shall be sick, as he shall give or dispose to give his money, so I grant that it be given ; and if prevented by arms or infirmity he has not given or disposed to give, then his wife or children, or parents and his lawful men, shall divide that for his soul's sake as it shall appear best to them.'   This clause is interesting as one of the first pieces of legislation that we have on intestacy and administration of the goods of the dying.   We seem to understand from it that *pecunia* alone was susceptible of testamentary devise ; that is, that the power of leaving land by will was already supposed by the common law to be withdrawn from the subject, and that whatever had been the case under the Anglo-Saxons, under the Normans bequests of land were impossible. Further, it reads almost as if it were by special favour that a vassal of the king might dispose of his personalty, and that the crown had some sort of claim on the goods of intestates.   If that were so, this claim resigns that power—a man may devise his personalty, and the king confirms his will.   If he dies without one, his relations, wife, children, or parents, or lawful men may divide it to the good of his soul; that is, one imagines, making proper provision for masses for his soul, may divide the residue among themselves. The legal importance of this clause is not great, for, as we know from other sources, the jurisdiction over wills and intestates' goods shortly after this fell into the hands of the clergy, and is regulated by clauses 26 and 27 of Magna Carta, in which, after the payment of the royal dues, the execution of the rest of the devises of wills is left to the executors, who are bound by religious duty, enforced by spiritual penalties, to carry into effect the will of the testator ; and in case of intestacy the goods of the defunct are to be distributed by his nearest relations and friends under view of the church. So that by the time of John the whole testamentary and intestate jurisdiction is under the view of the church, as indeed we know from Glanville that it must have been several years earlier. But in this article no mention whatever is made of the church or of spiritual matter, other than the duty of devising some part of the intestate's property for the good of his soul. It is therefore held that the doctrine that testamentary jurisdiction is a church right grew up between the reign of Henry I. and that of Henry II. I do not know that we need go so far as that, for there may already have been a common law practice for the bishops and clergy to see that a man's effects were distributed for his soul's sake, and of keeping executors to their duty by spiritual means ; but it is quite certain that the original duty of doing this did not belong to the clergy, but to the manors and perhaps to the early township administration. There are many manors at the present day from which the right of proving wills and granting letters of administration was only taken away by the recent Acts on probate and administration, and which had enjoyed and exercised the right quite as long as any ecclesiastical court had done, running in fact into remote antiquity. That the ecclesiastical jurisdiction on these matters was an unwarranted usurpation is one of the questions on which Prynne, who is in many points a constitutional authority, greatly relied, and which occupies in his tremendously heavy and numerous volumes a place somewhat in excess of its importance. It is, however, interesting, and this article is an interesting contribution to its history.

The 8th article, like some of the preceding ones, is intended to substitute a reasonable or fixed payment for an arbitrary and precarious one, in direct remedy of the tyrannical practices of the late reign. 'If any of my barons or my men has committed transgression, he shall not give wager or pledge in mercy of his money, as he did in the time of my father or my brother ; that is he shall not lie at the mercy of the king to exact entire forfeiture of all his personal estate, but, according to the measure of the delict, he shall make amends as he would have made amends before my father's time, or the time of my other ancestors. But if he be convicted of perfidy or crime, as shall be just, so shall he amend.' *Secundum modum delicti*, you may remember, was the expression introduced into the Exchequer copy of the 10 articles of the Conqueror, which allowed a man to be mutilated of hands, feet, eyes, &c., according to the measure of his fault. Here the rule is applied to fines and forfeitures, and the principle, which is of considerable importance, is found worked out in clauses 20, 21, 22 of the Great Charter of John. In this clause no standard is set by which the *modus delicti* can be estimated, and the offender might lie at very uncertain mercy under so loose a clause. But in Magna Carta here, as in other points, the reasonable discretion of the king is set aside for a more trustworthy determinant, and the amercement *secundum modum delicti* is to be made for ordinary freemen by the oath of good men of the neighbourhood, that is by jury, and in the case of earls and barons by their peers.

We now proceed with the concluding articles of the coronation charter of Henry I., which will not require much comment : e.g. 'All the *murdra*, all the murder fines which fell due before the day of my coronation, I condone, and those which from this date shall be incurred shall be justly paid according to the law of King Edward.' Note that this article seems fully to justify our belief, which is founded on the date given at the close of the charter, that it was issued on the day of coronation—*retro ab illa die* designates the past ; *a modo*, from now, designates the future—no provision is contemplated for the cases that occurred between the coronation and the issue of the charter ; therefore we infer that the division is exhaustive and the charter was issued on the very day ; and this agrees with the statement of Eadmer that on the very day the king issued letters sealed in confirmation of the coronation oath, in which the promise of good government was made in general terms, and in the language used in Anglo-Saxon times. Now Henry, we are told, was crowned on August 5, 1100, that is on the Sunday following the death of William Rufus, which occurred on a Thursday ; so that this extremely important document did not occupy in the drawing more than a couple of days : this seems a difficulty, and the date 1101, which appears at the head of the charter, may suggest a possible solution, namely, that although this appears as the coronation charter, i.e. the written and sealed declaration of the way in which the king meant his coronation promises to be kept, it is not necessary to suppose that the writing itself issued that day, only that the promises contained in it were to be operative from the day of the coronation. That, I say, is a possible solution, but I do not accept it myself. I think that the document, vastly important and comprehensive as it is, bears marks of having been hastily drawn up, and that there is really no reason to question its being the identical manifesto which Eadmer mentions (p. 96) as issued at the coronation. It is not at all necessary to suppose that all the copies which would be sent into the different counties were written on the same day ; but on the coronation the fiat was issued for the publication of these articles pretty much as they stand. The names of the witnesses support the conclusion. Maurice of London, the bishop who crowned the king ; Gundulf of Rochester ; William Giffard, whom on the very day Henry had nominated to the see of Winchester, would all be at the ceremony. Anselm, the archbishop, who returned immediately after and married the king to Matilda in the following November, would have surely attested the charter if it had been issued after his arrival in England. It is a point of more interest than importance, and the charter itself may have been republished from time to time as the king found it necessary to remind the nation of his good will towards them ; but as for the letter as it stands, I am content that it should stand as the contemporaneous and formal exposition of the king's coronation promises, and issued, or ordered to be issued, on that very day. That is the first point to note.

A second is the reference to the law of King Edward, on which I said all that need be said when I was commenting on the introduction of the murder fine. That amounts to so much; there are two points : had the law of Edward the Confessor been drawn up on the recognition of the wisemen of the county courts as described in the Leges Edwardi and assigned to the fourth year of the Conqueror ?—had the system of murdrum really been in existence in England under Edward or under Canute, and was it not introduced by the Conqueror ? Neither question admits of more than a doubtful answer. It is possible either way ; only if the Leges Edwardi were really codified under the Conqueror, I cannot think that we have as yet got hold of a sound text of them. As to the murdrum, I do think it possible that, as those laws tell us, something of the kind had been introduced by Canute ; certainly the wording of this clause shows that a tradition to that effect must have been current when the charter was drawn up. Clause 10 : 'The forests, by common consent of my barons, I have retained in my own hands as my father had them.' There were, as you of course are well aware, two great oppressions connected with the forests—the extension of them and the jurisdiction of them, the enlargement of the forest area and the enforcement of the forest law. The principal force of this article seems to refer to the former :

I do not know that besides the words of Stephen's charter there
is any evidence that William Rufus inclosed new forests; he may
very likely have done so, and if he did, then this declaration of the
king may amount to a renunciation of the forests that his brother
had made, with a retention of more which his father had enjoyed;
just as Stephen himself retained the forests of the two Williams
and renounced those of Henry I.; but if it were so, the same
evidence would prove that the promise so suggested had not
been kept. As to the severity of the forest law, we know from
the Anglo-Saxon Chronicle that whereas the Conqueror was satisfied
with blinding the deer-stealer, William Rufus made the offence
capital, and Henry II. in his Forest Assize refers to the legislation of
his grandfather as the settled justice that was to be taken on the
criminal; the plenary justice was mutilation and blinding, as we
learn from the Forest Assize of Richard I., issued in 1198, according
to the law of his father's grandfather. So far, then, as mutilation
and blinding were a modification of capital punishment, Henry I.
may be regarded as alleviating the oppressiveness of the forest jurisdiction exercised by his brother, but exceeding the severity which
marks his father's proceedings.

The 11th clause requires, perhaps, more careful reading. ' To
the knights who hold their lands by the hauberk, that is by knight
service, I grant by my own proper gift that the lands of their demesne
ploughs be quit of all gelds and of all work; that as they are relieved by
so great an alleviation, they may well equip themselves with horses
and arms to my service and to the defence of my kingdom.' The
words of the description are not surplusage : the holding the land
by the hauberk, that is the duty of serving the king in full armour,
is a sort of definition of the tenure of the knights ; the gelds and
opera are the money payments and personal services which were
required by the Anglo-Saxon law and by the Norman practice from
all landowners alike ; the lands of the knights that are so relieved are
not all their lands, but those which they kept in hand, their demesne
lands, the lands of their demesne ploughs. The exact payments
and services from which these lands are relieved would be no doubt
the Danegeld and special services of castle guard and the like. I
do not know that we can go so far as to say that they would include
the services of the trinoda necessitas ; but if the words are to be
construed literally, they would relieve them from part of that also,
that is the bridge bot and the burh bot, for the expeditio, the fyrd,
is the object to which by this general relief they are enabled to
devote themselves. In simple words, then, the demesne lands
of tenants by knight service are freed from taxation, the duty of the
holders being fulfilled by their equipping themselves with horses

and arms. Unfortunately we know so little about the exact terms
or dates of the introduction of the tenure by knight service into
England that we are unable to estimate the exact value of this
allevamen. But we do see that it is a moderate one, by no means
affecting all the lands held by that service, only the demesne lands ;
and we infer from that, that when in Henry IV.'s reign, or even
earlier, it became necessary to substitute a money payment for
military service, this immunity was lost sight of in the general
composition of scutage. I will not now take you into the vexed
question whether the scutage was a breach of this law, as has
sometimes been maintained. I do not myself think that it was ; for
although both the *auxilium militum* of Henry I.'s pipe roll and the
scutages of Henry II. were new taxes, the former cannot be certainly
said to have been hard by the king's tenants in chief, and the latter
was a commutation of an old obligation, not the imposition of
a new one.

Clause 12 : 'I place firm peace in the whole of my kingdom, and
enjoin that it be kept from this day.' Here we have the first of the
proclamations of the king's peace that are extant, and the importance of which lies in the fact that offences committed between the
expiry of the late king's peace and the proclamation of the new
king's peace were not regarded as breaches of the king's peace or
public law. On this I do not know that I have anything to say
that has not been said over and over again ; the peace here proclaimed is the general peace of the kingdom, not any special
protection of places or persons by the king's special peace, but
the general undertaking that the law shall be enforced on all
breakers of it. Of course the doctrine involved the necessity of
making the interregnum between the late king's peace and his
successor's as short as possible, and, as we have seen, it was all
over on this occasion within a week ; in fact the nation at a very
short distance from court would not have heard of the death of
William Rufus until they heard of Henry's coronation, the hurry
had been so great that only a very few of the magnates had been
able to assemble at all. In some of the later cases the space was
longer ; stress of weather in Henry II.'s case and business in
Normandy in John's lengthened the interregnum. Richard I.
seems not to have cared to hurry about his coronation at all. In
fact, whenever the government was strong enough, the theory of
the interruption of the peace was of little moment ; where the
government was weak, it was only alleged as a colourable excuse
for misdeeds that would have been done just as much without any
theory of excuse. We may, I think, add that the practical importance of the point had been altogether forgotten before the accession

of Edward I., although the form of proclamation of the new king's peace continued to be kept up as a part of the notification of a new reign to the nation at large.

Clause 13 : ' The law of King Edward I restore to you with those emendations with which my father amended it by the counsel of his barons.' This clause is worth noting, if it were only for this, that it is a distinct reference to the 7th of the genuine articles of the Conqueror, p. 84, which we examined so much in detail a few lectures ago. The emendations are those contained in that summary of 10 articles, and I think none other ; the mention of the counsel of the barons also seems quite fatal to the supposition that the Exchequer Charter, containing so much additional matter, as we saw, but not the statement of counsel and consent, could have been in existence when Henry I. issued this clause.

One clause remains to be dealt with—clause 14 :. ' And if anyone has taken anything of my goods or of the goods of anyone since the death of my brother William, the whole shall immediately without recompense be restored ; and if anyone has retained anything thereof, he upon whom it shall be found shall make heavy recompense to me.' This clause you understand of course in connection with the proclamation of the peace. What happened before William's death is condoned. Murder fines before the coronation are condoned, but acts of theft committed in the interregnum on the king or on anyone else are to be punished. A man may if he will make his peace by restoring what he has stolen, but if he is caught retaining it so much the worse for him. We wonder what peculiar mischief this clause, coming as a sort of appendix to other enactments of great and permanent importance, was intended to serve. Possibly even at this date there was a custom in king's courts for the attendants on the dead king to lay their hands on everything they could and run away with it, leaving the late object of their veneration and flatteries to be buried by the first comer. When we read of William Rufus's dead body being left by the attendants, of whom some went off to defend their homes, others to plunder their neighbours, others to welcome the rising sun, leaving the dead man to be carried by the rustics on an open cart, streaming with blood ; or when we read of the awful scenes at the funerals of William the Conqueror and Henry I. himself which the historians have recorded for us, we can understand the gist of the article. We remember, too, how Alice Perrers plundered the dead Edward III., and how, according to Shakespeare, Henry V. was in too great a hurry to step off with his father's crown.

However, there it ends, the most important manifesto that we have yet seen of the way in which the Norman sovereigns wished to rule the kingdom on which they had laid such a heavy hand ; a most valuable monument, too, of national history owing to the fact that it was upon its lines that Langton and the associate barons drew up their demands which were embodied in the Great Charter of Runnymede, copying the general arrangement of the articles, and paraphrasing, expanding, and defining their meaning. So that what Magna Carta was to England after the consolidating and organising work of Henry II. and his ministers had been accomplished, that the charter of Henry I. was to the nation before the era of reform had begun : it was the promise of a great king and law-giving statesman, who loved method and maintained justice wherever it did not conflict with the one mightier and stronger influence, which was his own despotic will, yet who saw in his hold on the magnates around him the only way as yet of directly benefiting the classes beneath them, the only reasonable hope that in time he might depress their overweening power. 'What I grant to you, you shall grant to them,' is the keynote of the most important articles, and by comparing that with the sentiment of the barons at Runnymede, who in the 62nd clause of the Charter extended to their vassals all the boons the king granted to them, we may measure the growth of national unity and the difference of idea that had grown up in the 115 years that intervened.

The next document that I propose to examine will be the charter of the city of London, which, in the manuscripts to which properly the title of Leges Henrici belongs, immediately follows the coronation charter. As I shall have to call your particular attention in a future lecture to the more important literary points connected with that valuable compilation, I will at once proceed to the text of the London charter, only premising a reference to the earlier charter of the Conqueror given in the 'Select Charters,' which simply grants to the bishop and the portreeve of London, as representing the burghers, the continuance of the rights which they had possessed under Edward the Confessor, and the right of inheritance, which, it would seem, if we are to construe this grant as a new privilege, had been somewhat limited by royal or municipal interference in King Edward's days. To this latter point I shall have to recur later on.

The text of Henry's charter runs thus: 'Henry by the grace of God king of the English'—for *Angliæ* in this place is simply a wrong expansion of the abbreviation *Angl.* for *Anglorum*, as you are doubtless aware, John being the first king who called himself in public documents king of England—'to the archbishop of Canterbury and the bishops, abbots, earls, barons, and justices, sheriffs, and all his faithful French and English of all England, greeting.' Observe here that we are dealing with a copy ; in the original no doubt the name of the archbishop would be expressed ; we may have occasion to consider this point as elucidating, or at least accounting for, some other difficulties of the text. You will find it convenient to divide the matter of the charter into fifteen subsections, as is done by Dr. Schmid. 'Know ye that I have granted to the citizens of London, Middlesex, to be held to ferm for £300 at account, to them and their heirs of me and my heirs, and that the citizens shall appoint a sheriff such as they may please of themselves and a justiciar such as they please of themselves to keep the pleas of my crown and to plead them, and no other justiciar shall be over the men of London.' That is the 1st clause. The administration of the county of Middlesex is assigned to the citizens of London in ferm. They are to appoint, or rather to be themselves collectively, the sheriff of Middlesex, appointing of course a sheriff to represent them and execute their powers, and a justiciar to keep the pleas of the crown, the justiciar in this respect answering to the later coroner, who in other county courts apparently about the reign of Richard I. was appointed to keep the pleas of the crown, to watch the interests of the crown that is, and so far to limit the jurisdiction of the sheriff. Besides this sheriff and justice no other person is to be justiciar over the citizens of London. We cannot but deplore here the total darkness that covers the history of London in the Anglo-Saxon times, and even in the reign of the Conqueror, for it obscures the meaning of what here might seem tolerably clear. We cannot see from what is in the text what has become of the portreeve, who was the head man in the former charter, or whether by the appointing of a sheriff we are to understand merely a sheriff for Middlesex, or one sole sheriff with metropolitan jurisdiction ; but if we look further on we see that when the pipe rolls begin London is under more than one sheriff, there being four in 1131, and during the first fifteen years of Henry II. two.

I have in the first volume of the 'Constitutional History' speculated on the possible history of the extinction of the portreeve, and the substitution of a shire constitution for the earlier municipal system which his name represents. You will of course understand that that is merely a speculation founded on the fact that we find the property of the cnihten gild, whose head the portreeve was, and whose jurisdiction was over the ward called Portsoken, was transferred by a charter of nearly the same date as the present to the monastery of the Holy Trinity, Aldgate, a priory of Augustinian canons whose prior was henceforth alderman of the Portsoken ward and one of the barons of the city of London. But I will not repeat what is down in print. The one unmistakable point in this 1st clause is that the Londoners are empowered to elect their chief magistrate, the sheriff answerable at the Exchequer for the king's ferm, and the justiciar, the officer whose function it is to look after and conserve the king's interests—his share in the fines of the law courts, the murdra, and possibly also the customs, such as they were, payable at the port.

The 2nd clause is an amplification of these judicial liberties. '(2) And the citizens shall not plead outside the walls of the city for any plea, and they shall be quit of scot and lot, of Danegeld and murder fine, and none of them shall be compelled to trial by battle.' We can understand the privilege of not being summoned outside the walls of London; it is a common privilege in later charters. They shall be quit of scot and lot is less clear, for scot and lot simply taken means proportionate taxation, and it is impossible to suppose that this clause means that where a sum is due from the city it is to be raised either by simple poll tax or by an impost levied without regard to the capacity of the payers. We must provisionally, however, understand that it means the arbitrary imposition which a few years later becomes known as tallage, which may from the method of its incidence be here designated by a more general and less appropriate term. We do know, however, that the question whether the citizens should raise their contributions by poll tax or by proportionate assessment was mooted a full century later than this, when William FitzOsbert set himself up as champion of the inferior commons in resisting the use of the poll-tax method prescribed by the magnates. The exemption from Danegeld, from the law of murdrum, and the trial by battle is clear enough.

'(3) And if any of the citizens has been impleaded of in any of the pleas of the crown, by the oath which shall have been judicially approved in the city he shall prove himself as a citizen of London exempt from such trial.' I think that this article is constructively connected with the last, i.e. if a citizen be appealed for an offence for which ordinarily he would be liable under the Conqueror's charter to trial by battle, he may obtain exemption by the customary oath of compurgation. This clause has the effect of making the custom of compurgation the most abiding rule in borough and city courts, to which the exemption from the trial by battle is granted in many charters; so much so that when by the great assize of Henry II. trial by battle in civil causes was generally superseded, and when by the assize of Clarendon compurgation itself in the courts of the itinerant judges was practically abolished, the town courts into which the itinerant judges did not force their way retained the ancient practice. The use of the compurgation in this way for the purpose of denying the adversary's right and traversing his cause, *disrationandi* as here used, was so common that in the Norman law the law of compurgation itself was sometimes called the *lex disrationis*.

Here it seems to comprehend both the appeal 'civis Londoniensis sum' and the denial of the charge.

'(4) And within the walls of the city let no one be lodged, neither of my household nor of another, unless the duty of entertaining him be assigned to some particular person.' That is, I conclude, unless some particular person can be found to be answerable for him, or unless the duty of entertaining him shall have been assigned to some one. The latter interpretation is probably the better. If the stranger came the magistrate had either to turn him out or to billet him on some citizen who would be answerable for him. No one much cared to entertain the members of the king's household, who as a rule treated their entertainers very badly. The practice common under William Rufus of the king's servants making themselves at home wherever they went is described in Eadmer in language of the utmost strength. Whatever they found in the houses of their entertainers they spoiled or carried away. Their wives and daughters they dishonoured, they burned their furniture, they washed their horses' feet in the wine, and let the casks run out. So bad it was that Henry, in an edict the words of which unfortunately have not been preserved, ordered the offenders to undergo the same punishment of blinding, castrating, and mutilating of hands and feet which was enforced against forgers and deer-stealers. The Latin of this clause, although obscure, is capable of interpretation by later charter law. It was intended to secure the safety and responsibility of the stranger entertained.

'(5) And all the men of London shall be quit and free, and all their effects, through all England and the sea ports, of *toll* and *passage* and *lastage*, and all other customs.' *Telonium* means toll generally, i.e. a duty on the merchandise carried about, more what we should call custom; *passage* would answer to the toll paid at gates and bridges, which would be the same whatever was the value of the merchandise admitted; *lastage* would properly mean a duty payable on weight. All three terms had better be explained loosely, for they may only mean the same thing applied to different descriptions of goods, and they are all more or less obscure. The privilege conferred is a very common one, frequently granted to the tenants of monasteries, and did not fall into disuse for more than a century. I have seen, if I have not got, a parchment pass granted to my great-grandfather, who was owner of a small property that had once belonged to the abbey of Fountains, by which he was empowered to remove his stock and go where he pleased without payment of the ancient tolls from which Fountains and its tenants were free by charter. I imagine most of those tolls are now extinguished, but the exemption survived the monastery for certainly two centuries.

Clause 6 is an interesting one, for it throws some light on the constitution of the city. 'And the churches, barons, and citizens shall hold and have well and in peace their sokens or jurisdictions with all customs, so that the strangers who are lodged in their jurisdictions shall pay their customs to none but to him whose soken it is, or to the servant whom he shall place there.' Here, you see, the city is certainly divided into certain sokens or privileged jurisdictions, which have a right to exact payments, customary payments from strangers and doubtless other rights such as belonged in the country to lords of manors. Some of these belonged to churches, in particular to the church of S. Paul, and the Augustinian canons of Trinity Aldgate, S. Martin's le Grand, and others; some belonged to hereditary owners, such as the lord of Baynard's Castle, the Baron Fitzwalter, standard-bearer of the city, and the lord of Montfitchet, who also had a castle in London, the warden of the Tower, and others, some of whom were barons of the realm, others barons in the limited sense of tenants in chief of hereditary estates in the city and as hereditary aldermen rejoicing in the title thus given; others were held by simple citizens. You will, however, observe that although these sokens represent the later wards of the city, there is nothing here that would lead us to suppose them to have either a recognised guild administration or a proper communa; they may have had what we call leet juries—township organisation, but there is nothing more. The city was a bundle of sokens, or manors, or townships, or parishes; but it had a collective organisation, as we shall see presently, in its husting court, as well as in its sheriff and justiciar. They have not yet arrived at elective aldermen, or a symmetrical arrangement of wards, or a merchant guild, or a communa.

Clause 7 : 'And a man of London shall not be amerced in misericordia, except in his *were*, i.e. 100 shillings. I speak of pleas that concern money.' This means that in suits in which pecuniary punishments or compensations are lawful (i.e. where death or mutilation does not come in) a citizen of London is not to be entirely ruined by arbitrary fines—as we saw in clause 8 of the coronation charter was granted to the barons—his weregild will be fixed at 100 shillings, and amercements *secundum modum delicti* will bear a proper proportion to that just standard.

Clause 8 : 'And henceforth there shall not be miskenning in husting court or in folkmoot, nor in any pleas within the city.' What miskenning is I have explained; what is here signified is this : if in the pleading in husting or folkmoot one of the suitors desires to amend either the form or matter of his plea, he shall not be liable to a fine for the liberty of altering it. I am not quite sure that the direct effect of the clause is not to forbid him to make the alteration altogether, and the result would be to make him begin a new suit or be non-suited ; but ordinarily this could be done on payment of a fine. Here the common interpretation refers it to the abolition of the fine ; so it comes to the same thing.

Clause 9: 'Husting shall sit once a week, that is to say on Monday.' This is the collective court of the citizens, which still subsists under the same title, although it would not be right to infer anything as to its history under Henry I. from its present business. The three courts of the city noticed in this charter are the folkmoot, the ward-moot, and the husting ; but the wardmote depends on an uncertain reading. I have conjectured that while the folkmoot would answer to the shiremoot in the country districts, the husting would answer rather to the proper meeting of the citizens, but I am not at all disposed to maintain this view if a better can be advanced, at least so far as the husting is concerned. Each of the later wardmotes was a proper hundred court, I believe ; but this passage is, to say the least, obscure.

Clause 10 : ' And I will cause them to have their lands and warde-motum and debts, within city and without.' The word wardemotum seems out of place, and there is a reading *vadimonia*, which repre-sents a sort of property more naturally associated with lands and debts, i.e. pledges or mortgages. I think we ought to read it so, and understand the passage to mean that the king will see that the citizens have their full rights in these matters. It does not amount to a corporate right, but it is vouched by the king ; and it seems as if clause 11 was intended as a supplementary or compen-satory clause. If the king was to secure them their rights, he would take measures to enforce his own—' of the lands which they hold of me I will hold right to them by the law of the city ;' or possibly— ' of the lands which they claim by resort to me, I will administer right to them according to the law of the city.' If the first reading is right, it will mean that the king will exact his rights ; if the second, that he will adjudicate on their claims, according to the constitu-tional custom that has prevailed immemorially in the city.

Clause 12 : ' And if anyone has taken toll or custom from the citizens of London, let the citizens of London take from the burgh or township where the toll or custom has been exacted, as much as their citizen has paid and has received of damages.' That is simple enough, however difficult to construe.

Clause 13 : ' And let all debtors who owe debts to the citizens pay them to them, or else prove in London that they do not owe them.' Rather hard lines on the debtors, but consonant with the idea of privileged jurisdiction as maintained above.

Clause 14: ' And if they will not pay, nor come to prove that they do not owe them, let the citizens to whom they are indebted take by distraint their pledges within the city, or of the county in which the debtor dwells. They must outside the city distrain the county . . . through the sheriff of the county in which the debtor dwells, holding him apparently responsible for producing the culprit.'

The next clause is the last. Clause 15: 'The citizens shall have their coursings for coursing as best and full as their ancestors had, in Chiltern, i.e. Buckinghamshire, Middlesex, and Surrey.' No doubt very good for them, and well calculated, according to modern views, to prevent the deterioration of the race. It seems curious that among these sporting districts thus placed at the disposal of the citizens, no mention is made of Essex, which to our fancy would be a better hunting country than any of those named. I think, however, that the citizens were not supposed to hunt the beasts of forest or beasts of venery, i.e. the hart, the hind, the hare, the boar, and the wolf, but the beasts of chase only, i.e. the buck, the doe, the fox, the marten, and the roe ; the former were *silvestres*, the latter *campestres*, and *venari* is the proper word for the one, *fugare* for the other. Now Essex, close as it was to London, was a forest district, the places mentioned here were open grounds. The forest was reserved for the king, the open grounds for the citizens. That is what seems to me to be the particular meaning of this grant, but it is quite possible that as time went on the privilege of the citizens developed. Now, of course, you will think of the recent transfer of the remnant of Epping Forest to the Corporation of London : a singular reversal of the arrangement which I suppose to have been intended here. I cannot, however, insist very positively on my interpretation of the clause, for although the word *fugatio* seems to be used in the restricted meaning, I find little or nothing among the civic records that helps to elucidate the point.

Before we quit this charter it may be as well to refer to the later charter granted by Henry II. to London, and printed in the Liber Custumarum, pp. 31, 32 ; for it will afford one or two points of comparison and explanation. The first of these is the exception to the general privilege of not pleading outside the walls, 'exceptis monetariis et ministris meis ; ' business that concerned those officers must be liable to treatment elsewhere. The article on reception of guests is amplified by the expression 'nemo capiat hospitium per vim vel per liberationem Marescalli ; ' there is to be no forcible billeting by the king's officers on the citizens ; further on *vadimonia*, not wardemote, is distinctly read in the clause corresponding to that on which the doubt arises in Henry I.'s charter : the other privileges are confirmed, and the further ones granted that the citizens shall be free of bridtolle or bridge toll ; childwite, the penalty for bastard children; yeresgive, or new year's gift, a bribe of some sort which the king's officers collected, but the meaning and growth of which is uncertain; and scotale, that is that the sheriff of London and no other bailiff shall make scotale, that is hold a compulsory beerfeast out of which he should make profit. All these terms are difficult in application, and as they do not specially concern our subject, I will content myself with referring you to the glossaries for such information as they can give.

We will now turn to what is perhaps the best known of all the documents of the reign of Henry I., the writ to the magnates of Worcestershire in which he orders the regular holding of the shire-moot. It will be found among the 'Select Charters,' and is dated between 1108 and 1112, the former being the year in which Bishop Richard of London was consecrated, and the latter the year of Bishop Sampson's death. The writ begins in the usual way, and it is a general writ, not restricted to Worcestershire, but this happens to be the Worcestershire copy of it. When the other extant copies see the light, we shall probably be able to fix the date more exactly. 'Know ye that I grant and enjoin that from henceforth my county courts and hundred courts sit in those places and at the same terms as they sat in the time of King Edward and not otherwise. For I, when I shall wish it, will cause them to have sufficient summons on account of my demesne necessities at my will. And if henceforth there arise a plea touching the division of lands, if it is between my own barons it shall be treated in my court; and if it is between the vassals of two lords it shall be treated in the county court, and that shall be done by trial by combat, unless there be some obstacle to such proceeding in the parties themselves. And I will and enjoin that all of the county go to the hundred courts and county courts as they did in the time of King Edward, nor for any cause retard my peace or quiet, who do not follow my pleas and judgments or ordeals, as they would have done at that time.' I do not think that there is any document in our history containing in twelve lines so much valuable information as we have here. It is really an invaluable link between the Norman and Anglo-Saxon treatment of the most characteristic of our early institutions, the county court and the hundredmoot; and although I am pretty certain that I must repeat to you several points on which you are fully informed, I shall venture to give a somewhat lengthened analysis and rationale of it.

The first point of importance is the order at the beginning and ending of the writ directing the conformity of the two sets of courts to the rule followed in the days of Edward the Confessor. They are to be held at the places, at the terms, and by the same constituent frequenters as had attended before the Conquest. The same rule had been ordered by the Conqueror in the article 'Requiratur hundredus et comitatus sicut antecessores nostri statuerunt.' If the national system required the reformation implied in the words of Henry I., the abuses must have crept in between the issuing of the Conqueror's order and the date of the present writ. Of course we lay the blame of everything of that kind on the broad backs of William Rufus and Ranulf Flambard, rightly or wrongly. Anyhow we are sure that the multiplication of the king's judicial transactions either *in curia* or *in itinere* must have had the effect of throwing the provincial judicature into confusion. Now, however, the old rules are restored. But what were the old rules? As for the terms, we know them from the laws of Edward and Canute. The hundred court sat every month, the county court twice a year. As to the places, we have no sufficient list of judicial centres for all England, but the cycle of meeting places might be made out from the hundred rolls of Edward I.'s reign, and from the local records of later ages, by which it appears that the several parts of each hundred or wapentake were visited turn and turn about for the hundred court, the greater county courts being held at the central town of the shire. That, however, is a matter of local archæology which need not concern us to-day; you will find some account of it in most of the better county histories, like Eyton's Salop and Whitaker's Craven. But the composition of the courts is a point on which unfortunately we have but little exact information on the Anglo-Saxon laws, which seem to state so much of the customs as too well known to need repetition. But it fortunately happens that we have in the Leges Henrici primi a full account of the composition of the county courts drawn up almost immediately after, and in conformity with the rule laid down in this edict. It is the passage printed in the 'Select Charters.' We will only look at the points needful for the illustration of our text. 'As it was framed by ancient constitution, by the salutary command of the king, it has been lately confirmed by a true record, that general courts of the counties should be assembled at certain places, terms and definite times, throughout the several counties of England, and should not be troubled with any harassing summons any more unless the king's own necessity or the common profit of the kingdom should make it necessary to hold them more frequently.' There can be no doubt that the *vera recordatio* here spoken of is the writ of Henry I., and that the use of the word *nuper* brings the comment into direct chronological relation with the Act. It is ascertained by a comparison of dates, to which we may refer when we come to examine the Leges Henrici, that that custumary was drawn up between 1112 and 1118, so that you have in the custumary an account of what at the time was meant by the ancient constitution of the shiremoots ; that is, the book of 1118 tells you what was meant in 1112, when, only forty-six years after the Conquest, the practice of King Edward's time and of the Conqueror's earlier years could not have fallen into oblivion. It is, then, not rash, but as safe as anything can be that is based on continuous links of inference, to believe that the description here given is a valid description of the shiremoots of the eleventh and even of the tenth century, for they are not likely to have undergone any material change since the time of Edgar. And if this be accepted, then every accepted point which it would be impossible to reconstruct definitely from the scanty particulars of the earlier laws may be illustrated and made more real by the casual mention of more early laws. If it were not for this link it would be impossible to prove and dangerous to argue on the presumption that the Anglo-Saxon shiremoots contained any element of representation, or had any fiscal or judicial authority but what is to be detected from laws in which everything of the kind is taken for granted, or on analogies which are by themselves insufficient historic evidence.

Well, the persons who are to go to the shiremoot are described in clauses 2 and 7, and the constitution of the hundred court in clause 8. The shiremoot is to be held twice a year and the hundred moot twelve times, the summons being issued six days previously unless the public interest or the king's necessities demand an earlier day. All bishops, earls, and lords of lands whatever are to attend. The lord may represent his tenants or may send his steward in his place. Where there is no lord or steward the reeve and parish priest and four best men of the township are to attend. That will do for the present on this point. Later practice will explain that what was here prescribed as an arrangement in case the lord and his steward were absent was really a rule for the representation of all residents within the area of the court's jurisdiction.

But we will proceed with the other clauses. The two meetings of the shiremoot and the twelve of the hundredmoot are the regular sessions of the court, but when the king's necessities require it they may meet oftener—*dominica necessaria*, demesne necessities. The word *dominica* in the language of this and the following century means little more than the word *mea*, or *ipsius*, the Greek ἴδια, though how the term gets that meaning it is very difficult to say, or when the exact usage comes in. Here, however, it need involve no question of meaning, for if you like to translate it sovereign you can, or royal. The point is that this proves Henry I. to have used the county courts for the purpose of raising supplies. We must not exaggerate the importance of it. It does not follow that the courts to which he applied had the slightest power of refusing to grant what

he asked them. The utmost we can suppose of voluntary action
which they had in the matter was the arrangement among themselves of the way in which the money required for the *dominica
necessaria* should be got together, very much like a parish vestry in
later times when a highway rate was made simply had to hear
what the sum of money wanted was and then to collect it, its only
real voice in the matter being the appointment of the collectors, or
a possible appeal against inequality of rating. Even so it was then.
Here is order, but not freedom; permitted action, but no spontaneity;
regular treatment, but not that measure of organisation which really
deserves in its most elementary shape the name of self-government.
It is a good instance of what in the ' Constitutional History ' I have
called routine, a step towards liberty, but only a step—the knowing
what you have to expect, the notice of what you are expected to do,
not the choice between doing and not doing. It is that first limitation of arbitrary despotism which consists in the self-limitation,
the restraint of caprice. And so far it is a thing to be thankful for.
To us, however, as I have said, it is most important as showing that
fiscal matters were in the country at large despatched in the hundred
and shire moots. Perhaps we need hardly have insisted so strongly
upon this because we know no other machinery by which this or
any other public business could be despatched at all. It is only
when we remember how ubiquitous the Norman administration was,
how Ranulf Flambard had found it possible to force the royal despotism into every county, ' driving ' the king's courts through all
England, that is probably superseding for all ordinary business the
action of the ancient popular system, that we can see what great
tyrannies might be exercised by irresponsible extortion fettered by
no ancient machinery and carried into effect by men of character
little above that of the bandit. Here we get order—a little order—
enough to show how great must have been the disorder on which
this is a remedy so acceptable. But the fiscal business, although
striking and important, is not all. The *dominica necessaria* may,
nay, no doubt did, include the arming of the shire contingent for the
fyrd when it was requisite. We know, however, of no occasion
during the reign of Henry I. after the date of this writ on which
such an application would be necessary, the first occasion of any
historical importance on which the population in mass was called
out being the levy for the war against the Scots in 1138; but from
earlier data of this and the preceding reign we learn that the shire
administration was applied in this department. The shires and the
hundreds furnished the 10*s. viaticum* which Flambard and his master
extracted from the pockets of the common soldiers, and the provincial forces attended Henry I. when he overthrew Robert of Belesme.

Still the judicial matters were the natural province of the courts. 'If hereafter there arise any plea touching the division of lands, if it is between my barons, *barones meos dominicos*,' where you see the word *dominicos* has no special meaning, the tenure in chief being adequately expressed by *barones meos*, 'the plea shall be treated in my court, that is either in that court of me or my justiciary which is held attendant on my person, or subject to the view of that court by an inquisition held under my writ by the officers of my court in the province itself.' The commission for hearing and ascertaining the truth as to trials about lands would be exercised in the presence of the county court, but by methods proper to the king's court— sworn recognitors of some sort, such as are found in some few writs of this and the preceding reign, anticipating the larger measures of judicial reform introduced by Henry II. If the suit arise between the vassals of two lords it will be settled in the county court—that is by the customary proceeding of the county court and the popular law—compurgatory oaths and ordeal, or more generally trial by battle. Here trial by battle is prescribed as the regular practice, recourse to other methods being exceptional, 'nisi in eis remanserit,' that is unless the objection to use that expedient arise from the litigants themselves.

The last clause we have considered in connection with the first: 'I will and enjoin that all of the county come to the counties and hundreds as they did in the time of King Edward, and do not delay for any cause my peace and quiet unless they are employed in following my courts and judgments; or otherwise so that men who do not follow my courts and judgments shall not delay for any cause my peace and quiet.' The construction is a little doubtful; we know that the persons employed in the king's judicial and fiscal business were excused attending the popular courts, and also from paying popular taxes such as Danegeld and the like. These words may refer to the exemption, or they may be used simply as a description of the persons who are most likely to defeat justice by non-attendance, and who therefore are to be compelled to obedience.

[*See Stubbs, 'Select Charters'; Pollock and Maitland, 'The History of the English Law before the time of Edward I.'; Vinogradoff, 'Villeinage in England.'*]

IV

THE 'DIALOGUS DE SCACCARIO'

I PROPOSE now to examine those passages of the 'Dialogus de Scaccario' which are supposed to throw light on the history of the Conqueror and on the legislation of the Norman period proper. It is probably unnecessary for me in a lecture like this to go into the elementary points of the history of the 'Dialogus,' but I may for a moment dwell on the reasons which should induce us to set a special value upon its statements, and at all events not to dismiss any of them as unfounded without careful examination and allowance for our own possible misapprehension of their meaning. The 'Dialogus' is the work of Richard, bishop of London from 1189 to 1198, who had been treasurer of the Exchequer under Henry II., and was son of Nigel, bishop of Ely, who had filled the same office under that king, as well as under Stephen and Henry I. Nigel was nephew of Bishop Roger of Salisbury, and was the original organiser of the Exchequer, the confidential minister of Henry I. before his accession, and his chancellor during part of his reign. As all the administrative work of that department was, before the 'Dialogus' was written, conducted simply by the personal experience of the officials and guided by the forms of the rolls of account, it is obvious that there was no small amount of traditional matter in circulation within a very narrow circle of officials. The body of ministers, and not the office of the Exchequer only, was a sort of family party, or a guild and mystery, and to some extent continued so for a generation after this book was written. The knowledge that was thus kept up in the family of the treasurer was not that of mere official routine; the men who worked that routine were statesmen, as the time was capable of producing statesmen as well as civil servants. Specialisation had scarcely begun in the region of government. Judges and bishops were as often employed as ambassadors or even commanders; a man like Glanville was not only a jurist, but a general; Richard FitzNeale himself was a bishop, a judge, a financier, and an historian too. Little bits of history almost of necessity intruded into even the most stupid routine of public office, and Richard was not a mere official; he wrote or compiled a history which he called 'Tricolumnis,' which is lost, and the loss of which is, for English history at least, one of the greatest losses of the middle ages; it must have been early lost, as not one of the many annalists of the next century cites it, and indeed may never have been in circulation at all, unless we suppose, as has been conjectured, that it may have been merged in one of the circumstantial histories of the reign of Henry II. which are known by the names of other authors. However this was, the author of the 'Dialogus' is connected, with but one intervening life, with the age of the Conqueror. His father, Bishop Nigel, may very well have conversed with men, like S. Wulfstan, who had been bishops, or with men, like Ranulf Flambard, who had been settled in England under Edward the Confessor. He must have had a good chance of knowing as much as any man did know, not only of the external history such as found its way into the pages of the monastic annalists, but of the legal history as developed in the public offices, and even of the secret motives of the court, with which as the king's most private counsellors the chief members of his own family had been very closely associated. This reason prepares us to give the greatest consideration to any fact which he mentions, unrecorded by the ordinary historians; and even where it cannot be explained consistently with received history, to search for an interpretation that may be regarded as subjectively possible. We are not going to regard him as infallible, because there is hardly any period of history about which a man is ordinarily so ignorant as the time of his own youth and early manhood, when as a rule he is too busy about his own concerns to look very far afield, and when the books are not yet written to which later generations will refer as authorities. But this must be allowed for in detail, and not set up as an objection to our author's general credibility.

The first of the passages on which I shall comment is that which concerns the resettlement of the land of England after the Conquest, and which can be read in the 'Select Charters.' 'After the conquest of the kingdom, when the king himself and his lords traversed the new territory, a careful inquest was made as to who, having been in arms against the king, saved themselves by flight: from all these, and likewise from the heirs of those who fell in the battle, all hope of retaining the lands and revenues which they had before possessed was taken away; for they thought it a great boon to enjoy the benefit of life under their enemies. As for those who, having been summoned to the war, had not come together, or had been prevented by private or other necessary business from taking part in it, when in tract of time they had by dutiful obedience won the favour of their lords, they began to possess their property for themselves alone, without hope of succession, and at the pleasure of their lords. In process of time, when those who were odious to their lords were everywhere dispossessed, and there was no one to restore what was taken from them, a common complaint of the natives was brought up to the king, as if, being hated by all and plundered of everything, they would be compelled to go to the foreigners. Counsel being taken on this, it was decreed that such property as by the intervention of a lawful bargain they could on their deserts obtain from their lords, should be conceded to them by inviolable right, but that they should claim nothing for themselves under the title of succession from the time of the Anglo-Saxon monarchy. How wise this provision was is clear, especially as thus for their own sakes they would be obliged for the future to purchase their lords' favour with dutiful service. Thus, then, whoever of the conquered race possessed land or anything of the kind, obtained it not because it was his due by hereditary succession, but because either by meritorious service or by some distinct bargain he obtained it.'

Now with this statement it would be well to compare what Mr. Freeman at great length has drawn out from the chroniclers and from Domesday about the redemption of the land ; it seems almost certainly to be the explanation of what is described in the Chronicle as taking place about the time of the coronation, when men are said to have paid the king tribute, and delivered him hostages and bought their land. There was no absolute confiscation of land except in the case of those who had been in arms against the king at Hastings ; but there was, if we understand the passage right, a general re-settlement. Those who recognised the king, and against whom no charges of rebellion were made, retained their lands by repurchase. As I have suggested in the ' Constitutional History,' the proceeding might be construed differently by different parties—the redemption broke the continuity of the title without necessarily breaking the continuity of the possession. But much more seems to be involved in the words of our author. It appears as if on the first negotiation the right of succession was taken away from the conquered race ; that is as if the Anglo-Saxon owners who were allowed to remain in occupation of their lands enjoyed them only at the capricious will of the lords, or at the utmost, to borrow a later expression, retained them only by a customary tenure at the will of the lord. I think that we are led into a slight misunderstanding of this by assuming this passage to contain a full account of the resettlement. It is really only an *obiter dictum* intended to explain the existence of the servile or villein class. You see how it arises—in the discussion on the murder fine. The legislation on that point drew a sharp distinction between Englishman and Norman—a much sharper distinction than subsisted a century later, when our author wrote. In his days Englishman and Norman had blended, and the result was that in every case of murder, every dead body found was supposed by custom to belong to the Norman or higher race, unless it could be proved English, and the only indisputable proof of its being English was to prove its being villein. What, then, was the rationale of villenage? Then follows the passage. It is an explanation of the customary tenure of villein property, at the will of the lord, without the right of hereditary succession. It is possible that more may at some time have been intended; the charter of the Conqueror to London, in which the king allows the citizens to have hereditary succession from father to son, may imply the presumption that even that proud civic aristocracy, in its lower members, was subject to the ordinary condition of succession in villenage—namely, the will of the lord, controlled only by custom of the place. But it would be unsafe to argue very positively about it; and, indeed, the further back we go into the primitive institution of land tenure, the more difficult we find it to disentangle the custom and law of succession as it must have existed in communities in which the land was regarded as the property of the tribe or township from the custom and law where it was regarded as all held at the will of a lord.

If, however, we are content to take the passage I have read with its context, confining its particulars to the point which it is introduced to illustrate, we shall conclude that it is a rationalised history of one portion of the Conquest proceeding. We know, from the later history both of reliefs in the freehold estates and of the creation of copyhold titles in the region of customary tenure, that the apparent severity of the accepted law was greatly modified in practice, and that the custom of the manor imposed a very strong and substantial check on the tyrannical caprice which might be supposed to underlie the *voluptas* or *voluntas dominorum.*

The next passage in importance is that referring to the murdrum, in relation to which this account of villenage is introduced; but as I have exhausted the interest of it in what I have said in previous lectures on the murder fine, I shall pass over it now.

The next is the account of the Danegeld. The account of the origin of the tax is only approximately correct. There can be little doubt that the origin of the Danegeld was to raise money to bribe away the invaders; for this purpose two shillings on the hide of land were exacted; after the exact pressure of the danger was removed the tax was retained, and possibly was represented, as it is here described, as a fund appropriate to national

defence, to the use of the mighty men who watched the coast and
kept the maritime defences of the realm in efficient order. It was
unquestionably one of those agreeable imposts, like the income tax,
which, having been originally imposed for an occasion of emergency,
have proved so convenient that they have been retained long after
their original occasion has passed out of sight—have, in fact, become
permanent. According to our author this tax was paid for the
maintenance of national defence until the Conquest, when the Danes
out of fear of William ceased to devastate the coasts; the Conqueror
then gave up the annual collection, but retained the right to use it
for occasional emergencies. And there the author stops, as he does
in some other places, in a very disappointing way; but we must
remember that the mention of the Danegeld, like that of the redemption, only comes in incidentally, to explain a word or particular
exemption which the master and pupil have found in the old pipe
roll they were using. As a matter of fact, we know that Danegeld
was abolished by Edward the Confessor, and that it was reimposed
by the Conqueror, not perhaps regularly, as our author seems to have
been aware, but intermittently, and therefore in larger amounts; that
it was continued under William Rufus and Henry I., who in an
alarm arising from a terrible dream he had in 1130, and in dread
of shipwreck, made a vow to abolish it. There is no reason to
suppose that he fulfilled his vow, or that Stephen's coronation
promise to put an end to it for ever was really kept. Henry of
Huntingdon, indeed, who records Stephen's promise, says that it
was not kept. So Danegeld went on in the old name and in the
old character of an ordinary tax until in 1163, in consequence
apparently of the quarrel between Henry II. and Archbishop Becket
at Woodstock, it ceases to appear in the accounts.

I will not now anticipate the controversy that arises on that
discussion, but it is interesting just to refer to the words of the
biographer given in the 'Select Charters.' There the tax in
dispute is not named Danegeld, but is described as a payment made
to the king's ministers who keep the counties in the place of sheriffs;
in other words, it is described as a payment to the sheriffs for the
conservation of the counties, a form which agrees closely with the definition of the 'Dialogus' as a payment to the *fortes viri* who provided
for the efficiency of defence. The exact point at issue between Henry
and Thomas does not come into our view just now, but I may add
that I think the most reasonable explanation of it is that, the Danegeld being farmed by the sheriff at a fixed sum, the balance collected
was either pocketed by him or spent on defence; or probably
appropriated on the understanding that he was responsible for the
defence, which for more than a century had been a nominal thing.

I conclude that Henry II. wanted to get this balance out of the hands of the sheriff—that Becket would not agree, and that in the event the character of the impost was changed, and a carucage substituted which all found its way into the Exchequer, no part being intercepted either by farming or by allowance of customary perquisites to the sheriffs.

The next passage we will turn to is in clause 16, in the portion of the chapter introductory to the account of Domesday—it refers to the character of the Conqueror as legislator and to the traditional accounts of his enactments. When that illustrious subduer of England had brought the further regions of the realm under his empire and had subdued the minds of the rebels with terrible examples, that no facility for error might be given henceforth, he determined to subject the people to written right and law. Having, therefore, proposed the English laws according to their tripartite distinction, that is Mercian law, Dane law, and West Saxon law, some he rejected, some he approved and added to them the transmarine laws of Normandy which seemed most likely to be efficacious for peace. Here, you see, you have the traditional story already referred to, and resting on the very apocryphal statements of the laws so-called of Edward the Confessor ; according to which the Conqueror gave the nation the choice of laws, only adding to King Edward's his own amendments. This is not one of the valuable passages of the ' Dialogus '—it shows, in fact, that the writer did not care by analysis unnecessary for the development of his thesis to go into the material points of the legislative history.

Look next at the account of the Domesday survey and Domesday Book in the same section. This is very clear and circumstantial, and, like every other passage of the book which can be compared with other documentary evidence, is exact. Set by the side of this section the heading taken from the Ely Domesday, and you will see by the exact agreement that our author had Domesday before him. I will not stay to construe the passage, for it is all quite straightforward, and as it does not give us any additional information, it need not detain us.

The speculation on the name of Domesday which immediately follows is worth a passing note. It is clear from it that the survey had already acquired its name of Domesday in the twelfth century. I think it is certain that the appellation is taken from the solemn day official account ; for in the Anglo-Saxon dictionary I find no use of Domesday for a day of man's judgment; it always refers to the day of judgment at the end of the world. Therefore we must not suppose that the name belongs to any other book of dooms or legal proceedings—it is the title of the great day of final account

borrowed here from its primary usage as a term of religion, not
vice versa. We must, therefore, accept our author's explanation of
it as used *per metaphoram*, for as the sentence of that strict and
terrible last account can be evaded by no art of tergiversation, so
when in this kingdom controversy arises about the things which are
here noted, when reference or recourse is had to this book its
sentence cannot be explained away or disobeyed with impunity.

This, then, is the primary application in secular matters of the
word Domesday. After this it is not unfrequently ascribed to other
similar compilations—there is a Domesday of S. Paul's drawn up
in 1180, and a Domesday of Canterbury also containing extracts from
Domesday and collections of documents accounting for the different
grants of land and the particular tenures of estates held under the
monastery. One more observation on this. You will notice that
our author describes the proceedings of the Domesday commissioners
in language which contains no words expressive of any very
exceptional proceeding. The king *communicato consilio*, that is
having laid his plan before his barons or *sapientes*, sent the most
discreet men from his own side through the kingdom in circuit.
Whether he did this or not is not the point—he probably did—but
if he did it was not in the eyes of Richard FitzNeale an extraordinary proceeding. It was a mission of fiscal commissioners exactly
answering to the fiscal commissions of his own day and to the
itinera of the justices or barons of the Exchequer. We should
not infer from it that the practice of those times was in his eyes a
novelty even in the days of the Conqueror.

This leads to a further point, the Rotulus exactorius of the
18th chapter. Domesday was the final rate book or valuation
book of the country, the Rotulus exactorius was the special rate
roll of the royal ferms—an abstract or summary of the several
amounts due from the sheriffs and other financial collectors of
the royal revenue. The existence of such a roll implies, as you
see from the words of the definition, a previous settling of the ferms.
This settling of the ferms belongs to the reign of Henry I. That
we know, not only because we find them fixed in the pipe roll of
1130 at pretty nearly the same amounts that appear in the rolls of
Henry II.'s reign, but from the exact account which our author
gives at p. 193. In Domesday the royal rights are often represented
as consisting of ferms, that is provision for so many days and nights;
and besides that, much of the rent paid by the tenants of the
crown lands was also paid in kind. The author himself had seen
men who had seen the country people bringing up their dues in hay
and straw, corn and meat, which was taken at a distinct valuation
in payment of the sums fixed in money. Well, of course that was a

very wasteful system, oppressive to the poor and embarrassing to the government. Henry I. by a similar expedient, *deffinito magnorum consilio*, sent *prudentiores et discretiores* men through the country to put a pecuniary estimate on the ferms, and by valuing the customary payments in kind to enable the payers to commute universally. The result of that measure was the fixing of the ferms —the Rotulus exactorius—a record and proceeding second in importance only to the Domesday survey itself. So far as touches our financial history, I am not aware that the original Rotulus exactorius exists, either in genuine copy or transcript; but as the ferms are easily ascertainable from any of the early pipe rolls it would not be difficult to reproduce it, and in the calculations of Norman and Plantagenet revenue which I have made in the 'Constitutional History' I have used a rotulus exactorius which I compiled myself from the rolls.

And this brings me to the last point which I shall particularly notice, the account of the institution of the Exchequer itself given in the 'Select Charters;' this is the vexed question whether the fiscal system of the Norman kings was brought from Normandy or grew up in England before and after the Conquest. It is said to have begun from the conquest of the kingdom by King William, its method, however, having been taken from the transmarine Exchequer; it is said so, but the English and transmarine Exchequers differ in many points, and those almost the points of greatest importance. There are some who say that it was a usage of the days of the native kings; that rests upon the institution of the blanch ferm, which some old men know from their fathers was an immemorial usage in their time; but that would prove only the nature of the ferm and not the sessions of the Exchequer to be older than the Conquest; and even that may be doubted, for Domesday does not say a word about the blanch ferm, neither is it mentioned in such finance rolls of Edward the Confessor as were extant in our author's time.

Now this being so it is not fair to quote the 'Dialogus' as authority for the Norman origin of the special Exchequer methods which the author is describing. When he wrote there was a Norman Exchequer, and the processes in it were, as he says, and as we know from the extant rolls of it, quite different from the usages of the English Exchequer. Still, as exchequer was a foreign word, it was not at all unreasonable to suppose that it may have come from Normandy into England. But we know now that no evidence has been produced from the vast mass of Norman charters of the reign of the Conqueror and his sons, that the word exchequer was used for the financial account court of Normandy until long after it was in use in England, not only for the great Exchequer of the kings, but for the audit court, also of the lords, such as the earl of Leicester and the archbishop of York. The name is older in England than in Normandy : the usages in England are different from the usages in Normandy, and the institution of the blanch ferm, which is not adopted in Normandy at all, is so inherently and intimately bound up with the Exchequer process in England as to prove that, except as both being audits of account, the two exchequers have nothing in common but the name, which, as I have just said, is older here than there.

I do not know that the matter is of other importance than as illustrating the growth of peculiarly Norman institutions on English soil ; a matter which has been rather complicated by the jealousies of French and Italian archæologists ; for the fact that the Norman kings of Sicily had an audit analogous to these exchequers, to which sometimes and loosely the name of exchequer is given, has been used as an argument that it was derived from a continental Norman source, and therefore that the English practice was also. But all this rests on a baseless conjecture ; the word *scaccarium* is not applied properly to the Sicilian *fiscus*, and if in its proceedings any resemblance to the English method of account could be traced, it might fairly be ascribed to Master Thomas Brown, the English counsellor of the great King Roger ; but the Sicilian antiquaries, either in their dislike to the idea of Thomas Brown, or wishing to maintain an independent origin for their own institutions, are intent on proving that the system of their *Dohana* is Saracenic rather than Norman, and try to attenuate Mr. Brown's importance in a very ungrateful way. But there we leave it. That Sicily was in the twelfth century indebted to England for her bishops, judges, and finance ministers, we know ; it was not to Normandy but to England ; the kings only were Norman, and they had been Italianised for more than a generation. Therefore if there is any common material, Sicily got it from England. If there is not, then the whole hypothesis falls to the ground. Certainly on no hypothesis can the introduction of Norman principles into Apulia be made the basis of an argument as to their introduction into England.

['*De Necessariis Observantiis Scaccarii Dialogus,' commonly called 'Dialogus de Scaccario,' by Richard, son of Nigel, Treasurer of England and Bishop of London. Edited by Arthur Hughes, C. G. Crump and C. Johnson. 8° Oxford, 1902.*]

V

LEGES HENRICI PRIMI

WE have now come to the hardest, if not also to the dullest and driest, perhaps also the most remunerative, part of the work which we have set ourselves, the examination of the so-called Leges Henrici primi. The subject is so full of matters of question that it is difficult to know which to take first. Perhaps the name has the first claim. Here is a collection of legal materials, extracts from early codes, canons, law books of all kinds; here a sentiment, there a statement of principle; here a list of names, and there a quotation from Scripture: possibly the commonplace book of a law student who has neglected to make an index; possibly the notes of lecture of a student of the age of Vacarius; anyhow a congeries of legal cram, and to it the title is given Leges Henrici primi, and, what is more, a preamble containing the praises of the great king and prayers for the welfare of his wife and children. To cut this part of the matter short, let me say that while there may be doubts as to the proper application of the title to the whole body of the book, there can be no doubt that it applied to the first two documents contained in it, which are the charter of Henry I. granted at his coronation, on which we have been commenting at length, and the charter of the city of London, which I have already treated. These are the first morsels of the collection, and it is even within the bounds of possibility that they were all to which the compiler in the first instance intended to apply the title. Mr. Freeman, in his essay on this topic in the fifth volume of the 'History of the Norman Conquest,' evidently inclines to a doubt whether there is anything more than an accidental connection between this part of the collection and the miscellaneous matter that follows. That doubt I myself do not share, because it would lead, as it seems to me, to still greater difficulties if we supposed the writer to have intended the panegyric of his preamble to apply only to two transcripts of tolerably well known documents. Perhaps, too, I am influenced by the fact that it is partly to the preamble that we owe the material for fixing the date of the compilation, which so far as

date goes seems to hang sufficiently well together. This consideration takes us so far.

Little important light arises from the question of manuscript
sources, all of which seem to be of at least a century later date
than the compilation itself, and are of the thirteenth century at the
earliest ; but no valid objection arises in this to the genuineness of
the work as a work of Henry's time, for we have in a much earlier
Cottonian MS. a full copy of the preamble, which, as I have said,
to the best of my belief belongs to the whole collection. External
evidence throwing little or no light on the date, we come to the
question of internal evidence, which has been discussed at different
times by very different persons with a singular tendency to a
common opinion. It has been discussed not only by the early
collectors, as Lambarde, Selden, and suchlike, but by Phillips in his
German history of the English law, by Allen the eminent Whig
constitutionalist, by Palgrave, by Freeman, and last of all by
Dr. Liebermann, who seems to me to have overcome all the difficulties that presented themselves to the earlier critics, and, as nearly
as anything of the kind can be settled, to have settled the question.

There are several points of literary as well as legal interest
touched in this settlement. The preamble, for instance, contains, as
I have said, a prayer for the life of Queen Matilda, and some expressions that seem to relate to the glories of the imperial marriage of her
daughter. If this were met by no questioning, it would fix the date
between 1110, when the empress was married, and the year 1118,
when her mother died. But upon this arose certain doubts as to
the character of the contents. In one place the number of English
bishoprics is stated as fifteen, which number was not reached until
the foundation of the see of Carlisle in 1133. In another place
references were made to decrees of the popes which were supposed
to be found only in the Decretum of Gratian, which was not put
into circulation before the year 1151. These considerations threw
the date on, and led Mr. Freeman to fix the compilation early in the
reign of Henry II., a supposition to which I also inclined at one
time, being, however, puzzled by the fact that the writer should
have been able to steer so clear of the legislation of that king as in
no case, even accidentally, to stumble across it. Dr. Liebermann
has got rid of both these points, calling attention to the fact that the
number fifteen is a various reading, with *multos* as the alternative ;
and that even if fifteen be accepted, still by counting in the see of
Whithern, which was in the ancient lists at the end of the ordinary
historical compilations such as Florence of Worcester, that number
might be made up without counting in Carlisle. What is of more
importance, he shows very distinctly that the quotations supposed

to come from the Decretum of Gratian are found with more literal exactitude in the Panormia of Ivo of Chartres, which I mentioned to you in an early lecture as the contemporaneous compilation of ecclesiastical laws. These difficulties being cleared away, he falls back on the dates of the preamble, and adduces in confirmation of his conclusion the use of the word *nuper* in the description of Henry I.'s writ for the holding of the hundred court, which also I have already mentioned. This being accepted, the date would fall between 1112, when Bishop Sampson died, and 1118, the date of Queen Matilda's death, and this is the conclusion now received. Of course the discovery of other manuscripts and the verification of other citations may lead to a review of this decision, but the old conclusion is now the favourite one; it is the one which Phillips early in the century inclined to, and is of course well accordant with a guess, made merely as a guess by some writers, that the real author of the compilation was a no less well-known person than our old friend Ranulf Flambard, who, surviving his wicked master and living a princely life as bishop of Durham, only died in 1129, six years before Henry I. There is no evidence, internal or external, that he was the author; but he certainly may have been, there is no evidence against it; still, it is a mere guess.

Leaving this, then, we come to the preamble. This is not printed in any English book, but was copied by me many years ago from the Cottonian MS., and has been very recently printed in Germany by Dr. Liebermann in the 'Zeitschrift der Savigny Stiftung,' iii. Its chief interest, as it seems to me, is that of a curious relic of literary work, but we may find that it has some value in relation to the question whether or no the preamble belongs to the whole compilation or only to the first two charters. The doubt which I have before mentioned as occurring in Mr. Freeman's discussion has been further noted by Dr. Brunner, the author of the very useful books on the origin of jury and on the Norman jurisprudence generally in Holtzendorff's Encyclopædia. I will read a freeish translation of this document: 'That the king of England is by singular majesty lord of his kingdom is recognised both by the intuition of manifest truth and the practical experience of individuals.' The king is emperor with singular majesty in his own island—a declaration of the peculiarly imperial character of Norman royalty as not only a fact of experience but a first principle of intuition. We go on to see how this arises from the renowned excellence of the king himself and from the fealty due to him of right from his subjects, but it is also promoted by the position of the country, shut in by the benefits of

L

nature and vicinity of the sea, so that without the licence of its lords no one can come in, no one can go out. ' Whence so great is the security of the people, so great the abundance of all good things, that if it were ruled by the honesty of true reason it would reproduce the pristine times of the golden age.' The silver streak, you see, struck our friends forcibly. The king was lord ; the people were in the trap tight enough ; as well make the best of it. But even he seems to be struck that it is rather ludicrous to speak of this reign as the golden age ; he remembers that there have been battles and such a person as Robert of Belesme ; and not so long ago. ' This, however, is a sort of drawback on so great privileges, and its blessings are almost too much for it ; when it is all free from molestation from without, yet such is the miserable condition of mortals always inclining to evil and prone to a fall, it has always been troubled with intestine seditions of ambition and a blind striving after novelties.' So true ; almost a forecast of the clôture. ' Hence from the very origin of the new-born world, those whom the Almighty Creator has enriched with equal liberty, have been cast out by the motives of inflammatory disobedience, as Adam and Eve were turned out of paradise, and those who could not bear the Lord of Heaven are made to serve the will of evil men, continually forced on from bad to worse in the prosecution of their evil courses. But although they are undeserving, divine pity so contrives the conformation of their masters that vile slavery may not annihilate them or impunity and security too great may not absolutely ruin them. Even kings who excel all others in ceremonial pomp, that they may not become insolent by the greatness of their powers, are frequently harassed by infirmities of the flesh and human necessities for a very useful purpose. For it is not . . . or raging madness, or infinite acres, or ingenious luxury, or money extorted from the lamenting people ; it is not the Tyrian vestments, nor gilded ceilings, nor the colour of the forehead or any royal mark that constitutes a king ; a king is he who has laid aside fears and the evils of a gloomy conscience, who is not moved by ungovernable ambition, or by the ever varying favour of the hasty multitude ; a king is he who casts away the sickening impulses of a selfish heart and desires in his benignity to benefit all. Such kings as have recently been raised to this pitch of dignity not by popular ambition, not by courting the favour of the people, but by moderation, are regarded and valued by good men.'

As Horace has said, ' If a man is a cobbler by nature, it is little use to call him a king.' Ah, well, we proceed. ' Temperance is good for lords and discipline is good for subjects ; for after the sagacious intention of men has penetrated all things, and nothing appears inconvenient that can be referred to a standard of money, with the increase of wealth, increases envy; from envy grows hatred, from hatred war; faith and almsgiving cease to have any virtue. But if any monuments of native goodness remained, men established laws and rights of living, built cities and trustworthy refuges where innocence might be safe among the wicked, and those who would not be kindled by exhortations to probity might at least be compelled to dread punishment.'

This passage is evidently an extract, possibly from some pseudo-Augustinian document which has not been verified, and of which the sense is more accessible than the grammar, although it is not easy to see what induces the writer to place it here. What follows is simpler. 'Law is of two kinds: one natural, which is the same among all; another of constitution, in which each several country has some vernacular rule of life of its own; but law we generally agree to call what is chosen by way of preference provided it be consonant with religion, agreeable with discipline, and profitable for the safety of men.' This is the emendation of King William on the English laws: 'Whatever you have proved honourable and useful on every side, our blessed king and lord ceases not to illustrate with daily praises, whence this book which I have compiled for the reproof of our times, I have arranged with a beginning only, not an end, as if in a garden of delights, among all the odorous pigments of pleasure, I would gather a single flower, and not like a thirsty Tantalus straining at flying waters, would praise the streams that flow conveniently enough for my lips. The king's successes in war and the glory of his children I have left for more skilful muses, thankful enough myself to contribute a pure stream of peace to the symposium of readers.'

Well done, Flambard, if Flambard it is; you may imagine how flowery his episcopal charges would be. Then follow the few lines that have been long in print. 'These then are the jocund dances of peace and longed-for liberty which the glorious Cæsar Henry by his writings and exhibition of good works pours down in radiance on his people, the king, moderate, prudent, righteous, and brave, whom may God with happy auspices and every wholesome blessing of body and mind, with his famous wife Matilda the Second and their children, make to reign for long ages of ages, and with the eternal peace of our nation.' The jocund dances that follow are the two charters which we have been commenting on. No doubt great national benefits, but scarcely to our minds answering the description. Yet there are men who regard legal writs as better than sensational novels, as our old friend Prynne found the *brevia de expensis* and other returns to parliament,

desirable, delightful, and most useful, and the Tower of London
merely a paradise of princely delights.

I hope that I have not spent too much time on this lively prologue, in which, perhaps, you may not feel quite so much interest as
I do ; but it is new, and, like every discovery of a relic of a most interesting age, a little likely to exaggerate itself in the eyes of one of
the first who gets sight of it. I will only add that, absurd as it
seems as the preface to a law book, it would be more incredibly
absurd if we retained it merely as the preface to a transcript of a
couple of charters. Whether it belongs to the whole of the following
material, or the original *unus flos* has been added to by successive
commentators until it reached its present size, I dare not venture
categorically to decide. It contains no less than ninety-four chapters,
all of them subdivided and paragraphed, but so far as one can ascertain arranged on no very definite principle, and extremely confusing
to work at without an index. I imagine that one of the first
exploits of our rising school of historical lawyers will be to give us
a thoroughly critical edition, with every extract referred to its author,
and all the difficulties of the text fully stated.

We will begin by a general survey of the materials used by the
compiler. These are primarily the laws of the Anglo-Saxon kings,
or rather, as Canute is the chief of them, the laws of the Anglo-
Saxon period ; of course, in translation, which makes the exact
identification of particular passages more difficult, and possibly not
directly drawn from these sources, but from some intermediate Latin
codification or arrangement of them not now accessible. There does
not seem to me to be any distinct evidence that the so-called laws
of Edward the Confessor were known to the compiler, for the occasional coincidences of language may be explained on the reverse
theory, and even without supposing any direct connection between
the two, through some intermediate work. But the laws of the
present reign, that is the charter of London, the coronation charter,
and the writ for holding the hundred court, are referred to in exact
citations. Next to this source of information come the canonical
collections of the eleventh and twelfth centuries, through which
alone also the civil law of Justinian seems to be known to the compiler. Of these collections that of Burchard of Worms was the first
of much importance known in England, and the commentators on
these laws both in the Government edition and in Schmid's are inclined to trace all the more important canonical extracts to Burchard.

Dr. Liebermann, whom I have so often referred to, prefers to look
to the Panormia of Ivo of Chartres, the difference between the two
being mainly this, that whereas Burchard knew the Roman civil
law only through the Theodosian Code, Ivo had been able to use the

Code and Pandects of Justinian.   On this particular point we have
not much light, because there are very few extracts, if indeed there
are any, from the Roman civil law in this compilation.   But it has
importance in this way : these laws do contain several citations from
the early canons in a form nearly approaching that in which they
are found in the Decretum of Gratian, which was published in 1151.
Hence the supposition, which I have more than once referred to, that
the book was drawn up after that year.   Dr. Liebermann, by a careful
examination of these, has come to the conclusion that they may all
be derived from Ivo, whose work was an anticipation of the Decretum,
and supplies several passages in a text in which they are not found
in either Burchard or the Decretum.   As I have not myself been
able as yet to complete the analysis, I rest content for the present
with Liebermann's theory, but I am bound to mention a third source
which may have furnished not only these canonical articles, but some
more distinctly secular ones.   Burchard and Ivo were not the only
collectors of ecclesiastical laws, and it may be questioned whether
our compiler did not live so near the date of Ivo that it would be
doubtful whether the Panormia had yet won the authority which it
possessed a little later.   There is a very famous collection of canons
called the Collectio Hibernica, because it begins with some synods of
S. Patrick, and may have been a compilation of Irish monks settled
in England or in Germany, which, like the collections of Burchard
and Ivo, incorporates extracts from secular legislation, such as the
capitularies of the Frank emperors.   We have in the Bodleian, in
the Liber Sancti Dunstani, a copy of this collection written in the
ninth or tenth century, containing, as it seems to me, more material
than is contained in the two better known collections, and certainly
containing large extracts from the capitularies.   Without, then,
denying that our author used Ivo—and, indeed, I should not deny
that he had used Burchard—I am inclined to add this as a rather
more probable source ; and some day, when I have less to do than I
have just now, I hope I may be able to work out the supposition into
something like a fact.   Well, through these mediums, whichever is
the first in importance, our compiler has access to the penitentials
of the early Anglo-Saxon Church, to the decrees of the popes, to the
civil law, and to the capitularies of the Frank kings and emperors.
The other books which he quotes, such as Isidore of Seville, and
occasionally early popes and fathers, come from the same source.
In saying this I am not denying our compiler the claim to original
treatment.   He has in most places made the material his own by
verbal alterations which leave the sense only of the common passages,
and that sometimes impaired.   But enough has been said, I think,
to show that his work is curious, and full of, at all events, second-

hand research; a work likely, as the study of ancient law progresses, to attract more careful attention than it has yet attracted, and with possibly some more curious results.

Having said all this as to its merits, I must now add that so far as arrangement goes it is a labyrinth of difficulties, so puzzling and unsatisfactory that it would be a waste both of my time and of yours to attempt a rationale of it. The best course, I think, will be to regard it for the most part as an undigested mass of detail, and to fix certain points of our own on which we may look for information running through the whole of the work. However, so far as the possibility of a general idea is concerned, we may run through the headings, a few of the first of which are coherent and orderly.

There are 94 clauses, including the two charters with which the compiler begins : clauses 3, 4, 5 are on the nature of causes ; 6, 7, 8 on the divisions of England and the character of provincial jurisdictions. Clause 9 returns to the classification of causes ; clauses 10, 11, 12, 13 are on the royal jurisdiction in general, in ecclesiastical causes, in matters capable of being settled by payment of damages, and in matters criminal, in which the person convicted lies at the king's mercy ; clause 14 is on relief of heriots ; 15–20, explanations of the vernacular terms of the Anglo-Saxon law ; and 21 returns again to causes ; 22 onwards to 42 are concerned with more minute directions for legal proceedings, crossing backwards and forwards with bewildering repetitions, and returning often in the same words to subjects that have been treated of before, such as royal rights, summons to popular courts, contempt or oferhyrnesse, and definitions of obsolete expressions ; 42 is on summons again, and with the same absence of order the articles down to 61 may be said to be expansions of the earlier rules for trials, both in the county and in the proper courts of the king ; 62 is on the distinction of legal terms, the division of the year into legal days and non-legal ; 64 is on the division and classification of oaths ; 66–76 are on homicide, including the murder fine ; 77–79 on emancipation of the unfree ; 80 returns to homicide ; 81, 82 are on the giving of peace, reconciliation, and the termination of blood feuds ; 83–90 on similar questions connected with the practice of private war, chiefly extracted from the capitularies, and referring to a state of society about which we are generally assured that it never prevailed in England, except under King Stephen ; 91 and 92 return to the murder fine ; 93 is a list of the payments to be made for injuries of limbs, and 94 on injuries inflicted without drawing of blood. There is no envoy or epilogue, the subject ends as abruptly as it begins.

If you trace any principle of arrangement here, you are more successful than I can claim to be ; all that I can see is this   the

author begins with a classification of causes, and immediately runs
into confusion between the forms of procedure and the matter of the
cause ; he then attempts the distinction of courts and runs into a
cross division again ; he then goes to the subject of offences, and
from that comes round again to procedure ; the last 30 chapters
seem to have a common factor, the treatment of murder, mutilation,
bloodshed, and bloodless assault. You will have noticed that, while
there is a show of distinction between secular and ecclesiastical
business, the two are mixed together whenever there is a chance of
doing so ; often the heading of the chapter refers only to the first
clause, the later sections, or sub-sections, referring to something
only incidentally connected with the matter. On the whole, I think,
my first definition of the work as a lawyer's commonplace book
without an index, or, perhaps, notes of a professor's lectures on
Anglo-Norman legislation that have not been submitted to the
lecturer for correction and arrangement, would be a fair account of
the thing. Bad and confused, however, as the method is, there can
be no doubt that the whole is a mass or a mine of information, out
of which we may get some ore in the remaining lectures, if we can
ourselves supply the principle on which to conduct the search.

The first of the selected points on which I now propose to dig
into the mine of information which the Leges Henrici primi contain,
will be that of the royal jurisdiction. And I take it first, partly
because it is the department of Norman legislation which seems
most distinctive, and, secondly, because it is the point which,
on account of the wonderful prologue, seems to have occupied
in the mind of the compiler the most important place. I will
add, by the way, that we shall find in this department most
abundant illustration of the conclusion which I came to, that
the author of the prologue was likewise author of such portions
of the work as are not simple extracts from other books ; the
style of these passages is so very similar, and is, in fact, so very
much like the style of the prologues to Anglo-Saxon charters, that
it almost suggests that our author was an English and not a
Norman or French jurist. Well, as popular or customary law is
one great feature of Anglo-Saxon constitutional history, the royal
jurisdiction is a great feature of Anglo-Norman administration, and
in this idea I propose to set to work first ; other points which we
may take will be the relation of ecclesiastical judicature to secular
judicature, and the actual procedure of the popular courts ; these
subjects cross one another, as you may well suppose from what
I have already said, and will involve repetition, but by this time
you will have learned to endure that minor evil.

The section with which we will begin is partly printed in the

'Select Charters.' The kingdom of England is divided into three ; the words *in regno Britanniæ* seem redundant, and may probably be one of those interpolations which were made about the time that we date our extant manuscripts. If not redundant, they are an expansion of the *regnum Angliæ*, and yet any *regnum Britanniæ* must have included Scotland and Wales, which do not come under any of the three divisions—these three are Wessex, Mercia, and the province of the Danes ; the kingdom has two archbishoprics, fifteen bishoprics, and thirty-two counties or shires. The counties are divided into hundreds and tithe socns ; the hundreds into deaneries or tithings and pledges of lords, that is into either collective frankpledges or manorial jurisdictions, in which the lords are sureties for their vassals.

We then proceed. Of English law there is a threefold division after the same lines. There is a law of Wessex, another of Mercia, another is the Dane law ; and besides this we recognise the tremendous imperium of royal majesty which we read of as continually presiding over the rest, and which we attend upon, or observe, as a rule to be regarded for the sake of security or public safety. This tremendous imperium Dr. Schmid freely acknowledges that he does not understand, and it is possible that it may be referred to the divine law. But I think from what follows it most probably is intended to represent the royal law or jurisdiction as presiding over and regulating the three customary laws, and in fact the very next words represent the four in terms that could hardly include a reference to the divine law, for he goes on, ' But in many things they differ, but in many they agree ; and even in the several provinces the rules of law of the several counties often differ, according as the greediness and malignant researches of professors have added to the legal statutes heavier kinds of offences ; that is, as the ingenuity of lawyers has invented distinctions of crimes and penalties. For so great is the perversity of the world and the overflowing of evil, that the definite truth of the law, and the permanent providence of healing art, can be rarely found out ; but to the greater confusion of all, new methods of impleading are sought out, new methods of injury are found, as if the old ones did not do mischief enough, and that man was to be judged of most value to society who had inflicted on it the greatest hurts.' Our friend now becomes so bitter as to be unintelligible ; ' nevertheless, to those whom we cannot do without, we do, by a sort of infernal hypocrisy, profess love and reverence ; whatever does not answer *pari passu* to our own crudelity (possibly credulity), *nobis natum* or *non reputamus.*' The reading is uncertain, and the sense absolutely lost.

The sentiment and the style belong alike, I am sure, to the author of the prologue. In accordance with the division given above, he now goes into the organisation of the local courts, clause 7, the chapter printed in the 'Select Charters,' which we shall recur to in discussing another head, if necessary, going on now to clause 9 : 'The quality of causes is manifold ; amendable, non-amendable, and those which belong solely to the jurisdiction of the king. The amendable are those which may be ended by the payment of a compensation ; the non-amendable those which require punishment by mutilation or death ; and besides these, which within certain limits are regulated by local and customary law, there is a department that belongs especially to the crown.' The same division is made in the fifth clause of the same chapter. The difference of causes is manifold : capital causes, causes in which pecuniary redemption is admissible ; transient, permanent, or mutual (that is apparently where one side is as much in fault as the other), and thirdly, those which belong to the *jus regium*.

Clause 9.—While the usages of the West Saxon law, Mercian, and Danish law are opposed to or vary from one another, the pleas of the king's court are in pretty much the same relation to them all, which court everywhere maintains its uses and customs in an unchangeable uniformity or uniform immobility. Then follows another division: the soke of pleas, that is the local jurisdiction and profit of lawsuits belongs either, first, singularly and solely to the king's fiscus or exchequer ; or, secondly, partly to that tribunal, the king having only a share of the profits ; or, thirdly, to the sheriffs and bailiffs of the king in their ferms ; or, fourthly, to the barons, who have sac and soke. That is another principle of arrangement, and is illustrated by abundant evidence. The first division is exercised in the curia regis ; the second by participation in the work done in the county courts by the sheriffs and judges itinerant as royal justices, in the way described by Glanvill when he draws a distinction between the two sets of functions of the sheriffs ; the third in the strictly popular courts farmed to the sheriffs ; the fourth in the private franchises of the territorial nobles. In connection with this I will read the first chapter of Glanvill's first book, which harmonises with this : ' of pleas, one sort is criminal, another civil ; of criminal, one pertains to the crown of the king, another to the sheriff of the county.' In his commentary or expansion of this passage Bracton, iii. 35, writing, you will observe, long after the jurisdiction of the coroner to keep the pleas of the crown had been introduced, explains that beside his functions as sheriff, the sheriff had others, *non ut vice comes sed ut justiciarius regis*, under which title would come all the jurisdiction that fell to him under new writs or in newly developed procedure under the system of recognitions.

To go into detail on this would be to run much too far ahead, and we ought now to be getting to our point, the illustration, viz., of what are called the pleas of the crown, the special points on which, for the sake of justice or for the sake of profit, have been even under the Anglo-Saxon kings withdrawn from the common law of the county and hundred; offences which were either in whole or in part infractions of the king's peace, and in which the pecuniary fines, either in whole or in part, accrued to the royal exchequer. The next clause gives us ample information on this, clause 10, *de jure regis*: 'These are the rights which the king of England alone and over all men has in his land retained for the sake of security: breach of the king's peace given by hand or by writ; Danegeld; pleas of contempt of writs or precepts; murder or injury of his servants; unfaithfulness and betrayal; every despite or evil speaking about him; *castellatio trium scannorum* [whatever *trium scannorum* may mean, *castellatio* has reference to the right of licensing the fortification of castles, the exact term is not explained]; outlawry, theft unpunished by death, murdrum; falsifying the king's money; burning, whether arson or merely ravaging with fire and sword; hamsoken or housebreaking, forestel or assault, stopping in the way or highway robbery; fyrthinga, the penalty of fyrdwite or disobedience to the summons to the host, flemenfyrthe, the sheltering of fugitive criminals, premeditated assault, robbery, stretebreche, usurpation of the king's land or money; treasure trove, shipwreck, seaweedrape, plunder; forest rights, reliefs of barons; fightings in the king's house or family, breach of peace in the host; neglect of burghbote, brigebote and fyrd; the entertaining of the excommunicate person or outlaw; breach of the king's protection; flight in battle by land or sea; unjust judgment; defect of judgment; prevarication of the king's law. All the great highways are the king's, and all places of public executions are altogether the king's and in his soke. And to all men in holy orders, aliens, poor and abject, the king ought to be a kinsman and advocate or patron if they have none other. These are the demesne pleas of the king, and do not belong to the sheriffs, apparitors, or other servants of the king in their ferms, without definite instructions. That is, they may be seen to by the sheriffs and others, but not *ex officio*, only when specially empowered. The proper officers for the administration are the officers of the exchequer or the curia, and the very existence of such a class of jurisdictions involves the existence of a tribunal and jurisdiction which is only to be found in the curia regis.

This, then, is the sum of the king's criminal jurisdiction, and the points enumerated are the original pleas of the crown. There seems to be very little change, as far as the list is concerned, from the usage of the Anglo-Saxon reigns; the list will be found, although not quite so long, in the laws of Canute, and of the additions many seem to be mere repetitions of the same points in different forms of Latin and English. One or two of the concluding ones may be worth noticing, especially the distinction between *injustum judicium*, *defectus justitiæ*, and *prævaricatio legis regiæ*. All three of these would, I conceive, come under the head of what in modern language we should call appeals, but on different grounds : *injustum judicium* could only be a decision which contained substantial injustice, the sort of case which in earlier times could be appealed only by a challenge of the court itself, but might now by writ of special grace be brought up for review before the curia regis, or have its execution stopped by a writ from the king himself ; *defectus justitiæ* would mean the delay or refusal of justice, either by the obstinate refusal of the local judges to hear the cause, or by delays interposed by the opponent, or by the failure of qualified judges in the court of first instance, or by inability in the court to come to a decision at all ; *prævaricatio legis regiæ* would mean perversion of the letter of the law to counte- nance unjust decision and would thus contain cases in which the receiving of bribes could be charged against the judge. I do not know that these distinctions are in legal history of much importance, but men are fond of such definitions, and much substantial injustice may be done even where forms are most carefully observed ; in the three, however, one may include all defeat of justice, whether by neglect of form, perversion of law, or material injustice.

The question arises, if these are merely reliefs of the more ancient law, what light can they be made to throw on the innova- tions of the Conquest ? I think they do throw light, if not on the innovations of the Conquest, at least on the new policy of Henry I. Under the Anglo-Saxon kings, the right of the crown in these criminal pleas had been little more than a financial right ; the sheriff conducted the trials and collected the fines. Now, we are told, except by special commission, the sheriff did not entertain them. Who did ? Surely the *justitiæ errantes*, the travelling justices of the time, whose visits are traceable now and then in the annals of the time, whom we have seen mentioned here and there in the ' Dialogus de Scaccario,' and who, few in number perhaps, and irregular in their proceedings under Henry I., were thoroughly organised and made a most important part of the judicial system under Henry II.

The next chapter, entitled ' De placitis ecclesiæ pertinentibus ad regem,' will be under our view more minutely when we come to that point of inquiry which concerns the church ; but I will call attention to it now, as it illustrates the *participatio*, the share which the king had in the jurisdiction and profits, of which he did not claim the whole. Just as in the customary popular jurisdiction he had a

share in the fines paid in the popular courts, so also he had in
the ecclesiastical. Neither the popular court nor the church court
owed its jurisdiction to him, although it would not be able to
execute its sentences without him or in contradiction to him ; but
in neither was he the source of judgment or justice, but he has a
share in the fines and in the punishments, and this chapter tells us
what that share was in the church courts. If murder is done in a
church, the peace of both king and church is broken ; both peaces
have to be amended ; the king and the bishop have the *weregild*, the
church has £5. If tithe be detained, the king's officer shall enforce
payment and share the penalty ; if Romescot is not paid, the king,
as well as the bishop, has a fine ; if churchscot is not paid, the same ;
if a married man commits adultery, the king has the man, the bishop
the woman ; perjury, false evidence, murder of clergy, refusal to
hear confession of the dying, working on holy days, detention of
church property, assaults and murders on church lands, and other
offences in which the church cannot secure her own without the aid
of the secular arm, there the king has a right to share in the fines
that his executive justice has enforced on the offender.

But we shall see by and by a better statement of the case than
this. The chapter on the king's rights in suits touching the church
is followed by two on the two classes of offences that may and may
not be compensated by pecuniary payments ; introduced by a transi-
tionary section, which is worth reading at length. ' Wherever
rightful obedience is refused to the law of God, according to the
statement of the bishop, there compulsion by the secular power may
be applied. Secular justice and compulsion are necessary in both
Divine and human institutions, since many cannot be otherwise
recalled from their vices, and many are unwilling to be inclined to
the worship and service of God ; whence for the greater punishment
of the evil, it is provided by the convenient dispensation of peace
that heavier offences and those worthy of higher punishment should
be assigned to the justice or mercy of the sovereign alone, that
pardon may be more freely given to penitents and punishment to
wilful sinners ; while in cases capable of compensation it is permitted
by the mercy of the saints that the lords of lands may venture by
their licence to exact pecuniary fines according to the law of the
country.' You will observe an attempt made in this section, confused as it is, to set secular justice on a religious basis, and to
establish thereby a somewhat closer connection than is ordinarily
allowed between ecclesiastical and temporal treatment of offences.
In point of fact every offence at common law which involves moral
guilt is also an offence against ecclesiastical law ; the common law
takes cognisance only of the damage, according to the idea of these

times; therefore the damage being compensated, the offender is left open to ecclesiastical penance, but towards this it is questionable whether the temporal law would ever be called in to enforce the observance if the injured party were satisfied and the infraction of the king's peace atoned for. Such, it seems to me, is the intention of the paragraph, which for inversion of style and complication of idea is well worthy of the author of the prologue. It is followed then by the chapter on amendable offences against your neighbour, atoned some by *were* and some by *wite*; that is some by payment of *weregild*, some by penalty, and some by a fine of 100*s*. I need not analyse this.

Clause 13 concerns the offences which place a man at the king's mercy; it is an expansion of the former brief enumeration, but contains some small points of interest besides. The unjust judge is condemned to a payment of 120*s*. and is to lose his dignity of judge. You seem to learn from this that there still was in the popular courts that class of judices or assessors of the sheriff which answers to the *scabini* of the continent, and of which I have spoken in the 'Constitutional History' as one of the difficulties in the early inquiry as to the development of the jury system. I do not think that a passage like this can be interpreted with reference to the judges of the curia regis, who certainly would not be let off for a fine of 120*s*. at any time, and who when they were disgraced fell with a heavier fall, like Geoffrey Ridel in the reign of Henry I., Glanvill himself at the accession of Richard, and Weyland, Hengham and Stratton under Edward I. Who these judices were we shall see better when we examine the structure of the shiremoot; another note—offenders who have neglected the observance of the *trinoda necessitas* have a choice of two procedures: they may either pay a fine of 120*s*., a *weregild* really, at once and have done with it, or they may go through a process which had been practised under Canute—let fourteen men be named by the court, and obtain eleven votes out of the number to back up his denial. This is one of the curious bits of procedure in which the system of compurgation approaches in appearance very near the system of jury, and on which accordingly the older investigators of the history of jury relied in support of their theories. Looked at carefully, however, and with caution against being misled by accidental analogies, it is seen really to be only a modification of compurgation, and not to have in it the essence of the inquiry by sworn witnesses which is indispensable to the historic jury.

I now proceed more rapidly to gather up the particular notes of the royal jurisdiction that occur in later chapters.

Clause 16, the king's peace, i.e. the peace of the court which is under his peculiar jurisdiction and special sanctions, extends in a radius of three miles three furlongs nine acres nine feet nine palms and nine barleycorns. That is curious, and likely when you come to the barleycorns to give rise to some disputes about measurement.

Clause 17, on the forest law, is perhaps the first authentic pronouncement since Canute ordered that every man should be entitled to his own hunting. It is clearly older than any text that we have on the subject and seems to be very true. Pleas of the forest are encompassed with sufficiently multiplied inconveniences ; they concern essarts, cutting wood, burning wood, hunting, carrying bows and darts—*de misera canum expeditatione*—if any one does not come to the hunt, if anyone leaves his stock shut up, buildings in the forest, neglect of summons, meeting men in forest with dogs, and the finding of hides or flesh. The section is merely a summary of the headings of a series of articles answering to the later forest assizes, but now lost. When I referred to Canute's law of the forest, I meant the single article that is found in his collected code, not the Latin articles which with an extraordinary neglect of all critical inquiry are still kept among the genuine laws of the Anglo-Saxon period, but which are obviously a forgery of much later date, and which, if they had contained any germ of genuine forest law, would have been discoverable either in this compilation or in the later assizes.

Clause 19, ' de justitia regis.' This refers to the extension of the royal jurisdiction locally. The king exercises immediate jurisdiction in all his demesne lands : where he gives a manor he sometimes gives soken with it, sometimes not ; and sometimes he retains the whole jurisdiction, sometimes only a part. Archbishops, bishops, earls, and other potentates have sac and soke on their own private lands, and on lands otherwise held they have manorial jurisdiction over their own tenants, the higher branches being apparently reserved for higher tribunals, as the hundredmote, the shiremote, and the king's justices. Over all capital cases arising in the courts of barons, senators, clerks and lay, whether the other parts of the jurisdiction belong to the king or not, he has direct control. This seems to me to make a difference between *haute justice*, power of life and death, belonging to the greater lords of franchises, and lower justice, belonging to lords of less dignity, among whom the *barones* are enumerated ; but by *barones* here I understand a translation of some such word as *thegen* in the corresponding Anglo-Saxon laws, and interpret it as merely meaning lords of manors ; and yet even to them occasionally judgment of life and death is allowed by special favour or on the ground of their peculiar merits : the lovely excellence of the king rather promotes than overthrows liberty, and therefore we may presume gives to those who deserve it by propinquity or dignity of deserts a right to hang one another.

Clause 29, on the king's judges, I propose to examine in another lecture.

Clause 35 refers to oferhyrnesse, or contempt of the king's summons, which also occupies clause 42.

Not much to notice in clause 43 : that no one impleaded by the king shall answer any other litigant. The king has the first right to be heard against any debtor or offender. No one impleaded by the king is compelled by law to answer anyone until he has satisfied him who is lord of all; and by corollary the king can warrant or act as warrantor for anyone in his service. Just as no one in the king's service can be excommunicated without his leave, so anyone in his service may depend on his protection.

So again in clause 52. A man impleaded by the king, whoever may be his immediate lord, must give security at once, or fall into the offence of contempt: his lord cannot intervene to save him from so much of responsibility. The great majority of the following articles are either expansions of the earlier ones or simple repetitions, and we go on to clause 81 without finding anything that much illustrates the royal power ; that chapter is entitled, 'De pace regis danda in potatione.' This chapter might open a very curious piece of archæology, bearing on the *scotales* and guild meetings in which money was raised for local purposes, and local disputes settled extra-judicially. I wish we knew more about it. ' In every potatio prepared for giving or buying, or of guild, or for any purpose of the kind, first the peace of God and the king shall be set among those assembled, and request shall be made that if any avoids any other then on any account, he will, if he please, make it known, and security shall be given him for his rights as shall be just to him. If they do not admit immediate agreement, let the man whose conduct has given offence retire from the company; if, after the peace has been thus set, anything shall be done by the drinkers [any wrong, I suppose], the penalty of oferhyrnesse is to be given to the master of the house or the person to whom such penalty is due if such person there be.' Now, this seems at first sight simply to refer to the maintenance of peace in public alehouses or fairs or the like; but it certainly throws a curious light on the purposes for which these drinking meetings were gathered ; and it runs very far back, for similar provisions are contained in the laws of Ine as well as in those of Ethelred, where the peace given in an alehouse has its special sanctions. But clause 87 concerns the same matter, and goes back farther still, even to the Salic law, which it is most curious to find quoted in an English custumary (§§ 9, 10).

The two subjects on which we should look for special information in the Leges Henrici which come next in importance to the royal judicature, are the relations between the ecclesiastical and secular jurisdictions and the history of the composition and proceedings of the county court. Both of these subjects we have examined in some detail in special reference to the innovations of the Norman period in the earlier lectures of this course, and, as there can be no possible reason for a recapitulation of the points taken in those lectures, it is not necessary for me to make any preface to the examination with which I am now going to proceed. I may, however, say that while we attempted to establish the fact that there was in the Anglo-Saxon Church an inherent and common ecclesiastical jurisdiction, and a sort of religious engagement on the part of the kings to give coercive force to spiritual sentences, there was some confusion or intermixture in the business of the courts on mixed questions, and possibly on simply ecclesiastical ones, which seemed to the advisers of the Conqueror to be opposed to the spirit of purely ecclesiastical jurisdiction. Suits were tried in the shiremoot by the bishops and archdeacons and with the co-operation of laymen which touched the *regimen animarum.* For that reason the Conqueror directed that the prelates should hold their courts apart from the shiremoot and hundredmoot, and according to the episcopal laws and canons, engaging the assistance of the temporal power to enforce their decisions. But it was not quite easy even under this peremptory act of reform to separate at once ecclesiastical from civil causes, or to determine what preponderance of the spiritual element gave an essentially ecclesiastical character to a particular plea ; e.g. questions about advowsons certainly touched the *regimen animarum,* and yet as certainly touched temporal rights of property ; accordingly questions of advowsons long constituted a debatable ground ; during the reign of Stephen it would seem they were constantly tried in the ecclesiastical courts ; Henry II. reclaimed them for the secular court by his Assize of Darrein presentment ; in the next century attempts were made to recall them to the forum ecclesiasticum, but in vain. And so with regard to offences committed by or against clergy, or in holy places or with reference to possessions of the church : where there was a breach of the king's peace there would be a question whether the plea came rightfully before the king's court, or because there was a spiritual point interested must come before the court ecclesiastical. Obviously there would be variations of dealing with these ; a strong lay minister of the type of the modern lawyer would insist on every plea that would bring the suit before the lay court, or would stop every proceeding that would claim it for the court Christian. And correspondingly, as *boni judicis est ampliare juris-*

dictionem, a powerful archbishop or ecclesiastical minister would draw every cause, in which spiritual man or thing was in question, into the court of the church, as Becket did with regard to criminal clerks, and the bishops of the next generation wanted to do with personal tithes.

In the passages quoted above describing the special rights which the king had in ecclesiastical trials, we saw some data for conclusions as to the state of things under Henry I. ; namely, that while the trial of the offender in an ecclesiastical suit was conducted for the most part by ecclesiastical judges, the king's share in the penalties was distinctly vindicated, and the king's duty of assisting in the enforcing of sentences was distinctly recognised. The passages to which I am now going to call attention presuppose so much ; the light which we shall look for in them will be on the matter of procedure, with reference to which you have to remember that the study of the Roman civil law procedure, on which the later process of the courts of the church was framed, had not yet to any extent made its way in England.[1] We begin with clause 5, of which the following is an abstract as touching this point. In all causes ecclesiastical and secular there should be accusers, defenders, witnesses, and judges ; and careful attention should be given to the nature of the cause, the intention of the accusers, the mode of testimony, and the choice of judges. There is an initial difference in the proceedings in secular and ecclesiastical suits : in secular suits, after a plea has begun, it cannot be withdrawn until the cause is finished ; in ecclesiastical suits, if it be necessary, it is possible to reject the judge as a suspected person, or to appeal on the ground of gravamen. The judges are to be persons whom the defendant is willing to accept ; they are to be persons well qualified to discharge the duty, and are not to act without a formal accuser. The accusers and witnesses are to be persons of good character, for none who is unfit to be a priest ought to accuse a priest ; if the first count in charges against the priest fails, the accuser is not to be allowed to

[1] Almost all these articles are drawn from the canon law, which must be supposed, therefore, to be so far received in England. The article which allows the clerk to appeal against gravamina is from the epistles of Pope Felix I. They are either derived directly from Burchard and so from the pseudo-Isidorian or other decretals, or through what is called the Excerptiones Ecgberti ; they are interesting enough, but cannot be read without a doubt whether they are really practical. No proper English manual of practice could possibly contain a regulation for trying a pope or cardinal ; and this obliquity affects a good deal besides. In point of fact, I should scarcely venture to go further than to say that they illustrate the knowledge of Roman canon law which had penetrated into England rather than anything which was actually in force in this church. It is, however, of the earlier canon law that I speak, not of the improved study under the influence of the revived civil law.

M

proceed with the others : a certain number of witnesses must prove a charge against a bishop ; the pope may be judged by no man. A prelate living against the faith should be accused before the pope ; if he be accused of crimes he is to be heard before the bishops of the province ; appeal is to be allowed him—some authorities allow a year and six months for such a defendant to prepare his case ; before a suit is canonically adjudicated the clergy are to be replaced in their rights, as in the case of appeal. I have given what seem to be the principal provisions. You will see at once that those of them which are excerpted from the old canons, such as the provision for the trial of a pope or cardinals, could only in a very limited sense be said to have any relation to English jurisprudence ; but those which refer to the selection of judges may be supposed to have such a meaning.

But what was the method of trial ? We know what we now mean by judges ; we have an idea of the proceedings of the popular courts at this time by compurgation and ordeal ; and we know that under the Roman law, after the preliminary work of the institution of the suit had been completed, and the work *in jure* had proceeded as far as the *litis contestatio,* or determination what point was to be decided, the prætor proceeded to *dare judices,* i.e. to nominate the persons by whom the point was to be decided. To which class of *judices* do the words of our laws refer ? I confess that the subject always has to my mind been one of extreme difficulty ; and it is one which it seems to me most of our commentators shirk. It is perhaps of less importance in reference to ecclesiastical matters because the period of its continuance is short, and we know that from a date very shortly following this, and possibly also before this, the only proper ecclesiastical judges were the bishops, and their officials archdeacons and chancellors, or the ordinaries as commonly known. But the *judices* here are not judges ordinary, but nominated or selected, and liable to be refused by the person impleaded as suspect. Unless we suppose these provisions to have been inserted without being understood from some canon that incorporated the Roman idea of *judices,* which is, I think, improbable, we must conclude that the *judices* who tried these cases were persons qualified in the same way as the *judices* of the shiremoot, the *judices* and *juratores* of the county court ; i.e. the persons qualified to act as assessors with the bishop and sheriff. We must, then, conclude either that the process in the ecclesiastical courts was in analogy with that in the shiremoot, or that these provisions referred only to that class of mixed trials which were still tried in the shiremoot. I think that the first is more probable, and the probability may be strengthened perhaps by the fact that it is more in analogy with the Roman law procedure. But on the whole it is most likely that they are simply a canon transferred from the collections without special reference to English usage; although there are in Glanvill traces of ecclesiastical *judices* who are not the bishops. However inviting, then, is the theory that the *judices* mentioned here may be the *judices* and *juratores* of the county courts, I fear we should be unwise to argue more than an analogy between them. They are the *judices* or delegates of appeals under the decrees of the pseudo-Isidorian decretal.

The next provision to which I will call attention is that which occurs in the order how business is to be taken in the hundred and shire moot (chapter 7): in which the first place is given to the causes that concern religion, 'agantur itaque primo debita veræ Christianitatis jura: secundo regis placita.' First church pleas, then crown pleas, third common pleas. What the pleas of Christianity were we have argued already: (1) They may either be the mixed pleas which, notwithstanding the edict of the Conqueror, had not yet found their way into the proper courts of the bishop; or they may be (2) the properly temporal actions in which subordinately ecclesiastical questions were entangled; or (3) supposing the bishops' courts to be held coincidently with the shiremoot, the bishops' business was to be taken first. It is possible that c. 11 may be intended as an amplification of this rule, 'De placitis ecclesiæ pertinentibus ad regem;' the chapter which I have already referred to in some detail as illustrating the cases in which the king, in courts in which he was not the source of justice, still had rights of fines and the power of enforcing sentences. The pleas noticed in this chapter are called pleas of Christianity, and yet many of them seem only to concern Christianity in that they accidentally concern the rights and wrongs of its ministers; they may, however, be the *jura veræ Christianitatis* that were still tried in the county court—they are homicide on sacred ground, detention of tithes, Romefee, churchscot, adultery, perjury on relics, false witness, injuries to ordained persons, refusal of confession, working on holy days, forcible detention of church goods, marriage of widows, reception of excommunicates. All these may be described as lying in the debatable ground between civil and spiritual judicature; and if their spiritual character be taken at its highest, they are different in kind from the merely spiritual pleas of immoral life, neglect of duty, non-residence, plurality, heresy, and canonical disobedience, or the penitential discipline of the confessional with regard to laity as well as clergy.

In the shorter articles that follow there are one or two particulars to be gathered up. C. 23. An abbot is responsible for his monks; i.e. in the same way as the lord is responsible for his villeins.

M 2

C. 31. The bishops, as well as the earls and other potentates, are still to attend the shiremoot;[1] after this there is little on the matter until we come to c. 64, which has to do with oaths and ordeals. § 3. The oath of the mass priest and the secular thegn are of equal value; the mass priest, I suppose, includes all ordained priests, whether monks or regulars, but there is a section for the regulars. § 8. A priest who leads a regular life may swear alone in a simple accusation, in a triple one he must do it with two of the same order: a deacon in simple purgation must have two companions; in a triple one, six. A plebeian priest is on the same terms with a regular deacon; a priest accused by his bishop or archdeacon must have six lawful priests, as compurgators, prepared for mass. That clause shows that compurgation was in full operation as regards the trials of the clergy. C. 66. If anyone slays a minister of the altar he shall be an outlaw to God and man and pay very heavy *weregild*; if a minister of the altar kill a man he is to be deprived of order and dignity and go on pilgrimage and do penance as the pope enjoins, or he may purge himself with a three-fold compurgation; so also in assaults on men in orders. If a man condemned to death desires to confess and is refused, a fine of 120*s*. is due to the king, or the refusing priest must purge himself with six compurgators. C. 68. § 3. Every priest, from whatever extraction he may be, if he leads a canonical and regular life, is in secular matters to have the estimation or rank of a thegn; but if he is killed, his *weregild* is to be estimated according to his real birth: if he comes of thegn's blood, he has the *weregild* of a thegn; if of villein blood, he is to have the *weregild* of a villein; his *weregild* is to be decided in all estates by the rank of the father, not of the mother. § 4. No one born in servitude may be admitted to holy orders before he has been lawfully emancipated; there you have a piece of much older law, best known, however, by being incorporated in the· Constitutions of Clarendon,[2] and about which at various times much nonsense has been talked. But, § 5, although the slain priest has only the *weregild* of his birth, there is a graduated tax additional put on him according to his orders, one pound on the first grade, up to seven pounds on the seventh grade, of orders; and beyond that, if any man kills a bishop, the final disposal of him is to be at the discretion of the king and his brother bishops. He who kills a clerk or monk is to be deprived of arms and serve God, that is be imprisoned in a monastery; if a deacon or priest kill a man he is to do penance and be deposed. These two directions are from the most ancient penitentials, and cannot be regarded as descriptive of

---

[1] *Select Charters*, p. 106.   [2] *Ibid*. p. 1 0.

existing law in Norman times, being merely added by way of illustration.

This is nearly the last article that concerns this subject. At c. 79, § 5, however, we find that homicide in a church makes a man *ipso facto* an outlaw; the crime cannot be atoned by any compensation; anyone who chooses may pursue and punish the culprit, unless he can obtain specially from the king the grant of his life, in which case he may, after proper penance, fine for breach of peace, and payment of *weregild*, *manbote*, and *wite*, be received again into society.

VI

THE SHIREMOOT AND HUNDREDMOOT

THE next subject to which we will now proceed is not less dry, but it may, perhaps, take your fancy better; I mean the constitution of the popular judicature, our old friends shiremoot and hundredmoot. The first articles on this head we have already examined, i.e. the edict ordering the courts to be held as in King Edward's time, and have argued from the words of it the identity of the later county court with the Anglo-Saxon institution of the same character. But there are still some minor points to note: in the description of the persons who are to attend, you get some curious names, not only bishops and earls, but vicarii, centenarii, aldermanni, præfecti, præpositi, barones, vavassores, tungrevii; and in some manuscripts herehohei, treingrevii, leidegrevii. This enumeration seems to be intended to include exhaustively all persons who, either as landowners or officials of any kind, could be expected to put in a personal appearance; it does not follow from it that there really were officials of all these names, or that, if there were, they were more than local names for the same functionaries. Vicarii, for instance; the only vicarii that we know of in England are the ecclesiastical vicars or curates of parishes: here it obviously does not mean that; if it means anything at all, it, as well as vicedomini, means the sheriff's deputies; but not at all improbably the terms may be borrowed direct from some foreign capitulary. Centenarii and aldermanni are both probably officers of the hundred, the hundredman and the hundred's ealdor; for the old ealdorman of great rank was extinct, or merged in the comes or earl, and the modern alderman of the town corporation had scarcely come into existence. Præfecti and præpositi again are reeves apparently of large jurisdictions, or they would not be put before the barones and vavassores; possibly of the king's franchises. The barones and vavassores seem to be lords of manors in their feudal relation; or the barones lords of manors, and vavassores freeholders or franklins holding under them. Tungrevii are the town reeves, tungerefas of rural townships. The other names given as additional, the herehohei, can be nothing else but heretogas, the old title of the ealdorman; the treingrevii are the reeves of the trithings or ridings into which Yorkshire and Lincolnshire were divided; the leidegrevii, the lathe reeves, the reeves of the lathes of Kent. These additional names, I conclude, are simply fancy additions put in to give an air of completeness to the summary, and probably interpolated. In c. 31 the attendance of these superior persons is included in the term *potestates*, which is at once clearer and quite as comprehensive.

These *potestates*, then, with the representatives of the townships, the reeve and five best men, constitute the popular courts; but the greater lords, who, having estates in different shires, could not be expected to attend every court in every shire, were at liberty to send their stewards to represent them and their men. The courts were to be held, the shiremoot twice a year, the hundredmoot once a month: notice was to be given six days beforehand—whether that was a summons addressed to every member, or only to those whose special duty, either as *judices* and *juratores*, or as representatives, or as litigants, was to attend, one cannot on the face of the thing say. It is more reasonable to suppose that, unless the place for the sitting of the court required to be notified six days beforehand, this summons must have been intended only for those whose attendance was indispensable. Certainly, where the summons was disobeyed there were heavy fines, heavier fines than we can suppose possible for casual disobedience, for not only does the Conqueror prescribe for the second neglect the seizing of an ox and so on, but these laws under the head of neglect of summons are strict enough in their demands. C. 51 is 'De summonitione hundredi.' If the person duly summoned does not come he pays 30*d.* for the first two neglects, and for the third a full wite or forfeiture; contempt of the summons of a lord to his court is equally criminal; and, c. 53, he who neglects to come when summoned to the shiremoot is guilty of contempt of the king.

We may doubt, however, whether these penalties would be ordinarily exacted so long as a sufficient number of *judices* and *juratores* were present to carry out the business of the court. Sometimes it was not so; then in the hundred court the business was transferred to the joint consideration of two or three hundreds or even more. But if this arose from the non-attendance of those who ought to attend, they were punished. Of course the power of fining for non-attendance was one which an unjust sheriff could use very despotically, and did so; for it is a ground of complaint to the king for at least two centuries after the Conquest, especially after the king began to grant to the knights exemptions from the duty of serving on recognitions.

We may, however, make one guess further, and suppose that there was in each shire and hundred a regular list of men capable of serving as *judices* and *juratores*, just like the list of men capable of serving on juries that is drawn out and stuck on the church door in every parish at the present day : from that list the constituent officer of the hundred court summoned those who either from proximity could most easily attend, or by wisdom and experience were most likely to be useful.

Anyhow, the persons so qualified constituted a special class of officers, and to them we must now turn. C. 29 is devoted to the question who ought to be the king's judges. ' The king's judges are the barons of the counties who have free lands in them, by whom the causes of individuals ought to be dealt with by alternate treatment ; but villeins or cotseti or ferdings, or those who are vile or poor, are not to be counted among the judges of the laws ; whence neither in hundred nor in county do they forfeit their money or their lord's if they leave justice without judgment (that seems to mean that their attendance is not compulsory on penalty) ; but the lords of the lands having been summoned, the plea shall be enforced at the competent term, whether or no they have been summoned.' [1] These judges are also called *senatores*, and it is on them apparently that the penalties for non-attendance are intended to fall, for they are repeated here as in c. 51, which I have already noted; and in § 4, if sufficient numbers are not in attendance, the business may be delayed rather than those present should undertake the examination of matters on which they are incompetent to judge.

If you would allow me to make another guess, I should like to advance the theory that those persons who are described as obliged by their tenure to attend the shiremoot and hundred, i.e. who held their lands by the service of attending at the three weeks' court of later times, were those whose services as *juratores* and *judices* would be most especially in requisition.

We ask very naturally, now that we know who these *judices* and *juratores* are, what is their function. I am strongly inclined to believe that their first duty, and that in which they reach backwards farthest into antiquity and onwards into the present, was the duty of presentment. I know that some doubt and some ridicule have been thrown on the old idea of the twelve senior thegns of the law of Ethelred, who had to swear that they would accuse no one unjustly, and who are popularly supposed to be the ancestors of the modern grand jury; but I still think that the existence of these *judices* can be accounted for most easily by supposing the institution to be continuous.[2]

---

[1] *Select Charters*, p. 106.   [2] *Ibid*. p. 72.

I will supply two parallels, one from the juries of the court
leets of manors, a customary institution so ancient that no statute
law even of the Norman reigns can be adduced as either creating it
or modifying it, the other from the practice of the most ancient
episcopal visitations, which followed unquestionably some popular
or immemorial process of the temporal courts : in both those
systems the first piece of business is to form bodies of inquisitors,
who take an oath to conceal no criminal for love or for fear, but to
declare the witness of the district on the point on which they
may be interrogated.   We may call these assessors of the
sheriff if we like ; but they are so, not as declaring the law, but as
qualified to report the facts or belief of the district, and in that
aspect the direct ancestors of the recognitors under the Assize of
Clarendon and the later grand jury.

The order of business, in which come first the ecclesiastical trials.
Next to them come the royal pleas : the subject-matter of them I
have already spoken on, and we have now only to add one or two
points which require further elucidation.   We have seen the nature
of the points reserved to the crown, and the means taken to secure
the whole or a share of the jurisdiction and of the profits.   C. 43
enacts that no one impleaded by the king shall answer any other
litigant ; the king has the first right to be heard against any debtor
or offender.   'No one impleaded by the king is compelled by law
to answer anyone until he has satisfied him who is lord of all ; '
and by corollary the king can warrant or act as warrantor for any
one in his service : just as no one can be excommunicated without
his leave who is in his service, so everyone in his service may
depend on his protection.   This rule is enlarged by Glanvill, lib. 1,
c. 27 ; and as a principle is the same as that which protects members
of parliament, acting as they are under the king's summons, from
being arrested.   So, again, c. 52, a man impleaded by the king,
whoever may be his immediate lord, must give security at once or
fall into the offence of oferhyrnesse ; his lord cannot intervene to save
him so much of responsibility.

The majority of the following articles are expansions or repetitions.   However, although the king had these rights in court, it
does not follow that offences against him, or causes in which he was
the complainant, would be treated in any other way than the *placita
singulorum*, which form the third item of county business, would be
treated.   It is very probable that if we could get a lawyer to put
down for us in simple language the principal features of Anglo-
Saxon and Anglo-Norman process, we should find that they did not
much differ except after the introduction of writs, of which we have

very few examples in Anglo-Saxon times and a very great number under the Anglo-Norman kings. I will for our immediate purpose postpone what little I have to say about the writ process, for after all it only guided and stimulated, did not alter the material character of the popular process. And I must repeat what I have already said, that at this stage there is no very deep difference between civil and criminal process, except where the criminal process is set going by presentment, if such were the case. The trials were trials of the evidence, the truth of the speakers; if it was an appeal of murder, the accused and accuser exchanged challenges as to the truth of the charge, and the compurgators swore to the truth of the oath of their principal. If it were a demand of right, the demander and the defendant exchanged challenges in the same way, and the compurgators swore again to the truth of the respective oaths. And if the oaths were insufficient, recourse was had to the ordeal in the case of the English, and to trial by battle in the case of the Norman, unless the court thought it necessary to call in witnesses. If the point in debate were a question on which the attestation of public witnesses was required, i.e. witnesses of a transaction which by law was ordered to be transacted in the presence of witnesses, as those cases of sale which we saw ordered in the laws of the Conqueror, such evidence would be at once procurable; but other evidence was given by the report of the neighbourhood *de visu et auditu*—they did not give evidence to fact, but to the report or belief of the neighbourhood as to the transmission of property and like matters of repute. These witnesses were produced by the parties litigating, not by order of the court, in Anglo-Saxon times; but in the Norman times, by the introduction of recognitions and records of court, or the simpler process which preceded the full-grown recognition, the importance of such party evidence was diminished, and the third sort of witness, court witness, as contrasted with transaction witness and community witness, was introduced and gradually supplanted the other two. Of course none of these (except in a modified way the transaction witness) answers to the modern idea of a witness deposing to his knowledge of a fact.

All these points would be no doubt much clearer to the legal mind; but the legal mind is very prone to take two things for granted: first that the non-legal mind is incapable of understanding a legal point, and secondly that, as it is hopeless to make it understand it, it is absolutely necessary that it should be made to accept it whether it understands it or no. This being so, I can only refer you for further distinctions and definitions on these points to the legal minds, and return now to the text of our authorities. I think we have examined all the places that mention classes of offences and variations of penalties and the right to exact fines, with the arrangements for the divisions of the fines. And we have likewise examined the practice of reckoning the lord responsible for the production of his vassal in court, and the collective responsibility of the frankpledge, which would seem in these laws of Henry to be then in full working. I think the main points that yet need to be touched on are those connected with the forms of oath and ordeal; and yet upon these in the earlier lectures I said perhaps as much as is in proportion to the rest of our treatment. However, on this I will read a part of chapter 64, of the Christian custom concerning spoken statements *secundum quod sunt*. 'Every accusation should be treated with a foreoath, *plano vel observato*, single or repeated as the custom of the place shall be; for all things are varied by the custom of places, the pleading of causes, and the method of the litigants. In some places there is much difference between oath and foreoath, as in informations and the like. In Hampshire he who swears *verborum observantiis* has to swear but once and stands or falls by his oath. In some places as often as he pleases he repeats the oath until he proves or fails to prove his point. It will also happen that the character of the foreoath may be altered by the nature of the matter in question, or by the dignity, nationality, or merit of the person who takes it. But owing to the violence of wicked men, and the conspiracy of perjurers, the *frangens juramentum*, the convincing and settling oath apparently *in verborum observantiis*, has been laid aside, and the accused prefers to appeal to the judgment of God, and goes to the ordeal of hot iron instead of purging himself with a company of ten compurgators. In Wessex, in cases of theft, murder, betrayal, fire, and housebreaking, and other crimes that are punished by mutilation, all swear by the *sacramentum fractum*; except thegns, priests, and others, who have never done anything to diminish their legal credit. These last, whatever the nature of the charge may be, swear the simple oath with of course the proper number of compurgators and due regard to the value of the oaths of their peers; the oath of the thegn being equal to that of six villeins, and his *wergild* being that of six villeins. The oath of the mass priest is equal to that of the thegn by English law. Frenchmen and other foreigners do not use the oath *in verborum observantiis*. If a man is accused of homicide and wishes to purge himself, he must produce compurgators according to his *were-lada*; those on his father's side to take the *fractum juramentum*, and those on the mother's the *planum*.'

Perhaps that will be enough. You will remember the difference between the *planum* and the *fractum*, which we came to the conclusion was the true theory. The *fractum* is the *solemne jura-*

mentum containing certain prescribed and dictated solemnities, dictated either by the parties, by the law, or by the judge, with a certain regulated form of words, from which the swearer may not diverge, or if he does his oath will go for nothing. The simple *planum* oath is a summary one, *sine delectu verborum aut locorum.* It would add very much to the interest of this part of our investigations if we could point to good examples of these oaths being formally taken. This we cannot do exactly, but our books do furnish us with a series of formulæ touching both oaths and ordeal which are worth knowing as illustrations of the sort of matters on which oaths were required, as well as the formalities of taking them. These forms are not contained in express terms in the Leges Henrici, but are preserved among the Anglo-Saxon laws, and are unquestionably the forms which are referred to in the Leges, and which continued to be in use with modifications of language as long as any part of the popular common law procedure continued.

As I have pretty nearly exhausted all the matters of interest in the Leges to which I should invite you, save and except the matters of mere archæology, it will be no waste of time to look back at these oaths and rules of ordeal. Eleven forms of oath are given, of which the first is the oath of fealty, a form which is tolerably well known both from its first appearance in the laws of Edward the Elder, which contain the injunction on the man who wishes to be in the king's peace, and from its later history in times which are more distinctly feudal. The oath as it here stands has no reference to homage for land tenure, but is a promise of faithfulness made by the subject to the lord and is called the hyld-ath, the distinctive words being the undertaking 'to love what he loves and hate what he hates, according to God's law and the world's judgments, and never of will or of power, by word or deed, to do anything which may injure him . . . as was in our agreement when I bowed to him and chose his will.' The oath is not, you see, exactly an oath of allegiance, for it assumes an initial contract, but it is not an oath of that sort of fealty which accompanies homage, examples of which you will find in the 'Constitutional History' in the discussion of the law of treason in vol. iii.

The second form is the oath by which a man asserts his right to a piece of property stolen from him and discovered in unlawful hands: 'I swear by God, to whom this relic is consecrated, that I prosecute my cause without fraud, without guile, and without any deceit, that this animal of which I speak has been stolen from me and that I found it in possession of so and so.' As a pair to this is the oath of disavowal No. 3: 'By the same God I was not by rede or deed, by wit or work, where by injustice he was robbed of his property. But I hold that animal as I by right acquired it, and I so claim it as he sold it to me, in whose hand he put it, and I so hold it as he sold it to whom of right it belonged ; and I so have it as it came to me of my own, and as by folk right it is my own property and my own rearing.'

The next pair of oaths contain the charge and repudiation of charge of theft, the accuser disavowing personal malice, and stating the charge as his belief, the other simply denying it. No. 6. The next is the oath of compurgation, which is simple and straightforward enough. By the lord, the oath is clean and unperjured, *clæn* and *unmæn*, which N. has sworn. No. 7 is the oath of the man who swears that when he bought a thing he bought it as sound and clean and with warranty against any other claim. No. 9 is the corresponding oath of the seller. No. 8 is the oath *de visu et auditu,* or party witness. 'In the name of Almighty God, as I stand here, for N. in true witness, unbidden and unbought [*sine prece et pretio*], so I with my eyes oversaw and with my ears overheard that which I with him say.' There you see the oath of witness, altogether different from the oath of evidence now in use as a promise to speak truth on questions put to you. This is simply a conjuratory oath to a particular fact, as the compurgatory oath was to the general deposition of the principal litigant. Nos. 10 and 11 are concerned with debt, the creditor's oath : 'In the name of the living God as I money demand so have I lack of that which N. promised me when I mine to him sold.' The denial is unhesitating. 'In the name of the living God I owe not to N. scat or shilling or penny or pennyworth, but I have discharged to him all that I owed him so far as our verbal contracts were at first.'

There were, as we know from other parts of our work, other oaths of a more modern character, such especially as the oath of the twelve senior thegns, which I have supposed to be the oath of the *judices, senatores,* or *juratores* of the county court ; and the oath of the peace, taken by all subjects of the age of fourteen, not to be a thief or receiver of them. But these oaths of good behaviour belong to another class, and not to the oath required in judicial procedure. From the brevity and simplicity of the forms here given we may, I think, conclude that they are the *planum* oaths and not the *fractum,* an example of which we still desiderate. The form for the ordeal is interesting, and we see in it how completely the institution was regarded as an ecclesiastical matter, and a solemn appeal to God as the righteous judge ; and so understand why the Conqueror in the edict we have so often referred to puts it entirely in the hand of the bishop : 'Concerning the ordeal we enjoin by command of God and of the archbishop and all the bishops, the fire is lighted in the church, and the church is closed to all but the mass priest and the person who is to go to the ordeal. A distance is to be marked nine steps, according to the steps of the accused, from the mark to the stake on which the ordeal, i.e. the hot water or hot urn, is placed. The kettle that contains the water may be of iron or brass or lead or clay [one would think that a lead kettle would insure a safe trial] ; the water is to bubble up before boiling, a stone is placed in the kettle. The culprit bares his hand ; if the accusation requires simple purgation, it is enough if he plunge it up to his wrist ; for a threefold one it must go in up to the elbow. Before the critical step is taken two men of each side are to go in and test whether the water is as hot as the rule enjoins ; then let a certain number of each party go in and stand in a row along the sides of the church. These witnesses must be fasting . . . the priest is to sprinkle them with holy water, and let them taste it, and give them all the book and the crucifix to kiss.' I do not know that we get the kissing of the book much earlier than this ; of course you will remember it in the history of Becket and John the Marshall. 'In the case of the ordeal of hot iron, the order is even more minute. The service begins with benediction ; the fire has been lighted, and the iron laid thereon. After the beginning of the benediction the fire is not to be stirred : the service proceeds to the last collect ; when that has been said, it is to be taken from the fire and put on the staple or stool, and there is to be solemn silence. Let there be no other speaking within, except that they earnestly pray to Almighty God that He make manifest what is soothest ; and let him go thereto, making the nine steps. At the first signal he must put his right foot on the staple, at the second the left foot, then grasp the iron at the third signal, and throw it forward, then hasten to the altar and have his hand covered and sealed to the third day. According to the state in which it shall be found on the third day, his guilt or innocence is proved. There is a good deal of literature on the ordeal, which went on as a regular institution until the Lateran Council of 1215, when it was forbidden. The prayers used on the occasion seem sufficiently long to warrant the belief that the water or iron might get comfortably cool during the ceremony. Baluze gives from the Benedictional of S. Dunstan the full ceremonial. In the case of the iron, it is carried to the fire during the singing of the Benedicite, after which the benediction begins. At the third prayer it is placed on the fire, then mass begins, the culprit being made to communicate. After the prayers are over, the priest again blesses the iron, and sprinkles it with holy water, after which the accused takes it in hand.'

VII

THE CHARTERS OF STEPHEN

THE reign of Stephen, I need hardly say, presents very little documentary material for either legal or constitutional history, and even the little which it does afford, in the shape of the two charters printed in the 'Select Charters,' is hardly of a character to detain us after the thorough examination that we have now given to the legislation of the preceding reign. There is indeed scarcely a point mentioned in these charters to which I have not by way of anticipation called your attention already in some earlier stage. As, however, both the class and the subject are becoming very much attenuated, and as the college statutes warn us, ' visibiliter tendunt ad non esse,' it would be useless to begin an altogether new subject now, and perhaps we shall find, as commonly is found, that however carefully we have gone over the same ground before, a new reading of the charters may find us some food for reflection, or suggest some new point of interest. Of the first of the two, that printed at p. 119 of the ' Select Charters,' nothing, I think, will come. It ranks among the charters of liberties, but is so extremely brief and so very jejune as scarcely to suggest a question. There are no difficulties in the construing, no difficulties in the form. All that King Henry had granted Stephen continues, and all the good laws and good customs that England had had in the days of King Edward he yields to his people, enjoining moreover on all that they have and hold these good laws and liberties of him and his heirs to them and their heirs, in freedom, quiet, and fullness, and forbidding that any one should do mischief, impediment, or diminution upon them. It is obvious that in the hurry of the accession or usurpation—for already to the mass of Englishmen the accession of Stephen must have seemed a usurpation—there was no time, nor any champion of the rights of the nation, nor any possibility of making any but the most general bid for the support of the nation, no opportunity, in fact, for making any definite step forwards. No doubt Stephen would have promised anything ; no doubt, as the historians tell us, he did promise everything that was put before him, but in his

charter he bound himself to very little. At the accession of Henry I.
four days had been sufficient to enable the king and his advisers to
draw up a manifesto, which was to secure him the support of the
baronage, and to protect him from any rival claim that might in
time to come be set up for his brother Robert. On that occasion
there was indeed ample room for hurry and anxiety; there might be
troubles ahead, but there was no imminent personal risk; no oaths
of fealty had ever been taken to Robert, no stain of perjury was on
the men who elected and crowned Henry.

It was different now. The late king had taken every possible
means to secure the crown for his grandson; no mention seems to
have been made of the possibility of Stephen's succession in the
public deeds of his uncle's life. He had been the first to take the
oath of fealty to Matilda and her infant son. We may be quite
willing to take the most charitable view of his proceedings, and to
attenuate to the utmost the guilt of the archbishop and the
ministers Roger the justiciar and Nigel the treasurer, and we may
even admit the probability of the truth of Hugh Bigod's story that
Henry I. before he died had disinherited Matilda and authorised
the succession of Count Stephen of Mortain. But were theory and
fact more conclusive than they are, it is certain that the burden of
the oath betrayed, and the necessity of making provision for their
own security, would prevent the prelates and ministers engaged on
Stephen's side from attempting to make with the king they were
creating any further terms than would indemnify themselves.
Possibly they sold their chance for the promise of continuance in
office; possibly, like the old reformers, Bishop Roger of Salisbury
thought that reform had gone far enough, and that even reaction was
better than letting the guidance of affairs pass out of his hands.
The excellence of routine, which was all that he and his master had
yet conceded to liberty, was contained in custom, and a promise to
retain good customs was all that was needed to bind the conscience
of the king. But it is quite possible that he also was carried away
by the simple desire of self-preservation, and that, in his heart
believing in the truth of Matilda's claims, he simply temporised,
and that to very little purpose.

Setting this aside, however, and granting that there are marks of
hurry and unpreparedness about the whole proceeding, let us go on
to consider what are the exact relations of the second to the first
charter. The chronology of the year is a little perplexing. According to Henry of Huntingdon, at the close of the Christmas festival
Stephen came down to Oxford and renewed the promises made at
his coronation, especially undertaking to renounce the unjust restraint on the free election to bishoprics, the Danegeld, and the

forest encroachments of his uncle. While at Oxford he heard news from Scotland that compelled him to go north and meet King David at Durham. After a hasty run to Durham and back, Stephen held a solemn court at Easter in London; shortly after Easter, Earl Robert of Gloucester, not yet having done homage to Stephen, came to England, and a few days after his arrival the king, at Oxford again, issued the new charter, the first witness to which among the earls of England is Robert himself. That is apparently the sequence of the events; the exact dates may perhaps be approximated to thus. They are curiously crowded, as our dates will be next term, by the occurrence of a very early Easter. Easter is on March 22, as early as it can be. Stephen's coronation was either on December 22 or on December 26; the evidence is conflicting. Before the end of Christmas he was at Oxford. What brought him there? Well, perhaps it was the funeral of the late king that brought him to Reading; that took place within twelve days of Christmas, i.e. before January 6, 1136. At Reading it is not unlikely that he would come on to Woodstock or to Oxford for the hunting. Anyhow, he did come, and before the end of the vacation, possibly that is before Epiphany, a day or two after the funeral, he received the news that led him to go northwards. John of Hexham gives us the date when he was at Durham; it was on Ash Wednesday, February 5, that he met King David, and he stayed a fortnight after leaving Durham, therefore on or about February 20. This gives him a month to come south and keep Easter, March 22, with great pomp at London, and then to come back to Oxford. There he had collected the barons and prelates for a great council, a *generale concilium*, as it is called. I have no hesitation in fixing this in the month of April; for having crowned the queen at Westminster on Easter Sunday, he seems to have brought the court with him.

After all this was done, just before the rogation days, the first of which was April 27, Hugh Bigod rebelled in Norfolk. When he was put down the king went into Devonshire against Earl Baldwin, and yet by the month of August he was able to go to France. The dates follow fast, but you will see they present no great difficulty. Stephen's marches must have been rapid, but we need not suppose that he led great forces about with him, or that the roads, as they then were, made any great difficulties in rapid cavalry movements.

A first look at the second charter will reveal to us something else that was being done at the same time.[1] We place it then at Oxford early in April 1136. It begins thus, in strict following of the precedent set by Henry I. in rehearsing his title; and this lets us into a good deal: 'I Stephen, by the grace of God, by the assent

[1] *Select Charters*, p. 120.

N

of clergy and people, elected king of the English, and consecrated by William, archbishop of Canterbury and legate of the holy Roman see, and confirmed by Innocent, pontiff of the holy Roman see, of respect and love to God grant that holy church be free and confirm to it due reverence.' What has Innocent, pontiff of the holy Roman see, got to do with the matter? We have already seen him recognised by Henry I. as apostolic pope under the pressure of Saint Bernard, who had supported him against Anacletus; he was owing then everything to Henry I., and now he is obligingly confirming the election of the nephew who has usurped the rights that Henry had so carefully conserved for his grandson. This is what has been doing in the meantime. The pope was at Pisa; there must be time for an embassy there to get the pope's recognition and to come back. No doubt one part of the business was to free from the stain of perjury the conscience of the prelates who had joined in the coronation; another was to obtain a clear recognition of the king's right. This was obtained, and Richard of Hexham gives a copy of the bill which contains it and which might form an important link in the catena of evidence that illustrates the relations between our kings and the popes. Henry I. had signified to Pope Paschal II. in 1103 his reception of the news of his election, and had promised that he should have in England all the honours that his predecessors had enjoyed under the reign of the Conqueror, but with this significant addition, called forth, no doubt, by the circumstances of the investiture struggle which was going on at the time. ' Your holiness will be pleased to take notice that as long as I live, God helping me, the dignities and uses of the realm of England shall not be diminished; and if I, which God forbid, should place myself in such abject condition, my optimates, yea the people of all England, would in no wise suffer it. Take therefore, dearest father, more useful counsel, and let your benignity so moderate itself towards us that you may not compel me to do what I should be very unwilling to do, depart from your obedience. That was plain speaking, very Henrician indeed; but now the tune has changed, and the king chosen by the English has, as it seems, to apply to Pisa for confirmation.

This is what Innocent says : ' The King of kings changes times and transfers kingdoms. The great King Henry we hear is dead, under whom religion and peace flourished. On his death religion and peace were endangered, and the kingdom was given over to evil men. Then Divine mercy put into the hearts of prelates, magnates and people, *communi voto et unanimi assensu*, to choose you Stephen for their king; so at least I am well assured by the letters of the bishops, of the king of France, and Count Theobald, your brother;

and considering that at your coronation you promised obedience and reverence to S. Peter, and because you are known to be of near degree of relationship to the late king, we receive you as the special son of the Roman church and S. Peter, and will that you should retain all the privileges of honour and friendship which your predecessor had at our hands.' A special son of the Roman church making at coronation special promises of obedience to the chair of S. Peter! Surely if Peter of Blois had seen this, it was sufficient warrant for him to tell Henry II. that he was as king of England in a special filial relation to the pope, and might extenuate, if it did not justify, the submission of John to Innocent III. Read this in conjunction with the claim set up by Gregory VII. and repudiated as distinctly by the Conqueror, and you will see that the times have changed.

Well, so much for Pope Innocent. Now how about the promises that the king had made on his first visit to Oxford, about canonical elections and Danegeld and forests? The first point is not absolutely left out of the charter. We shall see directly how very clerical in its character the charter is ; but just now we may observe that the only mention made of elections here is in the three or four words, ' donec pastor canonice substituatur.' About the Danegeld not a word. ' As for the forests, those of my grandfather and uncle William, I mean to keep; those of my uncle Henry, I surrender ; I give them up free to the churches and to the kingdom.' [1] Again you see how little that was wanted was really granted ; and then, again, how little that was granted was really given. The case of the Danegeld was very hard, for it was believed, nay known, that King Henry had vowed to release the people from it. The story is told on the best authority imaginable ; it was not the king's lawyer, but his doctor, that stood sponsor for it. As he was in Normandy in 1130 he saw three visions: first he saw in his dreams a multitude of rustics with their instruments run and jump on him and demand their dues; then he saw a cohort of armed men rushing at him with their weapons aimed direct ; then he saw a company of prelates with their pastoral staves threatening him. So startled was he at each dream that he jumped out of bed, cried for help, and drew his sword. Finding nobody handy to kill, he sent for the doctor, Grimbald, who told him to imitate Nebuchadnezzar, and redeem his sins by alms. Whether he took Grimbald's physic or not, he was in no hurry to take his advice, and it required a sound shaking in a storm at sea two years after to bring him back into the right mind. Then he vowed that for seven years he would release the Danegeld and do justice ; but whether justice or not was

[1] *Select Charters*, p. 120.

done, the Danegeld was left alone, and now Stephen contented himself with the custom of his uncle, vowed and did not pay.

But what, we further ask, did the charter contain? Again we find the chief lesson of these early charters is what the evils were that wanted remedy, rather than the nature of the remedies to be applied. The people without any difficulty could tell the evils, the king's ingenuity was tasked to invent the remedies. However, as we might expect considering the influence by which Stephen had reached the object of his ambition, the first and longest section of the charter relates to the clergy. So far as it goes it is very good. 'I promise that I will do and will permit nothing to be done simoniacally in ecclesiastical things.' Simoniacally, even under the better administration of Henry I., very much had been done. Freedom of election in an ideal state of church polity meant everything honest and true; but were the people, or the clergy either, fit for the use of such a privilege? The cathedral chapters were family parties, the monks of the conventual chapters were at the king's mercy. No doubt preferment was sold by the crown. No doubt the votes of the chapters, and even of the monks, were in many cases bought and sold too. Even a fair bishop did not think it a very bad sin to distribute among the members of the chapter which elected him the purse that he had been making by similar little transactions while he was one of their number.

Well, so far as royal promises go, simony was not only renounced, but forbidden; there is to be no more of it. Whatever we may think of the conduct of the leaders on the occasion of the usurpation, or election by surprise, as it would be more just to call it, it is certainly to the credit of the bishops that the first point of remedy they asked for was this grievous religious and social abuse. But the abolition of simony is by no means all that is demanded or granted.

The next sentence contains a recognition of the fullest kind of the right of the clergy to an independent administration and independent judicature. 'I recognise and confirm that the justice of ecclesiastical persons, and of all clerks and their property, and the administration and distribution of goods ecclesiastical, be in the hand of the bishops.' [1] The word *perhibeo* is peculiar—it is sometimes used as equivalent to grant, more frequently it means to assert —here it seems to be used in order to escape the actual use of the word grant, which would imply that this was rather the concession of a new privilege than the allowance of an old right. Anyhow, the right is allowed and recognised, and it would seem to some purpose; for not only are church councils much more free under Stephen

[1] *Select Charters*, p. 120.

than they had been under Henry I., but church courts also are more active and independent. The legation of Henry of Winchester, which was set up about three years after the issue of this charter, and which was regarded by the contemporary writers as an era of innovation in the practice of ecclesiastical appeals; the history of Archbishop Theobald and his attempts by means of the teaching of Vacarius to introduce the study of the Roman civil law; the correspondence of John of Salisbury, who, as Theobald's chancellor and secretary, transacted an immense amount of judicial business which would come under the *justitia potestas* and *distributio*, here recognised as belonging to the bishops: all show that the reign of Stephen was what Henry II. believed it to be, a period during which the limitations of his grandfather and great-grandfather had been forgotten or set aside, and the *avitæ consuetudines,* which had regulated the relations of spiritual and temporal power, had been practically disregarded.

This sentence, although it is not very much noticed by historians, is perhaps the first and most definite statement of the doctrine of ecclesiastical independence translated into fact. In comparison with it the next article is of smaller import. The dignities of the churches, confirmed by their privileges and their customs, had by ancient holding—'I ordain and grant'—to remain inviolate: the *privilegia* are royal and papal charters, which for the most part granted to the privileged churches and monasteries corporate rights, exemptions from ordinary jurisdictions spiritual and temporal, as well as their property and other honours. You will observe the distinction between the rights ascertained by charter, *privilegiis,* and those which depended for their validity on ancient prescription. The property, however, is subject to another clause: ' All the possessions of churches and their holdings, which they had on the day that William my grandfather was alive and dead [that is on the day of his death], without any counter-claim of other claimants, those I grant free and absolute; but if the church shall hereafter demand restitution of lands had or possessed before the Conqueror's death, of which she has now lost possession, those I reserve for my own indulgence and liberty of bestowal, to restore or to apportion between the claimants. Whatever since his death by the liberality of kings or the largess of princes, by offering, or purchase, or exchange at the hands of the faithful, has been bestowed on the churches, I confirm.' [1]

These three clauses divide the church claims into three divisions: the lands held from the days of the Conqueror with undisputed tenure; the lands the right to which accrued in the Conqueror's

[1] *Select Charters,* p. 120.

days, but is disputed; the lands which have accrued since the Conqueror's days. The first and last are freely confirmed; as to the second, the king reserves to himself the right of determining whether they shall be restored or discussed, subjected apparently to legal investigation and determination. The clergy were not to have everything their own way, but they do secure a good deal. This was the great era of Cistercian endowment, and unquestionably the king had the right to limit the bestowal of new endowments. The next article is the declaration of the peace, in much the same purpose as the proclamation of the peace at the accession of a new king, in accordance with the promises made at the coronation, and following the precedent set by both the Conqueror and Henry I.

The forest article which follows I have mentioned already several times in this course. ' The forests which William, my grandfather, and William, my uncle, instituted and held, I reserve to myself. All the others which King Henry added, I restore and concede quiet to the churches and to the realm.' [1]   We learn from this that Henry had made new forests as well as the Conqueror and William Rufus; and we learn from the express language of the historians that Stephen did not keep his promise, but almost immediately after making it, hunted in the grounds inclosed by Henry I. in Leicestershire. The quarrel about forest boundaries that seems to have revived at the accession of every king went on, as you may remember, a sort of perpetual sore, between the king and the landowners until the close of the reign of Edward I., when the final perambulations were made which defined the forest territory and left the unauthorised forest accretions under the name of purlieus or *purallee*, subject to a modified operation of the forest law, the study of which was a special subject of jurisprudence. The revival of forest claims under the Tudors and Stuarts should not be left out of consideration in a complete view of this point: a point which, although constitutionally simple and now obsolete, was practically a matter of very great significance long after the close of the mediæval period proper.

After making his futile promise about the forests, Stephen returns to church matters: ' If any bishop, abbot, or other ecclesiastical person before his death has made a reasonable distribution, or fixed that such distribution should be made, I grant that it hold good; but if he has been surprised by death before doing so, let distribution be made for the safety of his soul by the counsel of the church.' [2]   The curious privilege which the kings claimed of seizing the personal property of ecclesiastics after their death, of giving them power to make wills, and of authorising either beforehand

<hr>

[1] *Select Charters*, p. 120.   [2] *Ibid.*

or afterwards the execution of their wills, is an old and curious prerogative which I have nowhere seen fully discussed. It was certainly acted upon long after Stephen had pretended to surrender it. Henry II. seized the goods and money of Archbishop Roger of York, although before his death he had authorised him to devise it. So did John the property of Hubert ; so did Edward III. the property of Archbishop Stratford ; constantly we come across letters of licence allowing the prelates to make wills. Some time we must make it our business to try to get to the bottom of this. Certainly it seems to show that whatever extent of privilege the crown was willing to concede to the church as a sacred corporation, it would endeavour to make the utmost it could out of the individual parson alive or dead.

But we go on. 'While the sees are vacant of their proper pastors I will commit them and all their possessions into the hand and custody of the clerks or goodmen of the same church, until a pastor be canonically substituted.' This last article seems to be added as an additional guarantee against the misuse of the royal prerogative of prolonging vacancies of bishoprics and abbeys, of interfering with elections, and confiscating temporalities during vacancies. We have already noticed that the words *donec pastor canonice substituatur* are the sole words in the charter which seem to refer to the promise made by the king at Oxford, of allowing free elections ; nor is there any promise made not to hinder the election so as to prolong the vacancy. Perhaps Stephen thought that the word *canonice* implied not only freedom, but observance of the ancient canon which ordered elections to be made within three months. The guardianship of temporalities was a more distinct royal right, and one which for a long time occupies an important place in documentary illustrations of history. To conclude : 'All exactions and injustices and miskennings'—that is, as you remember, fines for not observing the exact terms of pleadings— 'whether wrongfully introduced by sheriffs or by any others, I altogether extirpate. Good laws and ancient and just customs in murder fines, pleas, and other causes I will observe and enjoin to be observed, and ordain.'[1] We gather from the special mention of the murder fine that Norman and Englishman were not so thoroughly welded together as the 'Dialogus de Scaccario' forty years after this represents them ; no doubt they needed the civil war of the next twenty years to produce the desired amalgamation. Consistently enough the charter ends with a saving clause : 'All these I grant and confirm saving my royal and righteous dignity.'

[1] *Select Charters*, p. 121.

VIII

THE DOMESDAY AND LATER SURVEYS

THERE is one sort of authority on the laws and customs of the Norman kings, of which we have made in this term's lectures less use than we might have done. I mean, of course, the Domesday survey. It is full of interesting matter, more or less directly bearing upon our subject; but to have attempted to read any part of it in the only way in which such things can be read in lecture would have been futile, and the few extracts from it which are printed in the 'Select Charters' are not selected as a specimen of the contents of the three huge folios that are known as the published Domesday, but are chosen as mere illustrations of the points (mainly set before the reader in the other parts of the volume) which are of constitutional importance. Of course I am not going in the last lecture of the term to attempt any general account of these volumes; but it has struck me that I might, by giving a few minutes to the several surveys of the century with which we have been dealing, set before you some of the points in which, when you have time and if you have the will, you may find your way to do some useful research. Among the day dreams in which I have indulged in the intervals of terminal courses, has been one of a Domesday Society: a devoted little band of forty savants of research, who might each undertake a separate county, and by adding up the sums, arranging the names and measurements, and identifying the localities, pave the way for a really true Domesday map. Then I have thought, by the help of later surveys such as I am going to speak of by-and-by, we might get a manorial map, which would show how the land of England was shared between the crown, the clergy, and the nobles at different critical periods of our history, and on that we might frame an 'honour' map, showing the distribution of family inheritances and local influences, some of which subsist to the present day. The thing would be possible now, for, notwithstanding the proceedings of late years, which have, by encouraging the enfranchisement of copyholds, done almost all that can be done for the effacing of manorial boundaries, those boundaries still subsist in men's memories and in court rolls, that still have some shadow of usefulness and legal force. But it may not be so much longer, especially if local self-government is, as seems likely, to be restored under new conditions and with little regard to organisation which is becoming archæological. Still, at the present day there is a great deal of interest felt in these local matters, and if we were to add to the concoction of a manorial map a codification of manorial customs, we should have erected a monument *ære perennius* of the continuity of English local institutions from the earliest times, to last until our American cousins have annexed us ; and possibly longer still, for those cousins, even more than most of our own countrymen, show a very lively interest in everything, legal, customary, or historical, that illustrates the cradle of the race, out of which evolution is going to produce the ideal man.

Well, that is a day dream, perhaps, quite as much as my Domesday Society may be ; but, returning to that, I propose to run over the materials that exist for reproducing surveys of this kind, with special reference to Domesday, but not with any attempt to analyse the idea of that work, or to present any of its results. We will make it just a lecture on documentary research. Of course Domesday is the beginning, but there are in the volume appended to the printed Domesday two documents which are historically prior to it, and out of which some portion of its materials were selected. These are what is called the Exeter Domesday and the Ely or Cambridgeshire Domesday. The Exeter Domesday is properly called the Geld Inquest, and if we only had it complete we should have a record which, as illustrating local history and nomenclature, would not be inferior to the great Domesday itself. It is a portion of a survey made in the year 1084 for the payment of Danegeld ; which, you will remember, William the Conqueror, according to the historians, in that year collected at the rate of six shillings on every hide of land. The Exeter Domesday then contains, with various degrees of exactness, a survey of the hidage of Devon, Somerset, Dorset, and Wilts, and nearly the whole of ancient Wessex ; and from it we get the hundreds and townships of some of those counties drawn out with great completeness. Although this Geld Inquest has no close connection with Domesday, it is one of the surveys cited in Domesday as an authority for the geld payable by every estate, and affords most useful illustrations and supplementary particulars additional to those which are in some cases given very sketchily in the more famous record. Domesday itself was the product of a survey made two years after the Geld Inquest, in the year 1086, and contains very much more information on social and economical points, as well as on local laws, customs, and privileges, although in the geographical information it might be improved if it had followed more closely the plan of 1084. The description of it given by Florence of Worcester, in the passage printed in the 'Select Charters,' answers so closely to the reality of the book, that we are tempted to conclude that he took it directly from a local survey of the county of Worcester analogous to the survey of the county of Cambridge preserved in the Ely Domesday.

As the preface to the Ely Domesday is also printed in the 'Select Charters,' [1] I need not now read it at length, but tell you simply what its relation is to the Great Survey, or Exchequer Domesday as lawyers call it. The Great Survey was made by small committees of surveyors, the barones errantes, or justiciarii errantes of the period, who went into every hundred and township and took the evidence of representative men from each district as to the extent, fertility, and agricultural value of every holding ; the inquiry is made on the oath of the sheriff of each shire, of all the barons, lords of manors, and Frenchmen, and assembly of every hundred, and of the reeve and six villani of every township. The villani here are the men of the township, the name not necessarily implying servitude, but simply that the six were representative hunagers of the manor, or members of the local organisation of the township. When each county had made its return by this machinery, the whole was abridged and codified and arranged. Unimportant particulars, or such as presented themselves to the codifiers at the Exchequer as being irrelevant, although to us they are very interesting indeed, were omitted, and the whole was arranged in the two beautiful parchment volumes which you may see any day at the Record Office in Fetter Lane, in a glass case and fireproof room.

Well, the Ely Domesday, of which I was speaking, is the earlier report of the commissioners for Cambridgeshire, out of which the chief commissioners made their abridged survey for the great book. It is in every respect much more full than the Exchequer Domesday, but of course its chief interest is local or nearly so. These, then, are the three great relics of the Conqueror's economical administration ; two imperfect, the other as perfect as when it was written, and constituting for Englishmen, perhaps, the most interesting record in existence ; on religious grounds less interesting than the gospels given by S. Gregory to Augustine, or some of the early collections of laws and chronicles, but in its completeness and uniqueness beyond all comparison with any record of this or any other nation of Europe. It is indeed to English history what the books of Numbers and Joshua are to the Bible. Domesday, as the

---

[1] *Select Charters*, p. 86.

chief valuation book of England, was never during the middle ages surrendered, and so long as the ancient systems of tenure had any practical importance was appealed to as an authority that could not be gainsaid. In particular all questions connected with the customs of ancient demesne, or the extent of that sort of holding, were resolved by Domesday. But it was not at the time regarded as possessed of such permanent authority; and one of the measures attributed to Ranulf Flambard, the famous minister of William Rufus, was the compilation of a new survey, in which the loose measurements of the hidage should be reduced to greater uniformity, and a basis laid for closer and heavier taxation. You probably know that it is one of the vexed questions of the reign of William Rufus, whether or no this second Domesday was ever drawn up, or whether the whole story may not have arisen on a mistaken notion as to the share taken by Flambard in the work of the real Domesday. It is said that there is still in manuscript a portion of a survey of the lands of the abbey of Evesham, which bears some signs of being part of such a second survey. Whether these signs are not merely indications of an improved and revised extract from the original Domesday, or whether the relic be not one of the many local surveys or rent rolls of the abbeys which were drawn up for the use of the monastery itself in the twelfth century, I cannot say, not having seen the manuscript, but it is most likely that it is an ordinary terrier or list of estates, with the special tenure, services, and rents of the monastery, and not a part of a general government survey. There are many such books, more or less complete, but generally somewhat later than the date of the Evesham fragment. The marquess of Bath has recently printed such a survey of the estates of the abbey of Glastonbury, framed very much on the lines of Domesday, but of at least a century later.

Archdeacon Hale, some years ago, edited for the Camden Society a Domesday of S. Paul's, drawn up by the Dean Ralph de Diceto in 1181, and the famous Boldon Book or Domesday of Durham, which is printed by the Surtees Society and also in the appendix volume to the Exchequer Domesday, contains an exact survey of nearly the same date of the lands, tenures, and services of the county palatine. But all these belong to a later system. There is, then, no certain evidence that the Domesday said to have been projected by Flambard, was ever really drawn up, and there is no producible portion of such a survey certainly forthcoming. But it is more than probable, almost an inference of necessity, that the changes of taxation and the improved administration of the reign of Henry I. would involve the drawing up of lists and rates which would, to some extent, be imitations of Domesday. Thus for the great aid taken by that king on the marriage of his daughter with the emperor, there no doubt was made a list of tenants of land, and of the number of carucates if not of exact knight's fees. I think that for the reign of Henry I. there must have been at least two such surveys, one in which the carucate-arrangement was adopted, and a second in which the knight's fees and their holders were enumerated.

The Liber Niger, the Black Book of the Exchequer, printed by Hearne in the eighteenth century, contains a survey of the carucates of Lincolnshire, made not later I think than 1127, and possibly as early as 1117, which must have been part of a general survey made to determine the incidence of a carucage or some tax levied on the carucate and oxgang. This is a very valuable local and genealogical record, and we owe to it nearly all we know of the hundredation and trithing arrangement of Lincolnshire. It is accounted by genealogists also as the most important temporal document that exists between Domesday and the first extant roll of the pipe, that of the thirty-first year of Henry I. But it is simply a survey of one single point, not a general description of the land and its capacities, and it is confined to a county which, although very large and full of anomalies, lay at the time outside of the more exciting acts of the historical drama.

The next thing of the kind is the pipe roll of which I have just spoken. This is the only roll of the kind earlier than the reign of Henry II., after whose accession there is a complete series, and for the most part in duplicate. It was published by the Record Commission in the early years of the nineteenth century, edited by Mr. Hunter, and contains an almost perfect account of the royal revenue of the year 1130, the amount of the ferms, and the sheriffs' expenses, the nature and profits of proceedings in the courts of law, the nature and incidence of general taxation, and light on almost every particular of interest in the constitutional history of the times. It is from it, combined with the Leges Henrici and the writs contained in the chartularies of the time, that we are able, so far as we are able, to reconstruct the public administrative system of the Norman period. Yet, curiously enough, it was not until Mr. Hunter edited it that the proper date was assigned to it. It was very commonly cited as belonging to the fifth year of Stephen, and is so quoted by Madox, the historian of the Exchequer, in a way which confuses the reader and unfortunately damages, to some extent, the usefulness, although not the authority, of Madox ; for that most industrious writer invariably gives his references, and so saves us from the risk of accepting his inferences as authoritative categorical statements. One result of the mistake was to represent the reign of Stephen as a much more orderly period than it was, a notion which still is traceable in some books, the writers of which were not aware of the error into which the misdate was leading them. But valuable as this pipe roll is, and although in many respects it supplies the place of a survey and furnishes the information that we look for in a survey, it is not a survey, only a most important link in the chain that connects Domesday with the later developments of the Exchequer economy. For an account of its contents and arrangement I must refer you to the 'Dialogus de Scaccario,' the second book of which contains a most lucid and exhaustive account of the method of account at the Exchequer; or to my own account of the book in the section on the Exchequer in the first volume of the ' Constitutional History.'

I said that the reign of Henry I. must have had two surveys made, but I mentioned only the fragment of the Lincoln carucage. The other, I think, must have been a complete list of the knight's fees of the kingdom, for that there was such a list we infer from the distinction between the old and new feoffment that is found in the accounts of the reign of Henry II. The knights of the old feoffment were those who had received their knight's fees in the reign, or before the end of the reign, of Henry I. The new feoffment included all that had been cut out and bestowed on knights from the accession of Stephen to the year 1166, the next date at which we have distinct memorials. This is, however, only an inference. No such list is now known to exist, nor have we any document of a similar character belonging to the reign of Henry I. or Stephen, besides those I have mentioned, and possibly early terriers of the monasteries and cathedral churches. When we come to the reign of Henry II. we are better off. Not only have we the perfect series of pipe rolls, which, although still unprinted, have furnished both local and constitutional archæologists with great wealth of material, but we have, in the collection known as the Liber Niger of the Exchequer, an assembly of documents which approach to the character of a new survey. One of Henry's reforms, as you may remember, was the substitution of scutage or taxation by the knight's fee for certain purposes for taxation by the hide, for the purpose of discovering what sum could be so raised, and who were the persons on whom it should be charged. Henry in or about 1166 issued writs to all the tenants in chief directing them to report how many knights they had of the old and new enfeoffments holding land under them. The letters in answer, one of which is printed in the ' Select Charters,' were collected in the Black Book, and occur also, I believe, in the Red Book, which is still in manuscript. These are most valuable as giving the skeleton of the feudal map of England ; and our lawyers and antiquaries have followed them up by tracing in the pipe rolls the transmission of knightly property wherever it is noticed.

Besides this record there is the Boldon Buke, or survey of the county palatine of Durham on the plan of Domesday, a survey of great importance socially as capable of comparison with Domesday, showing the differences which a century of important events had produced in the condition of classes, or at least between north and south England in corresponding classes of society. This and the other surveys, like the Domesday of S. Paul's and the volume on Worcester which Archdeacon Hale also published, are our chief authorities as to the condition of husbandry and agriculture in the latter part of this century, and thus have a value for that purpose far beyond mere lists of names and measurements of estates. And they take us a long way.

Alexander Swerford, the original compiler of the Red Book of the Exchequer, marks the next era and sort of material, although I should not forget the attempt made by Richard's ministers in 1198 to get a new survey made which would prove a more profitable rate-book than the Domesday. Nothing, however, came of that. In the Liber Ruber, Swerford not only copied our dear ' Dialogus de Scaccario,' but the returns of the Liber Niger to the writ of 1166, and continued lists from the pipe rolls of all the tenants in chief and knights accountable for scutage. It is probable that during the long reign of Henry III. there would be, as taxation increased or varied, new valuations of property. Certainly there were new valuations of church property, especially that called the Norwich taxation, drawn up by Bishop Suffield of Norwich about the middle of the century, and used for taxing the clergy until a new one was made in 1291 or 1292, but the Norwich taxation exists only in fragments, and would be of little use as illustrating secular territory.

With the reign of Edward I., as we might expect, we find ourselves again on sound economical footing and forthwith look out for new surveys. And this is the case from the very beginning of the reign. Very early in it, before the king had returned from France, where he was detained during the first year after his accession, it became necessary to ascertain what had become of the demesne estates of the crown under the lavish prodigality of Henry III. In order to obtain the requisite information, as soon as the king returned, commissions were issued for the purpose of examining into the condition of the local popular courts, the hundredal and manorial courts that claimed jurisdiction and profits. The result of that commission was the production of what are known as the ' Rotuli Hundredorum' or hundred rolls, a large return from every county in England, giving an account of the hundredal divisions and of the ancient courts that continued under that name to drag on an attenuated existence. This very valuable return is printed by the Record Commission in two large folios, and although, like other returns of the kind, it is a little puzzling, taking for granted on the part of the researcher a greater knowledge of contemporary law than is easily accessible, it is extremely valuable. What the Domesday survey is for general purposes, and the returns of the Black Book for the feudal allotment of estates, the hundred rolls are for the history of the surviving local jurisdictions. On these returns was based an Act of Parliament, passed in 1278, called the statute of Gloucester, and out of the statute of Gloucester arose another similar series of returns known as the quo warranto rolls, the result of a visitation under the statute, and this linked on to the rotuli hundredorum serves to complete the contemporaneous history of the subject.

A second great survey of Edward I.'s reign was what is called Kirkby's Quest, a grand record drawn up in or about 1284 or 1285, for the purpose of making out the tenures and numbers of knight's fees. Great part, if not the whole, of this record has been published. It will perhaps strike you that some of these surveys may have been very ordinary pieces of work, and that the extant remains of them owe their importance to the fact that most similar reports have perished, and not to any peculiar merit of their own. That may very well be the case, but without at all diminishing the historical value to us of the relic that has survived.

The third great survey of the reign is the ecclesiastical taxation, the taxation of Pope Nicolas, a new assessment of all church property, whether temporal or spiritual, that is whether consisting of landed estates or of tithes, offerings, and voluntary payments, capable of being reduced to audit. This was made in 1291 for the purpose of a papal grant which the king shared. It is very thorough and complete, and was the valuation book on which all ecclesiastical taxation was based until the reign of Henry VIII. With this the list of our great surveys ends, and nothing like a complete census of the landowners or taxpayers was as a census taken until modern times ; but the place of such a document for practical purposes was supplied by the extremely close and accurate way in which the returns for the taxes were kept, in what are called the subsidy rolls, immense masses of which occur in the Public Record Office, and some few of which have been printed by various archæological societies.

You may remember, if you have read that part of my 'Constitutional History,' that after the year 1334 no new valuation or assessment for the rating of grants from personal property was made but the sums levied that year on each hundred and township became the regular amounts henceforth demandable from such hundred or township, and so far as its separate incidence was concerned was reapportioned from year to year among the individual contributors by the local machinery.   The subsidy rolls are the returns made, for each tax, by the officers employed in the collection, and they give the names of the payers and the amount paid.   Some of them are extremely full, as, for instance, the roll of the poll tax of 1379, which contains the names of all persons above the age of sixteen on whom that unpopular impost was levied.   This roll is extant for the West Riding of Yorkshire, and has recently been printed by one of the Yorkshire societies.   Unfortunately other counties do not possess such a record, but this is for all questions genealogical and economical a repertory of facts of the greatest interest.   Well, so long as records of this kind were regularly made up from year to year, anything like a new survey for the purposes of practical business was unnecessary ; and as political economy had not yet set itself up as a science, men did not feel the want of a census for purposes of speculation and argument.   Still they might have found it useful at times ; if such a survey had been in the hands of Edward III.'s parliament of 1371 the ministers could not have made such a mistake as to suppose that there were 40,000 parishes in England, and the absurd numbering of knight's fees which was reputed in those times would have shared equal contempt.

So it is, however, that by the help of subsidy rolls, civil and ecclesiastical, we run down to the age of the Reformation without a new survey, and from the days of the Reformation onwards to the last century without the taking of anything like a census.   The great survey of church property taken between 1536 and 1540, and known as the *valor ecclesiasticus*, was one of Henry VIII.'s measures ; taken in connection with the dissolution of the monasteries, it superseded the taxation of Pope Nicolas, and continued to be the valuation known as the king's books, on which the payment of certain tenths, first to the crown, and after the time of Queen Anne to the augmentation of small livings, is made.   For other ecclesiastical purposes it is superseded by the returns made annually by the clergy, and by the particulars returned in the decennial census, in the tithe apportionments and the reports of the Ecclesiastical Commission.   Into the history of the census returns I am not going to intrude.   The return of the landowners of Great Britain, popularly called the New Domesday, was made in the middle of the nineteenth century to an order of the House of Commons, which wished to obtain clear knowledge as to the proportions of land held by large and small landowners.   It is a useful book for people who want to know what their country neighbours are worth, but for the real purposes of a Domesday scarcely worth even an incidental mention. Of course it does not lie within the scope of legal and historical inquiry at present to examine the numerous returns on agriculture which are annually furnished, and which form for economical purposes the closest analogy to the ancient Domesday; or the Ordnance Survey, which, if it would lend a hand to such historical maps as I have dreamed of, would add an invaluable section to national history.

IX

THE COMPARATIVE CONSTITUTIONAL HISTORY
OF MEDIÆVAL EUROPE

In beginning a course of lectures the purpose of which is to trace
the evolution of the chief European constitutions, and by comparison of their developments to attempt some view of the general
character of the growth of free government as exemplified in them,
it is perhaps necessary and certainly advisable that I should state at
some length some postulates or principles which will be usefully
kept in view by those who intend to follow my train of thought.
It is obvious at the outset that I must lay down an idea or two
which seem to me to be true, and on the hypothesis of which I shall
say much that I shall have to say, but which I by no means wish
to inculcate upon you as infallibly true, or indeed as my own view
so perfect as not to admit or even to require modification.

In the first place, however, I need hardly tell you that I am
no believer in what is called the philosophy of history. Philosophy
in its modern use is generally nothing but an attempt to discover
the wrong reasons for events or phenomena, to elaborate processes
by which the things that we see or know to have happened could be
accounted for, supposing that everything that produced them was
something else than what it is. History is, on the other hand, the
tracing of recorded effect and recorded cause ; and such philosophy
seems to me to be a contradiction in terms of the true readings of
history. If you think that I misrepresent in this definition the
philosophy of history, I bow to your decision, and will say only in
the second place that I am opposed to the school of thinkers which
exalts the generalisations of partially informed men into laws, and
attempts out of those laws to create a science of history. And the
reason of this is simple. I fully believe in the government of the
world by Divine Providence, and that the Divine Providence, acting
always for that which is right and best, by its very nature acts with
some uniformity of cause and consequence. But I also believe that
the Divine Providence acts in the government of the world through
secondary agencies, and the chief agency in the department of

history which we are attempting is the will of men, the aggregate of wills of individual men, than which no agencies can be conceived more capricious, more uncertain, more incalculable. It is the portion of history to trace the workings of these secondary agencies, and even to generalise from them; but to enter into the higher regions of Divine Providence is the portion of faith rather than of science, and I for my part should be very loth to bind as by a law the action of Divine Providence with any generalisation of mine from men's doings, as regards either past or future. No one believes more sincerely than I do in ' God in history; ' but I believe in Him so strongly that I dare not exalt even the most certain generalisations of history into laws by which to a certainty either past, present, or future is guided. Putting, however, aside the theological element, it is certain that greater and more minute knowledge reveals endless differences—leads to an impression rather of infinite diversity than of elemental unity; that although the eye of genius can descry the one in nature and the one in history, the admission must be made with two serious drawbacks: first, that it is not every student of history or one in a thousand who possesses the eye of genius; while generalisation is a most tempting process to all minds, and thence in nine cases out of ten a generalisation is founded rather on ignorance of the points in which the particulars differ than on any strong grasp of the one in which they agree. The more you know of any two persons or events, the less alike they seem ; perfect knowledge is independent of, and even inconsistent with, any generalisation at all.

We cannot study history without generalisation, but it is a great and fatal error to depend on such generalisations as a perfect and sufficient reading of history, still more to exalt them into laws, into necessary conditions of the moral government of the world. On this view you will not expect me to profess myself a believer in the ' education of the world,' as it is called, or in the ' unity of history.' On both these cardinal points I am to a certain extent a heretic. With regard to the former I need not say more than this, that I am averse to setting out ingenious and fanciful analogies as even guesses as to the way in which the world is led on from the worse to the better, and that independently of the agency of the church I can see no general progress of the kind in the world's history at all, nothing whatever that entitles us to regard the most advanced portion of mankind as representative of the whole race, the vast majority of nations and ages lying outside the sphere of the assumed process of the second. I may say a word more, because I was accused of having in my inaugural lecture neglected or despised a great truth, and also because the point lies close at the foundation of the subject we now have in hand. In my view as then expressed, the modern and ancient world are divided, and ancient and modern history set one against the other : in the opinion of my critics they are continuous, one of the chief links being the influence of the imperial idea of Rome.

Now, I do not for a moment dispute the continuity of many important influences, such as are describable under the general term of civilisation, including Grecian ideas of art, and the language and even the law of Rome ; but now, as then, I repeat that, firstly, the geographical area of modern history is for the most part outside of the geographical area of ancient history.   Rome and Greece are secondary and insignificant in the ages in which the chief place is occupied by England, France, Spain, and Germany ; and the Italy of modern Europe is a very different thing from the Italy of Roman times.   Secondly, I repeat that the actors in the drama of modern history are different from the ancient ; that. the nations are new to history at the opening of the new period, and that the main influences of their historical life are inherent in their own condition— are not derived from the continuous influences of the ancient world : the nations of modern history are new, and the chief characteristics of their history are their own, neither borrowed nor learned from the elder times.   But thirdly, and this I have always strongly insisted upon, the influence of Christianity, of the church, and Christian civilisation belongs far more to modern history than to ancient ; and in modern history it is one of the chief, if not in all respects the chief, ingredient.   In these three things, geographical area, national origin, and distinctive Christian civilisation, the world of modern history is self-contained, is divided from the old. Of course these things did not come into existence at the point of time at which modern history begins : Britain, Gaul, Spain, and Germany were portions of the known world, and the nations that come on the stage after the Christian era were known to the world before ; and the influence of the church itself, the spiritual process of successive dispensations which were leading up to the final one, were, or rather are, now traceable in the sacred history ; but for all that, the decision is a true one, and the distinction real for the purposes of study such as ours.   Nor is the continuity of the idea of Greek art and Roman law to be set in comparison for a moment with the entire novelty of scene, of action, and of influences which are what we have undertaken to examine.

Again, then, I say, our work of learning is here to deal with actual events, most efficient and powerful influences, and these are new, modern in every sense.   To take one example.   There can be no doubt that in many respects the ancient history of Greece affords parallels and analogies with modern history, especially in such constitutional questions as the formation of republics and the relations of sovereign and democratic or popular governments; and as men and aggregations of men are, whatever their actual history, amenable to limited sets and series of influences, there can be no difficulty in showing points in which modern and ancient institutions can be made to illustrate one another. But there is all the difference in the world between a casual coincidence or parallel such as might be traced between Carthage and Venice, for instance, however close the analogy, and a real case of recorded cause and effect. Even where, as in more modern times, the resuscitation of a political idea has really influenced the process of events, as we may imagine the mythical history of the Roman republic to have affected the actions of the founders of the mediæval Italian republics, or of the American republics, or even of the French revolutionary one, such an influence is itself a creation of the circumstances in which it finds room for itself; it is but an illustration, but a distant beacon fire which might have burned for ever and ever but for the existence of far stronger and innate influences which made the condition of things in which its usefulness became possible.

The freedom of modern Europe is based not on the freedom of Greece or Rome, but on the ancient freedom of the Teutonic nations, civilised, organised, and reduced to system by agencies of which Christianity and the system of the church are far the greatest and most important, in which the civilisation of later Rome is a minor influence, and that an influence apparent in the way of restriction rather than of liberation; in which the ancient philosophic freedom such as is exemplified in ancient Greece is an influence too infinitesimally small and remote to be worth calculating. And in general it seems to me that the bearing of the elder on the newer world was of this kind. I adduced this as an illustration: in reality it brings me to the point on which we are now going to set to work. If my principles are true, or even approximately true, or practicably useful for the study of one side even of modern history—and this much I may claim for them, I think, without gainsaying—we shall have to begin our study of the constitutional history of Europe with an investigation of the origins of the nations: that view we must illustrate by the history of their languages; and proceed through the history of their Christianising and progressive civilisation to the consideration of their common and written laws, their land system and their methods of government. The tracing of the changes, developments, or revolutions will form the main subject of the course, although I am not prepared to say that it will by itself occupy the largest number of lectures. I am induced to treat these questions in this way partly because I think that it may supply an element of life which is wanting in Hallam, and partly because it is to me the most fertile in interest, and that of a character not at present exhausted or likely to be so.

Now, no one can read Hallam without being sensible of two or three very astounding things ; in the first place, he deals with men and nations very much as if they were wooden figures pulled about by agencies and influences with which they themselves have very little to do. It may be that he was so deep a thinker that he took the distinctions of national origin and temperament for granted ; but if he did, it spoils the use of his work as a text-book. But it is more probable that he did not fully realise them—had not profited by the investigations of such writers as Palgrave, or even Allen and others whom he quotes so much, as at first sight would appear ; but in the second place he restricts, by giving so small a portion of his book to Spain and Germany, the interest of constitutional study altogether to England, France, and Italy ; while in his way of treating early English history he has shown his bias by giving to feudal history a share of attention not greater than it deserves, but out of all proportion to the importance of the earlier institutions, antecedent to feudalism, with which much that is of supreme importance in the mediæval constitutions is closely allied. Nor is there in Hallam any attempt at a comparison or generalisation on constitutional matters, except the most superficial and obvious ones between the effects of feudalism in England and France. Great as are our obligations to him, they are confined to the fact that he has brought together materials for generalisation. He has not even attempted the curious problem, how comes it that the barbarian nations, starting from very similar beginnings, and in possession of similar institutions, worked their way through not dissimilar histories to altogether different results in the way of government ; while others have arrived at a similar condition springing from different origins and disciplined by historical experiences which superficially viewed seem entirely dissimilar ?

This, then, is the theorem which we are going now to investigate ; and please to remember that we are going to attempt the task on an historical, not on a philosophical, plan ; to look at the facts as they are, not as they ought to be on the general laws of the science of history ; and that even in our abstractions and generalisations, when we shall draw off our attention from the points in which the histories we are comparing differ, concentrating it on those only in which they agree, we shall feel bound to adhere to historical, not merely theoretical, resemblances and connections, distinctions and differences. I shall not expect you to take what I say for gospel, but shall not overburden my text with authorities : authorities I shall be always ready to give when they are asked for. As to the

method, I shall not bind myself to either the synthetic or the
analytic ; but the latter will of course be the chief in an investigation naturally so short as can be given in a term's lectures to so large
a subject : several points will have, however, to be treated in direct
narration, and therefore synthetically. Illustrations, I fear, I can
only give through the medium of reference. As to proportion, if
I seem to give more than is requisite to the history of Spain and
Germany, you will understand that it is because these countries are
less clearly and exhaustively treated in our text-book, Hallam. I shall
then proceed to examine our subject in the following order.

First we shall ask what is the origin of the populations that,
within the ages we regard as the sphere of mediæval history, have
been known as the English, French, Spanish, and German nations ?
That question we shall treat with reference to both what history
records of these origins and also to the ordinary theories at present
in vogue about them, which theories in some cases, based on the
evidences of archæological conjecture, must either be met with sound
reference to existing authorities, or be left in suspension until new
data turn up. From this I shall proceed, secondly, to the question
of language as illustrating the historical origin, and show how that
which is puzzling and perplexing in the relations of language to
nationality may be cleared up by the plain reading of history with
ever so little recourse to conjectural causes. The third point to be
discussed will be the variety of sources from which the mediæval nations received the gospel and civilisation in union with
Christianity : we shall see how the source affected the full flow of
the stream, and how the church affected the state in various ways
determinable by the character of the initial source. The fourth
point will be the investigation of the origin of the laws or legal
system of the four typical nations ; in which I shall, in brief outline, attempt to give the relative amounts of barbarian, Roman, and
feudal law that are to be found in the mediæval law books, and to
draw some generalisations as to the ways in which they are developments and expressions of the genius of the several nations, or super-
strata imposed by conquest or imitation, or adaptations by the
national spirit of such superstratum when it has been laid over the
original customs of the race, which in time have had strength and
opportunity to grow through and assimilate that which was
adventitious. Fifthly, I shall attempt to show how the tenure of
land, the base of the great mediæval constitutions, varied in the
different nations and in different ages of the same ; how the mixture
of the two great tenures in different quantities affected the political
history, and how the constitutional history altogether springs out of
their combinations and oppositions. I shall try to show what

characteristics, moral and legal, belong to the two systems of tenure, historically and theoretically, and thence how the political or constitutional history varies with the working of those characteristics. We shall then look into the position of the sovereign as he was in the earlier and later middle ages, more especially with reference to his making and unmaking, his election, and the means by which his responsibility to his subjects for good government was secured.

In the following lectures I shall work out the constitution of the national council, first as to its powers, and secondly as to its constituents. The last lecture I shall devote to the question of judicature and a general summing-up of the course. You will observe that in this arrangement I have taken it for granted that there are a few very distinct and pronounced factors or ingredients, on the proportions of whose combinations the variations in the history of these nations largely depend : the land and the landless, the noble and the non-noble, the town and the country, the indigenous and the foreign, the Roman and the Teuton, the allodial and the feudal, the nation at home and the nation abroad, the nation heathen and the nation Christian, the power spiritual and the power temporal. On the working of these factors constitutional history is based ; but outside of these there is a great field of investigation, not the mere history of the factors and the proportions of their combinations, but how the factors come to be what they are, and how they are mixed in the proportions in which our survey of results sees them. This great field is that of political or general as opposed to, or rather as in itself distinct from, constitutional history ; and indeed it might, if our constitutional history could be made at all an adequate view of facts, be called the analytic, while the political would be the synthetic history of the same set of things. In this idea I should have been glad if I could, as I have done in the course of English and German history, have included within the scope of the series all that is essential in history, excepting wars and fightings and treaties. Almost everything else either belongs to the internal or constitutional side of history, or may be treated in illustration of it. Even wars and fightings and peaces sometimes are worth tracing in this view, as the constraining causes of internal movements, either by way of taxation, or of the levying of armies, or of the political action of parliaments. But, upon consideration, I found at once that this was impossible, and that at least four terms' lectures would be required for even the most scanty exhibition of such a design.

I have therefore, as I said before, without lending myself to either plan exclusively, drawn up this course on a comparative and therefore analytic plan, which will, I trust, serve as a programme for those who are beginning Hallam, and as a help to the critical understanding

of his real value, and of the relation of the different portions of his
'History of the Middle Ages,' while those who have read their Hallam
will be able to criticise me, and, comparing my views with their
own derived from him or from elsewhere, get new lights on the more
general and wider portions of the great field before them.   It would
indeed be a very valuable work if some of our historical writers
would, as Sir Francis Palgrave began to do, take the history of any
one of the four typical nations and show how its great features were
really developed.   It stands to reason that the form of government
into which a nation has educated itself must be the expression of the
natural spirit and genius of that nation ; supposing always that the
nation has had a free development, has not been tyrannised over and
brutalised by the dominion of another far greater than itself.   We
might almost say that where this has been so, the result has brought
out the weakness as well as the strength of the particular national
spirit.   Take Ireland for instance, where the national genius has
been, as it says, oppressed by centuries of English tyranny, by a little
over-nursing, and by constant misrule.   Notwithstanding the tyranny,
the over-nursing, and the misrule, the Irish spirit is unassimilated ;
it is not certainly what it would have been had it been left alone.
Foreign dominion has been one very influential factor in its history ;
it has brought out its bad points most certainly, and it has not less
certainly, if we would take pains to investigate it, brought out the
good.

On the relations of Hungary to Austria, and of Bohemia to
Germany generally, you may draw distinct conclusions.   In Hungary
neither race, or rather none of the three races, has been able to
extinguish the other ; in Bohemia, although it has been part of
Germany for nearly a thousand years, we see in these days the Czech
distinct in language : we know that three centuries ago there was
every probability that he would be distinct in religion ; and we can
with a little guessing foresee that, small as his nation now is, he
will not long be content without making a struggle for a distinct
political existence, and perhaps a distinct political system from that
of his neighbours.   But this is not the case in any of the four
nations that we shall discuss now.   In all the four, whatever may
have been the original elements, we have arrived at an amalgamation
which is equivalent to a new identity.   The Spaniard is a Spaniard,
the Englishman an Englishman, the Frenchman a Frenchman, and
the German a German ; his national character may or may not be
resolvable into conjectural elements, and it may be read different
ways according to the particular prejudice with which we approach
the study of it, but there is no question about the perfect amalgamation, there is no difference in England proper between Celt and

Roman, Briton, Saxon, Angle, Jute, Dane, or Norman ; nor in France between Celt, Aquitanian, Belgian, Frank, Visigoth, and Norman. The population is one, and the constitution, although its history requires investigation into its origins, is also one.   As for the modern character of the several nations, we may, I think, add that it also is one ; but we must not forget that it is as much indebted to the historic training it has received as the line of constitutional development is to it.

National character may be regarded as the result of national history, or national history as the development of national character ; either way we cannot fail to recognise the closest connection between the two.   Now, of all the evidence that can be taken, and that we shall attempt to take in this course, of the actual origin of each nation and of the persistence of the original character, by far the most clear and decisive are the customs of common law.   These customs spring out of the first movements of the race towards social and civilised life ; although not recorded in books, they are the most ancient portion of its lore, but they are not the earliest monuments of its literature.   They are indeed often not written at all until they are becoming obsolete, until the use of them is less absolutely necessary, and oral tradition in danger of dying out.   In the relics we have of the earliest unwritten jurisprudence, it may be we have only small portions of a much wider subject-matter ; but it may also be that, as nations feeling their way to a civilisation of their own take only short steps and use but little apparatus, we have a very large proportion of the whole.   And as the more closely we trace the origins of the modern nations, or say simply of the Teutonic elements in them, the more surely we come upon a few everywhere, and those common customs, I think we may fairly infer that these are nearly all that there is to know.   The modes of proving guilt and innocence, the modes of transferring or holding land, the assemblies of the tribe for counsel, for judicial work, or for military expeditions : these are common to the race, and they involve almost all the law that is needed by races in the condition in which we first find them.

But how about their persistency ?   Of course by their persistency I do not mean their absolute conservation—to expect that would be to expect a perpetual barbarism.   But I do mean that the changes and adaptations which the warm air of civilisation invites and necessitates should be developments from the original institution, should not be something merely mechanically added to it.   Train your plant in a particular way, if you please ; graft upon it, if you like, institutions which, because of their common and radical identity, there is no difficulty in adapting and making fruitful by the adaptation ; but do not hollow out your apple tree and make a tulip bed of the trunk, and then call the tulips a persistent growth from the apple stock. The English nation was at one time greatly in danger of having this done to it, but happily the tulip roots rotted, and the apple trunk put forth new branches and leaves and fruit. We might almost, I think, say that in the case of the thoroughly Romanised races of ancient Europe the process did take effect, and both perished together; but in England the old customs really continued, and new ones were developed out of them as the ages went on, and new occasions arose, and they showed their persistency and their vitality by taking new forms and bearing more abundant practical fruit.

Now, where there is this persistency and vitality of common law customs, this historical development of the new out of the old, we are surely very strongly tempted to argue a close connection between nationality of character and nationality of custom; and as there can be no question but that judicial machinery has been historically the training apparatus of constitutional working, we are equally tempted to discover in the constitutional development the characteristics of the national spirit : if persistent, strong and vital ; if much changed, pliant and feeble ; if altogether effaced, either too weak to live or crushed to death by some great affliction. It is, perhaps, natural to look for a greater degree of freedom, and therefore a more regular and natural development of these customs, this national spirit and character, where there has been less foreign interference, and therefore the purest breed, the most insulated history, will exhibit them in their most orderly growth ; and we are therefore inclined to ascribe to the strength of the character somewhat that might be as justly attributed to the freedom of the developments. In such cases one cannot be too cautious, but also one must not be too critical; of course the strongest plant will grow the most freely, and of course the plant which has the most liberty to grow in will prove the strongest. Our freedom may be indebted to the vitality and persistency of our primæval customs, or their persistency and vitality may be a consequence in some measure of our liberty of free growth; but for all that, if on examining more customs we find that they are in themselves, and not merely accidentally, akin to freedom ; if we place them side by side with those of other races of distinct origin and character, and without denying to those other races the credit which they claim, and which on the verdict of history they deserve, see that they really are based on a sounder principle of liberty and equality before the law, and on a clearer sense of a man's responsibility for his own acts, and on a fairer provision for the security of life and property than the other, we are bound to regard them as having the root of the matter in themselves. Nor shall I be going so far as to anticipate what I shall have to lay before you by and by

if I say now that I do trace in the old Teutonic system more germs
of real liberty than I can in the Celtic system, so far as we know it,
or in the Sclavonic, or in the Roman itself, with respect, be it said,
to all those who find nothing in civilisation that is not Roman.   I
do think that in the free tenure of land, the fixed obligations of
allodialism, the relation of the freeman to history as the impersonation of the race, the combination of the frankpledge, nay, I will add
the compurgation and the ordeal and the *wergild*, is to be found a
more likely basis of freedom than in the community of land, the close
tie of patriarchal or family unity, the enormous and disproportionate
estimate of blood nobility, and the clannish spirit that one finds in
the Highland Scot and Irishman, or in the Pole or Hungarian.

Of course you will understand there are two sorts of freedom ;
when I speak of these institutions as more akin, and the others as
less akin, to freedom, I do not mean that the Scot or Irishman
would fight for his country less bravely, determinately, or obstinately
than the Englishman, the Spaniard, or the German.   The love of
one's country's independence is one thing, the vital necessity of
political freedom is another.   One man will fight for his country,
another will fight for his master, another for the head of his house,
another for the one who pays him best, and all honestly and comparatively with honour.   But the Englishman and the German,
when they are fighting for their country, know and feel that they
are fighting for themselves, and even here the two sorts of freedom
show that they are very close akin.   The freedom that we contend
for as springing from our ancient free customs is, then, not freedom
from external control merely, but a freedom for internal development
and unfettered action, unfettered, that is, but by just laws and a
sound sense of responsibility : laws which are just because they are
accepted by those whom they rule as their own laws, which they and
their fathers have made and proved, and altered when they wanted
altering, and known by long experience to be good and fair to all ;
and a sound sense of responsibility, based on a knowledge of the
law, and a conviction of its fair dealing and experience of its honest
execution : influences which are no small powers in the training of
an active conscience, although they cannot supply the vital principle
of the active conscience when unhappily it is wanting.   These
remarks perhaps are more fitting for the conclusion than the
beginning of a course which will have in it little to relieve the
technicalities of the subject, but it is fair that you should know
my views at starting.

[*See Maitland,* 'Domesday Book and Beyond'; Round, '*Feudal
England*'; Stubbs,' Constitutional History,' *vol. i.;* Stubbs,' *Historical
Introductions to the Rolls Series,' ed. by A. Hassall.*]

X

THE ELEMENTS OF NATIONALITY AMONG EUROPEAN NATIONS

AT the very outset of our inquiry we are met by the common initial difficulty of all historical research. Naturally our first step is to determine, or to attempt to determine, the elements of the nationality of the several nations of Europe whose development we are studying, during the period of this development; and the main elements we shall have no difficulty in identifying. Nor perhaps will there be much that is problematical in the discovery of the process of civilisation in its main current and in its most pronounced influences. But we cannot wisely set aside the earlier question. None of the great nations of mediæval Europe can be said in the strictest sense to be indigenous; even the Germans, although within historic times Germany has always been German, have moved so much about the territory which bears their name that scarcely a tribe can be said to remain in the same seat in which we find it at the beginning of history. And as for England, France, Spain, and Italy, we know that a series of waves of conquest has passed over them, double, triple, and sometimes even still more complex. We cannot doubt that the earlier inhabitants of these lands had manners and customs and laws, as they had a language of their own. And yet we know of them from history only the names by which the Roman geographers called them, and have to elaborate from the scanty and uncertain data of archæology the details of their differences, their progress from the period of stone to that of bronze, and from that of bronze to that of iron; or the growth of the several tribes from hunting to pastoral, from pastoral to agricultural pursuits.

At every stage of such an inquiry we are met by tempting paths of research, each and all of which end after a few windings in the same perplexing obstacle. We cannot doubt that in each country the process of conquest and reconstitution involved a displacement of the original people and its civilisation, approaching at various degrees to, but in all cases stopping short of, complete extermination. Some relics of primeval custom must have been left, as some inter-mixture of indigenous blood must be allowed on any theory to have followed every wave of conquest or of change. We ask in vain how far had the original genius of the primeval races developed before it was overrun by the barbarism of a conquest, or forced into assimi-lation by the process of foreign civilisation. We ask in vain how far could the development of the genius of Celt or Cantabrian have advanced towards civilisation had it not been forced into the common groove of Roman customs, or what would have been the character of its civilisation, its arts and literature—for Celts and Cantabrians as well as Chinese and Japanese had arts and something like a literature —had it not been forced to bow before the transcendental but adven-titious genius of Rome and Greece and the more ancient sources in the East. We ask the questions, I repeat, in vain. We are forced to content ourselves with a few generalisations, or to sacrifice, as we cannot now do, the real practical lessons of history to the minutiæ of archæology. We have not time for both. We set out with two generalisations : one that, whatever were the actual developments of the primeval races, or whatever their possible ones might have been, they all had in common a defect or want of what we, educated by modern institutions, term civilisation proper, they were without the institutions of historical civilisation, they were in common barbarian ; the second that, whatever may be the proportion in which the blood of a primeval race is intermingled with that of the conquering or colonising race, and in whatever measure the manners and customs of the one may affect and modify those of the other, that must, for the purposes of constitutional history at least, be counted the paternal element of the race, whose laws, language, religion, customs, and institutions have succeeded in the historical period in working themselves to the chief place of importance in the national polity by an historical, not a philosophical or adventitious, process.

A people of German elements may be leavened largely by Celtic or Slavonic infusions ; but if, in spite of those infusions, the Ger-man element in language, law, and custom succeeds in winning for itself by historical steps the first place in the constitution of that people, I claim it as German, and German as the paternal element. If Roman or Celt has done the same, then that nation is of Roman or Celtic origin paternally and in the main. But, of course, I am not so foolish as to attempt so to determine the elements of a nationality or of an empire which is not thoroughly amalgamated. The German may be the strongest element in Hungary, and the English in Ireland, but the Hungarian population is not, strictly speaking, a nation, but a congeries of races, German, Slavonic, and Magyar.

Ireland is Celtic, notwithstanding the prevalence of Teutonic institutions and the intermixture of English blood. And I add that the prominence of the paternal element must have been won, not by a single measure or by a succession of separate measures, but by a steady continuance of custom and growth of principle. A Celtic nation may be conceived as adopting by one legislative act a German constitution, but that does not make it German. A German nation may, by successive developments and modifications, so vary its ancient programme that it can hardly be recognised as identical, except by painful antiquarian investigation, but it does not therefore lose one jot of its original Teutonism. This is not an unimportant point to remember, as we shall see, especially when we come to talk about feudalism.

There is all the difference in the world between a home-grown and an adventitious institution, as illustrating or illustrated by the subject of nationality. It will, however, not be lost time if, as we attempt to determine the national origin of our great peoples, we look by the way at the races that preceded them in their present seats, and point out their comparative degrees and sources of civilisation. As I said in the last lecture, I am not one who is tempted to exaggerate these influences. Modern civilisation is the work of Christianity, and has inherited nothing from ancient civilisation except what Christianity has gathered up into itself and preserved. Ancient civilisation, as we read history, springs from the East, whence Greece and even Carthage and Egypt believed themselves to have drawn the elements which, as modified by them in turn, were spread over the West, even before the iron sway of Rome forced Europe to accept her laws and institutions as supreme. Egyptian and Phoenician civilisation had reached Spain, and perhaps Britain, before the Roman—had modified the indigenous growth before they were themselves overpowered and assimilated or annihilated by that of the universal empire. But for our subject these things lie very remote: as, when our work begins, the Roman civilisation is falling before barbarism, as the earlier civilisation and earlier barbarism had fallen before it. Christianity brings a new life to the new races, and a new beginning to the world's history. Still, it is not wise to overlook these deep and most ancient differences.

Of the four nations to which we shall have most particularly to direct our attention I shall take the German first, then the English, then the French, speaking by the way of Italy, and last the Spanish. We shall try to determine two points: first, the nationality of the historical nation; secondly, its final settlement in its historical seat. 1. Of Germany I might content myself by saying that it always has been German. Various as are the differences between the accounts of Cæsar and Tacitus, and the scattered notices of the other Roman writers, they are all traceable to a series of developments or to varieties of developments in a race that continues substantially the same.   The Germans doubtless came in prehistoric times from the East westward, according to what may be regarded as the normal process of migration. Before them there were perhaps a Gaulish people, or some forgotten stock that fell before a short wave of Gaulish migration as the Gauls pressed on with the Germans behind them ; such a race as may have furnished the lake dwellers of Switzerland and the earliest war-riors of the flint arrows and hatchets.   In historic times modern criticism gives Germany entirely to the Germans ; engaged in war-fare often enough with the Gauls on the West, pressed on, and sometimes even hardly pressed, by Slavonic races all along the eastern frontier ; subject to invasions from Gaul, Roman, Slav, Turk, and Tartar, but gradually, or at once, repelling the foreign element, and revindicating to themselves all the territory in its widest acceptation known as German.

In more ancient times, as the same modern criticism now decrees, the Teutonic race must have covered a far larger extent of territory eastward ; the Getæ and the Daci, even the Thracians, were akin in origin to the modern people, the Getæ and the Goths ; the Daci and the Danes seem to have an original relation in nomen-clature and affinity at least of origin.   The student of Grimm will be able to adduce from the fragmentary notices of ancient writers a mass of vocabulary proving the kindredship of a language of the tribes known by these names.   So far forth, then, the Germany of the middle ages has always been Teutonic, but the conformation of its territories and the location of its several tribes have varied, the former from conquest and the latter from migration.   Its frontiers have been readjusted from age to age, east, west, and south, as they have been pressed on by Slav, by Gaul, France, or by Rome herself, for eighteen centuries, from the times of Cæsar to the congress of Vienna.   Since, however, the settlement of the nations, which may be placed roughly between the ninth and eleventh centuries, these variations of the frontier have been small, and diplomatic rather than national.   But the interior of Germany has been very variously re-arranged within and on both sides of that period, and to attempt an exhaustive account of those rearrangements would be work for years. I shall not meddle with it now further than it affects general or tribal nationality.

Germany at the moment that it became united politically was arranged in four nations, and this arrangement may be very usefully retained in the whole investigation of its history.   The four are the Saxons, the Bavarians, the Alemanni or Swabians, and the Franks ;

the fifth nation, the Lotharingians, is a political rather than a tribal creation, and it falls to pieces in time, losing itself in the kindred races out of which it was formed. Of these four the Saxons cover the north of Germany from the Rhine eastward, and southward as far as Hesse and Thuringia; the Bavarians extend from the river Lech to the eastern frontier, southward to the Alps, northward to the same border nations. The Franks occupy the northern half of Western Germany along the Rhine as far as the Main; south of the Main and west of the Lech are the Alemanni, the northern half of the Alemannian country becomes Frank. Now, all these are new names, or if not new, of new application. The races that bore them were confederations of tribes that earlier bore a different name, and they had migrated considerably before they reached their modern seats. The Franks appear in history first in the time of the Emperor Gallienus; they are already too strong to allow the supposition that they are a new people; they are doubtless races allied under the name of Freemen. The Alemanni, also a confederation of the tribes that had earlier borne the name of Suevi, and later fulfilled their mission under that of Swabians, appear to have been driven south in the time of Caracalla. The Bavarians also were the ancient Marcomanni, who had moved south through Bohemia into the modern Bavaria, pressed on behind by the Czechs and Wends, and displacing the Boii, who left their name to both Bohemia and Bavaria. The Saxons were a confederacy of northern and eastern Teutons moving on before the Wends.

I do not intend to pursue these tribes into the minutiæ of their migrations, as I did in the course of lectures on German history. These are the four historic nations of Germany: the little tribes such as the Thuringians, Hessians, Lusatians, and Misnians, themselves perhaps reconstitutions of the Elderenes, which lay between these greater ones, were politically unimportant in comparison with them, and were perhaps more anciently settled in their present seats; but there is no question of nationality among them. Their language, history, and laws, are all akin, are all German; nor do they affect the main current of German history otherwise than as slightly varying by their adhesion or separation the balance of power existing between the greater races.

How to account for these migrations is the one remaining point. The devastations of Roman conquest created a vacuum southwards, and the pressure of Slavonic tribes from the north and east forced the Teutonic races into that vacuum: a process repeated when the Gothic, the Lombard, and other barbarian conquerors had overrun and deserted the intervening spaces. So we have until the final settlement a constant pressure southwards and westwards. The

Alemanni settle in the *agri limitanei* of the Roman veterans, pressed south as far as Speyer; the Bavarians are settled in Bavaria by Theodoric as a counterpoise to the Franks; the Franks themselves, consistently though with varying degrees of earnestness allies of Rome, gain settlement and recognition from the emperors until they are strong enough to take their place. The Saxons only, unsubdued and enthralled by no engagements, are independent and self-dependent until the German power is itself becoming Christian, and preparing for its great mission of reconstructing Christendom and founding the new civilisation.

I have said on this, perhaps, more than enough already, but I must repeat that in German history there is no occasion to look for any other tribal element than the German. The race is pure, and although it may not from diverse circumstances be the Teutonic nation which develops with the most purity the original institutions of the stock, that result, if it be a fact, must be attributed to political and historical causes other than the influence of blood and race. It is to its association with the empire, and to a history which never succeeded in blending into one a congeries of tribes, one in origin and laws, but one also in a spirit of independence so strong that it refuses to coalesce even with its most close affinities: there were times when it might have been so, but the hand that should have done it was not there, and a national German unity has never been realised, nor, although it seems perhaps nearer now than it has often seemed before, can it be regarded as a certainty even in the future of which it is so strongly predicted. So far, however, as Germany is concerned, we have not to take into calculation the influence in blood, law, or custom of any antecedent races occupying the same soil; the only intrusive element is, as I said before, the Roman, which, however great as regards law and politics, is, and can be, held only in an infinitesimal degree to affect the blood of the race.

It is true that on each frontier of Germany there is, and has been for ages, an intermixture of German with foreigner, and a variation in language and physique as the German or Italian, German or Frenchman, German or Slav or Wend, has predominated in the mixed people. But this has only remotely affected politics, these border lands being held generally by the German princes with a strong hand. There are differences in this respect: German and Italian, or German and French, blend sooner, it would seem, than German and Slav; hence the Italian border varies, and the frontier has a mixed population, German in name, Italian in language, or *vice versa*. But the antagonism in Bohemia and Hungary between the German and the Slav seems to last, or to create at least a strong mark of separation. Hence the difficulties of Austrian and

Prussian governments, and the sad history early and late of Poland. But I have said enough about this, and can only repeat that it is from Roman influences that we have to expect the principal disturbances of the regular development of Teutonic institutions in the Fatherland itself.

2. We will proceed secondly to England, of which I have ventured to affirm that it is the country in which the Teutonic genius has most freely developed, notwithstanding the intermixture of the blood and the disturbances of foreign influences. And here the proposition that I have to lay down is briefly this : that the main and paternal stock from which the English and their constitution spring is Teutonic : Teutonic in source, as from the Angles, Saxons, and Jutes of the first conquest; and Teutonic in the additional streams poured in from subsequent invasions by the Danes and Normans, who, although by their different history and discipline they were made at the time of their introduction into England to exhibit an antagonism in language and institutions to the earlier stock, showed by the ease with which they mingled with it, and the rapidity with which within a century and a half they returned to it, that they were originally closely akin. In intermixing with the English the Dane within a very few years cast off all that was Scandinavian, and the Norman retained in some few departments of language only what he had contracted during two centuries of a French home and apprenticeship to French institutions. The Teutonic is the paternal element in the English race, as shown in physique, in language, in law, and custom. This is my firm conclusion. I need not tell you that it is one which has been and is still fiercely contested, nor could I lecture on the subject ever so superficially without devoting some time to argument on the points.

One or two topics I must put aside as too minute and remote from our general subject to be considered now, although in themselves of importance, especially the question to what extent was the British population before the great wave of Saxon conquest intermingled with German races from the opposite coast : were the Roman legionaries who occupied and may have helped in peopling Britain any of them of German origin ? Were the Belgæ or the Coritavi of Britain akin to the German or half-German tribes that are said to have borne similar names abroad, or were the pirates of the Saxon shore tenants or only depredators of the British coast? If these be answered one way, they strengthen my argument ; if they be answered the other, they do not weaken it. To constitutional history in the remotest way they cannot be said to belong. Between them and the Anglo-Saxon system spreads the wave of Roman occupation.

Granted, then, that Britain when we first hear of it was inhabited

by a race of Celts, to whom, perhaps, the name of Cymru is the
proper tribal name, and who were broken up into little states,
bearing names most of which are capable of reference to Celtic
roots ; that this race, partly by its own development, partly by commerce with the civilised nations of the Mediterranean and partly by
intercourse with semi-civilised Gaul, had arrived before the Roman
invasion at a sort of rude semi-civilisation which kept its enemies at
bay ; that it was subjugated by Rome with that cunning and cruelty
which marked all Roman aggression, and when conquered consolidated with that strong and kind policy that marks as distinctively
the hold which Rome maintained where she was certain that she had
conquered ; granted that when, in the decay of Rome, Britain was
deserted by those who had defended and developed her, she was left
with a mixed population and semi-Romanised institutions to work
out her destiny alone ; granting all this, what does history tell us
followed ? Like the other provinces of the empire, deserted by the
legionaries and incapacitated by long tutelage from self-defence,
this province lay open to the attacks of the barbarians of the land
and sea—to the Picts and Scots on the north and west, to the pirates
of Germany on the east. The ravages of the Picts and Scots
depopulated a country void of the power of defence. The immigration of the Angles, Saxons, and Jutes repeopled the desolate country,
and perhaps advanced even a step further the extermination of
the Britons. The Britons are driven gradually and at historic
dates westward ; their cities for the most part become deserts, and,
if not destroyed, are lost among the forests of the Anglo-Saxon
dominion. Their Christianity disappears all along the eastern half
of Britain, so does their language, so do their territorial boundaries,
so in a great measure the nomenclature of towns, rivers, and
hills. The pertinacity with which these things have maintained
their hold on the western side of Britain for 1,400 years, during
which the Welsh language and its local nomenclature have stood out
against English aggression, showing the strength and vitality of
the race as they do, show with it its utter extermination in those
regions where it has finally disappeared. I confess that I do not see
how such an argument can be answered.

If British elements continued to exist in the eastern half of
England after the Anglo-Saxon conquest, they were so small that
history knows nothing about them. Of course, in the west, along
the frontiers of what is now Wales and England, there was a greater
predominance of the ancient race, and more intermixture of blood.
The West Saxon kingdom, for instance, in Cornwall and Somerset,
included a large British population, and received Christianity in some
measure from it. But it was otherwise eastward, and what is more

it was otherwise in the main current. The main power was with the Teutonic race : they redivided the land, they renamed the towns and villages and rivers and mountains ; they accepted Christianity from a distinct source, not from the Britons ; they developed their own institutions without any mixture of aboriginal influence, and worked out the problem of liberty for themselves : it is from them that we have our language, our constitution, our names, and as I believe, for the most part, our blood. This theory of the repopulation of Britain by the English demands as its complement the further assertion, that the process was not one of mere conquest, but of colonisation, nay, of immigration rather, on the part of the new people. And such I believe to have been the case.

I believe, first, that the new names given by the Angles and Saxons to their new settlements are distinctly family or Gentile names, and simply the migration of a portion of the family in its integrity with wives and children. And I believe that the honour given to women among the ancient German races, although it was not such as to preclude the custom of polygamy and of concubinage, was still so vital an institution among them that it would preclude any indiscriminate intermingling with the subject race, supposing that subject race to have supplied material enough for a repopulation. I do not think that the Angles and Saxons are likely either to have married British wives, or to have admitted the children of British concubines to an equality of right, or to a share in the name and privileges of the race. Nor do I think that the Britons, proud and averse to intercourse with their masters as we know them to have been, would have endured an intermixture so degrading. It is, however, perhaps enough to say for it that it has no historical warrant. As soon as we find Angles and Saxons in Britain at all, we find their women with them. A woman, Rowena, plays as great a part in the traditionary history as do Hengist and Horsa : as soon as the country is settled we find princesses and abbesses in all their German dignity; but far more than this we rely on the tribal and family organisation as exhibited in the names of places and in the primeval institutions of the race transplanted in their integrity.

This is, then, a brief outline of the affirmative argument. It is capable of much corroboration ; it would be enough to insist on the point of primeval custom as showing the main constituent, the leading influence. But because it is so ardently controverted it must be examined from the other side. In opposition to it there are two considerable sets of arguments, for Mr. Matthew Arnold's ingenious attempt at the recognition of a Celtic element in our poetry as contrasted with that of Germany proper I set aside as simply an elegant theory, a peg for hanging clever criticisms, but unprovable and of no great importance if proved, for no one can doubt that there must be some intermixture of blood and constitution in races which have dwelt side by side for 1,400 years. That is not the question ; it is whether there is enough intermixture to make it reasonable to affirm that the characteristics of the English and their genius and development are largely indebted to such an intermixture.

The two lines of argument are marshalled in two books, ' The Origin of the English : a Prologue to English History,' by Mr. Lewis Pike ; and 'A Neglected Fact in English History,' by Mr. Coote. I say two lines, not because the train of thought is different, but because the two books supplement one another. Mr. Coote is strongest where Mr. Pike is weakest, and *vice versa*. Mr. Coote's arguments rest on the proportion of the influence of Roman law on the Anglo-Saxon system ; he attempts to trace all the distinctive features of Anglo-Saxon law to the civil law of Theodosius and Justinian ; and from that infers that Britain retained enough of the system of the earlier conquerors to leaven the whole policy of the newer race ; that the vast majority of the population during the Anglo-Saxon period was British or Romano-British ; that the Anglo-Saxon invasion was simply the assault of an armed post, of limited numbers but preponderating power ; that these succeeded in forming a sort of military oligarchy, not mingling with the subject people ; that these Romano-Britons continued Christian, and that to this may be ascribed the rapidity with which the missions of the seventh century are related to have accomplished their work, the real work done being simply the conversion of the kings, who were more than half converted by Franco-Gallican intercourse already. Such are the really monstrous conclusions of the book : so monstrous, so dead in the teeth of recorded history, that one is tempted to regard the argument as a joke, but that it is really supported with learning and acuteness, and supplies considerable matter for thought in its own strong line—that of law—which I shall examine in a subsequent lecture.

Mr. Pike's book is much less chimerical in its conclusions, and more moderate in its tone ; but I believe that it is, so far as its arguments are true, unimportant, and in the main line of its argument erroneous. I shall not analyse it, but say that its principal arguments are founded on physical phenomena, on the psychological analysis of the Celt and the Englishman, and on language ; that the most is made of the few historical particulars which seem to favour the writer's theory ; and that the argument does barely touch our great point, the customs of common law and polity. The question of language will come before us later ; the general sense of history seems to me to be what I have stated already; the arguments from physical and psychological analysis are too wide to enter upon in detail, but I must say, once for all, that all arguments of this kind, if they are to be applied to history at all, must be applied historically, and involve a great number of points which are historical as well as many that are physical.

In the first place, take any given skull, or any given brain, and determine which you will say are the German and which the Celtic elements in it. But you do not know the history of the owner by merely looking at it; true, his remote ancestors may have been mainly Celts, quite as probable that his grandmother was Welsh or Irish. You must know the pedigree of your skull before you conclude on its relative proportions, and infer its remote origin from them. And, in the second place, you cannot argue there are more black-eyed men than blue-eyed men in England, and more blue-eyed than black-eyed in Germany, therefore the English are Celts and not Teutons, until you have determined that the causes, physical and other, the air of the country, the nature of the food, the iron or other ingredients of the water, which Englishmen have been breathing, eating, and drinking for 1,400 years alongside with Welshmen, may not have produced in them the same physical conformation which it produces in the Celt, and which the German, with different food and water, does not experience. But it is impossible to argue on such data seriously; nor is there any nation in Europe of which physical uniformity can be predicated, or of which the ruling type, if there be one, is not broken so often by intermixture, that it is impossible to distinguish with certainty which is the rule and which the exception.

We have considered, so far as seems necessary to our main purpose, the question of the nationality of the two German-speaking races with whose institutions we have now to do. Our next task is to discuss the three Latin-speaking nationalities—the French, the Italian, and the Spanish, putting off, however, for the moment, the subject of the language. The theory in question is that the Angles and Saxons were a mere handful of military adventurers who succeeded in engrossing all political power in Britain, while the bulk of the population, Romanised Celts or Britons, subsisted continuously, gradually absorbed the German conquerors, and were the progenitors of the historic English, the people of the middle ages and our own selves; this being so, not only the influence of the original settlers, but that of the Norsemen and Danes and Normans, also Teutonic by race, becomes reduced to a minimum. The present English would be Celts or Britons mainly, with various infusions of Teutonic blood. The conversion of England in the seventh century was but the conversion of the chieftains. Now this theory, which appears to me to be with regard to England the wildest chimera, is to a large extent true with respect to France.

3. In France, as we shall see, the Teutonic conquerors only very partially mingled with the inhabitants of the subjugated provinces ; and those provinces were inhabited by Celts, brought under the sway, and civilised and Christianised under the influence, of Rome. There were, in fact, in France exactly the conditions assumed by the theory that I am combating to have been present in England : a large substratum of Celtic blood, a superficies of Roman education, a dislocating and disturbing superior flux, as we may call it, of German conquerors. This is *historical*, not theoretical, *in France*. If it were the case in England as in France, from the same elements the same results ought to have proceeded, the elements being *ex hypothesi* in about the same proportion. But there can be no greater contrast physically or mentally than the average Englishman and the average Frenchman ; therefore, what is true of the origin of the one is not likely to be true of that of the other. Or if the differences are to be ascribed to the climate, the food, the water, and other incidents of the country, then are all arguments that tend to disprove the Teutonic origin of the English based on the variety of physique &c. to be answered in the same way. I do not see how this dilemma is open to the usual answer, the *tertium quid*, unless you suppose a difference of proportion in the two or three ingredients in the respective races ; and if that be done, it reduces the question between us to one of local differences and variations, about which it is scarcely worth while, as a question of history, to argue at all.

Putting aside, however, the theory, let us look at the history of the French. I need hardly remind you that existing France has not a geographical unity, such as England, Spain, and even Italy, have. It has on the whole north and east but a conventional boundary, one that has varied largely, and may vary still more. It is thus one of the youngest political formations if we regard its territory, although it may be nearly the oldest state in Europe ; for its whole eastern side was within a few centuries a portion of the empire ; its northern boundary is settled by a more ancient arrangement, but by one which has no confirming warrant in the natural features of the soil ; and of the south, a large part was, during most of the middle ages, Spanish, Italian, and German by affinity, and can scarcely be said to have become permanently a part of France before the middle ages close.

Whoever may have been the inhabitants of France—and we will use the word in its loosest application just now—before the Gauls, we must leave for the archæologists to settle. We know from Greek and Roman history that the Gauls were a strong and warlike people four centuries before the Christian era, and although they may then have been in migration and not have fully and permanently occupied the country that they covered in the time of Cæsar, we have no reason to doubt that they were the identical race which that conqueror found in the Gallia which he describes as divided between Aquitania, Belgica, and Celtica. We have but few data as to the differences between the inhabitants of these three divisions; but we may argue from the name of the Aquitani, as well as from their subsequent history, that they were akin to the inhabitants of the Spanish peninsula, or intermingled with the Iberian races; of the Celts of the centre we may safely conclude that they were less mingled with border races, however much they may have modified their characteristics by mixture with the incalculable because unfixable earlier element; and as to the north, the Belgic portion, bordering as it did on a distinctly German population, and becoming as it did in historic times the stronghold of the Frankish kingdom, it may be fairly presumed that if not of Teutonic stock, as has been sometimes suggested, the Belgæ were somewhat intermixed with the Batavi and other hardly distinguishable Teutonic tribes who lived on the south of the Rhine and the Meuse. I think it is clear that the Belgæ were Gallic in the time of Cæsar, and as we have no other guide to follow, it would be manifestly unsafe to argue on the supposition that they ever were anything else but Celtic in the wider application of the name.

Well, the Romans conquered Gaul, this *omnis Gallia*, from the Rhine to the Alps, the Pyrenees, and the sea; the France, that is, of modern French aspirations, if not of future history, certainly not of the past; and when they had conquered it they subdivided it on a theory of their own into several provinces, Aquitania, Narbonensis, Lugdunensis prima, secunda, tertia, and quarta, Belgica prima and secunda, Germania prima and secunda, and Maxima Sequanorum. Into the land thus subdued and subdivided they introduced the whole machinery of Roman government, laws, language, municipal institutions, and therewith the elements more difficult of transplanting, arts and literature. Gaul was thoroughly Romanised, and in many particulars after the influx of the barbarians it was as Roman or even more Roman than Rome itself. Certainly much of the later Latin literature, over which the glory of classicality still seems to linger, was produced in Gaul; perhaps the larger portion of the later poets were either Gauls or Gallicised Romans. Now, what has this to do with the question of race? Why, this. It shows how completely a nation can be altered by exterior treatment; how it can be civilised, and tutored, and taught, so as to forget its former self, its history, and language and manners, without any considerable intermixture of the blood; for we cannot suppose that the Romans ever were so numerous as to afford to people to any appreciable extent the countries that they conquered. You may say, does not this apply to the Saxons and Britons, and may not the Britons have become Teutonised in language and polity without any considerable intermixture of Saxon blood, as you are here supposing of the Gauls? I answer, the cases are not parallel; for, first, in Gaul it is the uncivilised race losing their own superficial characteristics before a civilised one—in Britain the case is reversed; and in the second place, we have historical evidence for the statement, we know that the Romans were few and did not migrate, and that the Saxons were many and did migrate; we know also that the Gauls were a flourishing and the Britons a perishing people; and in the third place, we may add what I was coming to before, that the Gauls remained Gauls notwithstanding Roman institutions, and retained much of their ancient arrangements notwithstanding the remodelling of the omnipotent Roman administration. This will appear most clearly if you will remember that the Roman redivision and subdivision did not obliterate the ancient landmarks or tribal divisions of the Gauls. Narbonensis and Lugdunensis and Aquitania had subdivisions, and these subdivisions were drawn on more ancient lines, the lines of the little tribal kingdoms which were incorporated one by one as each was conquered. These little divisions subsisted down to the Revolution, through the Frank conquest and the Karling administration, and came again out of the Medean cauldron of the great break-up of that empire; nay, they exist still in the shape of the dioceses of the French bishops. Not merely the names of the cities, but the limits of the dioceses that belong to them, are Gallic for the most part, and even if there were no convincing proof that no general change has ever displaced the great mass of the Gallic people, they would be enough to make the history of the Celts under Roman government a contrast to that of the Britons under the Saxons and Angles.

Well, granted that the population of Roman Gaul continues throughout the Roman period Celtic or Gallic, civilised into the closest similitude with the real Roman, but yet identically Celtic in race, how does it pass through the ordeal of the barbarian invasion? To what extent is the race modified by Visigothic, Burgundian, and Frank conquest? The Visigoths occupied the south-west of France for the whole of the fifth century; the Burgundians conquered the south-east of it and never left it; the Franks extinguished the Roman power over the whole extent of it, swallowing up the Visigoths and Burgundians after a short series of wars in the sixth century. Did these nations to any considerable extent intermingle with the Gallic people, or change the proportion of Celtic blood in the race itself, the predominance of the Celtic or Gallo-Roman elements in the national character?

Take the Visigoths first, as the first in importance and also in time. They were the most likely of the three to amalgamate, because they were the most civilised and the most Romanised: we must suppose that already from their long association with the Romans they had come to use the Latin tongue as their own; at all events, whatever remains of them in writing is Latin. Matters of law and religion are rather beyond our present inquiry; but as we have not very distinct data otherwise, we must use them here. Of the Visigoths we know that their law was an adaptation of Roman law, that their Christianity was Arian. We know that they succeeded in imposing their law, and that they failed to impose their religion; the elements that were Roman amalgamated, those which were not Roman did not. The cities remained Romano-Gallic; the country was subject to Gothic lords; the bishops bore Roman names, the generals were Goths: this tells of no real amalgamation. Nor is there any need to look for it: the stream of Visigothic empire, Arianism with it, passed the Pyrenees, and left Septimania or Landgothia with indelible marks of Gothic occupation, but to all appearance tenanted by the same race that the Romans had found there, Gallic in base, but akin to the mixed population across the mountains, in which the Visigothic was only one ingredient additional to the Basque, the Iberian, the Celt, and the Roman.

The history of the Burgundians is more obscure; of their laws and religion the same may be said as of the Visigoths, but they were less civilised and less Romanised. Their tenure of their territory was a permanent tenure, unlike that of the Goths, but their numbers and power were smaller, and their struggles with the Franks much more pertinacious, their extinction as a nation more determinate and complete. Their name survived, and their law by the vitality of its Roman elements, but their language perished, and so far were they from being strong enough to impose Arianism on the people they found Catholic, that they were compelled to accept Catholicity themselves. They sink into the congeries of mixed peoples that inhabit modern Switzerland, so far as concerns the bulk of them; the nobles, where not extinguished by war, seem to lose themselves in the general body of Frank nobility after they once had succumbed to and became incorporated with the Frank state.

This brings us to the Franks themselves, who also have given their name to the great country they conquered, and imposed their law, but have failed to introduce their language, and have succumbed to the religion and the tongue of the conquered. Here the question narrows itself to very much one of proportion, and that varying proportion. In the centre of France the Franks simply succeeded to the position of the Roman masters, in the south-west to that of the Visigoths, and in the south-east to that of the Burgundians ; it was a conquest, not an immigration. In the north and north-east, the countries which had been their own original seat or the seat of the kindred tribes which had formed with them the aggregate Frank nationality, there can be no doubt that the Frank blood must have been stronger than elsewhere, yet it was not there strong enough to assert itself as it did on the other side of the Rhine against the Roman elements, and cannot therefore be regarded as unmixed. The Frank race continued an aristocratic race ; it ruled the land with pure feudalism, more pure towards the north, where it was less intermingled with Roman institutions. The nobles down to the Revolution prided themselves on Frank extraction, and bore the high old Teutonic names ; but the common people bore still mainly the apostolic names which had come down to them with Roman Christianity, or those of local saints, many of them equally Roman. There is no doubt much Frank blood in the French people now, for the Frank wave never passed away like the Visigothic ; but, arguing on the analogy of history, there is but a small proportion compared with the whole ; nor is there in manners, customs, or character anything that would assert the paternity of the race to be Teutonic. Still, 1,400 years of close intermixture and an historical discipline of singular uniformity have given to the people called French a more pronounced national character than any other European race can claim ; so far also as German elements are traceable in the polity, they are of a peculiar character—Frank as contrasted with the wider Teutonic type, feudal instead of allodial, but far more distinctly Roman in many important regards than Teutonic at all. We conclude, although the proportion of Teutonic blood varies in the north, south, east, and west of France, France, however young or old we may consider her, has a history and a national experience that seem to make her one and a peculiar people. It may be that the German element is worn out ; more probably it may be that it never to any very great extent existed in the bulk of the people.

For Italy a very few words must suffice. It would be very difficult indeed to assert for any single race a principal share in the origination of the modern Italian. Italy, like Rome, has been always a *colluvies gentium*. From the earliest times, when our school books teach us to refer the Etruscans, the Pelasgi, the Oscans, and so on to different tribal divisions of one great race, or to different great races altogether ; down through the Roman times, when the blood of the slaves of the great patrician houses must have mingled in vast proportion with the native blood of the born Italians ; through the barbarian ages when first the Goth, then the Lombard, then the Frank, then the German for century after century conquered, occupied, and governed the land ; through the later ages when it has been the refuge of strangers from all countries, the resort of perpetual pilgrimages, the geographical expression whose capital as the spiritual mistress of Christendom was thronged by crowds of foreigners as varied, if not as numerous, as when it was the home of the Cæsars ; through all these times the Italian people, so far as one can regard them as a nation, has been a mixture, a compound of endless different elements in the way of origin. That a race, undoubtedly so mixed, should develop into such a form as the Italian both physically and mentally has presented throughout history, is, to say the least, a curious phenomenon ; the process of natural selection must have been carried out on a large scale, or else the influences of climate and soil and so on exercise a power on the conformation of men and women more efficacious than that of race, and purity of race is no necessary condition of nobility either of body or mind. The Italian peasant, that class which must have sprung most completely from these intermixtures, is a nobler being in most respects than the Italian noble, whose blood in theory at least is less adulterated. Fortunately, however, we have not to pursue this question ; for, endless as are the varieties of race, endless also are the political types into which Italian constitutional history would have to run in anything like a general view. It is only by way of illustration that I adduce Italian affairs at all, and when I do adduce them it will be enough to indicate any relation that may exist between the polity and the nationality of the instance adduced ; for although Italian historians may assert that Italy has led the way of liberty in modern times, and exemplified every type of free government in its most perfect symmetry, it needs but a steady reading of history to see how utterly baseless this is, how little there is of original political action, and how little of constructive genius in the region of politics, in the Italian pure and simple. The feudalism of Naples and Sicily is Norman : that of North Italy is imperial, Frank or German : the republicanism of Lombardy with all its noble traits and all its wretched results is perhaps original, but it grew historically out of a system which was imperial and not Italian. There is no unity about the history, as there is no unity in the race.

4. So we come in the last place to Spain ; and of Spain much is true that has been said of France, and somewhat also that has been

said of Italy. It would be useless for me to attempt to enumerate the different theories as to the original inhabitants of Spain. We may say that they were Iberians and Celts, or a mixture of the two ; but which were Iberians and which were Celts, and whether the Iberians may not have been Celts, or in fact anything at all about the matter, is utterly in the dark. Two points I may mention in which the darkness, although not less dark, is more definite in its outline : first, the existence in the north of Spain of the Basque people and language, unique, I believe, on the face of the earth, and so possibly the relic of an earlier population existing before the Celts and Iberians, whom it may have successfully resisted, as it seems to have done both the Romans and the barbarians ; and secondly, the fact that the ancient Spaniards, having from the Carthaginians and the Phœnicians learned some of the lessons of civilisation, were more a match for Roman aggression than most of the other Western countries which they attacked. We may, I think, observe with regard to the Roman conquests that the more civilised the conquered race was, the more complete was the extinction of all former political life when the conquest took place : perhaps the civilised elements tended to amalgamation, perhaps they prompted to a stouter resistance and a more perfect extermination. In Spain it was the latter, so far as history has preserved any memorials. The Spaniards were more able to resist Rome, had better weapons and stronger fortifications, had stouter hearts, underwent greater hardships, and were more utterly and entirely Romanised. The conquest of Spain can only be compared, so far as the hardships of the Spaniards go, with the conquest of Judæa, and in some respects it is parallel ; but the Jews resisted the amalgamating power of Rome when they were conquered ; the Spanish nature, stout as it was, succumbed, having not the point and basis of unity and separation which the Jews had. Spain became Roman, exclusively and distinctly Roman ; all vestiges of earlier times, except in the remotest regions, were lost in one equable acquiescence in the Roman system ; nowhere was the resistance longer or stouter, nowhere was the subjection, nay the identification, more complete. Nowhere were the Romans more at home, or the colonies of Romans more frequent and prolific. In Spain we look for the largest infusion of Roman blood, the closest adherence to Roman traditions, the most entire solidarity with Roman Christianity, the purest dialect of the Roman language. The three best emperors of Rome were Spaniards : Trajan, Adrian, and Marcus Aurelius. Lucan and Seneca were Spaniards.

From the conquest of Spain to the reign of Honorius there is little in Spanish history of any interest as touching secular matters. It was thoroughly imperial, thoroughly Roman : perhaps as purely

Roman, or with as few ingredients other than Roman, as Italy itself at that period was. And when the break-up of the empire came Spain was the first to suffer and suffered the worst. In the year 260 A.D. it had had an experience of twelve years of ravages by the Franks and Suevi; but it had recovered from that before the great flood of the barbarians came. At the end of the fourth century it fell a prey to the Suevi, the Alans, and the Vandals: at the beginning of the fifth it was surrendered by Honorius to the Visigoths. The three smaller nations who first occupied it carried on a war of extermination against the Latin inhabitants: they were nations who, like the Saxons in England, were in search of a settlement, they migrated in mass, and depopulated the countries in which they intended to plant themselves. They proceeded to divide Spain among them: the Alans took the west, which is now Portugal; the Suevi, Galicia and the north; the south fell to the Vandals, from whom it is called *Andalusia*. There can be little doubt that Spain would have been entirely repeopled by these nations, which were, it would seem, of kindred origin with the German barbarians, had it not been for the arrival of the Goths as representatives of Rome. These mighty barbarians saved the remnant of Spaniards, and retaliated on the Suevi, the Alans, and the Vandals the cruelties they had inflicted on the natives. The Alans were extinguished, the Vandals were driven into Africa, there to work more terrible destruction still; and the Suevi settled down alongside of the Goths, under the nominal patronage of Rome. But the Goths did not yet emigrate, and the population, relieved from the Vandals and Alans, had time to look up. The Spanish Romans of this period do not make a great figure in history, but they did increase and multiply, and when at the end of the century the Visigothic monarchy migrated from Southern France into Spain altogether, it did not furnish a population large enough to displace or to exterminate the existing one. The Visigoths amalgamated with the Spaniards as the Romans had done, lost their language and their peculiar form of Christianity, and although they retained their ancient common law customs, as we shall see, and even after the invasion of the Moors reconstituted Spanish liberty on a basis which was Teutonic and not Roman, still we cannot view them, historically, as giving the leading element in the present population.

The great peculiarity of Spanish history as compared with that of the rest of Europe is, of course, the Moorish invasion, with its attending circumstances and consequences. At present I am only concerned with it as touching a narrow point; but it is worth while observing and anticipating what I shall have to remark later—that great stress must be laid on the period at which it occurred. The

Visigoths had only removed into Spain at the end of the fifth century, and the constructive effects of their policy, such as it was, could only then begin to be felt, and a thorough mixture with the people have commenced. The further fact that the Visigoths were Arians, while the natives were Catholics, until the year 587 A.D., when the whole peninsula became Catholic, must have retarded that intermixture for a century still; nor was the reputation of the Roman in the eyes of the Goth such that the two nations would mix on an equality. Before the distinction was forgotten, in a hundred and twenty years after the acceptance of the popular form of Christianity by the ruling nation, the Moorish conquest came. The Goths, enervated and demoralised, fell under it; but they had not forgotten that they were Goths; they could not combine with these conquerors as they might have done with the conquered, as the latter rose and their own national spirit declined. So the Gothic population was driven northwards, while the native continued under Moorish rule, and the task of recovering Spain for freedom and Christianity was left to the Goths as Goths, and before they had sunk the character of the Visigoth in that of the Spaniard.

Of the loss of language and of other points of interest I shall speak later, nor need we follow the history of Spain further at present than to remark one little point. I mentioned Christian names as illustrating the relations between Frank and Gaul. We may notice the same in Spain; although the language is Roman, the Christian names of the historical heroes of Spain are German; Alfonso is Hadefonsus, and its equivalent Hildefonsus, both pure German names; so is Ferdinand, so are Bermudo and Weremund, so is Roderick. Of course there are others, such as Garcias, Ramiro, and suchlike, the origin of which is obscure, and may be native; but I am inclined to look on Christian names as one of the most indelible marks of a nation's ancestry. I regard, then, the Moorish invasion as having stopped the process of absorption of the Visigoths into the Romano-Spanish people, as having thrown on the Gothic nobles the responsibility of recovering freedom, and as having led to the perpetuation of Gothic or Teutonic common law in Spain. I think it may also have driven in the Gothic race upon itself, and kept it purer than it would otherwise have been. Kept in the north, where also the Suevic race was more numerous, its Teutonic character strengthened until the whole population amalgamated, the distinction between Goth and Roman was forgotten, and a new era of national life began in the thirteenth and following centuries of which neither Gothicism nor Romanism can be distinctly and exclusively predicated.

Glancing·back now at the ground we have gone through in these two lectures, I hope you will not think that we have wasted time, although I have done little else than recapitulate and marshal bits of information which I doubt not you had already. We thus get clearly several stages of variation in our great mediæval nations as regards nationality. First, the German, pure and unadulterated Teutonic, with no infusion of conquering blood, moving about but not migrating beyond its own circle, unmixed with foreign immigrating races; its varieties of development therefore to be traced to the variety of historical experience—law, dynasty, religion, war, and alliances. Secondly, the English, almost as pure and unadulteratedly Teutonic as the German itself, but unlike the German a transplanted and colonising, an immigrating race; settling within its new circle for a permanency, mixed in a small degree with British elements, but modified in a far greater one by various successive infusions of Teutonic blood, as of Teutonic institutions—Dane, Norwegian, and Norman—developing itself since its last infusion, with no intrusion of foreign elements, and gradually eliminating all that could not amalgamate, amalgamating all that it was not necessary to eliminate; Dane, Norwegian, and Norman either losing their differences in the common race, or strengthening the weaker elements with an infusion of hardiness, or after a generation or two returning to the common type. In France you have a different state of things: a Roman population or a Celto-Roman population, with a Teutonic superstratum nowhere thoroughly united with the native race, but so modified by its relations to that native race as to lose all vestiges almost of its original Teutonism. In Spain the process is reversed: a Teutonic superstratum on a Roman substratum, but so modified by its relations to that race as to bring into relief its original Teutonism; to create out of the mass when it does amalgamate a new nation which distinctly could never have been what in its glorious period of history it was without the Teutonic element in it. As we proceed we shall see more distinctly how the German and English, the French and Spanish histories, diverge, and how the various influences expand or are restricted by other influences. So far as we have gone, however, do not think that I am speaking in parables. Nationality merely as nationality is a small motive power in history, but nationality considered as exemplified or expressed in customs, language, affinities, even in names, expresses a number of mighty influences, equivalent to all that move as mainsprings the internal life of nations, and affect in a great degree their external history also, their relations to other nations, their development in arts and literature as well as politics, their propension to or repulsion from ideas of political things and all that forms the historical interest of their national life.

Q

XI

THE LANGUAGES OF THE PRINCIPAL
EUROPEAN STATES

Any examination of the origin of the languages of the European states in a course of lectures like the present must be short and to a certain extent superficial; we can but look at them as they in their formation illustrate or are illustrated by history; it is quite beyond our province, and quite unnecessary to our present subject, that we should look at them from the point of philology. But some knowledge of their origin and growth is an almost essential requisite to complete our view of the nationalities, and there are some few questions touching the subject of nationalities which this will be found remarkably to illustrate. I will begin by a very short review of the history of the four languages of the four nationalities, and proceed then to the solution of the questions of their relations to one another and their illustration of the conclusions that we have arrived at on the nationalities in the two preceding lectures. And l will take them in the same order. The German language, the High German as it is perhaps more correct to call it, although by philologists it is divided and subdivided into periods and dialects, is, taken as a whole, one language from beginning to end, the lineal descendant of the Gothic or of some sister Indo-Germanic or Aryan dialect of which the Gothic is the nearest and most ancient representative. The Platt-Deutsch, or Low German, spoken in one dialect in Holland and in another prevailing at one time over the northern borders of Germany, is an offshoot from the same stock, differing in pronunciation and vocabulary somewhat, but not to be regarded as a different language unless you are prepared to give the title of language to every dialect. Very remote, even on the very borders of modern history, as must the period have been at which the Low German and High German separated, it is probable that the divergences have increased more rapidly since High German began to rank as a classic language and to be the language of literature. This, however, is beyond us.

The German language is the language of the German people ; it is historically one notwithstanding much alteration in grammatical forms and much innovation of vocabulary ; there is no case in which a German nation continuing on German soil has changed it or modified it by the adoption of any other language, and although it has freely absorbed into its vocabulary foreign words, especially Latin, it has not suffered the Latin to affect its structure either in the forms or in the arrangement of its words.   The modifications of German have been no doubt affected by the literary line that was taken by the writers of it from time to time ; and there is perhaps hardly any language which has been more constantly in flux, or later in acquiring a classical standard ; much of its literature is or has been imitative, and many of its developments dialectic, but all this only serves to bring out more the essential unity and purity of it ; we may say of it as of the German people, that though divided and divisible, and seldom attaining a demonstrable uniformity, it has an essential unity and singular purity from all foreign ingredients.   And the language is the only point, in addition to the purity of the race, of which in German history this can be said : the fatal union with Italy and the influences of the empire have adulterated German life and institutions in every other particular ; nor is the literature itself otherwise than a marked contrast in this respect to the language in which it is clothed.

Turn next to the English.   The English language as we have it now is a language of Germanic basis and structure, but with a vocabulary very largely intermingled with words of Roman origin, and some few very ancient forms of Cymric or Briton extraction. The question for us is how far can the introduction of these Roman words be associated with the historical or political changes that have befallen England ; and it may be a minor question how far the Celtic words in our vocabulary are of primeval or modern introduction.   As to this question I do not propose to say anything ; it is evident that the Anglo-Saxons coming into a new country must have adopted in many cases the native names for places, and even for articles of use and furniture which were not familiar to them at home and for which they had no specially proper expression ; it is also evident that terms of domestic life and furniture would be most easily introduced by the persons who were enslaved, and who might have the fostering of their masters' children, as agricultural ones would be by the men who were made to till their masters' fields. But the proportion even of these words to the original Teutonic ones is very small : far too small for us to suppose that this enslaving of the Britons could have been very extensively carried out ; far too small and in too humble regions of language to allow us to suppose that the two races could have allied themselves on anything like equality. In spite of the arguments of the Welsh advocates, I must, from a study of the language from its earliest to its latest forms, conclude that it is as I have described it, German in structure and German in the base of its vocabulary, although that vocabulary has been and is still being modified by the introduction of Roman words. The Anglo-Saxon remains, the remains that is of the earliest dialect of Teutonic England, are distinctly the precursors and lineal ancestry of the existing language. The first of these are more ancient than any Teutonic remains, save the Gothic Bible of Ulfilas, or perhaps the Malberg glosses: the fragments of Anglo-Saxon preserved in Boniface, Aldhelm, and in the life of Bede, are the most ancient written Teutonic, and from them we have in poems, or translations, or original works, or charters, a distinct and continuous current of English down to the present day, modified, as I have said, by an infusion of new vocabulary. Even, however, had the vocabulary been much more largely affected than it has been, so long as the structure of the language, its inflexions, its grammar, and the furniture of it, such as its prepositions and auxiliary verbs, remain what they are, it would seem impossible for anyone who is not very ignorant or very prejudiced to assert for it any other origin or the existence of any other strong influence in its origination. It is, however, very possible that a modification of vocabulary may be carried to such an extent as in time to put out of sight the fundamental structure of a language, and reduce it to a matter of theory. Happily this is not yet the case with English. In a language of whose literature we have such an abundant and continuous supply, we ought to be able to say whether the infusion of new vocabulary coincides in time with the political changes by which the external history of the people has been affected, and which may be regarded as possibly affecting the purity of the race and nationality.

Let us just look at this. We have as a nation passed through several phases of this kind: Anglo-Saxons to begin with, we have been crushed by Danes, Norwegians, and Normans; we have been converted by Romans, Scots, Burgundians, and Franks; we have been governed by successive dynasties of Frenchmen, Englishmen, Welshmen, Scots, and Germans. Are the infusions of new words synchronistic with any of those changes? Having abundant remains of literature to refer to, we ought to have no difficulty in replying. This question, although it sounds rather big as I have stated it, when analysed depends for its answer on a very small issue; for all the successive conquests, except the Norman, were by nations purely Teutonic, and so served, if they modified the language appreciably, only to introduce a few words which were as unmistakably

German as those with which they mingled. The Norman Conquest was carried out by leaders of Teutonic origin, whose posterity quickly consolidated themselves with the English, but it also contained a large infusion of French adventurers, who mixed with the English but did not speak the same language, and it further was the beginning of a series of connections with France which imported a large number of French ideas, customs, and legal doctrines. The question then narrows itself to this, did the Norman Conquest bring in such a flood of new words as to alter the character of the language from German purity to modern semi-Latinity or anything like it ? for if it did it may also have largely affected the blood of the race. Now I believe I am perfectly justified in saying that the Norman Conquest did not so affect the English language. It introduced a race of conquerors who spoke the French language full of Roman words and forms, and it led the way to a series of developments one of the remotest of which was the development in a Latin direction of one side of the modern English language. But the foreign language it introduced did not mingle with the English ; they continued side by side ; the English a century after the Conquest was as purely Teutonic as it was before the Conquest, and the English language was the language of courts of law and of charters during that century ; at least, charters were written in Latin and English co-ordinately down to the accession of Henry II. French was the language of the court, Latin the language of the church, English the language of the people. The courts of law and the sermons of the clergy were, of course, adapted to the understanding of the majority. No doubt the Norman Conquest did in a remote degree conduce to the adopting of Norman French as the legal language in the reign of Edward I., and matters had been looking in that direction since the reign of John, when our first English-French document now existing was written. Only mark, the infusion of French blood must, if it ever occurred, have immediately followed the Conquest ; the infusion of French into the language does not follow until nearly two hundred years. It is then to the adoption of French as the government language and as that of the courts of law, which began under Edward I. and continued until the time of Edward III. unbroken, and much later in different departments of the state, and to the use of Latin as the language of ecclesiastical ritual and general literature, that we are to ascribe the Roman element in our ordinary vocabulary.

Between the beginning and the end of the fourteenth century is the century of the influence of lawyers and the growth of universities, the century of continuous French war fought by English yeomen, each of whom, if he ever returned home, returned with a tongue accustomed to French forms and a quantity of new fashions of which the only names he knew were French. Thus we find in that century the causes of the modification of the language which is traceable in Wiclif and Chaucer, and which in a constantly increasing ratio has gone on until the present day, when we are privileged to see a strong reaction in favour of what is called pure Saxon English. The change is not connected with any modification of race or nationality, except in so far as it is a remote consequence of the Conquest, a consequence which might have resulted equally probably if there had never been a conquest, from other causes.   The foreign element of race was sunk in the native stock nearly a century before the foreign element of language enters into spoken English. Until then the two languages were spoken by different classes, but French was constantly being restricted to the court language. English was making its way upward, and strengthening downward, until our great English king by his use of the foreign tongue placed himself in the position of the father of modern English, as he is of modern constitutional history.   It is a curious thing that that English document of which so much has been, mistakenly I think, made, the proclamation of Simon de Montfort, should have been made by a foreigner, as Simon was; but it is still more curious that Edward I., a truly English sovereign, should have introduced French into the laws and the courts. I can only account for it by the great influence that the lawyers had with him, and suppose that as the legal views of Breton, Bracton, and Fleta were decidedly continental, their language was affected by that profession also.

I shall not dwell on the subject of ecclesiastical language; the infusion of Latin words through it was of course as old as Anglo-Saxon Christianity itself.   The English was a learned church: the English people throughout the middle ages was fertile in learned men; every little district had its monastery, the accounts of which were kept in Latin; the monks were drawn from the body of the people and associated with it.   Hence the people were accustomed to hear and learn new religious and learned words. In Germany this was less the case; learning was less active; the monasteries were more widely scattered; the monks and canons were drawn less from the body of the people; above all, the literature was of later growth, and it is through literature, whether religious, legal, or ordinary, that new words are introduced. The vocabulary of German was longer in becoming infected with Latin because it was longer in rising to the dignity of a literary language: as it was slow to rise, it was thrown more on its own fertility for the words to express new things; it is by itself, whether from the freedom of its developing or not, I cannot say, a more fertile language in new forms than the English, which has ever been prone rather to accept foreign names for new things than to coin them from its own mint.

As for the subsequent history of English, I need not say more than that in common with the other European languages it made a great step towards fixity under the early printers ; and before their influence was exhausted had taken up in the English version of the Bible, and in the unsurpassable diction of Elizabethan literature, a standard which it has been slow to alter, and to which probably it will look for some ages to come as the *jus et norma loquendi*. All modifications, developments, additions, since that period have been of small account as to the essence of the language itself. With matters of literature pure and simple, we have at present nothing to do. The question of language thus viewed does not affect our conclusions as touching the origin of the English. It would have been highly improbable that the language of the most adventurous, the most maritime, the most mercantile, the most warlike nation of Europe considering its population and the area of its occupation, should have remained unadulterated or unenriched, as you may choose to state it, by foreign ingredients. There are abundance of these, most of them of comparatively modern introduction, words of travel, of sea-craft, of commerce, of diplomacy, of war and military exercises. Most words of home use, however, are Anglo-Saxon still ; and the vast majority of words in any given paragraph of any familiar writer on non-technical subjects will, I think, be found to be English, notwithstanding all that has been said to disprove this. But anyhow I think we have seen that it is impossible to connect the ideas of a modification of the language with a modification of the main elements of the nationality. The French of Edward I., which marks the most distinct period of modification, a period at which England was more thoroughly English than she had been for 250 years, was a distinct and remote thing from the French of the Conquest.[1]

But it is time to go on to the French, Spanish, and Italian. These three languages, I need hardly tell you, are the own children of the Latin. It may be a question whether they are not the Latin itself a little knocked about in different ways. They all, I believe, are now regarded as standing in the same relation to the Latin ; that is, they are not derived from one another, but irrespective of one another from the parent Latin ; and I may add that they are all derived immediately from the Latin without any intermediate stage such as once was held to have intervened, on a theory by which the whole Latin world was supposed to go through a stage in which a uniform corrupt Romance language was spoken from which the

---

[1] *Select Charters*, p. 449.

Italian, Spanish, and French were formed as the grandchildren, not the own children, of the Latin. Anyone who wishes to investigate this matter on philological grounds may do so in Sir George Corne-wall Lewis's 'Essay on the Origin of the Romance Language,' and he will there find also what little historical evidence is forthcoming on the same point. The acceptance of this view simplifies matters a good deal. We have only to regard the Latin as having become the ordinary vernacular language of Spain and France, and to deter-mine as well as we can the cause of the disruption of uniformity, and the date and modifying influence that resulted in the formation of the new languages. The Latin from which these languages were derived was not, in vocabulary at least, what we are accustomed to regard as classical Latin: it was the vulgar Latin spoken over the empire as well as in Italy itself, during the whole time of which we have any data; no doubt it was the Latin of the lower classes as opposed to the literary Latin of educated society: the Latin of the camp and farm and suburb, just as in the modern language of America all that is regarded as distinctly American is vulgar and provincial English, the English spoken by or descended from that spoken by the Essex and Suffolk tradesmen and farmers who were the first settlers. As to this vulgar Latin and the process by which French was derived from it, you cannot do better than read Brachet's 'Historical Grammar,' a most entertaining little book, which has been translated by Mr. Kitchin, and which will furnish you with abundance of philological and historical thoughts that cannot fail to interest and be useful in your general reading. You will of course distinguish between the existence of a vulgar form of Latin existing universally wherever the Roman language prevailed, side by side with the literary Latin; and the existence of a Romance language succeeding to the Latin throughout the area of its extension, the idea disproved, it would seem, by Sir George Lewis. We may conceive, then, this vulgar Latin extending over the whole West as the vernacular of the countries under Roman sway. It had completely supplanted the original language of Spain and France, except where the Basque retained its hold, as it has done to the present day: it had as certainly not extinguished the British language in Britain, seeing that it subsists still in Wales, and probably covered at the very least a much larger breadth of the western side of the island. For several hundreds of years, from the time of the first conquest to the time of Honorius, it had been rooted in these provinces: the language that was spoken before these conquests was forgotten: here and there a few words remained to puzzle archæologists, some of which owed their preservation as Gallic words to the fact that they were not originally Gallic but German: such words as *ambactus*, for instance, which had been embedded in the Gallic language from the German and remained a Gallic word when the rest of the language was lost. The intercourse with Rome was continuous during these ages, and literature had its language in Spain and Gaul as well as in Italy. Probably the Latin of the empire went through as little organic change during these six centuries as any written language has ever gone through: idioms changed doubtless, but not grammatical forms. The event that put an end to this uniformity was of course the break-up of the empire under barbarian invasion. I do not mean the Goths merely, but the barbarian period generally from the fifth to the eighth century. That broke up the unity of the Latin language as it broke up the unity of the Latin empire: from that time Spanish, Italian, and French begin and go on diverging. The nature of the change was also disruptive; it broke up the synthetical character of language, that is the character which gives variations of case, tense, mood &c. by inflexion, and substituted for it an analytical character, which gives the same by the use of prepositions, adverbs, articles, and auxiliary verbs. It is true that in the more modern forms of these languages these auxiliary words have in many cases grown to the roots, and so made a second or new synthetic process. But the immediate effect of the Teutonic shock was disruptive. Instead of saying *scripsi*, for instance, they began to say *ego habeo scriptum, j'ai écrit*: instead of *scribam, ego scribere habeo, j'écrirai*, I have to write, for example. This process affects all the languages, and so far forth their history is one. This analytic character belongs to German in all its forms, and to this extent it affected the Latin to assimilation with itself; it furnished also a small number of new words to the vocabulary of the reformed languages. Anyone who knows French will by analysing a single paragraph be able to say how small the proportion of Teutonic words is in French; and I believe it is smaller still in Spanish, and still less in Italian.

Thus far, then, the history of the languages is one: here it divides. We may not forget that besides these three there were other Romance languages with quite as good right to be called daughters of the Latin, formed by the same process, some of which exist, such as the Provençal and the Latin of the Grisons; others too which are probably extinct. Italy itself has a number of such, dialects they are called, as we speak of Greek dialects, meaning co-ordinate languages, equally legitimate, although it has fallen to one of the lot—in the Italian to the Tuscan, as in Greek to the Attic—to be regarded as the language of culture. Well, the differences to be observed in the three main languages seem to have originated in three influences: 1. The period at which they cease to be Latin, and become what we call Spanish, French, and Italian;

2. The nationality of the race by whose impact, if I may so say, the change was produced; and 3. The character and circumstances of the people in whose mouths the language was so changed. 1. The Gothic invasion may have produced the original shock; but the subsequent developments were worked out under the races that followed the Goths: in France, under the Franks; in Spain, later, under the Visigoths; in Italy, latest, under the *colluvies barbarorum*. This—and I think I have said something like it before—was probably owing to the fact that the Goths were becoming rapidly Romanised in language and manners before they conquered the West. They seem to have taken to Latin both in Spain and Gaul as their ordinary language; and it is to the Frank conquest and the Frank empire that we trace the change in French. Hence it is the eldest of the three languages, and has also the most Teutonic words. The Spanish, which is Latin only modified by one Teutonic, the Visigothic, stock, is later in origin and has fewer Gothic words. The Italian is the youngest. The French appears in formation in the middle of the ninth century; the earliest bit of French being, I think, the oath taken by Lewis the German at Strasburg in 842. 2. The earliest Spanish, such as would be called Spanish proper, is of the twelfth century; and the earliest Italian is little if any later. There is much difficulty, however, in arriving at anything like certainty about these matters, simply because of the dearth of linguistic monuments. Charters are always in Latin, and charters are all that are preserved until something worthy of preservation as literature is produced. A language may have been spoken for centuries before it is written. But if we make the same allowances in all the three cases, we shall find the same results; literary French is a century and a half earlier than literary Spanish or Italian; the language itself is probably of as much earlier growth, and this earlier growth is owing to the fact that the Franks were less Latinised than the Visigoths or Lombards. Something is due, secondly, to the character of the race producing the change; no question that the peculiar character in which the mixture of Frank and Gaul has resulted has had to do with the elliptic and elisive character of French, both in structure and pronunciation. Most probably the difference between Suevian and Visigoth has affected the relations of Galician to Castilian Spanish, and so that of Portuguese to Spanish proper. The process in Italian seems rather to have been one of natural decay and development, the foreign element, as distinct from the intrusive force, being less distinctly apparent. 3. The elements of difference which may have been produced by the original constitution of the original race, or which may have been modified by the various

natural causes which we imagine do modify language in mountainous and plain countries, in maritime and inland ones, difference of air, of food, of water, of training and physical conformation, obscure as these are physically, are obscurer still historically, and making due allowance for them, you will not expect me to theorise upon them : the sonorous and dignified Spanish, the rapid, elliptic, incisive character of French, and the liquid, distinct, and musical Italian, are different in intonation and general effect, with a difference that causes purely historical, as opposed to physical, cannot account for. When more is known of the physical causes, we shall find an historical theory to account for it.

Of course you will understand that with these causes the great first cause of divergency and disruption was the break-up of inter-course and unity which had been maintained while the Roman empire lasted. As that intercourse ceased, the languages diverged and began to grow each according to its own genius. I think that we have now materials enough to enable us to answer the questions that arise from the fact that Europe is with so much common experience still divided into Latin-speaking and German-speaking nations ; to account for the facts at first sight so puzzling that in England the Teutonic tongue has beaten out of the field that of the British aborigines, of Roman civilisation, and of French conquest and migration ; that in Spain the Latin has maintained its hold after a German and a Moorish conquest ; that in France it has also maintained its hold, first upon a people whose native tongue it dis-placed and extinguished, and secondly on the conquering race, whose speech served to modify, but only to modify, hardly at all to alter materially, the speech of the conquered. That race and language do not vary together we must consider proved. The Celtic tongue, that has in Wales withstood Roman and German alike, in France and Spain has become extinct before the two. There can be little doubt of the Celtic origin of the bulk of the modern French, yet their language is Latin ; or that what in them is not Gallic is Teutonic ; yet the language of high and low is one. So great the power of the old Roman name and administration ; as Greece conquered her conquerors, so Rome in language at least assimilated both conquerors and conquered. Yet what the Roman has done, the Teutonic in the Anglo-Saxon form has done also in England. If we listen to the hypothesis of the Welsh scholars, it has assimilated the natives ; it has certainly assimilated the Norman race imported at the Conquest. But, as I have said before, this I do not uphold. I do not believe that the Britons were assimilated, but driven out or exterminated ; [1] and as for the Norman conquerors, I believe

[1] This view has been contested by Seebohm and many other historians.—A. H.

them to be greatly overrated in numbers and in extent of influence. I believe the Anglo-Saxon tongue had room to develop freely, and was never greatly disturbed by a foreign infusion in the way of admixture of race or forcible intrusion of new elements.

But the negative conclusion remains : we have seen that language and national origin do not vary together always, and we shall see as we proceed that neither do language and religion, nor race and religion, neither language and law, nor race and law, and in the same way politics and civil institutions. But here I am anticipating. The whole subject is full of anomalies that would puzzle anybody but a philosopher ; a philosopher will, of course, shut his eyes and so see nothing to puzzle him. It seems to me very curious that the Latin language with its hold on the church service, the law and literature, a hold so strong that it was able to permeate even the English vocabulary and very sensibly to affect the German itself, was not able to maintain its hold against dissolution and modification upon its own soil—in Italy, for instance, and in Spain. There it had every advantage ; it converted its conquerors, it preached to them, it administered their laws, and expounded their histories ; they forgot their mother tongue to use it, they went on using it, writing it, praying in it, and so on, and yet for ordinary purposes of life it varied and varied until it became new and mutually unintelligible languages, in different lands in which very much the same developments might have been looked for, and at very nearly the same period, as if it took just so many centuries to change from Latin into Spanish, and from Latin to Italian, and from Latin to Portuguese. After this same period of organic change it becomes literary ; it becomes vocal in all three countries, first in verse and then in prose. If there is a law in these things, it is in its working at least as curious as a chance. Well, the same thirteenth century saw the consolidation, as the fourteenth saw the complete regeneration, of the European languages : the English in its growth from the earliest ballads to the polished poetry of Chaucer ; the French through its poetical stage, past the period of its historical prose—the 'Chronique d'Outremer,' Villehardouin, and Joinville—to what is almost modern French ; the Spanish, like the English, from the ballads and poetical chronicles, under the creative genius of Alfonso the Wise, to the sonorous and majestic dignity of pure Castilian. As we proceed we shall see the significance of these names and analogies. We have, however, still another matter to discuss, and that in some detail : a matter that pervades every relation of mediæval life and runs into every political complication of constitutional history proper—the origin and variety of the relations of the church to the peoples.

XII

THE ORIGIN AND POSITION
OF THE GERMAN, ROMAN, FRANK, CELTIC,
AND ENGLISH CHURCHES

WE have all been educated on a system and under the influence of a civilisation which owes a great deal to Greece and Rome. In arts and literature our taste is formed in a great measure upon the principles and the models of the ancient world. It is so much so that in architecture alone perhaps of the arts will our artistic authorities admit any excellence to exist which is not calculated on the rules and lines of classical antiquity or developed from them. It is therefore difficult for us quite to realise the fact that historically the great civilising influence of our forefathers and of European life in one-half of its area was not that of Greece and Rome, but of Christianity. Northern Europe owes its civilisation to the church, and Southern Europe owes everything that is vital, sound, and good to the influence of the North one way or another exerted upon it. This is not the time for us to attempt any estimate of the old Roman civilisation. I stated my own opinion upon it strongly enough in the first lecture; it was a civilisation of a class at the expense of all other classes—a civilisation that had except for selfish purposes no power whatever or inclination to extend itself; it was not incompatible with the most debased life, the most tyrannical policy, the most monstrous vices, the most oppressive slavery and servility. It had no root of good in it, it had no religious element, its best ingredient was a philosophy which had no mainspring of benevolent action, no love of mankind, no principle of life in itself. This civilisation was in itself too far gone for Christianity to save it. Christianity supplied new motives of action, a new spirit of freedom and hatred of oppression, a thought of higher than sensual enjoyment, and an ideal of empire better than that of universal subserviency to the will of one pampered voluptuary or a hundred such. But the civilisation of the empire was decrepit, the system was rotten before Christianity forced its way even to toleration, much more when it had become

supreme. Nor could Christianity nerve the hands and hearts of a
people which for generations had been sodden with vice and infamy.
The church moreover was not unaffected by the state of decay, the
atmosphere of rank and rotten civilisation in which it fought its way
to the air ; and what with heresy and contention for civil power on
the one hand, and the influence of asceticism drawing better and
purer souls out of the filth of the arena on the other, the church
hardly seems to have exerted any quickening influence on the mass.
It was the *reductio ad absurdum* of the idea of progress, to end in a
mass of unsoundness which even the living influence of the Gospel
itself failed to vivify.   Then came the avalanche of the barbarians,
and the sons of the conquerors of the world were nowhere.   The
church itself, so far as it had rested on the temporal power of its
proselytes, fell with them, and the work of evangelising and civilising the world had to be begun anew—to begin from a new principle,
and to make a conquest of its conquerors.

It is not a part of my programme in this course to give a detailed
account of the evangelisation of mediæval Europe, but only to sketch
in outline the story and to go in detail into those points which affect
constitutional liberty and life, such as the position of the clergy and
the relations of church and state.   You all must know that it was
by the struggles of the church for liberty that during the middle
ages the remembrance of liberty was maintained at all.   I shall try
to show how the church and the clergy came to be in a situation to
claim and struggle for it.   Incidentally we shall come on several
matters that would illustrate a wider view.   With this idea I shall
depart from the order in which I have taken the nations in the former
lectures, and take them in the order of conversion, or nearly so—Gaul,
Spain, England, and Germany.   Both Gaul and Spain were Christianised while they remained parts of the ancient empire, and their
early Christianity has with a character derived directly from Rome
a character of its own that implies a relation to Rome rather of
co-ordination than derivation.   It is certain that Christianity
came to Gaul and Spain direct from the East, although there
was doubtless a stream from Rome after it became settled
and established in Rome.   The church of Lyons, for example,
under Irenæus was in close connection with the churches of Asia
almost as soon as anything is known of a church of Rome after
apostolic times.   The church of Spain has always claimed to be
apostolic, as the mission field of St. James, and although such a
mission was almost an impossibility, and may with that of Dionysius
the Areopagite be set down as quite apocryphal, the very tradition
proves an origin of unknown antiquity and irrespective of Roman
influence.   The traditions are themselves the fruit of a spirit, a

desire of proving antiquity of origin, which itself springs from an independence of Rome which is the major point in question. With the acceptance of Christianity by Constantine, the church of Rome became the rule and model of Christian churches, and the system of imperial Rome became closely allied with the ecclesiastical organisation. Hence in Spain and Gaul the dioceses of the bishops and the provinces of the metropolitans were exactly conterminous with the fiscal or political divisions of the imperial administration. The bishops in the cities became either the protectors of the people against the wanton tyranny of magistrates, or in many cases the chief magistrates themselves; the episcopate being a position of so great importance, both spiritually and temporally, fell hereditarily into the hands of great families and sometimes went in direct succession from father to son. Hence the clergy put on a secular character very injurious to their spiritual usefulness, and became imperial functionaries, statesmen, and even warriors. And in Gaul this state of things survived the Frank conquest.

You will remember how we remarked the strength of the town or municipal organisations as marks of the vitality of Roman institutions and of the strongholds of the Gallo-Roman society, or race, if it can be called a race. In the maintenance of that idea the early bishops under the Frank sovereigns are conspicuous; they bore Roman names, they were the chief citizens in the Roman cities, they obtained from the Frank kings privileges and endowments in the cities and in connection with them which gave them a secular character that they have never lost. This secular character is, it appears to me, more innate and inherent in the Gallican system than in the Roman itself; at all events, it is coeval with it historically. In the court of Charles the six lay peers are matched by six bishops—Rheims, Laon, Langres, Noyon, Beauvais, and Châlons. The voice of Romance sounds not out of accord with that of History. With the secular power the clergy, after the Frank conquest, seem to have taken up much of the barbarism of the new *régime*; and if it had not been for the rise of the monastic system, the civilising power of the church might have been deemed to be exhausted. But, partly by the influence of monasticism, and partly by the working of Christianity from a new centre, which through Britain and Germany affected for the better France also, this result was averted. The chief point to be noticed in the Frank church is its secularity and its close implication in all the evils of both the Roman and the Frank systems. It was in too close connection with a state which it failed either to strengthen or, beyond certain limits, to civilise. The Frank sovereigns on their conversion accepted Christianity in its Catholic form, and immediately they came in the

closest connection with the prelates. After a generation or two
Franks succeeded to the position, secular and ecclesiastic, of the
Gallo-Roman prelates ; to them also it was a matter of importance
to secure hereditary hold on a spiritual dignity so strong in temporal
appliances; and hence the exceptional strength of the clergy in
French politics from time immemorial. Their power and interest
were perpetual, in the midst of a world whose sovereigns and dynasties were ever changing. The measures of Charles the Great, who
would be master of the clergy as well as of the people, were ineffec-
tive under the rule of his posterity, and the same characteristic that
is traceable from the beginning pervades the history throughout.
By the influence of monasticism, and in a measure by the restoration
or foundation of a central power in reformed Rome, a religious
change for the better was brought about ; but its old form is not
eliminated. Secularity is the great mark of the churches which
sprang up under imperial Rome.

With the church of Gaul and France may be compared that of
Spain, for their origin was very much the same, and the first four
centuries of their history ; after that they diverge widely and signi-
ficantly. Of this early period what is true of France is true of Spain ;
there was an Eastern origin, and a constant flow of Roman influence ;
there were severe persecutions and martyrdoms of singular heroism.
There was great care for the maintenance of orthodoxy, greater
perhaps in Spain than in Gaul, because of the indigenous character
of the Spanish heresies. There were councils of great authority for
the same reason. Spanish scholars were of great weight in controversy. A Spanish bishop was the chief of the council of Nicea ;
nowhere was discipline more elaborated or conciliar deliberations
more generally accepted as authoritative. And we cannot doubt
that the same causes which led to secularism in Gaul were doing so
in Spain, when the shock of the barbarians altered the whole state
of affairs and gave to Spanish church history a peculiar character
that is quite its own. The barbarians overwhelmed Spain, and the
barbarians were Arians ; they were earnest supporters of that heretical
sect which the Spaniards at Nicea had been the first to condemn.
Now, how did this operate ? Why, thus : it made the Spanish
church, the bishops and clergy, so long as the Goths were Arian,
the leaders of opposition to the royal power in the Romano-Spanish
population ; and it prevented that extreme weighting of the church
by royal benefactions and secular privileges which we have seen was
too much for the Gallo-Roman church. The clergy could not be
sycophants to an heretical prince, nor was the heretical prince likely
to augment the powers of those who kept up the popular feeling
against his tenets. And this had a great effect in the maintenance

of a Christian standard in the Spanish people in morals and doctrine alike. The progress of the victory of the conquered over the conquerors was slow but steady; first the Suevi, and a few years later the Visigothic sovereigns themselves, became Catholic, and with that event a new tide set in. The clergy, who had been before in opposition, now became the most influential and trusty counsellors; without losing their hold on the people they became all-powerful with the kings; their secular power rose at once to the highest pitch; it became, as the school-books say, a theocracy, a perfect union of church and state; ecclesiastical councils made laws for Spain; ecclesiastical ministers governed the country; the old Gothic aristocracy lost political weight beside them; they were all-powerful. But with power came also a decline in moral and spiritual position. The kings, Catholic as they had become, had not laid aside their royal lust, or thirst for blood, or love of money and oppression; nor did they give their confidence or depute their power without a price. The church, by having to tolerate the vices of the princes, laid herself open to the influx of the same. There is no question that the moral condition of Spain during this theocratic period was bad, was becoming rapidly worse and worse, church and state conniving at each other's dereliction of duty, confounding their respective powers, and mutually buying of each other licence to sin; when another avalanche came down and altered everything, that Moorish invasion of which I have spoken before as the influence which, at the cost of seven centuries of toil and trouble, yet gave Spain an heroic history and a national character that in the present century could scarcely be said to be effete.

In some respects the secular power of the Spanish clergy is, up to this point, analogous to that of the French. It originates partly in the confidence of the subject population and partly in the patronage of the barbarian conquerors whom it has civilised; but the history of the struggles through which the position is achieved is different, and the catastrophe of the Moorish invasion has a consolidating influence as well as a salutary and reformative influence on the church as on everything else. Henceforth it becomes a portion of the intense Spanish national feeling: I might almost say of the intense Spanish nature. Henceforth Spain, under the Visigothic nature revived, and informing the mass, becomes intensely national and orthodox: the mass is welded together; the Christianity is a part of the heritage that has to be struggled for for seven centuries; the church and the people and the kings; Romano-Spaniard, Visigothic, and Sueve; Castilian, Arragonian, Galician, Navarrese, all are, in spite of territorial and dynastic divisions, one people, one church, one language, one outpost and defence of Christendom, one perpetual

R

unrelaxing, unflinching, watchful crusade. There is enough here to mark Spain off once for all from the rest of Christendom. As to the points in which her history may be compared with that of England in this respect, I shall speak after I have sketched the condition of England in the church aspect, as I shall now proceed to do. In Britain there had been, no doubt, a native or Romano-British church before the collapse of the empire and the invasion of the Angles and Saxons. The thing is provable from the writings of the Fathers, from the proceedings of councils, and from a few—very few but very distinct—evidences of monumental and literary sort. It would be absurd where we know so little to define anything as to the relations of this church with the secular government; it would be, no doubt, characterised by the same features as the Gallo-Roman church was. Perhaps, as the civil organisation of Britain was less minute and elaborate than that of Gaul, so far at least as we know, it was not in a condition to be tempted with secular advantages, as was the case with the sister church. If the town influence was less developed, so also must have been the municipal power of the clergy. This conclusion seems also deducible from a comparison of the condition of the Celtic churches when they first come into daylight; there is a patriarchal tinge about them, where secular and spiritual power are united, which is utterly unlike anything Roman. But the obscurity of the subject is great, and we have at present nothing to say about it except that, whatever it was, the Anglo-Saxon conquest must have made a clean sweep of it. It swept away its churches and their districts, its dioceses and provinces, if there were any; it swept away its bishops, clergy, and people, with their literature, their language, and their ritual. The church of England has to be built from the very foundations after the beginning of the sixth century; it is not that the seed of the Word has to force itself up through thorns, but that it has to be sown again as in a virgin soil. The mission of Gregory the Great was the beginning, and it was followed up, as soon as its success was ascertained, by a series of missions from other churches. Kent was converted by Romans, Wessex by an Italian mission, East Anglia by a Burgundian one, Northumbria from Kent. Subsequently, after an apparent collapse of the Roman missions, the task was taken up by the Scoto-Celtic church and carried out by it with such success that the work of organisation and consolidation was completed by Archbishop Theodore within considerably less than a century after the mission of Augustine. In this entire independence of imperial Roman influence, and in the variety of the agencies by which the conversion was accomplished, we see the first distinct characteristic of English church history; a second is to be found in the fact that the evangelisation begins from the kings, is carried on by their action, is adopted by their constitutional machinery and diffused effectively by them through the bulk of the people. It is not the religion of the conquered race forcing itself up, as in Spain and France, and conquering the conquerors. A third characteristic is the monastic garb of its ministers, which more than anything else prevents their assumption of that sort of secular power which is fatal to the spiritual work of the clergy in Gaul and Spain.

And I will add a fourth point; it was by the machinery of the church thus founded and consolidated that England became one kingdom; so much, at least, the prophetic genius of Theodore foresaw, and so it came to pass. The dioceses of the English church were the kingdoms and sub-kingdoms of the Heptarchy; but the provincial arrangement, according to which, from the seventh century to the Conquest, the whole, although divided into two provinces, was canonically subject to a single primate at Canterbury, did anticipate and lead the way up to a real union of the several kingdoms under one king. The churches had a unity under the successor of Augustine; in the great councils of the church men learned the way to hold great councils for the state; as in later times the principles of election and representation were maintained by the church to be the basis of future liberties for the people in general, so in earlier ones and in other ways the path of progress towards unity and good government was led by the ecclesiastical organisation. These things being so—and as they are known to most of you at least from your reading of English history, it is of no use my going into detail about them now—considering the great and speedy growth of Christianity in England, the humility and piety of its first apostles, the zeal and energy of its first nursing fathers the kings of Kent, Northumbria, and Mercia; considering the great learning and science politically and morally developed within the first generation of its converts in such men as Bede and Aldhelm; considering also that these, the kings and the clergy, seem to have had the same objects in view, and stood together in opposition rather to the uncivilised independence than the intentional hostility of the temporal chiefs, we cannot be surprised to find, both in ecclesiastical and civil concerns, the utmost harmony and the closest union between church and state. Ecclesiastically the kings sit in the church councils, nominate the bishops and abbots, divide the dioceses, and confirm ecclesiastical law. Civilly the bishops sit in the witenagemot, are, in fact, the leading advisers of the king, act as judges in the courts of law, sitting with the ealdorman and sheriff as the presidents of the folkmote; act throughout the Anglo-Saxon period as the standing council to the king; and after the Conquest take their old place in the parliaments of the new *régime*. Nay, to such an extent is this carried before the Conquest that ecclesiastical causes are themselves tried on the folkmote, the bishops and clergy by their influence there being able to secure fair treatment, and not yet requiring, as was granted by William the Conqueror, a separation of jurisdiction, the expulsion of the bishop from his seat in the county court, and the consequent withdrawal of ecclesiastical causes into spiritual courts. That for spiritual offences the bishop always had his court may, I think, be regarded as certain ; but until the Conquest ecclesiastical causes, as distinct from spiritual ones, were, it is believed, tried in the courts of the people. Are we to regard such a system as this as a theocracy, as at all an equivalent to the system of Spain under the Visigothic kings ? I think not. To a certain extent they were alike ; in both the union of temporal and spiritual authorities worked with very few difficulties, and in both there was some confusion as to the limits of the secular and the spiritual, which contributed to this easy working. In both the numbers of the prelates were small considering the extent of the territory they ruled, and thus contrasted with the countless hierarchy of Italy and France ; in both the weight of episcopal counsel in the national assemblies was out of all proportion to that of lay advisers.

But mark the difference. The councils of Spain, by which Spain was governed, in which the laws were made and promulgated, and on which depends the chief argument for the identity of church and state in Spain, were primarily church councils ; they are even, as I have said, church councils of especial authority, those of Toledo ranking but little below general ones. The forger of the decretals thought the name of Isidore of Seville a good name to recommend his forgery, so great was the reputation of Spain in church law. It is as church councils that they govern and direct the government of the kingdom. The clergy are all in all in them ; the laity, except as represented by the king, are of insignificant importance in them. There is abundance of governmental machinery, but the spiritual has dwarfed the temporal. The laws are of what is called the most clerical complexion ; the spiritual authority is accounted supreme. In the Anglo-Saxon church, on the other hand, although the personal influence of the clergy is perhaps as great, it is primarily as wise men, witan, counsellors, that they exercise it. The councils are national in character quite as much as ecclesiastical. In the witenagemot the bishops take a leading part as *sapientes*, not as spiritual potentates. The distinctively ecclesiastical councils do not bind the laity without consent of the witenagemot. As the bishops and clergy are so strong in the witenagemot, and the civil and eccle-

siastical councils can but consist of the same people in different
characters, it is not always easy to say which is a council of the
church and which a witenagemot; but there is in all decrees of
such assemblies, I believe, a distinction. The witenagemot does not
ground its claim to legislate on its character as an assembly of
spiritual men, but as being the collective wisdom of the people and
the counsellors of the king. Is not this in strict consonance with
what I have said as to the unsecular character of our early church,
notwithstanding its close union with the state? It was indeed so
closely united with the state that it needed no secular authority
exclusive of the state, but could safely leave the state to act by its
own religious instincts. Close as is the resemblance with the
Spanish system at first sight, it vanishes when the first test is
applied.

As I can in this lecture only indicate, scantily I fear, the *initial*
influences of Christianity on the politics of the nations, I must put
off any discussion of the developments of these influences in later
history. English church history is indeed almost the whole of
early English history, and one might spend terms on the illustration of it. As it is, we have hardly left time for the sketch of
German history which is necessary to complete our view. The
history of the German church lacks the unity which the other three
that we have discussed have, and so shares the difficulty of German
history generally. We may, however, roughly regard it according
to the national divisions which we adopted before—the Franks,
Bavarians, Alemannians, and Saxons. Of the church through the
Rhine countries, including the western half of the Franks and the
Alemannians, I cannot say anything more than I have said already
in speaking of the Romano-Gallic church. These countries had
been no doubt Christianised under the imperial influence. Treves,
Cologne, and Mainz were three great Roman centres, and they pre-
served the traces of their origin ecclesiastically, in the leading secular
position which their prelates maintained down to a late period.
What is true of the Gallic bishops is true of those of the Rhine, the
Mosel, and the Main. The Christianising of the rest of Germany
was due to other agencies, and has different characteristics; but it
has this in common, that it was never *Arian*. Although the earliest
Teutonic nations that were Christian were Arian, the Goths, the
Suevi, and the Vandals, yet the soil of Germany proper was never
polluted with that heresy. Those tribes either, like the Lombards,
Suevi, and Vandals, learned Arianism after they had quitted their
German seats, or, like the Goths, came from the East, took a southward
direction, avoiding Germany, and through Italy and France passed
away into Spain. In this way one influence which has considerably

affected Spanish history is eliminated altogether. Bavaria might, from its connection with the Lombards and Ostrogoths, have become Arian if it had been converted early; but it was suffered to continue heathen until the seventh century, and was then Christianised by the orthodox agency of the Austrasian Franks. Alemannia and Franconia were converted partly by the spread of Christianity and civilisation from their Western neighbours, and partly by the political measures of the Frank kings, but the spiritual part of the work was done by missions from Celtic churches of Ireland and Northern France under the discipline of Columbanus. Saxony remained heathen until it was conquered by Charles the Great, and it was then evangelised by missions from Saxon England; Frisia, the western part of Lower Saxony, by Northumbrian; and Saxony proper by West Saxons, under the influence of Pepin and Charles. It was to Boniface, the devoted English missionary, and we must remember also the devoted papal partisan, that these northern churches owed the character impressed on them throughout the middle ages, as most strongly national, most strongly German, and most strongly papal, in all points the least imperial.

Such, then, are the origins of the German churches, Roman, Frank, Celtic, English, so far as spiritual teaching with all its vast influences goes, and therefore unlikely to blend, in fact from the beginning arranged under different systems of organisation. The old Roman churches surviving in the three ecclesiastical electorates, their power strengthened and pampered with secular privileges by the emperors as a counterpoise to the power of Rome, and in secular politics faithful to the emperor, only liable to be checkmated after all successes by the spiritual powers of excommunication and deprivation exercised from Rome. The churches of Saxony, which had learned their first lessons of church policy from England, as I just said, were very religious, very papal, very national. In this relation of Saxony to pope and emperor, a relation so rooted and grounded in religious zeal, we have the key to the German history of the middle ages. The Saxons loved the pope, and unless the emperor were a Saxon they cared not a whit for the emperor; if he were a Saxon, then they were jealous of every moment he spent away from Saxony. Hence every anti-Cæsar was either Saxon or supported by Saxony; the anti-pope was strong only in the Rhine lands, and in the hereditary dominions of the emperors generally, that is, in the south. This is the great clue to Saxon history, and it is largely affected by the church relations in their origin and developments. For can we forget that this very Saxony, so Catholic while pope and Cæsar are struggling against one another, is the birth-land of Luther, greedily hurries into the Reformation, and most ruthlessly carries out the extermination of the older system which it had supported so long ? The national spirit of Saxony is strong against imperialism, and now that the papacy and the empire are at one the religious spirit of Saxony is strong against the papacy.

But here we get beyond the limits of mediæval history. And perhaps in what I have said I have gone rather beyond what is strictly constitutional history. The church in South Germany, in Swabia, and Bavaria has less individuality, and considering the large proportion of the number of emperors that were taken from the south, we cannot expect so much freedom of action. The Ghibelline spirit was stronger in the south than in the north Bavaria had always an eye towards Italy, as Austria has had in the later history, and even the character of southern religion is different from that of northern. The only prelate in the south whose position resembles at all that of the great prelates of the north and west, was the bishop of Salzburg, and he plays the same game with them. The laws, then, that had been the most imperial become at the Reformation the most papal. There the imperial hand is the strongest, and the religious instinct turns more readily southwards.

As regards the constitutional position of the prelates in Germany and the relations of church and state, I do not know that they present points of contrast or resemblance with the other churches that we have discussed to make it worth while to dwell on them. The German prelates are constitutionally secular princes, and their secular principalities are not their dioceses, but the accretions of endowments made at various times by the emperors to purchase their support, and confirmed for the same purpose by successive popes. The Saxon emperors founded great archiepiscopates in Saxony, to complete the system that they found existing on the Rhine, and to civilise, consolidate, and attach the north; but Hamburg and Magdeburg never equalled Cologne and Mainz, perhaps because the later emperors were southern and found that no such measures could propitiate the jealousy of the north. In the south the southern emperors were strong enough without this, and perhaps were afraid to strengthen the church too much. Hence there were differences of rank among the German bishops quite independent of their spiritual character. We have archbishops, electors, and prince arch-bishops, prince bishops, count bishops, and bishops simply. In a word, it was secular endowment and secular position that gave them their political status. They governed their states and commanded their armies as princes. The realising of so much of this is impossible without a reference to the history of the empire, which lies rather outside of my present speculations, and the peculiar character of the German ecclesiastical system is owing so much to its perfect assimilation with the German secular system, and both these are so foreign in later times to what we regard as constitutional history in other countries, and I may add I have so lately lectured at great length on them, that for the present I shall leave them alone, and only treat of them where they especially illustrate our comparative view.

XIII

THE HISTORICAL ORIGIN OF EUROPEAN LAW

ONE of the first questions that meet us in tracing the progress of
civilisation, and it is one that lies at the root of all government, is
the historical origin of the laws of the particular nation or nations
that we are contemplating. In theory this question, with reference
to mediæval Europe, might take precedence of the religious one,
which we examined in the last lecture, for, so far as the possession
of a code of laws went, civilisation had gone to great lengths before
the introduction of Christianity. But historically the civilisation of
modern society begins with its Christianising, and we have therefore
taken one aspect at least of that subject first. Our knowledge of
the laws of the nations before their conversion is very small, and
since their conversion Christianity and the institutions of earlier
Christianised society have, of course, had a conspicuous and in some
cases a controlling influence. The subject of law divides itself into
two—legislation and judicature—and of these legislation divides
itself into the process of law making and the substance of the laws
made. These cannot be considered in a single lecture even in the
most summary way. I shall begin, then, with the substantive question—the origins of the written laws of the middle ages ; I shall
treat the question of legislative process partly under this head, but
more at length when we come to the subject of government, and
that of judicature must in the same way be postponed.

Now, the fundamental systems of European law are threefold in
origin—are referable to three distinct sources : the original laws of
the Teutonic tribes exemplified in the more ancient portions of the
Leges Barbarorum, which may be explored at length in the collections of Lindenbrog, Canciani, and others ; secondly, the imperial or
civil law of the Romans, which must be studied in the Theodosian
Code and in the Corpus Juris Civilis containing the legal works
edited under Justinian ; and, thirdly, the feudal law, which, as being
customary, varies of course very much with locality and date, but
which may perhaps be found in its purest form, in its most theoretical perfection that is, in the Assizes of Jerusalem, the great body

of law of the feudal colonies established during the Crusades, in Palestine and Cyprus, and in the Grand Custumary of Normandy. These three sources, the law of the barbarians, the imperial, and the feudal law, lie at the root of all existing systems, and according as the intermixture of blood, of language, and of feudal institutions has varied, so will these elements be found to vary, although the two sets of influences do not vary together directly, or in some cases even approximately. Of these three—the barbarian, the imperial, and the feudal—the first and third might be described more properly as customs, partly written and partly unwritten, and according to date and locality more or less interpenetrated by one another and by the civil law. In the first, the Leges Barbarorum, which, of course, belong to an early stage of society, the element of custom is the strongest; in the civil law it is the will of the princeps, *quod principi placuit legis vigorem habet*; in the feudal law it is a combination of the two; as we should say in reference to copyholds, in which the feudal system has left its most distinct marks to the present day, it is the will of the lord and the custom of the manor. In truth, feudal law is a development of one part of the ancient barbarian law under the influence of partly Romanised institutions, and in the garb to a certain extent of Roman legal language.

Of this I shall have more to say when I speak of the feudal system in its original meaning in reference to the tenure of land; but it is impossible in a matter so involved as constitutional history is, to avoid occasionally anticipating. Now, there are theories of law which derive all modern law from that of Rome, either directly or indirectly, tracing both the allodial and feudal systems with their customs to the perversion or development of the institutions of the civil law. These theories are historically untenable, as I hope we shall see in this lecture, but at the same time it cannot be said to be easy to estimate the effect of Roman law. You must remember that, as we have just seen, all the leading nations of Europe begin mediæval history in barbarism, and out of various sorts of barbarism all have to win their way by one path to civilisation; that civilisation is won under Roman influences, the Christianity that effects it is Roman Christianity, speaking the Latin tongue and bringing in her hand the Roman law, suggesting new wants and new relations, new liberties and new restrictions, and clothing everything that is new in the new language. As the Latinised nations learned civilisation they lost their native tongue, as we have seen, in Gaul and Spain; that is, Roman civilisation had a retrospective and assimilating influence; even what these nations knew before and used before, they now learned to speak of in Latin language and incorporated with Latin usage. Just so the barbarians learning civilisation under the teaching of the Latin church : they learned to make new laws, and clothed them in the formulas of Rome ; if the substance of the law was not imitated from Rome, the language of it was ; much that is common to all civilised society thus got a specially Roman dress, and by retroaction and assimilation they began to write their earlier history in Latin and to assimilate their earlier law to a Roman shape. Hence the difficulty of estimating the real as opposed to the superficial influence of the civil law ; hence it is that only by insisting upon those particulars of judicature and practice which have no part whatever in the civil law, such as the ordeal, the *weregild*, and compurgation, we can distinctly eliminate Roman influence and say this or that nation's civilisation is not Roman, is at the base Teutonic ; and observing this, we look rather to the customary or common law of our nations than to the statute or written law, as a clue or as one of many clues to the identification of their origin.

With so much of preface, we will now go on to the laws themselves ; and I will here take England first, because our laws are the most ancient and purest specimens of the most ancient non-Roman law, and because our modern laws have developed from our ancient ones by a process into which very little that is Roman has ever filtered ; unlike Germany, which by the fatal union of its kingship with the imperial dignity became subject to the Roman law so far as it had any common system of law at all ; unlike France and Spain, which had the full benefit of the earlier law of Rome, and whose conquerors learned to legislate for themselves in the form of selection from the Code of Theodosius. You will remember that I am sketching very summarily, and not pretending to give you the substance of the laws whose authors I enumerate. Of the early English laws we have extant codes of considerable length from the hand of Ethelbert, the first Christian king ; Wihtræd and other kings of Kent ; Ina, king of Wessex, Alfred the Great, Edward the Elder, Athelstan, Edmund, Edgar, Ethelred, Canute, Edward the Confessor, William the Conqueror, Henry I., and every other sovereign from Henry II. downwards. The earliest of these are merely registers of customs. There were local judicatures and local usages preserved by oral tradition. As long as these sufficed, it would be hardly needful to have written laws ; but as the population grew thicker, and the little states coalesced, and superior jurisdictions limited the action of the local courts, and centralisation introduced conflicting tribunals, the need of written laws and the constant accumulation of new ones to suit new emergencies supervened. Hence the early laws are simply enumerations of fines and punishments for offences ; they then go on to prescribe and limit

jurisdictions. They proceed finally to define almost all relations and
direct the conduct of men in every province in which law is
applicable. So far as the influence of Roman law goes, it is only
very remotely and indistinctly traceable in any of the early laws;
even the canon law failed to introduce it in any considerable degree,
except in the ecclesiastical courts : these were only established in
their modern form at the Conquest, and the canon law itself is nearly
a century later in origin. The study of the civil law as science
dates in England from the time of Stephen. Putting aside the
indirect influence of Roman law, as traceable or said to be traceable
in the feudal system, I should place the date at which the civil law
began to affect English legislation and the proceedings of the English
lawyers as late as the reign of Henry III., just about the time at
which French began to be our legal language.

It is unnecessary that I should repeat what I have said as to the
influence of Roman institutions on our early history. I believe that
they had no more effect on England than was involved in the fact
that the common lessons of civilisation were affected by them
superficially rather than substantially. As our language at the
early period has no trace of such influence, and as there is no such
in the Anglo-Saxon blood, there is no such in the Anglo-Saxon law :
there is everything in the Anglo-Saxon law that speaks to its being
pure Teutonic : it is indeed of the purest Teutonic. It is not
uniform : the differing elements of Jute, Angle, and Saxon originally,
and the two conquests, or partial conquests, by the Danes in the
ninth and eleventh centuries made local and partial differences, so
that down to the reign of Henry I. local customs varied as the venue
lay in Wessex, in Mercia, or in what was called the Danelaw, the
eastern half of England ; but these differences only show how
thoroughly Teutonic the whole fabric was : differences in the murder
fine, and in the value of the oaths of the compurgator, and slight
differences as to the wager of law and ordeal. All these laws are
made by the king and people: from first to last there is no such
thing as a pretor's edict, a law made by the king on his own
authority : counsel and consent are the watchwords of Teutonic legislation ; *quod principi placuit* is by itself unknown to English law,
even at the time of the greatest abeyance of popular rights when
the king promulgated the decisions of his court in the shape of an
assize or a charter. And perhaps we may couple with this the fact
that English law throughout the middle ages was constantly growing : it was not codified, it was not restricted by statute law except
on certain points and at late periods : it was still in itself essentially
customary, and how great the customary element was may be inferred
from the growth of the practice of trial by jury, a mode of trial as

to the working of which we cannot argue in any particular case, unless we know the exact date of it, so rapidly did the plan and custom change.

The great English law books of the middle ages are not codes : the written laws remain clothed in the terminology of Acts of Parliament: Glanvill, Fleta, Breton, and Bracton, however high their authority and the authorisation under which they were published, are not codes but manuals of practice, attempts to embody the common law with its modifications ; not generally very successful or intelligible attempts, seeing that they fail altogether in giving us information as to points of the greatest interest. In all these points, in its antiquity, in its substance, in its characteristic differences, in its enacting authority and its character of growth and elasticity, the legal system of England is distinctly contrasted with that of the Roman law. Of course it has much in common in principle, if, as it is said, the Roman law is the clearest exposition of the common principles of all jurisprudence, of law in all the ways in which it affects all the relations of human life. English law and Roman law must have at all events enough in common to make them both entitled to the name of law.

As to the influence of feudal law on English law proper, I shall say only thus much, leaving further questions for future consideration. Feudalism touches the question of law rather in substance than in form : feudal government as affecting the enactment of laws, and feudal judicature as affecting the execution of them, I shall consider later on ; the feudal influence after these restrictions affects only the laws of land : as affecting the tenure of land only has feudalism had any influence in England since the reign of Henry II., and this influence has, like the rest of the customary law of England, been developed with the common law, restricted and modified in the written law, and embodied in the manuals of process. We have no book of English feudal law like the Grand Custumary or the Assize of Jerusalem, unless you regard Littleton's Tenures as such ; but at the utmost in England it is only a department of law, not a body of law distinct from the common law. There is no part of the country, nor any important interest, except land tenure, which is affected solely, or even principally, by customs of purely feudal origin. As it affects the tenure of land, I shall speak of it in discussing that subject.

In France the questions before us are much more complicated and abstruse. We have to recognise at the outset the permanent existence of a thoroughly civilised Roman society throughout Gaul : a society framed upon the older law which existed as the basis of the Theodosian and Justinian systems, a society which, though modified, subsists in its descendants and results to the present moment. Roman law is the most ancient basis of law in France. We have next to recognise the fact that the barbarian systems which in a measure superseded, but only in a measure, this earlier Roman law, were themselves also Romanised. The Visigoths and the Burgundians had clothed these laws in the shape of Roman law; they had selected from or adopted the Theodosian Code as soon as they began to feel the necessity of a law in their settled seats; and if, as I cannot positively say, the Franks themselves had not done something of the same kind, the Franks were becoming Romanised when they made their conquests, and when they became Christian became very distinctly Roman. Hence a great part of France was governed by civil law direct and immediate; the country of the written law as distinct from the law of custom—written law, i.e. Roman law as modified by the capitularies of the earlier Frank kings and emperors, and by the ordinances of the latter. The country of custom, or North France, was that in which the pure Frank and Teutonic were stronger; but, as I have said already, Frank as distinct from Teutonic, feudal as distinct from allodial. As in England so in France, feudality as touching law is rather a matter of administration than of substance, except with respect to land tenure; but where every provincial count and duke has a right to judge his own vassals, without the restriction of an ancient system like the Roman law, a various growth of customs does arise, and these when tabulated assume the appearance of distinct codes. Such are the Great custumary of Normandy, and the customs of Beauvoisis, the best known of the French custumals, a body of legal usages based on feudal jurisdiction, originally relating to tenure, but gradually extending to every relation in which land tenure touches the intercourse of mankind, and every sort of question which could be brought before the feudal court, a court bent, like every other law court, on asserting and exerting to the utmost its own rights and powers, powers that by their exercise became rights, too often tyrannies in practice, with that slight check that routine once learned imposes on irresponsible authority.

French law is, then, (1) Roman civil law, pure, and as filtered through the barbarian versions of the Roman codes; (2) customary, the law practised in the feudal tribunals; (3) the modifications of these laws, as exemplified in the capitularies of the early kings and emperors; (4) the ordinances of the kings of the third race, as they are called, especially such as had a general bearing, as the establishments of St. Louis and the acts of Philip the Fair and Philip of Valois, modifying and restricting the others. Of course the Revolution did away with all this, and the empire substituted for this variety the Code Napoléon. There is one peculiarity of French legal history which I have not noted—the fact that for several centuries after the Frank occupation the law was personal, not local; the decision, that is, of the law by which any person was to plead or to be impleaded, was according to his *nationality*, not according to *the locality* in which the trial occurred. It is thus opposed to the practice of English law, whose distinctions were local. This personal system seems to have existed in full force at the beginning of the ninth century, to have declined during the progress of it, and to have become entirely extinct in the eleventh. It is to this, moreover, that the accuracy of the separation of the *pays de droit écrit* from the *country of custom* is due. The population south of the Loire was chiefly Romanised; that north of the Loire was more thoroughly feudalised. In each case the personal law of the minority gave place to the personal law of the majority. Roman law became the rule of the south, feudal law the custom of the north.

The law of Spain, the common and fundamental law of the Visigoths, out of which, after the Moorish conquest, the Castilian and Aragonese jurisprudence developed, was of course originally Teutonic. The common law of Spain, the customary procedure, was, like the Lombard, the Burgundian, the Saxon, and the English, originally a table of wergilds, compurgatory regulations, and the like; but as the Visigoths very early became subject to Roman influences, their first written laws wear a Roman dress. The Visigothic kings adapted the Theodosian Code to the wants of their people, and embodied them with portions of the more ancient Roman law. Euric (466–483) was the first recognised lawgiver of the Visigoths; his laws, called sometimes *leges Theodoricianæ*, were improved on by his son Alaric, 483–506, the king who was conquered by Clovis, and with large additions also from the Code of Theodosius were incorporated in the compilation called Breviarium Aniani, the text-book of Visigothic law for both South France and Spain; each successive king after him added to this enactments bearing still more prominent marks of Teutonic origin, being, in fact, the admixture of the as yet unwritten common law with the adventitious Roman law. The body of law thus formed was called the *Forum Judicum* or *Liber Judicum*, in Spanish *Fuero Juezzo*; it was ratified by the councils of the Spanish church and in assemblies of the Visigothic people, and it formed the basis of the revived jurisprudence after the first shock of Moorish conquest had passed away. Between the development which it took in Castile and that which it took in Aragon, we may draw the same distinction as existed between Roman and feudal law in France. In Castile the Fuero Juezzo continued to be the body of law until it was superseded by the legislation of Alfonso the Wise and his successors; in Aragon it was very early superseded by the fueros or charters of towns and districts which answer to the customary laws of France both as to local operation and as to feudal origin. Aragon was, as you remember, feudalised; Castile was not. Well, the Fuero Juezzo, although in some degree superseded by the laws of the *Siete Partidas*, written by Alfonso, was not abrogated by them; it continued to be law until the present century, modified, of course, by the decrees of councils and by special charters and ordinances. The Siete Partidas was published by Alfonso in 1258. It is in this that the influence of the civil law proper, that of Justinian, first appears. Alfonso has in seven books drawn up an orderly digest of all the elements of law that previously existed: the Forum Judicum, the civil law, the local fueros, the decisions of councils, and the sayings of philosophers and saints. It is clear that in such a mass the early simple relics of Teutonic law would be very liable to be lost sight of, and in proportion as the civil law element wanes the old national common law wanes. We must not, however, suppose that even this elaborate treatise was accepted at once as the code of the nation; we may rather compare it with the works of our own great jurists who lived about the same time and brought similar influences to bear upon the modification of old English law; but, unlike the Siete Partidas, these never received any sort of legislative sanction. Alfonso was never able to promulgate them as a code; nay, they were discarded by his subjects as an attempt at innovation, and as by themselves unconstitutional; what legislative sanction the Siete Partidas received was by the act of Alfonso XI. in the middle of the following century.[1]

It is interesting to compare the spirit, for it is impossible to do it in detail, of the three great legal works of this same age: the Establishments of St. Louis, strictly feudal; the Siete Partidas of Alfonso; and the manuals published under Edward I., so strongly tempered with Roman elements. Perhaps we are inclined somewhat to undervalue the Roman element in the Establishments and to exaggerate it in the English law books, because it was to a degree natural in the former and adventitious in the latter; but the general impression derived from the literary or historic (for I cannot pretend to any legal) knowledge of them is what I have stated. But our Spanish and English books may be compared in a point still more interesting: I have just said that the latter never obtained legislative sanction, and the former only after long opposition, and then a quasi-

[1] An early compilation of his, the Fuero Real of 1250, was more generally received, but even it was only promulgated by charter, as a privilege to the communities that were willing to receive it.

sanction only; surely this points to the existence of a strong system of common or customary law in both countries which could not be set aside in a hurry, much less altered to suit the elaborate views of the civilians. The Teutonic element was still too strong for the lawyers, and it continued to be so in England; *nolumus leges Angliæ mutari* was the answer of the parliament of Merton when the lawyers wished to introduce the retrospective operation of marriage from the civil law. Although Breton writes in the name of Edward I., we do not receive him with the authority of Edward I. Edward I.'s laws are written not there but in the Statute Book, and that only is the proper exposition of his views, limited by the advice and consent of his parliaments, perfectly organised and duly summoned. To the civil law pure and simple, as to the canon law also, there was in England the greatest antipathy; nor were they ever introduced except into particular courts of technical law, as the ecclesiastical and admiralty courts. In Castile the introduction of the practice of Roman law was due to Alfonso XI., 1312–1350. Alfonso the Wise had given the professors of the civil law the rank of nobles; Alfonso XI. still further encouraged them, and gradually they undermined and eliminated the ancient Teutonic customs. With the growth of absolutism the practice of the civil law grew; with the disuse of the Teutonic customs the national hold on the conduct of the sovereign grew weaker and weaker; the old Spanish law remained, but it remained a dead letter. Happily this never became the case in England.

In Aragon, as I said, we see a different state of things; there the laws that were in real operation were simply special charters or fueros, like the assizes of the Plantagenet sovereigns, or still more like the Charter of John. The most ancient law of Catalonia is the *Usages of Catalonia* published by Raymund I. in an assembly of nobles in 1068. This is a mixture of Roman with Visigothic law; as usual the Gothic law prevails in the criminal part, the Roman in the civil portions; the laws of land are feudal. The *Fuero of Sopoarbe*, which belongs to both Navarre and Aragon, is probably of nearly the same date, and its elements of the same sort. Both were derived, no doubt, in great measure from the Fuero Juezzo. The laws of Portugal are little known, if at all, in this country; we can only infer from the tenour of the history that they contained less of the popular and free custom and more of the absolute authority of the king and his great barons. I have dwelt on the Castilian part of the story longer, both because its history is more accessible and its likeness to English law in many matters gives it additional interest. This likeness appears strongest, of course, in the fundamentally Teutonic customs I have glanced at. I believe that these are to be traced more distinctly in the fueros or supplementary charters than in the body of the codes : in fact, the codifier, from his altitude and the sublimity of his point of view, would naturally take the more advanced and refined form of expression, while the fuero, calculated for an occasional emergency or a local purpose, would be more distinctly of the race, racy. It is in the fueros, according to Sir Francis Palgrave, that we trace the long continuance of compurgation and the elaborate regulations of ordeal ; compurgation is not admissible into trials in the Fuero Juezzo.

But I have said perhaps more about Spain than I should have done considering the proportion that it deserves. Only please to remark that as in England, just as the national elements work their way through feudal law, and against the influx of the civil and canon law, liberty increases, the national genius for self-government expands and asserts itself, so unhappily in Spain the reverse takes place ; as the influence of the civil law increases under Alfonso X. and Alfonso XI., the Teutonic element fading out, even when no connection of fact can be traced between the two, absolutism increases, the influence of the nation in legislation and politics declines, and the way is made open as in France for a thorough tyranny. Surely here is more than a fanciful analogy. The history of Italian law is extremely complex, nor is there much besides its complexity that is peculiar. The Lombard law, like the Visigothic, is a mixture of civil and Teutonic legislation, and the Norman law of Naples and Sicily is distinctly feudal in its origin ; but the same causes that affected Spain affected Naples, and the same cause that affected Lombardy affected the great body of the empire.

The Norman laws of Roger Guiscard are extant in the shape of Constitutions, incorporated with those of Frederick II. in the collection of Peter de Vinea ; they were established in parliaments or general assemblies of the vassals, and had their authority from this source : although they included much from the civil law of Justinian, it was not as Justinian, but as the laws made, with counsel and consent of his barons, by King Roger, that they had their legal force ; and the same may be said of Frederick's legal enactments. The tendency of Frederick's laws, as may well be imagined, was, like that of the English the century before, opposed to feudal aggression, and directed towards the emancipation of royal power, coupled with a recognition of popular rights, the only certain bar to feudal tyranny and consequent disruption. The feudal law of the Milanese lawyers, which regulated feudal transactions, not only in Italy, but to a great extent in Germany also, is referable to the end of the twelfth century ; it contains far more of the Roman law than the feudal customs of England and France, as, indeed, might well be expected, seeing that it was a part of the imperial system. This law, embodied in what are called the Libri Feudales, is often found appended to the Corpus Juris Civilis; it is not of the nature of a code, but, as I have described the customary books of France, the legal treatises of England, and the Siete Partidas of Alfonso, an authoritative compilation to regulate customary practice in matters of feudal business.

We turn, however, in the last place to Germany; and here, I am sorry to say, we can only look at the subject briefly, and in the points in which it contrasts with what has been said. The several nations of Germany had originally, that is, as soon as they became known to us, their own laws, varying in expression and custom, but with the general likeness of the race. The laws of the Saxons, of the Bavarians, of the Alemanni, of the Thuringians, of the Mecklenburgers, or what were afterwards so called, are extant either in their earliest forms, or else as modified by the Karling emperors, under whom they were combined and permutated, and sometimes treated as one nation. I need not add that these laws, wherever we know them to be modified or added, were modified or improved in the national assemblies. Well, as in France, so in Germany, the substratum of native law was overruled by the capitularies of the Frank kings and emperors; and what elements of Roman law were introduced into the Saxon Code were so introduced. The Bavarian and Alemannian Codes were much derived, like the Visigothic, from the Theodosian; but the Saxon was free. Unfortunately, with the termination of the capitularies we lose all unity of law in Germany, save and except what the civil law created, or the imperial constitutions supplementing the civil law. As the capitularies had altered the written law of the nations, so the action of the Missi Dominici or of the Comites Palatini altered, generally in the direction of the civil law, the customs of judicature and civil process. But with the same paralysis of central power that puts an end to the capitularies, the central jurisdiction, both in itself and in its provincial operation, is paralysed too; everything, both law and judicature, falls gradually into the hands of the princes or the cities that are strong enough to extort or rich enough to purchase from the emperors exclusion from their nominal jurisdiction, or from all intermediate jurisdiction that is neither more nor less than perfect independence.

To trace the history of German law would be to trace the history of law in every little state, every little municipality, in Germany, and this is for us out of the question if we were to give our lives to it. Few of the German princes of the middle ages were lawgivers. From Frederick II. to Albert II. and Maximilian, no general law was passed affecting the whole empire. The Golden Bull and a few

s 2

260 THE HISTORICAL ORIGIN OF EUROPEAN LAW

similar documents are not worthy of the name of law, either from their scope or from the efficiency of their operation. During this long period also the courts of central jurisdiction were extinct; although the idea of such central jurisdiction lived, and attempts were made at times to establish general peace and a common supreme tribunal; but it is not until the time of the Reformation that we see the diets actually uttering edicts, and expecting them to be obeyed. The result of this was to leave the law to the mercy of the lawyers. Some few princes were lawyers enough to draw up codes, Lewis of Bavaria, for example, but few were strong enough to get them obeyed. The lawyers became a privileged caste, and as the tendency of the lawyers always was to adopt the hard and sharp, the lucid and definite, principles of the Roman laws, the Roman laws gained a general, though not universal, acceptance, to the exclusion of the ancient but varying and obsolete traditions. This, I believe, has extended so far that modern German law has less in common with the ancient system than any other in Europe. The difference, however, of allodial and feudal still subsists in the matter of tenure. So much, then, for the present.

XIV

SYSTEMS OF LANDHOLDING IN MEDIÆVAL EUROPE

It is upon the possession of land that the governmental system in all the mediæval nations depends ; and it is according to the way in which land is possessed that the character of many of their political institutions is determined, their political feelings turned one way or another, and their party combinations formed. There are but two ways in which, on first principles, land can be held : it can be held allodially, of God alone ; that is, the original title being in the possessor ; or it can be held feudally of some person or persons, the original title being in the gift of the one to the other, and being maintained by the performance of certain duties by way of acknowledgment. In the one case the proprietor is his own master ; his land is a sign and token of freedom ; he is a member of the nation to which he belongs, in the fullest sense of member-ship, and his possession of land involves him only in the duties that a subject owes to his sovereign or to his people ; as an indivi-dual he is subject to the laws of his country, but as a landowner he is no otherwise subject than if he had none ; nay, in general he is more entirely free. In the other case, the feudal possessor is subject to a lord who may or may not be the sovereign of the country that he belongs to ; that is, he has at least one lord over him besides the king, unless his lord be the king ; his land is a sign and token of service and obligation instead of freedom, and besides his duties as a subject to the sovereign and to the law, he has obligation and duties to his lord which may or may not always agree with those which he has as a subject.

Now, both these systems of landholding may be found all over the world. It is, indeed, an exhaustive division of all possible tenures ; a free possession with no service other than that which every subject owes to his state, and a non-free service where the title comes from some other source, and that source a single over-lord, or a whole nation, or an association of people, or a particular family. You get something like feudalism in Turkey and India, and in fact everywhere where there has ever been a conquest or an immigration ; but although this distinction is a logical one, historically, for the purposes of mediæval history, both allodial and feudal tenure are traceable to ancient German institutions, traceable in the earliest accounts we have of our ancestors through German, English, French, and Spanish history ; that is, although viewed generally it is a distinction in the nature of things, viewed historically it arises out of the nature of things as they existed in the ancient home of the Teutonic races. The *allod* or *ethel* was the piece of land which each head of a family possessed as entirely his own ; the *feod* or *fief* was that which the powerful lord or warrior bestowed on his retainer by way of fee or reward for his services, and to be held on the condition that those services should be continuously performed ; the obligation on the lord's part being to maintain his vassal in possession of the land that he had given him, and that of the vassal to defend his lord. The foundation in this case of the tie between lord and vassal is land held by both in good faith ; the privilege of the allodial is the freedom from all earthly service.

Now, it is obvious that according as either of these systems existed in any particular country, it must form the local or national character very considerably. In the allodial system is inherent the germ of all the institutions of freedom. In the feudal is inherent all that generally we should loosely term loyalty ; that is, all that in rude ages furnished the cohesive influence in a nation, the subordination of classes by an actual hold of one upon another, over and above the tie of race, language, and religion ; and with the subordination, all the benefits and also the evils that are sure to arise where men are entrusted with power over one another which there is no central force strong enough to regulate. Land, as I said, is in the one case the sign and pledge of freedom, in the other it is the bond of union but the type of service. Each has its political characteristics : therefore, with the allodial we invariably associate the patriarchal rule of the king, the fixed obligations which no subject of the state can elude, the *trinoda necessitas* as it is called : the right and duty of all free men to bear arms ; the divisibility of estates of land ; the equality of all free men in the national councils, the limitation of the royal power by the collective wisdom of the nation. Morally the characteristics are the love of the soil, the hearty attachment to the national leader as the head of the race or the chosen magistrate, and the preference of the life of the country to that of the town. The corresponding phenomena in the feudal tenure are the substitution of homage and fealty for the voluntary and genuine tie of tribal unity—that is, of an artificial for a natural bond ; the infinite subordination of classes each less than free in relation to its superior, with the inevitable curse of servitude at the bottom of the scale ; the limitation of central power by councillors whose qualification is not wisdom but the feudal relation to the lord and to each other, and who each is jealous of both inferior and superior ; the balance of power between the king and vassals—a balance of power which is never preserved, for when the king is strong enough to enforce authority the vassals are too weak to keep him responsible for the use of it, and *vice versâ* ; the substitution of the feudal court of justice for the popular one, of the indefinite aid for the fixed obligation, of a strict succession by primogeniture for the divisibility of estates ; and morally, the love of the court and camp, the essentially military policy of a nation governed in accordance with it, and servility instead of freedom.

It is obvious on such a view that the allodial system is that of a nation abiding in its native lands, with no foreign element to deal with, at home and in peace; if moving at all from home, moving in mass and carrying all the institutions of home with it into an empty land. The feudal as clearly belongs to a nation at war, a nation of warriors, of lords who have to reward their followers by gifts of land, and to maintain their hold upon the land by such followers so rewarded ; or of settlers who by the strong hand have taken the mastery to themselves, and allow the old owners to cultivate their lands or parts of them subject to service to themselves. The allodial system we are accustomed to regard as exemplified either in the Germans who stayed at home, or in the Anglo-Saxons who migrated in mass; the feudal, in the Franks, whose dominion was founded in military conquest and held by military tenure. And although other barbarian conquerors, the Burgundians, for instance, and the Visigoths, maintained their hold on the lands they conquered in the same way, still, as the feudal system of history was the result of the Frank conquest and worked out its characteristics most conspicuously in the Frank empire, we do not generally apply the name of feudal to any system but what was either Frank or derived from the Frank, as the Norman in Italy and England.

It does not, however, follow necessarily that because the land in a particular country is held feudally, the country is governed feudally ; but as a nation's form of government generally, where the nation is independent, is coloured by its political and moral principles, and as these are considerably affected, as we have just seen and as we all know, by the way in which land is held, we may be sure that the instincts of government which are peculiar to these tenures, and the capacity which each has of being made the machinery of a system of government, are not thrown away. The system of land tenure is not in itself a governmental system, but as a matter of fact it has generally proved the basis of one —generally and ultimately, but not without considerable growth and modification. Both these principles, then, are German; the allodial remains distinctly so; the feudal system, presenting points of analogy to Roman law, becomes modified by it, and that to a degree which has caused the civil lawyers to claim it entirely as their own; for in Roman law there is a theory called emphyteusis, under which a double title to land is held to subsist, a superior title in the lord and a subordinate one in the holder; and it is said by the lawyers that we must regard this as the origin of the fief. Combine with this double title the practice of commendation among the Germans, by which an inferior placed himself and his land in the protection of a powerful lord, making himself thereby less than free on condition of being supported by a stronger hand than his own, and you get, we are told, the idea of feudalism.

I do not quite hold this, although I am willing to believe that in many cases such has been the process, in England especially before the Conquest; but strictly speaking the feudal tie ought to originate in the gift of land by the lord, not in the adoption of a lord by the vassal. The relation, as I said, is one of universal occurrence, and hence I am rather inclined to regard the civil law theory as the Roman version of a common condition, and am quite willing to grant that as the barbarians became acquainted with Roman law, they adopted its formulas and translated their own customs into its precise and definite language; and I also hold that as the relation of clientship subsisted at Rome, it would be as fair to reverse the order of this theoretic combination and suppose the double title to be originally German. But I have said enough of this and on this principle in the other lectures.

We have now to see how the tenure becomes the key to the form of government; and first as to theory. We may imagine a government based on the freedom which we associate with allodial ownership: such a government as is drawn in outline in the 'Germania' of Tacitus, and elaborately filled up in Kemble's 'Saxons in England;' in which tribal assemblies exercise the powers of judicature, legislature, and military councils; in which magistracies are elective, and public business the business of every free man. We may imagine a feudal state such as that exhibited in the Assize of Jerusalem, in which all the land is divided in strict subordination between lord and vassal, in which every lord rules and judges his

vassals in peace, and leads them in war; in which the king is
supreme lord, supreme judge, supreme lawgiver, supreme general,
and supreme politician. In such a condition of things we should
say that government was worked altogether by the machinery and
on the tenure of land ; but historically, as opposed to theoretically,
there are other things to be considered. The alod and the feod
may be an exhaustive division of land tenure, but the allodial and
the feudal are very far from an exhaustive division of governments.
Not only may there, must there be countries in which the two land
tenures are intermingled, and in which practical views conflict, and
the government is determined by a balance between them ; but
the historical German or allodial system of government makes its
appearance in a world governed on a totally different plan at the
beginning of mediæval history, and historically the feudal system
of government, so far as it has ever existed at all, has grown up into,
through, and out of another system quite foreign in origin to it.
I mean, of course, the imperial system which the barbarians found
governing Europe when they conquered it, and which, when they
had taken to themselves the empire, they in a manner adopted
and modified and Teutonised, and ultimately feudalised, within
certain limits. There is thus another principle or set of principles of
government, which belongs entirely to neither of these ideas of land
tenure, but which may grow out of either system, or from a balance
of the two, in which the managing and regulating power of the
nation is placed in the hands of a sovereign or a ministry, who
do not owe their position or define it by the possession of land,
which may develop out of either system, or may even subside
into either, may dispense with the governmental agency or may
unite what is useful in both. For such a government, entirely independent of land considerations, we have to go back to earlier than
mediæval times : in mediæval and modern times it has grown in very
different ways out of feudalism, by the elimination of feudal
judicature, legislation, finance, &c., as in England during the Plantagenet period, and in an increasing ratio down to the present day :
in France it may be said to have been the result of a series of re-
actions ending in the military one, which is at present supreme. In
general the chances are greatly in favour of tyranny, resulting from
the forcible destruction of the old basis ; England alone has a history
in which ancient freedom has made its way through, and utilised all
that is good in feudalism, widening from precedent to precedent into
perfect political liberty.

But I am becoming too general. I return to the point at which
historically feudalism begins to be a system of government. I have
said that it belongs to Frank government, that is to the Frank

empire in its later developments: therefore the geographical extent of historic feudalism is co-extensive with that empire, or extends beyond it only in cases where its system was imported by colonisation and conquest, as by the Normans and the Crusaders. In England, then, it existed only after the Norman Conquest for a short time. In the greater part of Spain it never existed at all strictly speaking, only a system analogous to it; but in France and Germany it did exist and, although in different ways, worked out its destiny. We will, then, take France and Germany first and at length, and then say a word about Spain and England. The Frank conquerors both in Gaul and Germany found a system of law and government existing: they found in Gaul the Roman, and in Germany various systems; in Saxony, for instance, and Bavaria, pure German governments, barbarian if you like, but still systematised, and in the more Romanised regions systems more or less approaching the model of Roman civilisation. We do not imagine that either Clovis when he conquered the Alemanni, or Charles when he conquered the Saxons, repartitioned the whole of the lands or introduced full-grown feudalism; but they did carve out feudal estates for their chieftains, to provide for the men who had to govern the conquered countries as their representatives: they provided for their followers by the gifts of such fiefs, and where it was expedient to forfeit great tracts of land they planted them with feudal colonies.

Now, the problem is to trace from these small beginnings of feudalism the growth of a system of government such as I have described as feudal. How did feudal estates grow into the size and secure for themselves the jurisdiction of imperial provinces or nations, or groups of nations, and finally expel the imperial jurisdiction altogether; the risk of escheat or forfeiture being the only hold that the central power had on the great feudatories, and the suzerain himself being only *primus*, and sometimes *infimus* as well, *inter pares*? And how, this growth being thus traced, are we to account for the difference of the result in France and Germany; in the one ending in complete union, in the other in complete disruption and disunion? These things are among the most interesting and not at all the most obscure questions of mediæval history. (1) The gift of the early benefice bestowed by the Frank chief on his vassal as a reward for faithful service; (2) the office of an imperial minister employed in provincial jurisdiction; and (3) the position of an allodial owner living among his own dependants, are in theory three different things, yet in practice the three would not unfrequently be found together. Take, for instance, such a case as conquered Saxony in the time of Charles the Great. Suppose him anxious to maintain his hold on the conquered land by fair means, and that he finds among the chiefs able and well-endowed men willing to be faithful; or that he marries one of his own retainers to some Saxon heiress, and establishes him as imperial lieutenant in the conquered land. This imaginary vassal will unite the local influence of an allodial or indigenous noble with the beneficial or feudal provision of a *comes* of the great king, and may add to that the title of an imperial officer. Let the benefice become hereditary, and the chance is the imperial office will become hereditary too; the three characters interpenetrate one another, the whole tenure becomes feudal, the jurisdiction becomes hereditary instead of deputed, and the local influence strengthens him still more; the prince, duke, or count becomes practically irremovable; and when the central power is removed, which originally set up this provincial power, he becomes independent. And the character of the jurisdiction will itself become feudal, that is the duke will judge his vassals not in that he is their king's deputy, but in that they are his own dependants. This was so much the case already even under the Karling emperors, that they found it necessary to assert their own central jurisdiction by the mission of counts palatine or imperial judges; but so inveterate is the tendency that these also quickly became hereditary and feudal officers, the rivals of the dukes of the nations who had originally possessed a title analogous to their own.

Now, this became very early the rule in France: the counts and dukes very early became hereditary princes, engrossed all provincial jurisdiction, and reduced their sovereign to a nullity. In Germany it became so more slowly, and other causes were at work to modify the result. And how? In France all the land was held feudally, and the nation, although its constituent elements were widely different, speedily took a tolerably uniform character. In Germany the allodial ownership of land continued much longer; consequently an indigenous nobility continued to exist in the midst of their own people; and the five nations of which the body of Germany was composed grew less and less coherent. Every Frenchman was primarily a Frenchman, but a German was primarily a Saxon or a Bavarian or a Swabian. The ancient tribes of Gaul had under the Roman domination moreover been ground and welded together, while the nations of Germany had until the conquest by Charles scarcely anything in their history in common, however much they might have in law and language. We might imagine in France a perfect system of feudal government set up at once: we cannot imagine the same in Germany: the disruptive tendency in France grew up from feudalism, and when feudalism became effete the disruptive tendency ceased; but in Germany the disruptive tendency was anterior to feudalism, and survived it. The indigenous nobility, the allodial tenure, and the strong sense of national independence existed before the feudal system of government was introduced, and it exists still now that the feudal system has been long extinct.

Now, there are in the theory of the thing four stages of feudal government, and to one or other of them almost every phase of it may be referred, although every feudal nation does not by any means go through all the stages. In the first of these we may suppose every lord and vassal doing their duties to one another without infringement of right or dereliction of duty. In the second we may suppose the vassals to have taken advantage of the weakness of the central power, to render themselves independent in all but name, and possessed of entire jurisdiction, the right of private war, coinage, and other powers belonging properly to sovereignty. In the third we suppose that the central power, which is in every conceivable case the longest-lived, and has at its weakest some power of manipulating the vassal states by escheat and perhaps marriages also, has succeeded in creating for itself a real dominion, is able to engross to itself jurisdiction and all the other powers of which we have seen it deprived, and, in fact, to create a tyranny. A fourth state is when the subjects of this absolute prince have compelled him to give way to constitutional restraints, and have vindicated for themselves constitutional rights. When this is the case feudalism will remain only, as in England, a machinery of land tenure.

Now, as to the first of these stages, we may say that it existed perhaps in Germany under Frederick Barbarossa, and he had some difficulty in maintaining it; in theory perhaps it existed even in France under the Karlings. The second stage existed in France from the tenth to the thirteenth century, when Philip Augustus and St. Louis began to absorb the great fiefs : in Germany it was the normal condition of things from the deposition of Frederick II. in the council of Lyons. It was never so in either Spain or England, but it was so in Italy almost continuously from the break-up of the Roman empire ; but in this last case it was not owing to feudalism, the feudal character was superinduced on the original condition of disunion, and we may leave it out of the calculation. The third stage was arrived at in France under Louis XI. and continued without much change to the Revolution : if it ever existed in England, it was under John. And the fourth stage is peculiar to England, in which kingdom only has constitutionalism worked its way out of feudality; but even here we must make the exception that feudal government, strictly so called, never existed in England at all ; it was rather that the national spirit worked itself free of trammels that were feudal in character, and might have enslaved it. I connect, then, the distinction between French and German history with the difference of the degree in which, first, the constituents of the population were amalgamated, and, secondly, the institutions of the constituent races maintained their ground, the index of which is allodial tenure, with the continuance of an indigenous proprietary and system of law. In short, France under a feudal government breaks up into hereditary principalities which only require escheat to unite them; Germany, a collection of four or five distinct nations, unites under a thin superficies of feudalism to break up for all history into its original constituent tribes. And I believe that this might be exemplified at length by a comparison of the different parts of Germany, and that I could show how strongly the Saxons and Bavarians retained their peculiar and contrasted policy; how each had its own attitude to the empire or imperial centre, and how in each this feeling varied with the rise or extinction of the allodial nobility. Henry the Lion of Saxony was a great feudatory, an imperial deputy, and an allodial prince; and his attitude towards Frederick Barbarossa was distinctly that of the Saxon nation from the time when they ceased to give an emperor to the empire, that is since the middle of the eleventh century.

England before the Conquest retained the allodial tenure of land with such modifications as grew naturally out of it by the processes of commendation and subinfeudation, as princes grew powerful and received independent landholders as their clients, or as they divided their overgrown estates among their children and dependants. The truth of this statement would not be affected if it were true that not an acre of land was held allodially in England in the reign of Edward the Confessor; for the results I have mentioned grow naturally, and are not properly or historically termed feudal, though in the eye of the law they come to the same thing. The feudal tenure of land was historically a result of the Conquest, when the Conqueror and his successors took to themselves the ultimate title, and the custom grew up and prevailed that all land was held either mediately or immediately of the king: the state of things under Canute and Edward no doubt rendered the change easy, but the change came all at once and did not grow up out of those circumstances. One result of the Conquest was the extinction of allodial tenure, although many of the customs connected in idea with it continued. Unless, then, William had been very careful in his policy with respect to his vassals, this universality of feudal holding might have introduced a general feudal judicature, and feudal government with its universal disruptive result. But he avoided this, as is well known, by distributing the fiefs of his great feudatories over widely extended districts, in which no very considerable continuous tract belonged to one noble; by dividing the offices of provincial administration from the possession of feudal estates, and by retaining the ancient laws and methods of procedure in the law courts. He knew what feudal vassalage was in France, and would have nothing of the kind in England. The object of the feudatories during the reigns of William Rufus and Henry I. was to emancipate themselves from these checks, to unite great continuous estates, to make provincial jurisdictions heritable, and to establish feudal customs in the courts; and in the anarchy of Stephen's reign they succeeded in a measure, and every baron, as the chronicler tells us, was king in his own castle : he coined money, judged, tortured, taxed, and hanged his dependants, and fought private wars with his equals. But Stephen's reign was short ; the estates of the barons were not large enough to enable them to resist the uniting policy of a strong sovereign, and their anarchy and pretensions were put an end to by Henry II., who pulled down their castles, abolished their coinage, and by the mission of his judges altogether superseded in important causes their jurisdictions. Under him, too, many of the great Norman fiefs, either by escheat or forfeiture, fell in, and he was able to create out of them a new ministerial nobility, which readily recognised the central authority and its duty of supporting and guiding the people. It was this nobility that armed against the kings John and Henry III. when they were disposed to misuse the authority that Henry II. had won for them, and preserved, or rather developed, the constitutional liberties of Englishmen from the combination of all that was free and living in the older system with what was uniting and forbearing in the feudal. So it came to pass that in England there is and has long been feudal tenure, but not feudal government. The judicature of the country is developed from allodial Anglo-Saxon, Teutonic institutions ; the representative system has arisen out of the judicial ; and the power of taxation, legislation, and political deliberation of the nation has been vindicated and exerted through the representative system.

But this is to anticipate. You will mark how, the ancient tenure ceasing, the ancient institutions by the policy of William the Conqueror and Henry II. survive. They place, in fact, a feudal superstructure on an allodial substructure ; they take the strongest and most cohesive parts of each, and make their pyramid strong throughout with the king at the apex. As England, never having been part of the Frank empire, escaped altogether the evils of feudal government, and only tasted the fruit of the system at all by a sort of violent dose administered by the Normans, so Castille also escaped the horrors of historic feudalism. Yet there was very much in the land system of Castille during the middle ages that closely resembles feudalism. Castille had in great measure to be conquered from the infidel. The conquests so made were bestowed on barons to be held feudally—that is, with the duty and burden of defence—and this system grew up into something like general usage. But the same causes that in England prevented the further steps worked in Castille. The fiefs were scattered and the central administration strong; the barons were strong enough to thwart and overwhelm the royal authority, but never strong enough to oust it altogether; while the system of the Cortes, which, as we shall see, rested fundamentally on the royal charters of privilege, not on the feudal tenure of the land, had a tendency to deprive the great nobles even of what might seem their legitimate share of administration. This country lies, then, very much outside the scope of our present discussion. And perhaps Aragon scarcely less so, for although the land tenure is feudal, and the composition of the Cortes also feudal, the territory is too small to allow of rival principalities existing; nor is there in Aragon that contrast of feudal and allodial tenures which existed in England and Germany, and probably also in Castille. The tendency in Spain was not at any time to disruption: although the kingdoms were long in uniting, they were distinct in origin, and long maintained their separate condition and their separate institutions. The kingdom of Aragon contained, for instance, three subkingdoms or provinces: Aragon proper, Catalonia, and Valencia; and these each had its own Cortes, and did not unite like the German states, which also had distinct provincial assemblies, in a single diet, or like the French in the States-General. But the absence of a disruptive tendency is not equivalent to the presence of an amalgamating one. It was seven centuries from their foundation before the kingdoms became permanently one; and even when so united they retained their distinct constitutions. When they united, it was by a royal marriage, not by a movement of political sympathy or by an exertion of central authority.

But in these remarks I am straying away from the point in discussion, which is but little illustrated by the history of Spain at all. Whether the influence of Teutonic customs originally connected with land tenure, and long preserved in Spain—preserved, in fact, until the advance of the principles of absolutism and the practice of the civil law together wiped out all that was Teutonic in the Spanish institutions—may not have contributed to give somewhat of the sturdy independence and self-possessed dignity that is said to be the character of the pure Spaniard, quite as much as the consciousness of the long battle that his people had to wage for very existence against the Moors, and quite as much as the extensive privileges by which the kings sought to interest their subjects in the acquisition and maintenance of new territory, I do not know sufficient about Spain and Spanish character to enable me to say; but if we may believe the statements of legal writers such as Palgrave and Hallam, and the recondite authorities on which their conclusions were based, I should hold that this was not by any means unlikely, nay, that it was probable in the highest degree that a nation which was so isolated from Teutonic influences, and so formed and affected by others quite foreign to them, and yet retained its Teutonic customs for so many centuries, must have been very tenacious of its nationality, and most likely to gather from those customs all the strength and nerve that the nationality itself possessed. Its tenacity and the nature of that of which it was tenacious must have combined to give it an air of self-possession and self-respect.

XV

THE EARLY EUROPEAN CONSTITUTIONS

WE are now come to a point at which we shall be able, I hope, to utilise the speculations that we have gone through—to that point of constitutional history to which the name is frequently, but wrongly, as I conceive, appropriated, the department of government; and I propose to give this lecture to the consideration of the upper range of government, the king and his highest class of counsellors, leaving the later and lower developments, such as the origin of representation and the origination of bodies to be represented, to another lecture. We have seen, if not explicitly, by inference that in all the mediæval European constitutions of which we are taking cognisance, the ruling people is Teutonic, the Anglo-Saxon, the Frank, the Visigoth, and the German generally. We look, therefore, in this highest range of personnel for German institutions least modified by Roman ones; and even where we do find coincidences in this latitude between Roman and German, we incline to ascribe the actual origin of the questioned point to a German source. We begin, then, with the king, and ask, what is the origin and the limit of his power, what are his actual powers, and where are they circumscribed ? Now, a king in the old Teutonic sense was not an irresponsible ruler, nor an unlimited one ; he was at the top of the social scale, but he was not supreme as regards influence, either in war or in judicature; he did not name the magistrates who acted under him, nor could he determine without check the policy of his people ; he was not the primary landowner as in feudal times, nor the head of the religious system, nor the generalissimo, nor the fountain of justice. Nay, although he was a very desirable and influential appendage to a state, he was not indispensable. Although in the time of Tacitus most of the Teutonic nations—not all, for he mentions some tribes especially as *quæ regnantur*—had kings, by the time of Bede many of them had found out, as the states of Germany have constantly found in modern times, that they could do very well without one, and that the whole machinery of their simple polity could work without a head. This is very different from the Roman

T

imperial system, in which the emperor stood alone, irresponsible and without limit to his power; separated, however, not the less from the older machinery of government, the senate and the popular assemblies, or only united to it by the frail link of the Lex Regia, the supreme lawgiver and supreme judge. Still less does it resemble the feudal idea, in which the king is the sole and supreme landowner, general and judge, the source and fountain of justice and the supreme politician. Nor can we trace the feudal idea to a combination of the two. The feudal king historically owes his character to the fact that he superadded to the functions of the old Teutonic king those of the successful herzog or leader of armies, and eliminated in the increase of his power the old Teutonic checks; he came into a new land and left behind him many of the most precious institutions of his fathers; his servants become his counsellors, his word becomes, with certain limitations, law.

The first point to be considered is the selection of the king, and by corollary from it the power of deposition. Tacitus tells us the principle: *Reges ex nobilitate sumunt*: that is, first, the kings are chosen, they do not succeed by right; secondly, they are chosen *ex nobilitate*, that is, for descent; in other words, they are elected out of a single noble house or group of houses—noble, as we know from later history, by a presumed descent from the gods, from Woden as in England, or perhaps from some other-named impersonation of Woden's attitudes in other lands.[1] This restriction of selection accounts for the extinction of royalty in some of the German tribes of which Bede speaks, the semi-divine house died out, and the people found they could get on without one; of course only for a short time, for in peace some neighbouring king would always be happy to annex or revendicate; and in war, if a dux or herzog had to be chosen, he would not rest, as the mayors of the palace did not, until he had the name as well as the substance of sovereignty. The same was the case in England in one or two cases—in Northumbria, and especially in Kent, where the royal house died out—and after an interval of anarchy the kingdom was annexed. Within this family, then, the king had to be chosen, in England a son of Cerdic; among the Goths an Amal; among the Franks a Meroving or a Karling. The tendency under the circumstances is always (1) to a gradual extinction of the semi-divine house; (2) to the transmission of the chieftainship from father to son. Jealousy of power and frequent intermarriages tend to extinguish a family every member of which may be rival to every other; and if the king lives out his life, he has, in nine cases out of ten, a son to leave behind

---

[1] *Select Charters*, p. 56.

him who is fitted by education and an inchoate possession of power to fill his place. The tendency is thus to hereditary government, and the son will scarcely ever be set aside if he be grown up and not labouring under some disgraceful defect. That rule we see operates in all these states. In England, even under the Heptarchy, it is the rule, with very occasional exceptions; and after the consolidation of the kingdom it is the rule with only such exceptions as are necessitated by the difficulties of the case. If Alfred succeeds, to the detriment of his nephews, and Eadred, to the damage of the children of Edmund, you must remember, first, that those children were minors; and, secondly, that it was a time of war and trouble, while against these we have the case of Ethelred to set, a minor and the son of a murderess. In the former cases the nation wanted a leader as well as a king; when they only wanted a king, the claim of the child Ethelred was admitted. So also in the case of Harold, although there they went out of the house of Cerdic to seek for one.

Now, in France you do not find this except in the great cases of change of dynasty, when the Karlings set aside the Merovings, and the Capetings set aside the Karlings; the descent was hereditary because the mayor of the palace supplied the place of the herzog or leader, and the king was a cypher. Son succeeded father. In the imperial succession in Germany it was the same, except in one or two later cases down to the extinction of the house of Hohenstaufen, when the empire became a burden rather than a prize. The Saxon house from Henry the Fowler went on to Otto III. and Henry II.; the Franconian followed, when the Saxon became extinct, representing it, however, in the female line. So on the death of Henry V., after the intercalation of a single reign, the Hohenstaufens enter representing the Franconian house, and hold the sceptre for four generations; nay, in the empire so far is the elective system, until the middle of the twelfth century, liable to be overridden, that the dying emperor sometimes names his successor, and that not always his own son. In Spain the case is different. The theory of election and the practice of hereditary succession were broken into by frequent revolution and usurpation : the chiefs supplant the king by a chosen leader, and the king, instead of being superseded as in France by a nominal servant, is murdered or sent to a convent. With all this distinction, however, the theory of election remains, and in form and ceremony subsists, in England at least, to the present day. With the introduction of Christianity an ecclesiastical sanction is added to the simple act of choice; and with the influence of feudalism a further recognition and the renewal by the vassals of the oaths of homage and fealty. These three things are part of our coronation service, and although the crown is now and has been for ages hereditary in certain lines, they are legally necessary to the full title. Until the reign of Edward I. the idea of the heir becoming king on his father's death was unheard of, unless a previous election had been made of him. Henry II. and Richard I. and John are only dukes of Normandy and lords of England until they are elected, and then crowned, and finally have homage done to them. Hence the extreme solicitude of the Norman kings to have their sons recognised before their deaths; the great pains taken by Henry I. to secure the crown to Matilda and her son; Henry II.'s securing of the succession to his sons William and Henry in their infancy, and his refusal until he was dying to allow the same to be done for Richard. The succession of John can hardly be regarded otherwise than as a usurpation.

And we may add a further parallel to this. The kings of France, for several generations, did not content themselves with obtaining the succession for their sons, but actually had them crowned and admitted to a partnership of power. Philip I. so shared the power of Henry I., Louis VI. was king seven years with Philip I., Louis VII. was consecrated king at Rheims six years before the death of Louis VI., and Philip II. was actually sole king before the death of Louis VII. Henry II. tried the same plan in England by having his son crowned, and although it turned out fatally for him, still the plan was in itself not an unreasonable one. It prevented a disputed succession, and it also prevented the recurrence and prolongation of the periods of anarchy between the death of one king and the proclamation of peace by his successor, which occurred once or twice in England, to the great suffering of the people and damage of the royal influence. This plan of securing the succession was probably imitated from the Byzantine court, in which it was usual to have two or three co-ordinate emperors; it had been adopted also by the Karlings, and at a later period became the rule in the Germanised empire, the heir of the possessions of the reigning emperor becoming by election king of the Romans and coadjutor with the right of succession; not to be set aside, therefore, although not fully recognised until coronation at Rome made him sole emperor. Against this the German princes struggled as long as the imperial title conferred any substantial power. Though the emperor was called emperor and king, he was in reality also the elected general, the herzog of earlier days, to the perfectness of whose character it was necessary that he should be elected for a fitness which could not be hereditarily transmitted; nor as a rule was a man allowed to become king of the Romans who had not shown himself possessed of some of the qualifications, or the promise of them, that befitted a future emperor. The idea of the military fitness, of the character of the herzog chosen *ex virtute*, as Tacitus says, as well as *ex nobilitate*, may also be supposed to enter into the idea of homage paid by the feudal vassals to the newly crowned king; it had become a condition of the tenure of their lands, but the oldest theory of land tenure of the kind was that of the comites or companions of the successful general, not merely of the king; for the herzog they fought, and by him out of his domain they were provided for. Probably the idea, which might be historically worked out, never occurred to a single one of them throughout the middle ages. As the homaging, however, it may have been considered, was in its very nature the act of the warriors of the nation, the coronation, unction, and consecration were in their history and theory ecclesiastical. It was the bestowal of the power, or the recognition of the bestowal of power from above, as the election and homaging were from beneath. Into the origin of it I cannot go; it may have been taken from Scripture history, or it may have been one of the universal customs of antiquity; but it is the same throughout. The emperor must receive the crown of Germany at Aix-la-Chapelle and the imperial crown at Rome; the king of France must be crowned and anointed with the heaven-descended oil from the sacred ampulla at Rheims; the king of England must be crowned by the archbishop of Canterbury, and in later times necessarily at Westminster, and on the sacred stone which had been Jacob's pillow at Bethel. Each kingdom had some sacred relic which formed part and often the typical part of the regalia. The iron crown of Lombardy was made of the nails that fastened our Lord to the cross; the lance of St. Maurice was the sign and token of the royalty of the kingdom of Arles; the spear of Constantine was given to Henry the Fowler with the kingdom of Germany; so in England there is still St. Edward's crown, and in Hungary that of Stephen.

But a more important part of the office by which the consecration was conferred was the oath taken by the king to govern well and do justice. This is found in the earliest pontificals in the form of an adjuration or an exhortation, but it early assumes the character of an oath, a compact with God and the people to maintain peace and to do justice. It is emphatically a limitation of irresponsible power, imposed before the responsible power is conferred; for the king is not king until he is crowned, nor is he crowned until he has taken the oath. Our own coronation service is in origin the oldest in Europe, that of France being taken from it; in it the archbishop exacts the oath in a twofold character, first as high priest, and second as chief of the king's counsellors; he represents for the time both God and the people, and the theory of the oath is that it is to God for the people. I need hardly remind you how much import-

ance this position of the primate has occasionally assumed; the case
of Lanfranc and William Rufus is enough: then we know that notwithstanding William the Conqueror's bequest of the crown of
England, William Rufus could not obtain it until he had taken to
Lanfranc the three oaths, *Justitiam æquitatem et misericordiam in
omni re servaturum; pacem libertatem securitatem ecclesiarum
contra omnes defensurum; præceptis atque consiliis ejus per omnia
et in omnibus obtemperaturum,*[1] which so long as Lanfranc lived he
compelled Rufus to keep, though he broke them all once and for ever
as soon as the archbishop was dead. So Archbishop Theobald
secured the succession of Henry II. Thomas Becket, on the ground
of the primate's right of crowning, upset the whole policy of the
same king, lost his own life, and posthumously avenged his own
death. So Hubert Walter, in a speech of truly Teutonic freedom,
obtained the election of John; and Stephen Langton, a true Englishman, although a papal nominee and a cardinal, secured the rights of
the child Henry III.

I need hardly, except as a matter of archæology, refer to the
claims put forth by Henry of Blois, that the crown of England is
the special gift of the church; or that of the monks of Canterbury,
that it was their privilege and right to bestow it. But these matters
are of interest when you compare the theory of the thing with the
theory of the present day, when the king of Prussia crowns himself,
or of that of Napoleon Bonaparte, who, having dragged the pope to
Paris to crown him emperor, took that honour unto himself without
a call, and set the crown upon his own head. The coronation had
anciently always a religious connection: even when the emperor by
his word recognised a duke as a king, such as in Bohemia, Hungary,
or Armenia, the pope sent the crown, and the pope sent crowns
to the anti-Cæsars in a more venturous way and with less happy
results.

Connected with the question of election is that of deposition.
I have not said anything yet about the people who were supposed to
have the right of electing the king; but it now becomes necessary
because only they could have the right to depose who had the right
to elect. No doubt anciently, prehistorically, when the German
kingdoms were small and education and rank pretty equal, the
election was made by the people; in theory all the people, but as
the hereditary principle prevailed and there was less occasion for
speculation or room for competition, the election, which was often
only the recognition of a previously settled arrangement, devolved
on the wise men of the race: after the feudal system prevailed,

when it was necessary to depart from the hereditary succession, it fell to the feudal baronage and the prelates; and as parliament in England has succeeded to that position constitutionally, it has been settled by parliament. In Germany the crown was settled by the nations first, speaking through their dukes, then by the dukes themselves, and lastly the electoral body composed of three prelates and four electoral princes, the same composition of clergy and barons, although on a much restricted scale. In France and Spain the succession has been strictly hereditary since the beginning of the historic middle ages; and although there have been disputed successions, the strong hand has generally decided them. In the great changes in the Frank sovereignty, that from the Merovings to the Karlings, and that from the last French Karling to the house of Hugh Capet, although there was unquestionably some process of election gone through, as well as the process of deposition, the acceptance and confirmation of the new aspirant by the nation and by the pope occupy a more prominent part in history than the election. We can easily see how that is; few kings have ever been deposed for their own demerits unless there were some prominent person at hand to push the measure and take advantage of it. He is strong enough to prevail on the nation to depose his predecessor, but the element of choice does not come much into the acceptance of the successor, a point which I think is worth observing throughout modern as well as mediæval times. As a matter of fact, then, we may allow that the same persons or powers that could choose a king for a nation could also depose him; but it does not follow that in the received theory of the kingship any such provision was contemplated, or that the right was ever regarded as a part of the common law of any country. It was not, so far as I am aware, a part of any mediæval constitution that the king was responsible to his subjects for his good behaviour. There is no doubt that if it had been so, much bloodshed might have been spared, and much tyranny that was patiently endured for fear of civil war would have been effectually prevented. But it was not, the person and office of the king were always sacred. When it was necessary to get rid of him, the dagger or the poison cup was the easiest and most efficacious way; or a forced submission to monastic vows, which involved for all classes alike a civil death. Otherwise the change of a ruler was both in fact and in theory a revolution; and a revolution is a thing not provided for in any constitutional system. It is a suspension of the constitution, be the constitution rough or thoroughly and definitely organised.

We cannot afford to run through all the cases of deposition in detail, but take them together: the many changes in the sovereignty of the Visigoths were simply usurpations: the successful usurper put his predecessor out of the way, and the council of the kingdom received him as successor, elected him if you please to say so, but elected him because there was no one strong enough to compete with him: the whole proceeding, so frequently repeated, was one of force, and cannot be pleaded on constitutional grounds.   In France, the setting aside of the Merovings and Karlings on account of their faineancy was quite justified by the facts; but, as I just said, the necessity was made to appear only by the urgency of the new competitor.   In England between the union of the heptarchic kingdoms and the Conquest there was only one case, that of Ethelred the Unready, who was deposed by the witenagemot of England in order to make room for Sweyn, who had virtually conquered the country, and who, if he had not been elected, would have easily dispensed with the process.   This case is one, if not of revolution, of conquest.   Nor can I allow that either the case of Edward II. or that of Richard II. can be regarded as legally justifiable.   There was in neither case a simple act of deposition uncomplicated by actual treason or rebellion: in neither case was there fair trial: in both the subsequent murder of the deposed king must be regarded as a proof that the usurping successor was not satisfied with his constitutional title until his predecessor was destroyed.   In point of fact the obtaining of a fair trial for a king in the condition of either Edward or Richard was impossible: when a king has fallen so low that he is liable to be tried by his subjects, he has fallen too low to expect fair treatment; but he cannot fall so low as not to be dangerous as long as he lives, and thus death is the natural consequence and supplement of the deposition.

This, then, is what I conclude with regard to England: the theory of deposition may exist involved in the theory of election; but the power has never on that ground been constitutionally used, it is not in the nature of things that it should be.   The only case in which it is conceivable that it would be is the case of insanity, and there may have been insanity in Richard II., although he was not deposed for it.   In such a case there would generally in modern times have been not a deposition, but either a regency or a devolution by the mad king, or his counsellors acting in his name, on the next heir if one was at hand, or if not on some able and prominent noble willing to conserve the succession for the lawful heir.   So it was in the insanity of Henry VI.: the arrangements for his lunacy were strictly provisional; nor was his deposition broached.   His subsequent deposition is quite a distinct matter, the cause alleged being usurpation not lunacy, and the whole proceeding violent and revolutionary, to a greater degree than was the case with either

Edward or Richard. The proceedings against Charles I. were not only revolutionary, but in the very highest degree illegal and unconstitutional : they may be justified, by those who take the opposite view, by necessity, or by the declaration that the case was one for which the constitution had not provided, and that there is an expediency and a necessity above both law and constitution, but no special pleading can justify the sentence of death passed on Charles. The revolutionary proceedings in James II.'s case I need not go into : the question is not, has the constitution provided for a deposition ? but, have the transgressions of the prince reached such a pitch as to justify revolution ? There is in the selection of a king, or in the acceptance of an hereditary succession to a dead one, in the form of election or in the homage of the vassals, or in the oath of allegiance of a free people, and in the coronation oath of the king, an express compact of obedience on the one side and justice on the other : each makes the promise to cleave to the other, and the coronation and consecration were regarded as the sealing by God of a compact that was indissoluble except by death. The breaking of the compact by either might morally justify the other for the dereliction of his part, but neither could abolish the Divine sanction : the king might, however, shirk the difficulty by abdication, which was of course a mutual renunciation of it. Such a condition of the relation may be held to justify the deposition of a king, and in some cases it certainly does so.

Turning to Germany, we find the question complicated by other influences than constitutional ones : one especially is the claim of the popes to ratify the election of an emperor ; another is the complicated character of the emperor himself as emperor and king of Germany ; and another the equally complicated law of election, which rendered it almost impossible to produce a title in which no jurist could find a flaw, and consequently the deposition would be rather a declaration of nullity than an actual deprivation. The case of Charles the Fat is an exception to this generalisation, but then it falls outside of the period during which we can look at the imperial dignity, as thus complicated by election, papal acceptance, and the German kingship. Charles the Fat certainly was deposed, but he was insane, and it was necessary that his person should be under restraint : he was not set aside in favour of any pretender. It was an act of necessity, and may perhaps be regarded as an instance of the exercise of an admitted right on the part of the nations over which he claimed to rule. If you just run through the list of deposed or deposable emperors after the reconstitution of the empire by Otto I. you will see what I mean about the complication. Henry IV. was deposed, but by whom ? By the pope assuming to dissolve the tie which God had been held to sanction at the coronation at Aix-la-Chapelle, and denying to the king the character of an emperor, which indeed he had never duly received. True, there was a party, a large party, in Germany that accepted the papal release ; but the influence of a pope so exerted is not an element considered in the compact between a king and his people. The pope could deny the title of the emperor, and could absolve his subjects for a breach of their oath, but that did not constitute legal deposition, nor as a matter of fact did legal deposition often result from such a mixed procedure. Like complications affect the cases of Otto IV. and Frederick II. Otto IV. was first the favourite and then the victim of the popes, and they succeeded in depriving him to a large extent of the status into which they had helped to force him. But Otto's election was a disputed election, and it is questionable how far he can be regarded as having ever received the acknowledgment of the German people. The pope had crowned him, it is true, but the mere word of the pope could not uncrown him : in this case you get the threefold complexity—uncertainty of original title, complication between the offices of emperor and king, and complication between the pope's claim to confirm the imperial election and his claim to release nations from their allegiance. The deposition of Frederick II. by Innocent IV. is a simpler matter, but equally out of the pale of constitutional law : historically you can but view it as a piece of ecclesiastical assumption, which was taken advantage of by the mal-contents of Germany to bring about their own revolutionary ends.

But as we proceed we do find cases more colourable : that of Adolf of Nassau for instance, and that of Wenzel, one at the end of the thirteenth and one at the end of the fourteenth century. These cases are free from the papal complication ; Adolf and Wenzel were only kings of the Romans or kings of Germany, not emperors. Adolf, by his want of management and unprincipled conduct, had incurred the hatred of the princes who had chosen him ; and Wenzel, by his drunkenness and neglect of Germany, had justified the same feeling generally ; and in the latter case there was no prominent candidate for the position that Wenzel forfeited. In both these cases—and they are very exceptional—I think the diet and electors acted fairly and justly ; and in neither was deposition followed by murder, as in England and Spain. Adolf fell in battle, and Wenzel enjoyed many years more of tyranny and revelry. The case of Lewis of Bavaria is one of the most complicated imaginable ; it was a disputed election, it had no papal sanction : the coronation was by an anti-pope ; the empire was divided, it was indeed practically as well as legally in abeyance. These cases of Adolf and Wenzel are the really important ones because in them the process was not revolutionary, but steady, fair, and legal ; putting together the facts that at these times the imperial dignity was really elective, and the depositions legally carried out, you have the strongest cases of the inter-relation of the two rights.

Now, although I cannot, as you will see, hold so strongly as some historians do, the actual right of subjects to depose bad rulers, as being an explicit constitutional right, I am far from disputing the necessity and expediency of such processes : only I believe them to be cases *supra legem* and *extra legem*. But there were some peculiar cases in which the subjects had on their king a constitutional hold that almost amounted to the same thing : a conceded right on the part of the king that if he failed to do his duty in certain matters, his vassals might compel him to do it by force of arms. This right you will find in Magna Carta, not as a general stipulation, however, only as a provision for the carrying out of that particular agreement ; and Magna Carta has it not as a charter, which it is primarily, but as a treaty between John and his barons, which it is virtually, as may be seen if you look for a moment at the articles presented by the barons and prelates on which it is founded. It was a treaty made after a struggle ; and like every treaty of those days it contained a provision for the machinery by which its execution was to be enforced. You will find, in the treaties for instance of Henry II., a certain number of bishops and barons always introduced as sureties, who swear that if their king fails to perform the obligations he enters into in the treaty, the barons will renounce his allegiance and the bishops will put his lands under interdict until he complies. Now the clauses in Magna Carta are not so strong as this, but they do provide that the execution shall be put in the hands of twenty-five barons, and, if the king or his officers shall transgress the charter and persist in transgression after due remonstrance, then the twenty-five, with the *communa* of the whole land, shall distress and aggrieve the king by all means in their power, by seizing his castles, lands, and property until they shall receive amends, ' saving the person of the king and queen and their children.'

Now, I do not know of any other case in English history in which this implement was used, but it was quite reconcilable with the feudal theory of mutual obligation. Here, however, it is a concession by the king for a particular emergency : the barons acted on it : John did transgress : they rebelled and renounced allegiance, going so far as to bring over Louis, the crown prince of France, as a rival to John. This looks like a rough exercise of constitutional right, as exceptional as were the circumstances of John's election to the crown ; but the origin actually of the right and its justification must be sought in that executory clause of the charter. Now with this you must compare the privilege of union of Aragon, which was granted by Alfonso III. in 1287, and was not abolished until 1348. This was not an occasional article, but a deliberate concession of constitutional right: it contained two articles; one absolved from their oath of allegiance the members of the union of nobles, in case the king should proceed in arms against them without the sentence of the justiciary: the other related to the holding of the cortes, which they bound him to do every year at Saragossa.   You will find the history in Hallam, 'Middle Ages,' ii. 46.   This is a very curious coincidence, and may be partially explained by the thoroughly feudal character of the Aragonese government.   Some such provision exists also in the coronation ceremonial of the Hungarian kings, I believe, but I am not able to give the words.   In England, you are aware doubtless, the allegiance of the barons, as feudatories, was never the sole tie between the king and his subjects: there was over and above the homage and fealty an oath of allegiance to be taken by every free man from the reign of William the Conqueror downwards, continuing on the analogy and in imitation of the oath prescribed in the Anglo-Saxon laws, and determining the king's position to be not merely that of sovereign landowner and feudal superior, but the king, the cyning, the child of the race, the accepted ruler and father of the whole free nation.

[*See Stubbs, 'Historical Introductions to the Rolls Series,' ed. by A. Hassall.*]

XVI

THE KINGS AND THEIR COUNCILS IN
ENGLAND, FRANCE, AND SPAIN

THE constitutional limit of the power of the king is the council of
the nation, and the effect of that constitutional limit will vary
according as the council is composed of men who owe, or do not
owe, their place there to causes within the king's power to control.
In the freest ideal state the councillors will be men who do not owe
their position to the king; in the most despotic, the councillors owe
their position altogether to the king's will, and may be removed at
his pleasure. In every form of government which comes between
these two there must be some sort of compromise, tacit or expressed,
between the irresponsible authority of a king and the powers of the
nation as expressed in its chosen councillors, or by councillors who
do themselves without election represent the acting and paying part
of the community. We have seen how limited was the power of the
king in the primeval German constitution as described by Tacitus;
that he was not the determiner of peace or war, nor the general, nor
the judge; that he did not appoint provincial rulers, or exercise
without limit any function of modern royalty. He was simply the
representative of the unity of the race, simply a man with great
opportunities and influence who might by innate gifts take to himself power as a general, a judge, or a statesman, which he had not,
and was not supposed to have, *ex officio*. The constitutional limit
on his action was the deliberation of his counsellors, of which
Tacitus, in a short way, describes two sorts: *De minoribus rebus
principes consultant, de majoribus omnes; ita tamen ut ea quoque
quorum penes plebem arbitrium est, apud principes pertractentur.*[1]
On minor matters the princes consult; on greater matters all (that
is, all the grown-up free men); but the princes also give a thorough
discussion to the matters, the absolute decision of which rests with
the mass of the people. We may infer from this that there were
two sorts of councils, one of the *principes*, and one of the whole

---

[1] *Select Charters*, p. 56.

mass of the people, including *principes, nobiles, ingenui,* and all *liberi*; that in the more select assembly ordinary matters of routine were managed, and other measures prepared for the acceptance or rejection of the people; in the wider assembly apparently every matter of national importance was, after previous handling perhaps by the chiefs, deliberated, discussed, and decided. Tacitus further describes the way in which the greater assemblies were held. He tells us that they were judicial assemblies, and that in them were chosen provincial rulers, who were to administer justice in the smaller divisions of the territory.[1] It is, in fact, clear that most of the business of a small free nation at peace must be of such a character that it will have little more to do than to elect magistrates, to try criminals, and to regulate the transfer of lands. Taxation there is none that is not amply provided for by the *trinoda necessitas*; and as for legislation, the laws existing are immemorially sacred, and require no improvement or alteration. It may appear that Tacitus describes a state of things necessary in a condition of semi-barbarism, and by no means peculiar to the German genius; but it is no drawback to the truth of the description that it is more generally applicable.

But it is obvious enough that a state of affairs in which all the free men can join and deliberate in a single assembly belongs only to a very small organisation, and that as civilisation increases, the share of the great mass in deliberation will be confined to assenting to or differing from the conclusion of the chiefs; their attendance will become impossible, and at last, unless some system is devised in which representation can be substituted for actual presence, the whole authority will be engrossed by the chiefs. Such was the case in every great nation: the general assembly with universal suffrage survived through the middle ages in some of the smallest communities, such as the little republics of Switzerland; but we may trace the existence of the idea in the twofold annual meetings of the Frankish and German kings, in one of which national questions were treated by the princes, and in the other a military levy of the whole force of the nation was held. Now, in the earliest witena-gemots in England you can still trace the presence of the plebs, the folk; and it is rehearsed in the preamble of the laws that were made in them, that they had the assent of the whole people. They were made by the great men, with the suffrages of all; King Ina of Wessex, with the counsel and teaching of his bishops and earldormen and the most distinguished wise men of his kingdom, and also with a large assembly of God's servants, does command so and so.[2] It is

[1] *Select Charters,* p. 57.   [2] *Ibid.* p. 61.

probable that in all these early parliaments, and in all countries where they were used, there were considerable concourses of people who were loosely held to represent the nation; but the supreme deliberation was engrossed by the smaller class, the *principes* of Tacitus, the witan or *sapientes* of historic German institutions. The meeting of these was in England called the witenagemot, and on the Continent was known by similar names, *concilium sapientum*, or *mallus*; or *magnum concilium*, or *curia*, and so on. You will remember that it was not a representative assembly as we now understand the word; taken altogether, it did represent the people, but it was because, by a sort of fiction, it was supposed to be the people; the members of it did not sit as delegates, nor were they chosen by any larger body to represent their interests there.

In the lower courts of the nation representation was a regular institution. The judicial function was entrusted to a select body of judges or assessors of the judge in the folkmote, and the districts were at a later time represented in it by some of their own members elected so to serve; but the principle of representation reaches the highest order of assembly last of all. The members of the witenagemot owe their position to their personal qualities. They are what are called the wise men, the *sapientes*. Who now are they? First: after the conversion of the nations, wisdom is almost engrossed by the clergy, and the nations have a very proper consciousness that it is so. With the introduction of Christianity war has ceased to be the normal state of things, and the council of warriors the only practicable council; the arts of peace are those in which most of the work lies, and these the clergy understand, they also know the laws, and have the art of writing. The bishops are an indispensable element in the witenagemot; so are the ealdormen, that is, the great magistrates who administer the justice and taxation, and lead the armies, the magistrates who are either, as the theory suggests, elected by the people in their provincial assemblies, or nominated by the king and witan, magistracies with a constant tendency to become hereditary, and therefore to constitute an hereditary nobility. Besides these two there is a third element, the king's friends and servants, his *comites* or *gesiths*, or *antrustiones* or *thanes*, those counsellors who owe their position to his choice, his vassals as under a feudal government we should describe them.

The assembly of these three classes, bishops, princes, and *comites* or *ministri*, is the witenagemot—is the assembly that canvasses with the king every national measure, makes laws, levies taxes, determines war or peace, nominates bishops and ealdormen, executes high justice, gives or forfeits lands, and regulates the transfer of them, and on a vacancy or on misbehaviour chooses and deposes kings. It is limited in number, neither bishops, nor great nobles, nor the immediate dependants of the sovereign being very numerous at the early time. It is elastic also, for it will admit, besides these, princes of the blood royal, and even foreign advisers whose ability and good faith can be relied on. The qualification of the councillors is wisdom. Time advances and matters change. The king becomes more powerful; his *comites, thanes,* or *ministri* increase in number; all the public land in the country goes under his name, and he bestows it as he pleases, and the new holders are his vassals, and the ealdormen whom the witan appoint are chosen from his vassals; and either gradually the whole system becomes feudalised, or by change of dynasty, as in England, feudalism comes in *per saltum*; and then the character of the royal council changes, or is seen to be changed, and it is now one in which every member holds his place by a title flowing from the king. Even the bishops, the most ancient element, are made to hold their lands feudally, and to risk the loss of their immemorial character by joining to it the baronial. The witenagemot ceases to be an assembly of the wise, and becomes the assembly of the king's tenants in chief, his barons, his feudal council, who, like the homage of a manor, are attached to him by attornment, by homage and fealty, the basis, however, of the tie and the basis of their qualification being land, the title to it derived from the king as supreme landholder.

So far, I think, the development of this principle runs pretty equally through all the polities; as feudalism or its equivalent prevails, the supreme national council changes its character. In some countries it develops still further into representative institutions; in others it breaks up into groups of feudal jurisdictions; in some it advances a certain way in either direction, and ends in the monopoly of power by the king. In our typical states we may say: in England and Spain it developed into representative institutions; in France and Germany it broke up into an infinitude of feudal jurisdictions; the form of the royal council subsisting, however, for certain purposes, and with a certain deceptive appearance of unity. But the steps of these developments were very different, and no generalisation will comprehend all. Each has a history of its own, and to get some idea of this in outline we must go now into separate detail; and for this purpose it is unnecessary to recur to the older state of things, during which the councils were of a character common to the four nations. We saw that in Spain the church element under the Visigothic kings was supreme; and we may say that during that period in France and Germany the military element was, in conjunction with the clerical, the most influential. In

England the wisdom which gave name to the assembly could hardly be of a more advanced sort in either direction than it was abroad. It may have originally implied acquaintance with the laws, and prudence in affairs; but if it did, it simply implied qualities that were supposed to belong to all counsellors.

We will therefore now suppose all these distinctions to have merged in the feudal qualification; the king is the head of the state, and his council is the assembly of his tenants in chief. Let us sketch very briefly the history of the institution, first in England, second in Spain, third in France, and fourth in Germany. Taking for granted that the feudal tenure became under the Norman kings the common tenure in England, their council was composed of their tenants in chief. But neither William I. nor William Rufus troubled himself much with other men's advice. They went their own way, they held their courts and wore their crowns, and published laws as had been done before with the counsel and consent of their wise men; but they were despots, and even under Henry I. the only restrictive power of the king was that of routine and a strong determination on Henry's part to enforce law: the enforcement of law implies a law to enforce and a habit of respect for it. During this period the great feudatories were constantly rebelling, desirous to establish their own minor jurisdictions and to break up the kingdom into their own fiefs independent of a central jurisdiction, or only nominally, as in France, dependent on the king. The failure of these rebellions and the forfeiture and breaking up of estates increased in a very large ratio the number of tenants in chief of the king; and accordingly, when in the reign of Henry II. the liberties of the nation began to look up, and the great council to show some opposition to royal caprice, it became necessary to regulate in some way or other the numbers and nature of the assemblies; nor was it easy or advisable to compel the attendance of all the vassals, many of whom were poor and uninfluential. To secure, however, a meeting of barons, and perhaps to give the king a proper influence in selection, the form of summons was adopted. The greater barons were summoned specially, and the minor tenants were summoned generally by the sheriffs in the county court. This plan enforced the attendance of the barons, whose presence was really important, and left it open to the minor tenants to attend or not as they happened to have business or leisure to make the journey. This is the system described in Magna Carta, and was probably devised during the reign of Henry II.[1]

In the reign of John first, and in that of Henry III. in an

---

[1] *Select Charters*, pp. 163, 299.

increasing ratio, the principle of representation, which had been previously adopted for judicial and financial business in the county court, was applied to this ; a custom had grown up of electing in the county court two knights to select the juries for the great assize, to assess or assist in assessing the taxes, and for other such business. Now, in order that the minor personages who in theory had the right to be present at the national councils might be really represented, each county was ordered to appear by two knights ; and these knights, being chosen in the county court, in which every freeholder had a vote, were really representatives, not merely of the king's tenants, but of the whole county, and as such they voted supplies that affected the whole county which they represented. This is the origin of knights of the shire, the first representative element, to which were added, first by Simon de Montfort and afterwards by Edward I., representatives of the towns. These two representative elements, conjointly with the barons, lay and ecclesiastical, composed the parliament of England ; if in addition the judges and other advisers of the crown were called in, it took the title of great council ; but great councils differed from parliaments both in the manner of summons and in the extent of their powers.

Early in the fourteenth century these elements split off into two houses, and although each estate continued to tax itself separately for several years, it remains still the parliament of England—the house of lords and the house of commons. By these are represented the three estates of the realm—the clergy, the barons, and the commonalty—the clergy represented by the bishops, the barons representing themselves, and the house of commons representing the commonalty of both country and town. Without the joint assent of the two houses, no measure since the reign of Edward I. can become law ; no taxation can be legally made without the same since the confirmation of charters by Edward I. in 1297 ; and on all subjects of national interest the two houses have, except by mutual agreement, a right to be heard and to discuss—a right enforceable by them against the ministers, whose supplies they can stop, or whom by votes they can displace, on a principle of usage and compromise generally understood, although not a formal part of constitutional law. This is an outline of the growth in England of the limit on royal power merely as touching form ; the exact details of the steps by which each part of the constitution got its present place, by which it was qualified for power, and by which it obtained, held, and increased it, involve a long series of narrations which, if I were to attempt now, would destroy all chance of our being able to compare the history of other states with them. Be it sufficient to say that Henry II. defeated the disruptive working of feudalism as we shall see it in France and Germany, and that Edward I. consolidated by representation of counties and boroughs a symmetrical and definite constitution of parliament which, having the command of the purse-strings and the confidence of the people, was sure in the long run to make tyranny impossible. It had a hard struggle to realise all its rights, and under both Tudors and Stewarts the older history of both king and parliament was obscured; but in theory little has been assumed beyond the letter of law and authority of precedent as it was recognised by Edward I. The constitution was complete then as regards its machinery; it has only added strength and elaboration of detail and power of easier working.

Thus in England, out of the feudal court of the king, which succeeded to the place and incorporated the elements of the old witenagemot, which by successive steps received the modifications which made it a fair representation of the church, the nobles, and the commons, sprang, defined and completed by the genius of this great king, the modern English parliament. Mark, however, three points before we proceed.

1. The name of parliament properly signifies, not the assembly, but the purpose or employment for which it is called, as we might say, the session. Hence the word parliament, when it does become applied to the members of the assembly, as in each country where it was used it did come to be applied, may have a different meaning according to the actual constitution of the body, or the purpose for which it was called. It means simply a talking, and when it is applied to the talkers its meaning varies. The parliament of England, the parliament of Paris, and the parliament of Naples were three very different things.

2. Observe that although the English parliament is a practical representation of the three estates, it is not called together on the same principle on which the states-general in France and the Netherlands were called. We have traced the process and seen how it sprang from the combination of the witenagemot with the king's council and the representatives of the counties and boroughs. That the organising and defining genius of Edward would gladly have made it also a representative assembly of the three estates, we know from the fact of his summoning the clergy to appear by their representatives, a summons which, known by the name of the clause *præmunientes*, appears still in the writ addressed to every bishop at the beginning of a new parliament, and which has not since the fourteenth century been attended to. This summons is altogether different from the summons to the convocation, which is a purely ecclesiastical assembly. If Edward's plan had taken effect, we should

have had either three chambers of parliament—the lords, the clergy, and the commons—or the two houses of lords and commons, the latter divided into the knights of the shire, the proctors of the clergy, and the burgesses. As the thing came to nothing, we cannot argue as to what line it would have taken had it really succeeded. As it was, you know the clergy neglected to send deputies, and the right of taxation therefore by a compromise devolved on the house of convocation, which retained it until the reign of Charles II.; the bishops sitting in the house of lords was regarded as political influence enough for the clergy at the time; and considering their other ways of affecting politics, it certainly was, for at the time the ministers of state were always clergymen, and they had moreover the right of sitting in the house of commons as representatives of shires or towns. If, however, the plan had been successful, we should have had in our parliament, besides its character of witena-gemot and of the king's court, a perfect theoretical representation of the three estates.

3. Mark that although in England we had for certain purposes provincial or county courts, we had never since the days of the heptarchy provincial assemblies of estates either for legislation or taxation; the provincial courts shared the judicature but not the other powers of a national assembly; the elements were the same, but the powers were different. Had it been otherwise, no doubt the hold of feudalism, slight as it was, on the provincial jurisdictions would have broken up the national unity as it did in other lands. I mention these three points because by pointing them out before we proceed to sketch the national councils in other countries, we have points of contrast made clear which will save much repetition.

We will now look at France; and as I have said so much about the early French system, which became extinct with the Karlings, I will very shortly characterise the proceedings of the third race. Up to the reign of Philip the Fair there was no national council in France except ecclesiastical ones, with which we have not now to do, except in so far as they may have afforded a pattern for the lay councils. During this time the king had a feudal court of his own great vassals, which seldom met, and then not for much business; he had also a court of the vassals on his own demesne states, in which he despatched business like any other lord of the manor, or any duke of Normandy or count of Anjou. And in each of the feudal principalities which had made out for themselves a practical independence under the nominal suzerainty of the king at Paris, there were feudal courts often partaking of the character of assemblies of estates. But there was no general assembly and no estates-general until 1302. As the kings Philip II. and Lewis IX. gathered in the great fiefs, they did not collect the provincial estates into one assembly; they conducted their deliberations just as when they had independent rulers, the king merely stepping into the seat of the count or duke. Philip the Fair, perhaps observing the reforms of Edward I., or perhaps seeing the expediency of extinguishing the irregularities of government produced by these multitudinous assemblies—having, moreover, a purpose to serve, to unite the whole spirit of his nation against the outrageous proceedings of Boniface VIII.—summoned the three estates to meet in 1302, and sometimes afterwards, for the purpose of taxation. These estates were the prelates and the representatives of the clergy, the nobles, and the deputies from the chartered towns.[1] Of the functions and later history of this council I shall have something, not much, to say in other lectures. You will observe, however, that it differs radically from the development of English institutions which were almost contemporaneous with it; it does not grow out of any preceding assembly, national or feudal; it had, no doubt, its prototype in the petty provincial assemblies, but it did not develop out of them, and from the beginning its history is different. Nor did it extinguish the provincial estates either.

Now, Philip the Fair instituted or developed another assembly, which I merely notice now that you may not be tempted to confound it with the states-general—that is, the parliament of Paris: remember the distinction I have drawn as to the use of the word parliament. In France it was applied to the merely judicial sittings of the king's court, the aula regis; this Philip, by the admixture of a large number of lawyers, erected into a supreme court of judicature, which, moreover, had the privilege of registering, for it had no power in modelling, the ordinances which under the despotic rule of the kings of the third race took the place of laws. The parliament of Paris was simply analogous to the curia regis (judicial council of the Plantagenet kings) and other courts of Westminster; it had nothing to do with the government, although it sprang directly from an organisation (the curia or aula regis) which might under favourable circumstances have grown into something like a real national assembly. I say it might have done so, because if we look to Spain, or indeed if we look to Flanders and other provinces actually cut off in the middle ages from the body of France, we see that a similar institution was the germ of a real parliament of the English form. In Aragon, certainly, out of a feudal council of the king's vassals grew the Aragonese cortes, a definitely organised and definitely empowered national assembly.

---

[1] States-general in 1302, barones, prælatos, duces et comites, abbates et procuratores capitulorum, decanos et custodes ecclesiarum collegiatarum, vicedominos, castellanos, majores et scabinos civitatum.

But we will take Castile the first, because it is the largest and has the most importance in history; it springs too more certainly than that of Aragon out of the old Gothic liberties. The origin of the cortes is in the ancient national assemblies; but the whole history of the transition from the thoroughly ecclesiastical organisation which under the Visigothic kings assumed the character and powers of the national assembly, to the state of things in which we find the mediæval cortes in full working, is very obscure indeed. We can merely say that, while in the beginning of the eleventh century we can find only bishops and barons taking part in it, some time before the end of the twelfth century it contained a very large ingredient of the deputies of towns and chartered districts. These towns and chartered districts or communities were, as we shall see, privileged corporations established by the kings for the consolidation of the country newly wrested from the Moors, and one part of their privileges was that they should not be taxed without their own consent given by their deputies in the general council of the nation. They had reached this eminence before the year 1188, at a time when no other people in Europe practically enjoyed the like liberty, and no doubt they had gained it from the policy and the exigencies of the kings, their need of money, which the growth of settled commerce enabled the towns to supply, and the desirableness of interesting such important bodies in the business of the kingdom. They owed their summons, then, not to their indefeasible character as freemen, not to their tenure of lands and houses as feudal dependants of the crown, but to distinct acts of royal policy, recognising natural right and sound policy, but not developing the system out of a previously existing one, as in England and elsewhere. And, strange as it seems to us, as time went on, the representative elements of the cortes ousted the two elder estates from a share in their deliberations; the bishops and nobles were free from taxation, and of course it would have been on first principles unfair for them on the strength of their own immunities to join in taxing the people; but there was no reason why they should have been deprived of their right to legislate. The prelates were excluded from the cortes in a long series of sessions which Hallam enumerates from 1295 to 1505, and from most of these the nobles also; but it does certainly seem that such an exclusion was founded on an abuse, and that the deliberations of the cortes must have lost greatly in importance when so influential a constituent of the nation took no part in them; while their determinations must have been weakened in point of efficiency when such large bodies of interests would feel themselves free to act in opposition to them.

And this probably explains the fact that through the middle

ages the deliberations of the cortes are far more important as deliberations than they are efficacious as political causes. They were brisk fighters, and they discussed all manner of business, but in the end, in struggles with the royal power, well backed by the nobles, they had to give way. It is evident, however, that the natural tendency of the Castilian cortes was somewhat democratic; but the king had the great advantage in being able to determine how many and which of his communities should be summoned to each cortes; and in general the plan, as well as its principle, was too flexible to be in itself a lasting check on a powerful monarchy.

In Aragon the cortes was the feudal court of the king divided into four branches or estates: *ricos hombres*, or greater barons; *infanzones*, or lower barons; prelates and clergy, and representatives of towns. If you consider that the first two branches were simply two divisions of the same class, you get a symmetrical meeting of three estates, just as they were in the provincial estates of France or Flanders. In Aragon, I believe, the existence of these may be traced further back than in France, but the thing is the same. Now, in England, by Magna Carta, you may remember, a distinction is drawn between the greater and lesser barons, the former of whom are to be summoned to parliament by writ, and the latter by a general summons addressed to the sheriff; these greater and lesser barons may be supposed to answer to the *ricos hombres* and *infanzones*; but there is the radical distinction that in Spain all these were noble, while in England nobility of blood gave no title whatever to a share in government apart from the tenure of land and the royal summons. Moreover, while the English lower barons came soon after Magna Carta to be represented by the knights of the shire, the *infanzones* in Aragon were not represented; they appeared in person, as in theory all the free tenants of the crown appeared in Henry II.'s great courts in England. Into some of these points I shall have to go again in our further lectures.

The parliaments of Naples and Sicily were also strictly feudal; there the distinction into estates, however, was not adopted: the members sat in two houses, the lords and the commons, according to Giannone; the upper including bishops and barons, the latter lower clergy and representatives of towns; but I cannot be confident about this, because the tendency of all constitutionalists of Giannone's age is to try to bring the ancient form of the continental constitutions into as close a conformity as possible with that of England, at that time the model free government in Europe.

The Germanic diet sprang out of the assemblies of the nations at the imperial court on the great days of the year; the assembly that we saw assisting at the promulgation of the capitularies, and also taking part in the election or ratification of the election of the German kings. As the feudal idea advanced, the diet got some of the characteristics of a feudal assembly ; but it was far too unwieldy to exercise much real influence except where it expressed the real sentiments of the nation, as it did once or twice in the deposition of impracticable sovereigns. The details of the early diets are obscure in the last degree ; they are stated in the same general terms which make the history of the early English parliaments so hard to unravel. We may, however, safely conclude that they contained all the elements of the national life, and that those elements which at a later period are not found in them have been excluded by neglect or superseded by some other organisation. When the diet appears definitely arranged, we have it in three branches or divisions : the bishops, the princes, and the towns ; the lower nobles are not allowed to take part in the deliberations and are not represented. This is the case, I believe, as early as the last decade of the thirteenth century, which is indeed the time to which we should naturally look in any attempt to compare the rising institutions of freedom in our pattern nations.

I should not omit to mention that in all the constitutionally governed nations, besides the great council of the nation, which only sat intermittently, there was an ordinary or privy council, an assembly of ministerial advisers who attended on the king to despatch the regular business of government : a body often viewed with jealousy by parliaments and cortes, but of course indispensable to the conduct of public affairs. But the history of this council is distinct from that on which we are now employed, and I either have noticed it already under the question of the royal power, or shall hereafter in discussing the powers of parliaments.

XVII

THE FUNCTIONS OF THE NATIONAL ASSEMBLIES

THE functions of the national council, parliament, assembly of estates, diet, or cortes may be resolved into four: legislation, taxation, judicature, and deliberation on politics generally. Taking these in their widest sense, legislation implies every act of law-making or amendment, whether it proceed directly through the legislature or only by the restriction of the king's action, and all alterations in the common law of the country where such alterations proceed from the competent authority; in taxation also we will include finance generally, and that both in the form of collecting revenue and in that of controlling expenditure. I do not of course mean to say that each of the nations that we are at work on had a national council possessed of power to discharge all these. We take our own as the best specimen, and then measure how far those of the other countries come short of it.

As for legislation, I must, at the risk of a little repetition, run through the history of English legislation, but I will make it as short as possible. (1) The earliest English laws are made by the kings with the advice and help of their witan; of that we saw examples the other day: they were published in the shape of codes of law, and articled like the canons of a church council, on the model of which they were perhaps drawn up. Such, with some minor variations, is the form of enactment until the eleventh century, when Canute adopted a more imperative style, but still retained the form *cum consilio sapientum*. (2) The second form adopted by our lawgivers is that of charter, and this comes in at the Conquest. There are two forms of William the Conqueror's acts: one is a confirmation of the laws of the English as stated to him by a jury of each shire sworn to declare the ancient customs; that is, in the form of their declaration, and his confirmation is stated historically; on the whole nothing can be argued from it for want of historic authority.[1] The other is

[1] *Select Charters*, p. 81.

directly in the form of a charter: Willelmus &c. to all whom it may concern. Know ye that I, with the advice and consent of my barons, have established so and so. (3) A third form is that of the assize, which was in use under Henry II. and Richard I.   This is rather of the nature of a prætor's edict, the laying down of certain rules to be observed in judicial matters, or for the collection of a tax; and it is published in this way: This is the assize which Henry made at Clarendon with the advice and consent of his archbishops, earls, barons, and all his freeholders. (4) The new legislation of the thirteenth century takes the form of articles, and therefore of a sort of compact between the king and the nation.   This is really the case with Magna Carta, although it is technically in the charter form, and it is the form of the Provisions of Oxford and some other documents of the kind issued by the king with what is called counsel and consent, but is really the strong compulsion of his barons.[1] (5) With the reign of Edward I. the modern form of enactment begins, the king stating at the opening of the act that he with the advice and consent of his barons and prelates assembled in parliament enacts so and so; but in this reign we find examples of almost every form; nor is it easy to distinguish between the statutes drawn up with consent and counsel of parliament, and ordinances published with the advice of the royal council. (6) The reign of Edward II. witnessed several improvements.   1. It saw the introduction of petitions which had to be embodied in new laws or ordinances; 2. The preamble of the acts begins as a rule to express the participation of the commons in the legislation; and 3. By an act of the seventeenth year it was provided that nothing should be received as law which did not pass both lords and commons. (7) Under Edward III. we have a more precise clue to the share ascribed to the commons; the acts are made by the king with the advice and consent of the lords, and at the request of the commons; bills are framed thus on the petitions of the commons.   This goes on with some variations until the twenty-seventh year of Henry VI., when it becomes advice and consent of lords, request of commons, and authority of parliament. It was in this reign also that the commons' initiative ceased to be clothed in the form of petition and took that of a bill.   The request of the commons, however, is specified until the first year of Henry VII., when the form becomes what it has generally continued, the assent and counsel of lords and commons in parliament, and by authority of the same.

You may observe if you please that the more important of these

---

[1] A similar conclusion may be drawn from the writs of summons—ad tractandum, or ad consultandum, or ad faciendum.

alterations are introduced coincidently with the assumption of greater powers by the parliament or by any branch of it; but all I can stay to remark now is, the permanence of the form counsel and consent, the necessity which even a despotic king like the Conqueror felt to express it in what was intended to be received as law, and the usefulness of the term itself to express the function continuously assumed by the national council in legislation, whether that national council be the witan of the allodial king, or the barons of the feudal one, or the estates, the parliament, of the constitutional one. How the same form seems equally to have covered every degree of strength and weakness in both the parties contending for power, we cannot now explain in detail; it is enough that counsel and consent are the theory of the thing, and such a theory obviously could not coexist with the great principle of Roman law, *quod principi placuit legis vigorem habet*, the legislative power being, with no restraint of counsel, with one consent devolved on the emperor. In other words, the principle of the constitution was Teutonic; the enacting power on which the laws rested was not Roman, but German, Anglo-Saxon, English.

Let us look now at the case in France, where also the historical government begins from the German starting point. The early capitularies of the Frank kings are edicts, published frequently in synods, and no doubt with the advice of the synods, but on the royal authority. I do not wish to argue strongly from these, because I am not certain as to the genuineness of the existing forms, but so far as I can judge by the absence of the expression of counsel and consent, I should say that in principle they resemble the imperial rescripts from which they were probably copied. It is under Carloman, the brother of Pepin, in 742, that I first find the form; that is, under the Austrasian, thoroughly German, as opposed to the semi-German influence of the Neustrian court. 'Ego Karlomannus dux et princeps Francorum, cum consilio servorum Dei et optimatum meorum,' his chief bishop being Boniface, mark you, an Englishman; it may be observed, however, that Carloman was not king, only *dux* and *princeps*; and secondly, that his capitularies were issued in ecclesiastical councils. But you get the same form under Pepin two years later: 'Pepin cum consensu Francorum et procerum' divided his kingdom; Charles the Great enacts 'hortatu et consultu; consentiente sancta synodo: omnes unanimiter consenserunt;' but when Charles became emperor he changes the tone; he publishes the laws for the Lombards by his own authority, and in several of the capitularies omits the mention of any counsel but his own. But these may be explained as referring to matters of private authority: Lombardy he held as a conqueror, and so legislated. But there is an act of A.D. 818

preserved in due form, modifying the Salic and Roman law on some points, and particularly declared *cum consensu consilioque*; the council containing bishops, abbots, dukes, counts, and all faithful. This is as strongly expressed by Louis the Pious, Charles the Bald, and Louis II.; and of these, all but the last refer to Germany as well as France.

From the time of the Emperor Louis there is little material to argue on until we come to the third race of the kings; the form still subsisting, and even strengthened occasionally by a declaration of Pragmatic Sanction. But under St. Louis and the following kings we lose sight of the form with the reality of the influence, and instead of the counsel and consent of the bishops and nobles, the style becomes *par nostre conseil*, just as in the English ordinances the king allows his council—that is, his private council—to be mentioned. It is the feudal council, in fact, reduced to little more than the ministers and specially appointed advisers of the crown. Hallam does not hold that the form had any real meaning in France from the end of the Karling dynasty, and it certainly was not made a reality by the proceedings of Philip the Fair: his assembly of the states-general was simply for the purpose of taxation, and as these states-general are the only occasion on which the representative principle was tried in mediæval France, we may conclude that the influence of the nation on legislation had long ceased. It had while it lasted rested on the feudal principle alone, and that was not sufficient to give it vitality. If the estates in 1302 had had the power or the will to imitate the conduct of the English parliament in 1297, they might have turned the history of France altogether in a different direction; but they failed, and with them the representative theory failed.

The ordinances of the kings of France run henceforth as done by themselves and their council. The parliament of Paris, however, exercised in modifying the form of the royal ordinances an important check on legislation of this sort; still it was regulative, not initiative; it was rather suffered than recognised as a right; and the body which exercised it was a body of professional lawyers, not national representatives or even feudal barons. The immense influence gained by the kings through their consolidation of the great fiefs, on which they entered by succession, escheat, or forfeiture (and entered into not the mere reality of royal powers, but the inheritance of all the privileges which the former holders had wrested from them in the time of their weakness), made the kings rich as well as independent; and the advantage was improved by them until they became absolutely despotic.

Looking next at Germany, we fail to find after the end of the

Karling dynasty any instance of collective participation in legislation. The nations had retained very much their own laws, and over these was laid a superficies of the immutable civil law. The civil law was occasionally modified by an imperial recess or rescript drawn upon the model of those of Constantine and Justinian, and the local laws by the action of the local rulers; but there was no central life, no real centralisation for any of the functions of government except judicature, and the ministers of that function were not strong enough to carry the imperial jurisdiction into the feudal states. The emperor might hold a diet at Nuremberg or at Frankfort, and in it publish a recess or a rescript in German or in Latin, but they were imperial acts, such as the inoperative proclamations of Frederick II. and the Golden Bull of Charles IV. In Italy he might do the same at Roncaglia if he could bring the assembly together; but in general we may say that as in France the feudal system, so in Germany the imperial system, was fatal to the exercise by the nation of this first and most important of its functions.

Into the history of legislation in Spain we went sufficiently in a former lecture. There, if the influence of the cortes was great in other matters, it could be brought to bear on the administration of the law as well; but the modifications of the laws themselves were few so long as the real strength of the cortes lasted: the regulation of everything by royal charter and the codification of the charters by Alfonso the Wise in the Siete Partidas, the introduction of the civil law by Alfonso XI., are the great features. But every new law and modification of the old had to pass the cortes: the Siete Partidas did not receive even their formal confirmation until 1348. The theoretical perfection of the code of Alfonso the Wise once accepted left little to be altered, and hence it is that this is the function in which the influence of the cortes appears least. Such, however, was their power during its period in all branches of state that we may be sure, if a modification of an existing law had been required, it would have been done with their counsel and consent, for the Teutonic idea so far forth was as prevalent in the south as in the north of Europe.

I will proceed to our second head, that of taxation, and pass the four states in review as before. There is no point on which the allodial, the feudal, and the constitutional systems are more distinctly separated and more easily distinguishable than this of taxation. Under the allodial system there are three distinct obligations, beyond which all taxation must be granted by the witenagemot. The *trinoda necessitas*, the obligation to build and repair bridges and castles and to take part in the national armament, was incident to

all possession of land, and these obligations are in fact the inse-
parable mark of an allodial tenure.   Whatever was needed over and
above this was matter of legislation ; nor under the Anglo-Saxon
kings was much needed.   They were rich in domain and they were
frugal ; for any increase of a permanent character in their own
expenditure a new grant of folkland could be made, as was made
to Ethelwulf.   There were no great occasions of expenditure except
for war, and for war a tax of two shillings on the hide of land was
sufficient.   Such was the tax raised to bribe off the Danes, and in the
same way money was raised for the maintenance of the ships.
These taxes were laid on by the witan under the general name of geld
(Danegeld and shipgeld), and apportioned by them also ; sometimes
with the assessment payable in arms and ships, sometimes with a
demand for money.   With the feudal tenure of land William the
Conqueror and William Rufus introduced the feudal taxation : of
this, also, one part was fixed and settled, another depended on an
act of the person who would have to pay it.   Aids and reliefs were
specific incidents of feudalism ; but even aids were commonly asked
as a matter of courtesy—not taken without asking ; and reliefs,
marriages, wardships, and suchlike were the only source of revenue
which the king could take without a gift from his barons.   The
Norman kings, entering into the position of the old English sovereigns, did not commute the allodial taxation for the feudal, but
simply added the one to the other.   They still exacted all the rents
that had been paid from the shires to the kings in lieu of corn
and produce ; they exacted the allodial obligations ; and they per-
petuated the Danegeld.   These things they found in use ; they
added the reliefs and the profits of wardship and marriage, which
they took quite capriciously, and having taken these, they came with
irresistible courtesy on their feudal lords for aids, and on their
towns in demesne for taillages.   The limitation of this irresponsible tyranny was begun under Henry I.   He by his great charter
of compact with his people consented to limit the reliefs to a reasonable amount, and abate the other hardships on women and children.
He condescended to ask for an aid to marry his daughter, and
received no denial.   But the maintenance of Danegeld and the
recurrence of bad seasons during several years made his reign a
period of poverty and hardship.   Stephen's was one of anarchy.
Henry II. abolished Danegeld like a true English king, but he asked
for and got large *aids*—the same thing under a less hateful name.
Richard I. and John collected large sums by aids, asked for generally in a tone that admitted of no denial.
    At last Magna Carta stopped the progress of royal assumption
that way.   By it, as you know, John was compelled to assent that

besides the three customary aids none should be taken or any tax levied without the consent of the common council of the nation to be summoned for the purpose in a particular way. Although that clause does not appear in the confirmations of the charters, it was struggled for and vindicated during the reign of Henry III., for notwithstanding the unlawful levying of large sums, they were not levied without discussion or declamation ; and had it not been that the demesne lands were not yet freed from arbitrary taxation in the shape of tallage, the crown might have been starved into submission. It is just at the time that the towns began to be regularly summoned that tallages are distinctly abolished, and from the reign of Edward I. no tax has been constitutionally levied without the consent of parliament, the estates rating themselves separately for a long period, but at last joining in a regular administration of taxation, pulling together to make taxation a leverage for all reforms, and finally in modern times leaving that taxation entirely to the representative or commons house. In England, then, the development of legislation and taxation has moved in a groove with the increase of freedom and free institutions. Exactly as feudalism is eliminated, representative taxation is introduced. Henry II. instituted scutage instead of personal service, and destroyed the military power of feudalism thereby. For a century the counties and towns were asked for their contributions separately, when the king and barons made the laws ; as soon as they were assembled for taxation they vindicated their claim to a share in legislation.

There are several points of secondary importance which make the process of taxation in England extremely interesting to trace : the changes from fixed aids and gifts, entirely dependent on the tenure of land, to the grants of tenths and twentieths of movable or personal property, a change which by itself would mark the extinction of the feudal idea ; the change of tenths and fifteenths for subsidies of wool, wool fells and leather ; the progress from direct to indirect taxation ; the different proportions in which the barons, knights, and burghers taxed themselves, together with the progress of self-taxation before it began to be transacted in the national council or parliament, when the king treated with the several towns singly for their grants, and each baron rated himself by a cartel of his freeholds ; the long-continued severance of the taxation of the church from that of the body of the nation, transacted in convocation ; but many of these points are remote from our immediate subject, the power of the national council, and demand to be treated at large. We will therefore proceed to take a glance at the power exercised in this direction in the continental states.

And first in France. The revenue of the French kings was chiefly derived from lands in demesne, or from the gift of the states of the provinces which the king ruled immediately without a feudal middleman. These gifts were granted by those states on the ordinary feudal principle, as aids or donatives, some of them expressly demandable without process of consultation as the feudal rule was everywhere, some requiring a special grant, and therefore applied for only in special emergencies. From the time that feudalism became fully established, and the old allodial taxation, which of course had been used under the Merovings and Karlings, was entirely superseded (as, you remember, was not the case in England), the support of the king and of the framework of government depended legally on demesne lands and the proceeds of the feudal incidents. While the kingdom was very weak, it made government cheap and war difficult, and taxation accordingly small. Hallam, however, points out that some of the kings, by debasing the coinage and exacting money from the Jews, managed to do without any direct taxation, except of their demesnes, which could be tallaged at their will. Philip Augustus, following the example of Richard and John, levied taxes on the vassals to the amount of a third part of their goods. But the precedent was too dangerous ; and the following kings down to Philip the Fair were greatly enriched by the acquisition of new provinces. But Philip the Fair, having called together the states-general for a political purpose, would fain utilise them for a financial one. In 1314 they granted him a subsidy, in which both nobles, clergy, and towns joined, the barons thus surrendering their privilege of immunity, and the towns for the first time being consulted whether they would give or no. The towns before this had been tallaged at the will of the king, now they vote money as a free estate.

Hallam has traced in detail the history of the influence of the states-general on taxation, and their remonstrances as affecting political business. It would seem that the kings occasionally asked their consent, as they occasionally consulted their opinions, but quite as frequently taxed without consulting them, and acted without asking advice. The power was practically reduced to remonstrance ; redress of abuses must be seized by the strong hand, not pleaded for or bought. It was under John and during his captivity that the remonstrances were most efficacious ; on one occasion, in 1357, Charles, the son of the king, being regent, was obliged to enact an ordinance conformable to the petition of the states ; but the general tenour of the history is a struggle against overwhelming odds and rapid strides of the kings towards absolutism. In 1380 Charles VI. repealed all taxation that had been imposed since the reign of Philip the Fair; but there is no question that he and his successors did impose taxes at their will. The deputies of the towns, moreover, do not seem to have had full power; their constituents had to confirm the grant when the states had made it; it being uncertain whether they could guarantee payment, they could not of course insist on the fulfilment of their petitions; they fell, therefore, into contempt, and so into disuse. The states of Tours in 1484 were a remarkable, and the last remarkable, assembly of the kind. This was divided for the time into six nations, Normandy, Burgundy, Paris, Aquitaine, and Languedoc and Languedoil; and demanded that no tax should ever be levied again without the consent of the states. They tried for too much and came to an end in a not altogether inglorious way. Henceforth the king took his taxes as he wanted them. The failure of the states-general to make good their ground was doubtless owing to the fact that it was for taxation alone that they were summoned; they had never possessed the right of legislation, that the king could do without them; nor had they any way but petition of remonstrating; it may be added that they never seem to have reached the point of refusing a tax demanded.

It was different with the cortes in Castile and Aragon; a word will suffice to show it. In Castile, as I have several times remarked, the nobles and clergy were free altogether from taxation; only the communities were taxed, and these were therefore the most important element in the cortes from an early period. Legislation and political deliberation required the consideration of the united body, taxation required the deputies alone; but this did not result in the deputies losing their right to interfere in the two higher branches of government, possibly it might have been so had they been called up only to be taxed. It resulted in the withdrawal of the other two estates, and leaving the whole business to the deputies; the nobles and clergy by their immunity lost the power of affecting either legislation or politics in the same way as the third estate; they saw that their counsel was valueless because they were not going to back it with a grant. Up to the close of the middle ages and to the middle of the reign of Charles V. the cortes retained their independence; but it was rudely shocked by the wars between nobles and the revolutionary junta which in 1522 attempted to bring them under taxation, and it came practically to an end in 1538, when the emperor, in great need of money, found them obdurate as to making a grant, and dismissed them in great indignation. From that time only eighteen cities were summoned to the cortes; and means were taken of making the thirty-six votes certain as soon as money was wanted; the third estate was not really strong enough to stand by itself. In Aragon the taxation was strictly feudal; the

independence of the cortes there came to an end about the same
time.

Germany remains, and there it would be difficult to say that
there was any general taxation through the middle ages commonly
so called ; the emperor was, as a matter of fact, entirely dependent
on the proceeds of his own estates and on the money voted by his
hereditary provinces.   These estates were originally very large ; but
by the time that the Hohenstaufens came to an end, they were all
either given away or sold.   Conradin parted with the last of his
paternal allods to make his expedition into Italy ; and from that time
the hereditary succession ceased.   The emperor, if popular, could
sometimes get a gift from the imperial towns ; and could, until that
resource was exhausted, improve his position by selling privileges
to princes, prelates, and cities ; but as a rule the imperial court
was very poor.   The institution of circles by Maximilian placed
a small revenue and a small standing army for certain purposes
at the command of the emperor ; he could raise 4,000 horse
and 20,000 foot, and about 100,000 crowns as procurations for
his journey to Rome ; but none of the successors of Maximilian
took the journey.   The diet also during the reign of Charles V.
voted him considerable sums in supply for wars against the Turks ;
but these were certainly extraordinary efforts, and so far as I
know there is no precedent for them before the reforms begun by
Maximilian.

A necessary corollary to the right of taxation is that of directing
expenditure and exacting an account of it ; impeaching dishonest
ministers, and making the grants of money dependent on the redress
of grievances.   I think it would be difficult to find that any real traces
of such privileges lasting a long time or in an increasing ratio existed
anywhere else than in England ; nor in England were they secured
within the limit of the middle ages beyond the risk of gainsaying.
In France hardly an attempt was ever made to acquire the right.
Germany gave no scope for any such action.   In Spain the parallel
with England holds good part of the way ; but if we may judge of
the earlier by the later history of the cortes, it does not hold good
in these respects.   The cortes of Aragon in 1519 granted Charles V.
a sum of 200,000 ducats to be applied to the payment of the debts
of the crown ; but it does not appear that unless money was
demanded for a special purpose, it was usual to make special mention
of it in the grant.   If the Spanish cortes ever attempted to make
their powers of taxation a leverage for the removal of abuses, the
king with the nobles and clergy would be strong enough to resist
them successfully ; and hence we cannot rate their influence in
general politics, the fourth of the heads under which we ranked

the powers of the national council.[1] It was, of course, always and everywhere in the power of the kings to determine what should be brought before them, nor until late on in the constitutional history of the middle ages had the parliament, cortes, or diet any way of initiating measures except petition ; beyond that stage the states-general of France never got. Even in England and Spain only legislative improvements were otherwise initiated. If the king wanted political advice, he asked for it ; if not, he did without it. If he wanted advice and money too, the people had their chance of giving the one and withholding the other. In the earlier times, the twelfth century for instance, before the third estate was summoned to the royal council, it may be remarked that in England the king asked advice of his parliament on subjects which now could not come in that shape before it : the marriages of his children, even where no parliamentary provision was asked for ; and occasionally a question of arbitration between foreign powers. It does, indeed, show that the king's confidence in his own absolute power was too great to allow him to be jealous of advice, and he was therefore consciously free to ask it when he thought he wanted it. Much later than the twelfth century, however, even in the fourteenth, we find the commons trying to avoid advising the king on the subject of war and peace, as matters too wonderful and excellent for them ; doubtless had war or peace been made without such communication their jealousy must have been roused. From this period, however, there is no public matter in which, when they are strong enough, or sufficiently excited about it, they are not able to prove their right to interfere. I should say that generally the diets of Germany were more like political councils than merely taxative or deliberative ones ; they took cognisance certainly of the behaviour of their emperor, and joined with him in the publication of his recesses or edicts, which generally had reference to internal politics ; they certainly advised him about wars from the crusade of Frederick Barbarossa to the wars of Charles V. with the Turks ; and, as we saw a lecture or two ago, they visited his incapacity or neglect with remonstrance and even with deposition.

In the last place we have to notice the office of the national council as touching judicature. I cannot now attempt to show how the judicature of the English councils led the way to their organisation for other purposes, but we must start from the point that the

[1] Hallam, ii. 33. *Inter alia*, cortes of John II. in 1419 claimed the right of being consulted in all matters of importance ; the king replies that in weighty matters he has always acted and shall act in conformity with their advice.

feudal council of the king was his high court of judicature. That feudal council was the court to which all his vassals had to do suit and service, and in which in the last resort their quarrels with one another had to be decided. Out of this feudal court, which we have seen took on itself the character of the witenagemot or national council also, were developed the royal courts of justice, the curia regis, the exchequer, the king's bench, the court of common pleas. All these courts were either a selection of the learned lawyers out of the body of the royal council, or committees, as we should say, of the feudal court itself. But however many courts of justice were cut out of it, it retained, in its own integrity, the character of the highest judicature. The great council of the nation, as called under the Plantagenet kings before it was superseded by parliament strictly so called, contained all the elements and exercised all the powers of the feudal court. After it was superseded by parliament, its jurisdiction seems to have fallen partly to the house of lords and partly to the inner royal council, out of whose jurisdiction the court of chancery sprang. The house of commons was as jealous of the appellate jurisdiction of the house of lords as it was of the right of the privy council to legislate in the shape of ordinances or to try causes as a supreme court co-ordinate with the house of lords, but it never succeeded in getting judicial power into its own hands. The judicial power of parliament as the king's court is exercised by the peers, so far as it continues to exist. It is only by impeachment or by act of attainder that the commons can take part at all in an act of judicature.

Compare with this the state of things in France. The abeyance of the national assemblies, which caused the calling of the states-general to be regarded as a new invention, had left the judicial power of the king's feudal court to be exercised by lawyers and clerks; yet that power was exercised by them under the title of parliament. The parliament of Paris was the assembly of the king's legal advisers, and the organisation of it was a reform of Philip the Fair, and a pair to his summoning of the states. The title of parliament alone seems to survive to show that in the distant past both inventions had a common forgotten origin. It is enough to say for this that this parliament was not the national council, and that the states-general made no pretence of or claim to judicature. Nor was judicature any part of the regular business of the German diet, although it was ready to decide disputes between the states of which it was composed, to declare public enemies, and to put to the ban of the empire those who were accused before it. But otherwise Germany had no central judicature for many centuries. The diet was the feudal court of the emperor, and in the general indeterminateness of its functions it is impossible to say that any business whatever was withdrawn from its jurisdiction.   We cannot now discuss the power of the cortes in this respect, but you will remember that in Aragon the power of the *justizia* was supreme in judicature—a check on the tyranny of the king as well as on the feudal judicature of the cortes and the distinct tribunals of the nobles, while in Castile the king was regarded as the fountain of justice, and his magistrates, the royal alcaldes, had a supreme jurisdiction, with which any such power on the part of the cortes as the house of lords retained in England would seem to be inconsistent.

[*See Stubbs, ' Constitutional History,' Vols. I. and II.; Hallam, The Middle Ages.'*]

XVIII

THE GROWTH OF THE REPRESENTATIVE
PRINCIPLE

THE origin of the idea of representation we need not attempt to
define, it would seem to lie at the foundation of social life; but the
history of the introduction of the principle into a particular department of a particular national government is fair matter for inquiry.
One portion of that inquiry we have already investigated; we saw
how and when the representative system was applied to the national
council in the countries in which the necessity of a limit on royal
authority was recognised. There still remain two portions of the
inquiry: (1) The origin of the communities which became represented in the national council, parliament, cortes, states-general, or
whatever the form might be; and (2) the growth of the principle of
representation itself before it was introduced into this the highest
function of the body politic. We can afford, I fear, to give only a
very succinct account of either. The three estates of the realm
are the clergy, the nobles, and the commons; this is a principle
recognised in the European constitutions, although some divide
the commons into peasants and burghers, and so make a fourth
division. Into the representation of the clergy and nobles I do not
propose to enter: the former would open a series of discussions about
councils and convocations, synods, and so on which would take us
away from our main point; and as to the nobles, it is only on a very
limited scale that the principle of representation has been applied to
them. In England they always appeared in person without representation except by the custom of proxy; in Germany the orders
which did not appear in the diet were not represented at all.

The representation of the third estate will be sufficient for us to
discuss now, and this question breaks itself up at once into two—the
burgher and the peasant; the burgesses and the knights of the shire;
the town and the country; the origin of the country communities and
the origin of the towns. Now, although in England the system of representation was applied to both these sorts of communities within a

very short space of time, it is scarcely too much to say that up to that time they had had hardly anything in common. The country or village communities are a system common to all Teutonic races, and their whole administration is founded in freedom, in the spirit and discipline of the ancient free allodialism. The town or burgher communities are, on the other hand, founded on privilege, spring from a state of servitude through a stage of protection into a stage of freedom that we may compare with what S. Paul says about his own—the cities with a large sum of money obtained their freedom, but the country communities were free-born. The village or country communities originate in the primeval condition of settled life. The unit of this settled life in the Teutonic system was the mark, that is the circle of inclosed and cultivated land which was surrounded by the forest out of which it had been cleared, and was arranged for the use and property of the handful of freemen who had cleared it, men probably of one *mægth* or kindred, among whom the eldest of the race would be the natural magistrate. In this mark we may suppose there would be ten or a dozen families, each with its homestead and allodial estate, each with rights in the common wood or pasture. This is the origin of the English township; and when the country became Christianised this was the basis of the parish. Also for judicial purposes it would be the district of the tithing, the ten men would be bound for one another with the frankpledge; and when the land became feudalised that which had been the free jurisdiction of the mark would become the manor. I do not mean, of course, that townships, parishes, tithings, and manors are identical, but you will as a rule find them divisible into the same subdivisions. One manor may contain several parishes, and one parish several manors; but generally you will find that the one division is divisible into the others without remainder. A number of these townships—ten, perhaps, originally—formed the hundred, a division common like the mark to the Teutonic races, and with a like organisation. The hundred judicially has its hundred court for trial of offences, and it also, as the country becomes feudalised, changes its administration into the form of a bailiwick. Ecclesiastically it is a deanery. In the court of the hundred the townships appear by representation; the reeve and four men represent each township in the English hundred court, and I believe the same sort of arrangement was German also.

Well, rising higher, we come to the *shire*, or as it was in Germany, the *gau*, which was a collection of hundreds, with its own officers, the shire reeve or sheriff as judge, the ealdorman as military leader, the archdeacon as ecclesiastical head, or, where the dioceses were small, the bishop. The court of the shire is emphatically the folkmote or meeting of the people; but the hundreds are represented by the hundred men, the townships also by their reeve and four men, the church by the parish priests, and the feudal lords by their stewards. The court of the shire has a regular organisation : for judicial purposes the sheriff, ealdorman, and bishop preside; but there are twelve assessors, who hold the law in memory, and sit with them to declare the law. In these two points, the representation of the hundreds and townships by the reeve and four men, and in the representation of the whole body for the judicial purpose by the assessors of the sheriff, the *scabini* as they were called in France, *échevins*, and by other names, we get the earliest employment of the principle in the direction which it ultimately took. Thus far the rural organisation is common to England and Germany. In Germany it went no further, for at an early date the rural communities fell into the hands of hereditary reeves, or grafs, under whom they were quickly feudalised into little territorial principalities. But in England the sheriffdom never as a rule became hereditary, and the whole bent of the law was to make it an annual office ; nor was it allowed to fall into the hands of the largest proprietors of land, as it would have done had it been simply elective. The sheriffs were during the historic times appointed by the crown from year to year with few exceptions. Higher than the folkmote the principle of representation did not rise. The witenagemot was not actually representative ; it may be that in the primeval times, when the shire was an independent organism, or a little kingdom, the supreme council may have been representative ; in historic times it was not till the growth of freedom had made it so.

Still, I think when the time came for the country to be governed by representation, the machinery was at hand. The institution of a new method of judicature by Henry II. substituted for many purposes the election of two knights to direct the business of the shire ; these two knights nominate the grand jury, and become therefore the highest form of representation in the shire : they are elected in the county court, they are consulted by the crown as to the feelings of the county, and finally they are brought together in a single assembly to express the wishes of the county, to tax themselves, to join in the making of laws, to direct and control politics, to make themselves indispensable as a part of the constitution. In this development of the rural element we get a history unparalleled in Europe, the direct growth of the perfect system from the earliest forms and origin of ancient liberty : it is truly Teutonic without a taint of the Roman, truly free without a touch of the feudal. And it is peculiar to England among the four countries that we are discussing : a representation of the peasant class did exist in Scandinavia generally, and does still, I believe, in Sweden ; but as to our four countries, we may say that in France and Germany the towns only were represented in the assembly of estates : the country was indeed feudalised under the nobles ; while in Spain two plans were adopted : in Aragon every tenant in chief appeared in person, whether noble or not, and the under-tenants were nowhere ; in Castile the country districts were represented, but it was not on the basis of ancient freedom, but by the operation of a royal privilege, exactly analogous to the charters by which in England, Spain, France, and Germany the towns and cities were incorporated and made into units capable of voting by representatives.

Now, the origin of towns is quite different, and is altogether the result of privilege ; but the history of towns is so different in the different countries of Europe that we must separate our inquiry as usual into four branches. In the Romanised parts of Europe, that is in France and the Rhine country of Germany, many towns or cities have been towns and cities from the Roman times, and so have retained an administration which, whatever changes have been introduced into it in machinery, may still historically claim a corporate identity. In the north of France, England, and Spain such places did exist under the imperial system, but they were extinguished uuder the Teutonic barbarians, and even if they ever revived, they revived with institutions altogether altered, there is no corporate identity about them ; most frequently, however, in England and Germany the modern cities are on different sites from the ancient.

We will, however, divide and take England first. Now, in England a borough grew up under the protection of a lord : it might be the king, or a bishop, or a great landowner, and the centre of population may have been constituted by a castle or a church, or a port, or convenience of trade ; but as a rule the boroughs were demesne lands of the king and nobles, inhabited by people desirous of their patronage and protection : the soil on which they were built, the jurisdiction of the district belonged to the lord, and he was their judge in peace and their leader in war. As tenants on the demesne of the lord they were his homagers, less than free therefore ; their reeve was his steward, and by him and his reeve they appeared in the county court. He could demand and take of them what feudal dues he chose. They were, in fact, vassals of the lowest degree. Some organisation was necessary for them, and that organisation they had in common with the shire ; they had a reeve and his assessors, sometimes twelve in number, who maintained peace and order by the lord's authority. By the time of the Conquest most of the towns of England had become demesne lands of the crown : there were not a large number, but there were of course the county towns and the ports ; a few of these were in the demesne of the bishops and earls, but most in that of the king, and the kings were always ready to sell privileges, even if they were not, as the wiser ones were, anxious to foster the towns for the sake of trade and the revenue derivable from it. The steps by which the towns emerged from absolute servitude to comparative independence in the two hundred years that followed the Conquest are traceable. The liberation had begun, indeed, before the Conquest, for under the semi-feudal jurisdiction of the native lords there were towns which had made a good stride towards emancipation : the first step, however, at the Conquest was to obtain a confirmation of their existing status, such as William the Conqueror granted to the city of London.[1] We do not know very much about that existing state, for London is quite an exception, more like an aristocratic republic than a mere capital city ; but the earliest town charters generally are confirmations of the existing state of things. The first step in advance is the purchase by the burghers of the *firma burgi* : that is, instead of paying individually their taxes to the sheriff for the king, they compound for a regular sum, which they apportion afterwards among themselves. They became answerable to the sheriff as a unit.

Now, the question is, what body was already in existence in the boroughs that had a personality, that was representative enough to deal on behalf of the whole community with the sheriff or the crown ? and the answer is, that in some places there were merchant guilds, voluntary associations with their own privileged organisation, containing, in days when merchandise was restricted and trade quite elementary, all the chief men in the place ; and in other, if not in all, places there was the ordinary judicial machinery, the reeve and the lawmen, the *scabini*, the assessors of the lord's steward in the court leet. Of course where there was a merchant guild, the members of it, as the most influential and richest burghers, would be the leading men in the leet ; so that either of these bodies, or the same men in either character or both, would be fit and able to deal as representative bodies ; they were in fact the magistrates of the borough. When, then, the guild of the town by its leet had bought of the lord the firm of the borough, they had got a basis of independence on which to go much further : they were now excepted from the machinery of the county as regarded taxation, they next procured an exemption as regarded judicature, and so emancipated themselves altogether from the rule of the sheriff : the series of charters begins with the reign of Henry I., and you can trace in them the gradual purchase of new privileges, the largest under Richard I. and John. First the privilege that the burghers shall

[1] *Select Charters*, p. 82.

not be compelled to plead outside of the main walls; then that they shall have the merchant guild and hanshouse, that is their right of making by-laws and executing justice among themselves; then that they shall be allowed to choose their own magistrates: this point they reached under John: they had common property then, and a common chest; they could make and enforce their own by-laws; they could resist the sheriff, or even refuse to receive the king's judges, except at legal times. They grew stronger and richer, and more inclined to a freedom every step of which they had purchased; and the last remnant of servitude pinched them in the tenderest part, for since they had bought the *firma burgi* taxation had grown amain, and the towns, as parts of the king's demesne, were liable to him for tallages in a way which the country had been freed from by Magna Carta: hence their struggles for freedom, and the importance to the royal cause of propitiating them. When Simon de Montfort wanted an assembly sure to provide funds, he summoned the towns;[1] and when Edward I. found that to exact tallage without a grant of the people's representatives was becoming an impossibility; that the voice of the knights of the shire was not enough to warrant the collection of taxes from communities which were out of the shire, although these were in it; when he found that the old plan of canvassing the towns individually for money was made an excuse for hanging back rather than a reason for rivalry in benevolence and patriotism; when in fine he found that he must work England in a representative parliament if he was ever to be strong and just, he made the representation of the towns a part of the constitution; and as he summoned two knights for each shire he summoned two burghers from each town to his parliaments.[2] But until modern times the variations in the borough representation have testified to their foundation in privilege and servitude; for the king could increase or diminish at will the number of towns sending representatives, and even the sheriff or the boroughs themselves could limit this branch of the legislature. The towns were glad to be excused the expense, the sheriff could arrange matters as suited his party. There was not the same unaltered basis of representation that there was in the counties: the franchises differed in the towns; sometimes the magistrates, sometimes the tenants of the burgage houses on which the original *firma burgi* was fixed, sometimes the whole body of freemen returned the members; sometimes the lord of the manor, the town continuing still in private demesne. If it had not been for the county representatives forming a body of independent men, unvarying in number and position, the representative system might

---

[1] *Select Charters*, p. 415.   [2] *Ibid.* p. 486.

have died out altogether, or become powerless as it did in other countries. Of the subsequent developments of the boroughs; of their being incorporated, that is made capable of perpetual succession instead of personal only; and of their becoming in several instances counties in themselves, I need not speak here, for they do not affect the point of representative government at all.

The history of the estates which in the other countries of Europe were represented in the national assemblies, is somewhat simpler than that of England, because either the towns alone were represented as in Germany, and, as compared with the country, in France also, or where, as in Spain, the rural districts were represented, they owed their right to the concession of privilege by the sovereign, and not to the old Teutonic birthright. There were of course towns which more or less represented the rural interest, but they did not represent it as country, but as towns privileged by charter or *fuero*. We need not, then, say anything about the other elements of the states-general, the diet, or the cortes, but confine ourselves to the origin of the towns and cities.

And first France. Hallam, in a very good note on the history of French municipalities, taken in great measure from Guizot, gives four distinct origins for the French towns: 1. The prescriptive possession of civic right, handed down from Roman times, in the government of decurions, with a *defensor urbis*: the cities which had this ancient constitution were all in the South of France, where the Roman and Gothic elements were stronger than the Frank, and where the greater proportion of people were living in the personal enjoyment of the privileges of the civil law. 2. The German system of guilds spreading to the whole community for a common end: this is analogous to the influence of guilds in the early English towns, but I cannot agree in making it an independent source of civic organisation; the reeve and his assessors, the *schultheiss* and the *scabini*, the *schout* and the *schepens*, were not necessarily connected with the idea of the guild, but with that of the township or vill, which was no doubt indebted to its identification with the guild for much of its cohesive power, but was not originally the same thing. 3. The forcible insurrection of the inhabitants against their feudal lords; and 4. The bestowal of privileges by charter. Now, the two latter divisions are illogical; they are in fact only two of the ways in which the privileges otherwise originated were secured. There are really only two origins, the Roman and the Teutonic: the Teutonic may be worked into a perfect development either by the voluntary act of the ruler, or by the extorted privilege, for actual independence won by insurrection is not a result ever found in the French municipalities. The history of the Roman municipalities is peculiar to itself; that of the others has every element in common with that of the English towns which we have just discussed : the emancipation from external jurisdiction, purchased by the payment of regular imposts ; the by-laws of the individual community, confirmed by charter; the privilege of·electing magistrates and conducting their own judicature. The distinction between the commune and the bourgeoisie, of which Hallam says a good deal, and on which the French jurists are strong, is almost exactly analogous to the difference in England between chartered towns and boroughs in demesne. Both have a good deal in common ; but the borough in demesne and the bourgeoisie are not, as we should now say, incorporated : they have not the *communa* or corporate identity which in mediæval times was the great feature, the essence in fact, of a chartered borough ; and in France, where more frequently than in England they were subject to other lords than the king, I question whether they were represented in the states-general, though they doubtless would be in the provincial estates. The distinction of communes and bourgeoisies is a cross division to that of Roman and Teutonic cities ; for both the latter might belong to either class, according to the tenour of their charters. If they had no charters they necessarily belonged to the bourgeoisie class. It is hardly necessary to account for the fact that the lower nobles and the towns only were represented in France, the noble class being so large, and all the land except the towns belonging to the noble owners ; for the lower order of freeholders, which must have existed at one time, was either altogether lost sight of, or sank in the general mass of servitude which lay at the root of this perfectly feudalised constitution.[1]

---

[1] Thierry divides France municipally into five zones :

I. North—Pays des communes jurées, communes proper—filiation of charters in Picardy as in the model charters of Derby, Norwich, Oxford, in England.
Rouen, mayor, 12 échevins, 12 counsellors, 75 peers.

II. South—Italian, consular régime.
Podestat in Marseilles, Anguen, and Arles, a foreigner, as in Rome.
Consuls established, Arles 1131, Béziers 1131, Montpellier 1141, Nismes 1145, Narbonne 1148, Toulouse 1188 (first appearance).
Bordeaux, mayor, 50 jurats, 30 counsellors, 300 défenseurs.

III. Centre—Orleans, Maine, Anjou, &c.
Constitutions won by revolt; aimed at commune or consular, but not reaching it ; emancipated towns.
Chartres, 10 prudhommes.
Orleans, 10 prudhommes.
Le Mans, first case of insurrection ; against bishop ; chartered by Louis XI.
Tours, 2 boroughs, with 4 prudhommes each.
Bourges, also 4 prudhommes, freely elected for a year.

But it is interesting to ask in what measure were the towns represented in the states-general, and by what machinery were the representatives elected?[1] I wish that we had data for forming such a conclusion as would give a reality to our idea of the thing; but all I can say is that, so far as I know, all chartered towns, all bourgeoisies or boroughs, and sometimes even unwalled towns and villages, appeared by deputies in the states-general; and as these chartered towns had by their charters the right of electing their own officers, the deputies to the states-general were so far certainly elective, and elected by that part of the community to which the privilege was given by the charter in unchartered towns; probably the magistracy, by whatever form appointed, were the most likely persons to appear as deputies, so that it matters little whether the deputies were specially chosen to be deputies, or were, as in later times, the chiefs of the local magistracy *ex officio*. I need hardly tell you that it was for purposes of taxation only that the states-general were ever called after their first summons by Philip the Fair; that they had no political authority, except the very indirect one of stopping supplies, only a part of which they furnished, and in the voting of which they were largely outnumbered by the clergy and nobles; and that consequently they are of less constitutional importance than the corresponding branch in any other national system of Europe. The dates are simple: the Roman municipalities and the bourgeoisie towns are of remote antiquity, the former springing from the ancient empire, and the latter from the feudal system in its first stages: the charters of the communes or corporate towns begin under Louis VI., almost at the same time as they begin under Henry I. in England. The states-general were called first by Philip the Fair in 1302, and from time to time during the century, but the

IV. West—Brittany, Poitou, Saintonge, Angoumois, &c.
    1. Peculiar Breton institutions, régime à la fois ecclésiastique et civil; parish church the centre.
    2. Poitou &c. derived the constitution from Normandy, on the plan of the Rouen system; under English domination.

V. Alsace.
    Enemies hostile to municipal independence where it was created by revolutionary means; acts of Frederick II. against them.
    Besançon. 7 quarters or bannières; each chose 28 notables, who named 14 magistrates for the year; prudhommes; the 14 current prudhommes + the 14 of last year + 28 notables were the council of state.

Lyons—Droit Italique (Jus Italicum) charter in 1320 from Peter of Savoy preserves ancient status; sec. 13; council of fifty = Roman curia; concentrated in council of 12; called sometimes échevins, sometimes consuls.

[1] Hallam says the lower nobles were represented in the states-general by deputies.

king gradually engrossed the power of taxation, as well as of legislation, which the states never had possessed. The history of Philip the Fair is a curious travesty of that of Edward I.[1]

The history of the German towns is in some respects opposed to this; some points it has in common. As in the case of the churches, so here, those districts which had been thoroughly Romanised retained the institutions which the South of France retained. The great cities of the Rhine retained the character of Roman municipalities, in some cases overlaid by ecclesiastical or feudal superincumbrances, but still a continuous identity. The Germans themselves were not a city-loving race, and accordingly in those regions which had never been Romanised there were very few cities or towns with any constitution at all until Henry the Fowler and Otto I., by way of colonising and consolidating the north, founded cities with very extensive privileges, intended to invite settlers. The two points to be remarked as to these are: (1) That the purpose of foundation was well defined; (2) the civic constitution did not grow up, but was a creature full-grown at its birth, the creation of royal policy and privilege. The subject territory, the noble burghership borrowed from the Roman patriciate, the titles, perhaps Teutonic in sound, but meaning far more than merely met the ear, the very great extent of the favours heaped upon them, purchased by them, or given in gratitude for the help so freely and constantly bestowed on the emperors by the cities, all these things marked out a great future for the German cities, a future shared and most brilliantly exemplified in those of the Netherlands and Flanders, the origin of which is partly Teutonic, partly French. And the German cities, instead of being excluded by the nobles from the diet, actually superseded a great part of the native nobility. The diet consisted of the prelates, the princes, and the cities; counts that were not of the rank of princes did not sit there and were not represented.

In theory, then, the German diet was a very popular assembly; that is, the popular or representative element in it was strong. And occasionally we do find the election of an emperor, although it was not a point on which the diet as a diet was competent to treat, considerably affected by the support or antipathy of such a city as Nuremberg or Frankfort, much as might be the case with London in the chance of a disputed succession in England. But the diets, as you know from your German history, were a very disunited body and were called together but seldom; when called together they had

---

[1] States-Gen. 1302. W. de Nangis. Barones, prælatos, duces et comites, abbates et procuratores capitulorum, decanos et custodes ecclesiarum collegiatarum, vicedominos, castellanos, majores et scabinos civitatum.

little power to execute their own sentences. The country which
they were supposed to help to govern was really divided into a
variety of independent states, each of which had a little diet or
assembly of estates of its own, just as was the case in Flanders and
in France also. The provincial estates were more lively and
influential as a rule than the diets or states-general. And as they
were also more squeezable, great part of the business that could be
transacted without general discussion was transacted in them. The
diet was very often merely a magnificent show; where it was not
merely that, ·it was in many cases a tumultuous gathering. The
cities, however, as I said, were in most cases on the side of the
emperor, from whom they could expect only privilege, and against
the local ruler, whom they resisted as an aggressor even to the
waging of war. The appearance of the cities in the diet of the
empire dates from the end of the thirteenth century. Here, also,
the right of representation belongs only to imperial cities, and there
is no doubt that the election of the deputies was made by the ruling
class or burghers.[1]

What I have said of these is true, and to a larger degree, of the
Netherland cities, the charters of which raise them to the rank
almost of independent states confederated voluntarily for certain
purposes. There are differences as to the extent of privilege and as
to the purposes for which they were granted, and as to the ways in
which they were extorted, but there is little difference as to their
origin. And here the provincial estates were powerful. It was not,
indeed, until the gathering in by the dukes of Burgundy of this
large agglomeration of territory that any framework of unity was
formed ; and when it was, the states-general were but the representatives or proxies of the several provincial bodies.

The history of the Italian cities lies outside of our present subject,
but I may say of the northern ones that their origins differed, as did
the French. Some were Roman, some were the creation of the
German emperors, but they were all separatist in tendency and
character ; they would not combine except under a force seldom
strong enough to exert itself, such as Frederick I. could bring to
bear when he held his diets at Roncaglia. Then the Italian system
was in its infancy ; but it was disruptive, as was the German: disruptive, with a strong dislike to the empire, and herein opposed to
the German, to which not unfrequently the empire was indebted for
its continued existence. As to Southern Italy, there is, I believe, no
doubt that Frederick II. did summon representatives of his cities in
Naples and Sicily to his great courts. It would be improbable that

---

[1] The votes in the diet of the towns were reduced to two in 1474, the
Rhenish and Westphalian benches.

THE GROWTH OF THE REPRESENTATIVE PRINCIPLE 321

a plan which was already in use in Spain, and was coming into use in England, should have no recommendations in the eyes of so ingenious an organiser and so far-sighted a politician; but the facts are obscure, and the duration of the system depended on his own energy. Whatever he organised perished with his dynasty.

We come, then, last, to Spain; that is, (1) Castile; (2) Aragon, with its three constitutions, the Aragonese, the Catalonian, and the Valencian. (1) In Castile, as in North Germany, the origin of the towns is historical. They were created for defence and colonisation; they were created by privilege, *fuero* or charter, not by the operation of common law. One of their privileges was the right of being represented in the cortes; their charters and their enjoyment of this privilege are as old as the eleventh century at least. Nor were the towns the only communities possessed of this right. The country was carved into *behetrias* or chartered divisions, privileged by *fuero* in the same way. And this is the only one of the four countries in which the rural as well as the urban population is represented except our own. It differs from ours because our representation of the counties is not a matter of charter, but of the very essence of the constitution. The representation of the *behetrias*, as that of our towns, is the result of privilege. And it was in Castile a privilege which varied according to the exigencies of the times. The cortes were complete whether the number of communities represented was great or small. The sovereign had thus power far too great to allow the cortes to be a perfect or an independent representation. Still the cortes had for five centuries very great power, and in them the great power was not that of the nobles or clergy, who were reduced to insignificance by their privilege of freedom from taxation. The cortes represented the taxpayers, and so were able to make their influence felt. They were not outnumbered by the non-taxpayers; their authority extended to all the business of the nation; laws were subject to their approval, and all political matters discussed in them. They came, in fact, the nearest of all to our English parliament; but their history is not that of the English parliament, for it both begins and ends differently. Yet through mediæval history the Castilian cortes are a great power. They fell before Charles V.; but rather by intrigue, such as the nature of their constitution left them liable to, than by any misconduct of their own. Their later history in their revived form is not such as to deserve praise.

I should not omit to mention that in Castile as in Germany, in times of weakness of the central authority, volunteer combinations were both sanctioned and patronised by the law. The Hermandad under Ferdinand and Isabella, for the maintenance of justice in troubled districts, is exactly paralleled by the leagues of the counts, cities, and bishops of Germany in the fourteenth and fifteenth centuries, the league of St. George's Shield, or the Swabian League, or the Wetterau League. And as, when peaceful times came, the Catholic princes Ferdinand and Isabella restored to the cortes the functions that the Hermandad had usurped ; so Albert II. and Maximilian constructed out of the leagues the system of the circles by which Germany was regulated as long as the empire continued to exist.

(2) In Aragon the cortes consisted of four states : the *ricos hombres* or barons, the *infanzones* or knights, the clergy, and the chartered towns. The constitution was entirely feudal ; the barons were the large holders of land ; the cities were chartered towns in demesne ; the *infanzones* were the class which in England sent the knights of the shire to parliament, and in Castile the deputies from the country *behetrias* ; but in Aragon, as in England under Henry II., they were not represented except by their own personal attendance. Moreover, they were very few in number, and although they escaped the extinction which the corresponding class met in France, they did not develop, as in England, into a county representation at all. In Catalonia and Valencia the cortes consisted of three estates only, there being no *infanzones*, but the system was purely feudal, as in France and Aragon. The actual power of these bodies in these small kingdoms was, however, disproportionately great, as we shall see, or have seen already, under our other heads.

XIX

EARLY JUDICIAL SYSTEMS

THE subject of judicature lies so deep at the root of all constitutional development, and it is so commonly through the machinery of judicature that the constitutional instincts of people are trained and modelled, that we must not, even at the risk of compressing and omitting other important matters, let the course finish without some attempt at the examination of it on the principle which we have hitherto followed. We have seen in several points the assistance that it has given in English history to the growth of the representative system, and how in all the municipal systems powers bestowed for the carrying out of judicial proceedings in the newly chartered communities have been the basis of the independence afterwards erected there. Nor would it be difficult to show how it was in this department of civil administration that the three ideas of delegation, representation, and election became combined. But any such lengthy speculation we have not time for now. I shall therefore briefly sketch, at some little detail in the case of England, but in the others as shortly as possible, the growth of the more elaborate judicial system.

Judicature is among the Anglo-Saxons purely a matter of local or self-government. The court of the township, or, as it was afterwards called, the court leet, settled disputes between the men of the township; the reeve, the elected head of the village, or tithing, or township, or if it were a village in the franchise of a lord his steward, presided; the law was declared by the oral testimony of the elders; the compurgators swore to the innocence of the accused, as the witnesses deposed to his guilt; not much judgment was required, the guilt or innocence being decided by the value of the oaths, and in some cases by ordeal. Above the court of the township, the business of which was of course very small and unimportant, was the court of the hundred, and above that of the hundred that of the shire or folk mote, in each of which the township was represented by the reeve and four men, while the presence of the thanes, the parish priests, the bishop, sheriff, and ealdorman gave to the united body a completeness which for the most part satisfied the litigants. Very few causes ever went higher than the shiremoot; the sheriff, within historical times a nominee of the king, represented the judicial element in the presiding trio, the bishop the religious sanction, the ealdorman the national recognition; but the suitors were themselves the judges, the functions of the body being confided to twelve thanes sworn to declare the law, as assessors of the sheriff.

The compurgatory system decided guilt or innocence. If any cause could not, either from the equality of the compurgations or from the ambiguity of the law, be settled in the folkmote, there was no other resource but the king in person, who from time to time made judicial journeys, or could be caught and made to act as assessor while he was travelling about to his different allods. This was a primitive mode of action, and before the Conquest we find cases (1) of the king appointing high reeves to hear and settle matters occasionally in the provincial courts; and (2) by writ calling the suitors to his own audience, or otherwise interfering with local procedure. This is not very certain, however, but it does seem clear that no cause could on the theory of the law come before the king except by way of appeal. After the Conquest, the local courts continued to maintain their jurisdiction side by side with the manorial courts of the feudal lords. No doubt in these latter some feudal customs were introduced, but the main processes continued for nearly a century the same, compurgation and ordeal, wager of law and wager of battle; the act of William the Conqueror also modified the constitution of the national courts so far as to relieve the bishops from taking part in them.[1] These local or national courts were strictly representative bodies, and their judicial authority was from beneath and not from above; their jurisdiction was not derived from the king, although by nominating the sheriffs and other functionaries he gradually absorbed the management into the supreme government. But under the Conqueror and William Rufus the supreme sovereign or appellate jurisdiction of the king became a great feature of government, and as the business increased the royal justiciar took his master's place at the head of the curia regis, that curia regis being, as it is commonly stated, the feudal vassals of the king in the first instance, but devolving its legal business on certain learned members of its own body, who in their judicial character were called justices of the curia, and in their financial capacity barons of the exchequer. At the head of these, in both their capacities, was the chief justice or justiciar, who acted as the

---

[1] *Select Charters*, p. 85.

king's representative in all matters, just as the reeve or steward of a manor represented the lord of the manor, and as the sheriff or *vicecomes* represented the royal functions in the shire at the head of all business, judicial, taxative, military. The chief justiciar was regent in the king's absence, judge of the court, prime minister of the treasury, commander-in-chief of the forces. By the justices of the curia and the 'barons of the exchequer,' Henry I. began to exercise provincial jurisdiction over the heads of the county courts, not as a regularly settled system but rather by an occasional special commission.

An assize or provincial session of the justiciar is mentioned in the Anglo-Saxon Chronicle under the name of witenagemot, and one of them signalised itself even in those murderous times by hanging eighteen robbers, a fact which shows that they were acting judicially, even if, as would seem from the pipe roll of Henry, their expeditions into the country were chiefly and primarily financial. We gather from this that the taxative machinery of the exchequer—that is, the visits of the barons to the different towns and county courts for the purpose of rating the feudal aids and assessing Danegeld— was made available for judicial purposes also, and that thus was laid the foundation of a new system, emanating from the king as fountain of justice, which gradually absorbed all the important functions of the ancient folkmotes, while it superseded in all serious matters the action of the feudal courts of the great vassals. If in this we see cause to grieve over the diminution of the importance of the old national institutions, we must set against that loss the great gain of the reducing to insignificance the manorial courts of the nobles, whose jurisdiction had a tendency to constant extension and interference with the rights of the people. This was accomplished by Henry II.'s organisation of itinerant judges, who united financial with judicial powers, and who under his successive assizes of Clarendon and Northampton introduced a new system of process superseding compurgation everywhere but in the chartered towns, and retaining in the institution of the grand jury the principle of election and representation. The same points were kept in view in the institution of the grand assize [1] and in the several modifications of it under Richard I. and John. Out of these reforms we might, if we had time, trace the growth, on the one hand, of trial by jury; on the other, of self-government in matters of taxation, the representation of the taxpayers for the purpose of assessment,

step towards their being assembled for the purpose of voting the taxes. All this is familiar enough to you who have read English

---

[1] *Select Charters*, p. 161.

history with me. I cannot now state it at length without displacing matters that have a prior claim to our present discussion.

In these systems we have the germ of modern provincial jurisdiction by royal judges; in the curia regis and exchequer that of the supreme central judicature; the royal audience constantly throws off new courts, still retaining its own supremacy. Henry II. limits the number of justices of the curia, reserving appeal cases to himself; under John the curia breaks up into three permanent courts, the bench, the exchequer, and the court of pleas; under Henry III. each of these has a staff of judges to itself, and at last a chief of its own, the ancient justiciarship being broken up into three. The royal audience, again, under John, remains, as under his father, the personal tribunal of the king and his curia; under Henry III. it is united with the great council of the nation, giving the origin of the appellate jurisdiction of the house of lords, but still continues to exist by itself. Under Edward I. it originates the equitable jurisdiction of the chancellor; under the later princes that of the privy council, the star chamber, the judicial committee of privy council that exercises us so strongly at the present day. The principle is that of a central power, constantly, as it were, throwing off from itself functions of jurisdiction, but as constantly retaining its own original power unimpaired.

Now, there is not, I believe, in any other nation anything so complete as this; but it has many complexities, and from beginning to end there must be difficulties where there are so many co-ordinate jurisdictions. It is far from easy to determine the mutual relations of the courts of the hundred and shire, and those of the manor and honour, or the co-ordinate departments of the bench, the pleas, and the exchequer, or the rival merits of the chancery, the house of lords, and the judicial committee of privy council. But that very complexity is a sign of growth; simplicity of detail signifies historically the extinction of earlier framework. That which springs up, as our whole system has done, on the principle of adapting present means to present ends, may be complex and inconvenient and empiric, but it is natural, spontaneous, and a crucial test of substantial freedom. Perhaps, however, in our present connection, the point we have chiefly to remark is, the entire prevention of the feudal lords from obtaining jurisdictions over their vassals in causes of any kind. It is only in very unsettled times and in very uncertain conditions of the law that any feudal baron can hang, fine, or beat his own dependant, even the poorest and the meanest. Of course, where law is paralysed, such things are done, but not by virtue of the law, as in foreign countries where the feudal tenure has carried feudal jurisdiction, either under the royal supervision or independent of it. Neither as under the king nor as against the king could the possession of land or heritable jurisdiction give one man any judicial hold upon another save according to a common process of law.

Now, in France the case is very different: both in France and Germany we find the great feudatories ousting the royal jurisdiction from their domains. In the Karling empire, much that I have described as Anglo-Saxon, but which was really Teutonic or allodial, subsisted and worked fairly. There was thus abundant local machinery, while for the central machinery there was the imperial court with its officers, and, as a link between the two, there was the jurisdiction of permanent counts palatine, exercising their functions in the several nations, and occasional *missi dominici*, whose commissions were special and extraordinary. We saw that the tendency of the palatinates was to unite with the local hereditary jurisdictions and split off into territorial principalities; the paralysis of the centre gave them complete independence; the *missi dominici* came to an end; and the rest worked without control. Such was the state of affairs in France until the monarchy began to gather the provinces and clothe itself in administrative strength. Such was the permanent condition of Germany from the restoration of the empire by Otto to the fall of Frederick II., under some control; from the fall of Frederick II. to the reign of Maximilian, without any. The point of time at which the territorial judicature became a matter of feudal privilege cannot be ascertained, or rather it grew up during a long period, and only acquired its full growth when the central power became paralysed or extinct. In France not only the great feudatories had high justice, but the barons and castellans also: a right which the turbulent barons of England were prevented from obtaining by the policy of William I. and Henry II., the middle and lower justice being held by the vassals of lower rank over their unfortunate dependants. The cruelties of these feudal courts were ameliorated by several expedients, but the title to jurisdiction was the same, and all great feudatories ignored any supreme centre. The attempt to recover the royal status in this respect was made in France by Louis VI., whose institution of itinerant judges, almost contemporaneous with the like act of Henry I., may have had a common origin. Philip Augustus in 1190 established royal courts of justice in his domains, on the plan of feudal courts rather than of the provincial extension of central jurisdiction as it was practised in England, and thus made each of his demesne baronies a fixed centre of law and justice, which attracted and gradually engrossed the great share of territorial judicature.

On the other hand, the royal council of barons, which in England took the form of the curia regis with its manifold developments, grew up in France later and less spontaneously into the parliament of Paris, a strictly legal body, formed on the basis of the court of peers, but gradually adding lawyers and eliminating barons, until it consisted of the former only. The history of this parliament is important, not only judicially but legislatively, for in its character of registering the royal ordinances it acquired a power of wording or modifying them, just as in England the chancellor made his way to jurisdiction by having the duty laid on him of drawing up the writs of the king's court. And there can be no doubt that as the knowledge of jurisprudence marched along with the growth of the power of the parliaments, very much that was unjustifiable in the local and feudal courts was remedied and prevented. It was by these means the extension of royal demesne till it covered the whole area of France, the establishment of royal courts gradually as the demesne increased, acquiring supreme territorial jurisdiction, and the growth in power and fame of the parliament as the central and highest court, that took away the abuses of baronial jurisdiction, and made impossible the excesses of royal tyranny. It is clear, however, that in France the judicial system had retained very little of the ancient character; it was overlaid in the north by feudal custom, and in the south by Roman law; and accordingly it was scarcely able in the slightest degree to modify the constitutional process. It was, in fact, extinguished; and the restoration of law and order was managed irrespective of it; law and order were restored not by the workings of the nation, but by the increase of the power of the king, and they ended as the royal power must ever end when the needful checks are wanting and the deeper forces depressed and bound down in despotism, resulting in an explosion, a revolution, anarchy, and, as action and reaction are correlative, a series of such phenomena, which has never in this world's history been summed up except in national extinction. It remains to be seen whether the experience of the ages and the development of political knowledge has anything better in store for France in our own time.

As for Germany, it would be hopeless to attempt to discriminate the various petty and local jurisdictions which the princes, each supreme in his own territories, and the barons, subject only to their princes and sometimes not even to them, had engrossed in their own hands; nor can I pretend to say what amount of local independence remained during the middle ages as a check on this from below; but probably there was some everywhere, and through North Germany, where both the allodial tenure and the local self-government retained their vitality, as in Friesland and Holstein, that check was doubtless very considerable. But there was no check from above. Between the princes and nobles the right of defiance and private war flourished for three centuries, the very measures taken for the prevention of it being used to legalise and strengthen it. Nor were the central courts established by Maximilian, the imperial chamber and the aulic council, accessible to the subject except through long and tedious transactions and by way of appeal. Their chief object was to settle disputes between the states, and the territorial jurisdiction of the states was left to themselves. Thus every state in Germany has a separate history; nor can any generalisations be drawn from them illustrative of a state of things which in England, and indeed in France also, was so very different.

More important analogies, in this as in all other constitutional matters, meet us when we turn to Spain. Spain, in its two kingdoms of Castile and Aragon, does in the article of judicature afford some most important parallels with the English practice in its two stages of Anglo-Saxon and feudal, and to the French systems of the two great periods of the second and third race. Taking Castile first, we distinctly get in the scanty sketch given by Hallam both the ancient local and the modern central system, the former of which preceded in England, and the latter of which superseded the feudal judicature. The alcaldes of the towns, at first elected by the community and later by the governing body, seem to answer exactly to the reeves or provosts of the early English townships, or the steward of court leet in the rudimentary municipalities; the officer who in the county communities was elective because they were free, and in the towns was nominated by the lord because they were less than free, until by charter the right of choosing their provost or mayor, or town reeve, or port reeve, was conferred upon the community. Sir Francis Palgrave has shown that one peculiarity of the Castilian system was the election of both military and naval commanders by oath of twelve men; that is, the principle of election was recognised, and the principle of representation by jury, although applied there in the choice of officers, here in the declaration of law or fact at different times. We cannot, then, doubt that the institution of lawmen in some shape or other was germane to the Spanish system. The jury of good men was indeed an actual part of trials, in which the decision of the single judge who first heard the case did not content the parties. The existence of a chosen judge and a jury of twelve men to declare the law was thus common to the Anglo-Saxon and Visigothic systems; and so were the more ancient expedients of compurgation and ordeal. This is perhaps as far as it is wise to carry this point, because it might be difficult to show an exact analogy in the application of these factors.

Again, as in England before the Conquest there were lords of franchises not strictly feudal, but possessing summary jurisdictions, so in Castile there were communities where the lord nominated the alcalde. This he did, says Hallam, not by feudal privilege of common law, but by express gift of the king, just as at home it was by royal charter that the Anglo-Saxon franchises were conferred, sac and soc, tol and them, infangtheof and outfangtheof. These were feudal in character, not in origin, in both countries. In the thirteenth century, Hallam proceeds, the king began to appoint *corregidores*, local judges with royal jurisdictions; the same principle which in England was worked by the king's nomination of sheriffs, and the later supersession of the sheriffs by judges of assize; although the analogy is more strictly with the former. Alfonso XI. is requested to remove all *corregidores* from chartered communities that had not petitioned for them; in England the same appears in the exemption of chartered towns from the sheriff's jurisdiction, and their refusal, except at intervals of seven years, to receive the visits of the itinerant justices. An appeal from all these lower courts lay to the *adelantado* of the province, and thence to the tribunal of the royal alcaldes, if we suppose the jurisdiction of the adelantado to correspond in range (for it did not in origin, and we happily had no *adelantados* or counts palatine) with that of the judges of assize; you get the appeal from them to the courts of royal audience, the king's bench, the exchequer, and common pleas of later days: this court of the royal alcaldes continues an ultimate appeal in criminal matters, civil ones being transferred in the fourteenth century to a new court of king's audience, just as in England in the thirteenth crown causes continue to belong to the king's bench, civil ones go to the exchequer and common pleas. At the head of justice in Castile is the constable, who here, as in England the justiciar, is supreme representative of the king on the land. Curiously the Spanish and English systems of judicature retain the same title, the latter in the lowest, the former in the highest, department of justice; we have to recall the fact that the judicial use of the word constable in England has descended from the lord high constable to the humblest parish officer; both are derived from the Byzantine *comestabuli*, an office that would be difficult to distinguish in itself from the marshalship, which has had somewhat the same history.

The Spaniards long and steadfastly maintained in their common customs of law the ancient Teutonic superstitions of compurgation and ordeal, and if you read the history of Spain carefully you will find in it the reason why the countries that longest retained the customs of which these are a part were those which made the longest and most effective fight for political liberty. Now, in Aragon you get a purely feudal judicature, with a *justiza* at the head, answering so far as the extent of his office goes to the English justiciar, at the head of the king's feudal council, and supreme over all courts feudal or otherwise ; but the *justiza* of Aragon has a long history of his own, and does make historically a more important figure than his English counterpart. Two important and peculiar points Hallam mentions in which the power of the justiza was used for purposes which in England were otherwise met : the process of *juris firma* or power of withdrawing a cause from the lower to the higher court, and in the meantime issuing an injunction for the protection of the suitor at whose instance the writ is issued ; this is distinct from the right of appeal, it is an appeal perhaps before sentence ; the second, that of manifestation, which applied to the person the same protection which the *juris firma* applied to property, analogous, perhaps, to our court of habeas corpus ; in these two points the Aragonese law seems a little in advance of the English in point of time. The power of the justiza has been in some books a good deal exaggerated ; up to 1348, when it became tenable for life, the office does not really differ much from the chief justiceship ; and even when held for life, it did not exempt its holder from responsibility or even from a commission of inquiry at the demand of the king and cortes. In 1461, the *justiza* had a court of seventeen councillors appointed to hear complaints against him ; as the courts of Westminster are liable to review by the exchequer chamber, and the house of lords in its appellate jurisdiction. These particulars help the parallel, and serve to complete the illustrations I have given already of a royal central judicature superinduced on a lower feudal one.

This, then, is as far as we can for the present go in our attempt to compare the constitutional origins of the mediæval nations, and it is as far as I propose to carry this course on this plan. At some future time we may perhaps attempt a comparative view of the political history of the four nations, or even take one or two more into the list; but to do that with good effect, it would be necessary to have more thoroughly in hand the general history of the nations than can fairly be expected from an elementary course like this. I feel that even as it is I have attempted too much, and must send you back to your Hallam for much of the material that will fill up the sketch that I have attempted to draw. If, however, you have given me a fairly reasonable amount of attention, you will find your Hallam much more easy, connected, and interesting reading than is wont to be to those who begin Constitutional History in it, and are perplexed at the want of method and unity which is the most evident fault of the book. You will begin by seeing how much the

nations of mediæval Europe have in common, and how very much of
what they differ in can be and should be accounted for by the events
of their history.   But you will also see how persistent the genius
of the paternal race is in one nation, and how pliant in another ;
and you will venture to allow that that persistency may be owing to
the blood, the language, the freedom from external conquest, or
the growth through the conquering stratum by the conquered, and
the assimilation of the former to the latter.   You will not miss
the lesson, distinct enough in itself—and perhaps rather obscured
than brightened by the halo of universal praise—that of all constitutional systems the English combines the greatest political with
the greatest personal liberty.   You will accept this on the testimony
of foreign writers on politics, to whom for centuries our polity was
the model of free institutions.   You will not be less likely to accept
it after reading the history of the newer constitutions in Europe
and in America which have copied many of the leading features of
our own, but have not tempered them or adapted them so wisely to
their own circumstances that they seem a natural and spontaneous
growth, or have not calculated their forces so well as to secure an
equable and uniform working.   You will further, I think, realise
the fact that a national polity is not the creation of a single brain
or of a royal commission of brains, but grows with the growth and
strengthens with the strength of the nation ; cannot be changed
without changing much of the spirit of the people, and is strong in
proportion to the distinctness of its continuity.

Our own English constitution is like many old country houses
which have a great history of their own if they could tell it ;
have been now castles, now abbeys, now manor houses, or farm
buildings ; in which every room has often changed its destination,
and the granary become a dining-room, the chapel a billiard room,
and the dairy a bath ; about which many little turrets have been
run up and tumbled down ; some have been battered down by
enemies, and some pulled down because they made the chimneys
smoke ; in which chimneys themselves are a novelty, and drains
and hot-water pipes a new development of luxury ; in which no one
room now answers the purpose for which it was built, but has
answered many others and more useful ones that were not contemplated.   Such a house is generally beautiful, sometimes a little
inconvenient to people whose ideas are bounded by a front door and
five square windows, but it has its history, it has seen a great deal
of happiness, and would not be what it is unless it had seen and been
adapted to many changes.

Well, so the constitution begins with the little farmhold in the
Teutonic clearing ; it grows up and becomes a feudal manor ; it

builds a national church and a court of justice, and towers and crenellates its roofs and walls ; the church becomes the mother and nurse of liberty, and then liberty takes on itself to reform and remodel the church ; the court of justice develops into a parliament ; trial by jury grows out of compurgation and ordeal. It retains much that it could do without, and goes without much that might be well added if it were not that the addition would stop the working of some more important part. It will, however, like an old house, also stand a great deal of alteration and adaptation without losing its identity. To put away the parable, however. You have seen how small are the early institutions of a race in the process of civilisation, but how great is the difference between working out the civilisation of which the germs are in its rude condition, and receiving civilisation even ever so tenderly by the teaching of a more advanced race ; and from first to last the lesson has been, the more continuous the growth the stronger the result. I do not mean to tell you that the knowledge of this is in itself as valuable as the discussion by which we arrive at it ; if it were, all knowledge might be distilled into a few brief rules, and the world need do nothing more than write and read novels, or pictorial histories evolved by the light of nature. Such principles are but guides and clues in the pursuit of real fact knowledge, and to the student who tries to apply them so they will be useful clues, because as he realises the application of them in one branch, he will use them more skilfully and confidently in the investigation of another. But the very generality of such generalisations is in itself a proof of their insufficiency to convey real knowledge. The scantiness of the generalisation surely suggests the consideration not merely of the existence of some common formula, but the infinite variety that history must afford when its chief formula is so very general : if the national histories have so much in common, how infinitely more must they have that is peculiar to each ; if on that common formula so much can be ranged, how diversified must the histories be that have created the enormous differences.

You may have been sometimes impatient when I have gone into detail about petty legal institutions or small municipal distinctions ; but when you put all together and see how often a petty little institution comes to answer a purpose which was never contemplated at its creation, and how out of the petty distinctions of municipalities have arisen differences of training of the men who were to work out, or to fail to work out, real liberty, you will think that nothing of the kind is too small to be worth remembering, and grieve that one memory cannot contain more of what is so full of what is memorable. You may also think that I have an unwise and undue bias against ascribing civilising and politicising influences to the Roman Empire. To an aversion to ascribe anything directly to that agency that cannot be shown by probable evidence to belong to it, I certainly own; and I think that I have read enough to warrant me in that aversion. I prefer to refer the civilisation of England and Germany to the working of non-Roman causes—to the ancient land system with its judicial and social peculiarities, and to the teaching of the church, through which teaching most of the Roman elements that are at all traceable are to be traced. In France and Spain I grant that it is very different; both those countries were thoroughly Romanised and got their civilisation that way; but the distinction in history between France and Spain is not owing to the difference of Roman ingredients—they were the same in each—but to the difference of Teutonic ingredients, and to the fact that it was by the Teutonic-Visigothic ingredients that Spain worked her way so far as she did work it to liberty; while it was by Teutonic-Frank ingredients, or feudalism, that France worked her way to absolutism and servility. It is easy to say, and within certain limits it may be true, that Europe learned a lesson from each system; from the Roman the equality of all men before the law, and from the Teutonic the right of every man to join in making the law that is to bind him. But I do not see that we learn much from the generalisation, and I think that it would be a very difficult one to prove inductively or circumstantially. I do not wish you to leave me with the impression that I like to knock down other people's nine-pins, only to set up my own instead of them. It is not my place to force upon you principles which I can give no reasons for. I am to lead you on to make out such generalisations for yourselves, and to read history intelligently. I naturally exhibit most prominently the principles in which, as it seems to me, the truth of history has shown itself to me, but you are quite at liberty to get out of my premisses conclusions diametrically opposite to mine. The good will have been done by your going critically and honestly through the work.

XX

THE GROWTH OF THE CONSTITUTIONAL PRINCIPLE IN THE THIRTEENTH AND FOURTEENTH CENTURIES

TRUE patriotism is like that true self-love which builds its happiness on a good conscience: it is not like that base self-conceit which can never see or own itself to be in the wrong. It does not require of any man to believe that his own country is in the right always; it does not require him to go with public opinion against his better judgment; but it does require that he shall himself do his best to make and keep his country in the right. Whether he succeeds or is obliged to yield, he can still do his duty, and this duty is in a soldier obedience, in a citizen submission to government in all things lawful. So neither does a patriotic view of history, of the history of our own country, at all require us to take always the side of the victorious cause: ' Victrix causa Diis placuit sed victa Catoni ; ' nor does it at all when we have taken a side require us to see no faults or weakness in that side, and no virtue or truth in the other. History has been written very much in this style, but it is not history that the matured conscience of a people can ever approve as true. In particular, in viewing the struggle by which our fore-fathers won their liberty, we ought to be careful in this respect. They were our countrymen on both sides. Honour and truth, and perhaps also dishonour and falsehood, were peculiar to neither: it may be that the object in present dispute did not, to their minds, fall incontrovertibly into one of two classes, right or wrong ; perhaps at times both sides were seeking only private ends ; rather, we may gladly believe, at other times, both were fighting for what they believed sincerely to be the right cause.

There is an Almighty Judge and Ruler of nations who gives victory to which He will; but the victory is no more a necessary token of His favour than the chastisement of defeat. He sees men fighting for the shadow of good, and oftentimes gives the reality to those who have striven lawfully. There is in the Carolinenplatz at

Munich a monument set up by King Ludwig to the memory of those Bavarian soldiers who fell in Napoleon's army in the Russian campaign. The inscription is (I cannot remember the exact words) to this effect : 'These also died for the deliverance of their native land,' an expression which is puzzling enough to those who look only at the outside of things. They died under the banner of the tyrant, but fighting bravely and enduring manfully for what they believed to be the right cause. They were mistaken in their cause, but God saw and gave to their country the liberty for the shadow of which they perished. So also in the review of every struggle for freedom that has been fought out at home, we can claim great and noble spirits on both sides, high and honourable motives. In the Great Rebellion some fought for what seemed to them religion on either side, some for fancied freedom, some for loyalty ; when the time came peace and freedom were granted, though not the peace or the freedom that either had pictured as the object of his struggles. The blood honestly shed in pursuit of the shadow did not lose its reward when the substance of peace and freedom was bestowed.

The cause of freedom in England has been a consistently triumphant and progressive cause, and so has been checked by fewer mistakes and disgraced by fewer crimes than are to be found in the struggles of other nations for freedom in the whole of history. Those crimes that have disgraced the partisans of liberty have never been ultimately conducive to liberty itself. The murder of Charles I. was not only a crime but a blunder, and it is impossible even for the most acute advocate at this day to prove that the act was in any way or degree conducive to the freedom of the country : nay, more, the horror that it inspired and still does inspire gave rise to a reactionary feeling that will see nothing but admirable in the martyr, nothing but what is detestable in the persecutors. Most happily, however, such crimes and blunders are rare. There were no unlawful means used in the real winning of our liberty : we have no causeless rebellions, no secret assassinations, no going to war for ideas, no sentimental conspiracies, no justifications of means by ends. We are indebted to no foreign interventions, no bloody revolutions, no violent revulsions. If there were nothing else in our constitution of which we might be proud and happy, we might glory in the way in which it was won, grew up rather, we thank God when we say it, without a stain if not without a flaw. The fabric of the constitution was, as I understand it, perfect under the Tudor sovereigns ; whatever crimes or errors have taken place in our internal government, have been rather owing to the mistakes and faults of those who had to work the machine, than to any vice of the machine itself. The Tudors were strong tyrants ; the Stuarts, it may be, were weak tyrants; but neither spoiled the old machinery. Cromwell is looked on by some as a liberator, William the Third by others; but neither introduced anything new into the machinery of the constitution. The Declaration of Rights was, as its name implies, a declaration, not an institution or enactment. What these later struggles did was this: they made it impossible for the machinery of the constitution to be worked by men merely for private and selfish ends, they produced a better state and atmosphere of political morality in England.

We think at the present day that we could not bear to be governed as Lord Liverpool governed; but compare Lord Liverpool's government with Lord North's, Lord North's with Sir Robert Walpole's, Walpole's with Harley's, Harley's with that of the statesmen of the Revolution; theirs, again, with that of the Cabal, with the military despotism, the reign of terror of the Rebellion, the unprincipled extravagance and caprice of Buckingham, and the Machiavellism of James I. I think that we must see a gradual change—an elimination of bad means and measures, a greater and more widespread purity of political character. Not but that men are at all times men; not but that the progress of political morality has been often and may again be disturbed and wayward; still I think we should be undervaluing our own happiness if we refused to recognise it. Whig as we may be, or Tory as I am for my part, we would not exchange a government by Palmerston or by Derby for one either by Strafford or Cromwell; nay, more, highly as we value order, we have no desire to be ruled by Metternich; precious as liberty is, we are glad that for us it was not won by a Cavour.

True liberty is the freedom for every man to do as he likes within the limits of right defined by laws which he has a hand in making; the liberty of doing what you please, without infringing the liberty of other people. We have seen in our first lectures how far our fathers were in possession of the conditions requisite for the winning of it: their German origin and the institutions that the Anglo-Saxon race had developed being a very strong basis of independent character, and the discipline of the feudal system a pretty strong training towards self-restraint. We may say that as Anglo-Saxons they had a good notion of doing as they liked, and that under the Norman princes they were broken in to the habit of regarding the likings of other people. They were taught unity, loyalty, sympathy; they found out that they were one people. We have seen also in our last lecture the terrible slavery under which they found themselves when they awoke to this truth; and how with the commencement of Henry II.'s reign they began to get glimpses of the dayspring.

z

Our first question must be, what elements of freedom were now existent ; where were the memories, where the hopes of freedom in this latter half of the twelfth century ?   The first circumstance that was beginning to make freedom possible was the amalgamation of the people : Anglo-Saxon and Norman were becoming one English nation ; nobles, freemen, and villeins were drawing nearer to one another, and finding out that personal security, limited taxation, and some check on the irresponsible power of the government were alike needed by all three classes.   Let us see how this was coming about. The union of the royal blood of both races in Henry II. was typical of a like union going on among the older nobility.   Many of the followers of the Conqueror had been mated with English heiresses ; the impoverishment of the Anglo-Saxons was not so great but that still the fortunes of the daughters of the richer natives were an object of ambition to the younger sons of the great houses ; half Eng-lish, perhaps, by birth themselves, they were content that their children should be more than that—three-quarters English ; and this acted in two ways : not only did the descendants of the Norman nobles become anglicised, but by the peculiarity of English custom, the titles and offices of nobility being settled by primogeniture, the younger sons settled down at once into the rank of commoners, so that noble Norman fathers had sons who were not only commoners but English, surrounded by English of the same rank, and united more by sympathy and common interests with them than with their more elevated relations.   In like manner, though by a different process, the villeins were being raised nearer to the rank of free-men.   Not only were they gaining a vested interest in the lands they had cultivated from generation to generation, becoming in fact copyhold tenants instead of serfs ; but the work of emancipation was going on to a great extent by which the serf rose at once to eedom.   Immense numbers of monasteries were founded by the repentant warriors of the Norman kings, and slavery was a thing always discouraged and to the utmost forbidden by the church even in its greatest depression.   The emancipation of serfs followed almost immediately on the founding of a monastery.

Again, the nobles were, partly by extravagance and partly by extreme taxation, almost as much impoverished as the native land-owners : they were glad to sell a serf his own liberty if he could produce the money to buy it ; further, a service in arms on a crusade made a man free ; the towns held out safe asylums for run-away villeins who being unclaimed by their masters for a year and a day became free men ; pious people on their deathbed freed their servants ; many ways were open now for the abolition of servitude, and while it continued, the serfs were beginning to have relations and friends in the class of freemen who would not stand by and see them oppressed.

In the second place, the liberties of the church, though oppressed by the Norman sovereigns, had never been quite extinguished and were now beginning to revive: I do not mean only those pernicious liberties which were the subject of the contention between Henry II. and Becket, but the more reasonable ones which had existed under the Anglo-Saxon kings. Among these was one in particular, the election of bishops and abbots. This right, as far as bishops were concerned, had not been exercised in the churches under the Anglo-Saxon kings—the bishops were nominated by the king and witan, and elected by the chapters of the churches much as they are now. But the Norman kings, by always thrusting Norman prelates into these places of trust and honour, had provoked the spirit of resistance among the clergy, who were almost universally English by birth and always supported the native party. Men who had no notion of supporting the pope against the king in general, yet supported Anselm in his struggle for investitures : to them the choice was not only between a nominee of Henry or William Rufus and one of their own election, it was the choice between a Norman allied in birth and habit with the tyrants, and an Englishman united in sympathy and blood with themselves. Anselm, fighting the battle of the pope as he thought, was in reality fighting the battle of the inferior clergy and of the nation through them. In like manner every act of plunder and oppression exercised against the church was exercised against the nation, and as the clergy had a stronger *esprit de corps*, firmer organisation, and more united action than the laity, they were the first to cry for liberty and to understand that against a Norman ruler the liberty of one is a hope at least of liberty for all. I have already referred to the liberalising tendencies of monastic education and civilisation, and to the work of emancipation carried on by the clergy and monks.

The third element of liberty is to be found in the rise and increase in power and independence of the towns as contrasted with the country population. The towns were not, as you must have remarked from my omission of mention of them, a prominent element in Anglo-Saxon society ; still there were towns and boroughs united perhaps for purposes of commerce and mutual defence, and enfranchised in Anglo-Saxon times. Either they grew up on demesne lands of the king or under the castle of some lord, who saw a little further than his neighbours ; or they were on the sites of old Roman cities like Colchester, and retained some sort of measure and recollection of municipal independence. In Domesday Book the burghers of the towns are already a different class from country churls : their tenure—burgage tenure—was akin, as we saw, to socage tenure, and the service they paid for protection was free and fixed : they were, however, subject also to tallages, arbitrary taxation at the demand of their king or lord.   Their first step towards independence was to exchange the many fixed rents due from the single burgage tenants for one settled rent for the whole borough, and that a perpetual and fixed rent.   This was done in Huntingdon before the Conquest, possibly in others also : a town thus let to the burgesses at perpetual rent was said to be let at fee farm to them and their successors for ever.   The lord ceased to have any right of property in the town, and the tallages which he continued to set were always regarded as an oppression.

The next step was to incorporate these boroughs, a measure largely carried out under the first three Plantagenets—it gave them local self-government and exclusion of every foreign jurisdiction : they elected their own sheriffs and justices.   The material groundwork for these corporations is often found in the guilds which for purposes of commerce or religion had existed from very early times : hence the guild hall is equivalent to corporation court house.   It is unnecessary for me to go to first principles to show how such communities, once formed and enfranchised, were sure to become centres of liberty, and, acting singly or together against oppression from king or lord, to attract multitudes of new citizens.   The city of London e.g. has always been strong on the popular side in all public questions, right or wrong.   To these three elements, the memory of liberty in the church, the amalgamation of all classes of society, and the foundation and development of towns, we are to look for the origin of English liberty, as revived under the Plantagenets, and flourishing and to flourish we trust as long as the world lasts.   I have given a loose definition of liberty—it would take volumes and years of lectures to go into detail either of law or history on the development of these little seeds into the full-grown tree : I shall not attempt to do it : but supposing that the three great gifts of the English constitution are, security of life and property by law, the right of taxation and taxing ourselves, and the existence of a supreme court of parliament, to which all officers of government are responsible and in which all classes are represented, I propose that we sketch shortly the process by which these possessions were won.

And first, of personal security and freedom.   You have not forgotten, I hope, the description from the Anglo-Saxon Chronicle of the wretchedness and misery of the people in the reigns of Henry I. and Stephen.[1]   The worst troubles of these times fell on them in the civil war, but there was throughout the feudal period, throughout the reigns of the Norman princes, no adequate prevention, no adequate remedy ; it was the weakness of the feudal system that to be properly administered it required angels and not men. The barons in their strong castles, in a thinly inhabited country, un-fettered by public opinion, unchecked by equal neighbours, presiding in their own courts, with assessors too much in their power to venture a word against their decisions, at once the aggressors and the judges, they were to all intents and purposes irresponsible. If they did an injury, imprisoned or ill-treated a vassal, they were strong enough to get their own way in the county courts ; they were their own judges in their courts baron ; it was a long way to the king's court, and there even, when it was reached, much was done by money. A poor man had little chance against a rich one. It was better to submit than to provoke further oppression by appealing to so distant and untrustworthy a protector. On the king's own lands it was little better : his officers were of the same class and sympathies as the barons : justice was only to be bought, and, unhappily, injustice was quite as ready to be sold. Thus it was not so much the existence of any institution hostile to per-sonal freedom as the absence of remedies and securities that caused the evil.

There were thus two things peremptorily required : 1. A re-cognition of the rights of freemen to liberty and security ; 2. Free, cheap, open, impartial administration of justice on that principle. Neither of these could be sufficient without the other ; yet it was tried first to make justice acceptable without the previous recognition of the right. Besides the courts of the hundred and the shire which remained from ancient times, and the manorial courts and franchises, which were, as I have said, almost inoperative for good and certainly afforded no guarantee against unjust administration, there was until late in the reign of Henry I. only the king's court to appeal to—that is, the assembly of princes and lawyers and state officers who attended the king whithersoever he went ; a man might, if he was not shut up in prison, appeal to the king, after he had been cast in the courts of the shire ; when the king was absent from England the grand justiciary supplied his place. This court consisted of the grand justiciary, the chancellor, the constable, the marshal, chamberlain, steward, and treasurer, with any others whom the king might appoint. In one apartment of the palace they sat as a court of exchequer, and judged all suits arising from questions of revenue ; in the reign of Richard I. it began under another form to take cognisance of common pleas, i.e. matters cognisable by common law ; under name of the court of common bench it took cognisance of all matters in civil disputes in which the king's interest was not concerned, and no matter of a criminal nature. Here you have the origin of the three courts—king's bench, exchequer, and common pleas.   It was certainly a great step in advance that there should be such courts, but their efficiency was greatly impaired by the fact that they were obliged to follow the person of the king or his vicegerent : by Magna Carta the courts of law were settled at Westminster.   But previous to this—as early as the reign of Henry I.—justices of assize, justices *in itinere*, were commissioned to go through the country and hear appeals from the county courts, or other suits which the suitors on the payment of a fine were allowed to bring before them.   The immediate benefit of this institution was, of course, delayed by the civil war of Stephen's reign, but the permanent establishment of these courts we owe to the early years of Henry II., and we may ascribe them, as well as the destruction of the strongholds of the tyrant barons, to the powerful administration of Thomas Becket.   These judges went their circuits annually, and their assizes were expressly confirmed and their jurisdiction enlarged by Magna Carta.   To the same great foundation of liberties we owe the recognition of the right which I spoke of as the necessary complement of accessible justice.   It declares as follows : 'No freeman shall be taken or imprisoned, or be disseised of his freehold or liberties or free customs, or be outlawed or exiled or any otherwise destroyed, nor will we pass upon him nor send upon him but by lawful judgment of his peers or by the law of the land.   We will sell to no man, we will not deny or delay to any man justice or right.'[1] Trial by jury is thus recognised as a part of the rights of freemen.   We have seen that it was not of Anglo-Saxon origin.   It had been growing up in the meantime.   It was in the development of amelioration in civil justice that we find instances during this period, where a small number were chosen out of the county court to declare the truth in civil suits.   Thus, in suits for the recovery of property the public mind was gradually accustomed to see the jurisdiction of the freeholders in these courts transferred to a more select number of wellinformed men : it did not become a matter of right, however, until Henry II. brought in the assize of novel disseisin in 1176.[2] We owe it to Ranulf de Glanvill.

The use of juries in criminal cases dates from the reign of Henry II.   Thus personal liberty was secured in its simplest form ; it took ages more to get the ordinary rights recognised which we connect almost inseparably with it, such as the right of disposing

---

[1] *Select Charters*, p. 301.   [2] *Ibid.* pp. 152, 164.

of property by will or transfer, into which as matters of law rather than history we cannot enter. We shall see by and by how Magna Carta was won; but before we turn to that we will consider the subject of taxation, a matter which also was regulated on the side of freedom by that great act. We have had occasion to remark in our first lecture that under the Anglo-Saxon system the only universal taxes were for the building of fortifications and bridges, and for the maintenance of the militia. All lands were subject to taxation for these purposes: the folcland, so long as it continued to be let out in benefices to the nobles by service, paid other dues analogous to feudal reliefs and aids; but the whole expense of the administration was very small. The king was supported by his demesne lands; justice was administered on the spot at no cost whatever; the only tax that could be construed into an oppression was the Danegelt, which was originally a sum collected to purchase peace and immunity from Danish invasion, but was continued, like most taxes, long after the original occasion for it had passed away. These taxes (those of the *trinoda necessitas* and the Danegelt) were levied on the whole people—so much for each hide of land, the sum required being most probably declared by the witenagemot, and the collection and assessment of it being left to the local magistrates. With the Norman kings this system was partially continued; but the weight of taxation, as we saw the other day, terribly increased: Danegelt was continued and increased sixfold, and besides it all the land, being placed on a feudal footing, became liable to those feudal exactions, reliefs, fines in aid &c. under the colour of which any extortion might be, and was, practised. Tallages were imposed on the towns; the king or lord announced to his tenants that he wanted so many thousand pounds, and they were obliged to raise it, sometimes by a poll tax, more frequently and justly by an income and property assessment on all the tenants of the town. As soon as military service was commuted for escuage, the lands of the church and the estates of the nobles became liable to similar arbitrary calls for money; tallage and escuage were levied by the justices *in itinere* when they were established, and this may be considered as one step towards remedy.

There were also from time immemorial other taxes exacted by the crown, tonnage and poundage on the import and export of merchandise, of which the prisage of wine, two casks out of each ship, was the most important. This, with the Danegelt, was probably a remnant of Anglo-Saxon taxation; escuages, tallages &c. were strictly feudal and arbitrary. I told you that William the Conqueror professed to restore Edward the Confessor's laws; one of the articles of his charter was relative to taxation: 'We will enjoin and grant that all freemen of our kingdom shall enjoy their lands in peace, free from all tallage and from every unjust exaction, so that nothing but their service lawfully due to us shall be demanded at their hands.[1] We have seen how this promise was kept—not at all; still it is important as a recognition of the right. Henry I. made still better promises, for he undertook to fix the amount of feudal incidental taxes, so that they should be no longer arbitrary. He did not keep his word any better than his father. Stephen bought the crown with still better ones, but these he had not the power, if he had the will, to fulfil. Henry II. confirmed at his accession the charter of his grandfather. His long and troublous reign was, owing to the difficulties of his position and the weakness which was consequent on his quarrels with the church and with his own children, not a very oppressive one. Noble, gentle, and simple were being drawn together, and the commonwealth was gaining strength. But with Richard I. troubles and exactions began again: he was in constant want of money; he wanted it first for his crusade, then for his ransom, then for his wars with Philip Augustus; he raised what he could by torturing the Jews, by feudal exactions, and by the sale of dignities; he sold the earldom of Northumberland to the bishop of Durham, his right to the homage of Scotland to the king of Scotland, and, what is more to our purpose, he granted a great number of charters to corporations, a measure which, we have seen, was destined ultimately to conduce in no small degree to liberty.[1] Well, Richard died, and John followed him on the throne, and in his days matters came to a head. He waged wars in France, Wales, and Scotland: he was generally unlucky, but his defeats cost the country quite as much as other men's successes; instead of learning wisdom by adversity, he fought and intrigued so much the harder. All this, however, and all the tyranny and exaction that he brought to bear on the nation, were borne for years, until, after the country had been under an interdict and matters were everywhere wearing the complexion of the old Norman reign of terror, he was compelled to grant the Magna Carta, one of the provisions of which was that all feudal aids should be fixed and definite according to the estate of the tenant, so also should all amercements in punishment be made according to the magnitude of the offence, and required the great vassals to concede to their dependants all customs and liberties as freely as they were granted to themselves; that no aid or escuage except the three great feudal aids should be imposed without consent of parliament. Tallages, however, were not mentioned. Still, the right of the taxpayer to

----

[1] *Select Charters*, p. 265

be taxed only by the expressed will of the national assembly was recognised.[1]

Now, how was Magna Carta won? Stephen Langton, archbishop of Canterbury, and the barons of England met on November 20, 1214, and drew up their demands for a redress of grievances. The king first tried to divide the confederates, to set them one against another, but failed; then he tried to set the church against the barons by first emancipating it—that failed too; then he tried to get the pope to censure the archbishop and barons; the pope complied, but the archbishop was firm; the king continued to shuffle. May 24, 1215, the barons entered London. June 15, Magna Carta was signed—signed, but not secured. As soon as it was signed the king began to intrigue against it; hired mercenary troops to put down the barons; he even offered the Saracens to turn Mahometan for assistance; persuaded the pope to annul the charter, excommunicate the barons, and suspend the archbishop. Then came the crash. One party among the barons had recourse to the king of Scotland, others to the king of France; the crown was even offered to Louis, the son of the king of France, and he was in arms in England when John most happily saved the constitution and liberty and the very independence of the nation by dying. His son, Henry III., was a child; the ministers of the new king were glad to gain unanimity by renewing the charter; the French invader was sent about his business, and from that time to this the Magna Carta has been held as the basis of the constitution. It is still, says Hallam, the keystone of English liberty. All that has since been obtained is little more than a confirmation or commentary, and if every subsequent law were to be swept away there would still remain the bold features that distinguish a free from a despotic monarchy. It has been lately the fashion to depreciate the value of Magna Carta as if it had sprung from the private ambition of a few selfish barons, and redressed only some feudal abuses: it is, indeed, of little importance by what motives those who obtained it were guided; the real characters of men most distinguished in the transactions of that time are not easily determined at present; yet if we bring these ungrateful suspicions to the test, they prove destitute of all reasonable foundation. An equal distribution of civil rights to all classes of freemen forms the peculiar beauty of the Charter. In this just solicitude for the people, and in the moderation which infringed upon no essential prerogative of the monarchy, we may perceive a liberality and patriotism very unlike the selfishness which is sometimes rashly imputed to those ancient

[1] *Select Charters*, p. 296 *seq.*

barons; and so far as we are guided by historical testimony, two great men, the pillars of our church and state, may be considered as entitled beyond the rest to the glory of this monument—Stephen Langton, archbishop of Canterbury, and William, earl of Pembroke. To their temperate zeal for a legal government England was indebted during that critical period for the two greatest blessings that patriotic statesmen could confer—the establishment of civil liberty upon an immovable basis, and the preservation of national independence under the ancient line of sovereigns which rasher men were about to exchange for the dominion of France.

We are now come to the third article of our liberty—political liberty as secured by the existence of a representative parliament. It is obvious that, notwithstanding the great admissions and concessions of the Charter, in the hands of a strong, irresponsible, and unscrupulous king, all would be a dead letter unless supported by an authority that could limit the actions of the monarch within the bounds of law and public expedience. Nor could any council nominated by the king himself have authority strong enough even if inclined so to limit his power and compel the observance of his promises. An assembly was required which should represent the taxpayers and check public expenditure by drawing the purse strings close or relaxing them in emergency— a council, moreover, which should fairly represent the wealth and wisdom of the country as well as the land, and so should be able to advise and compel the redress of grievances, draw up bills for the king to authorise as laws, and see to their execution, not by minute interference, but by securing the responsibility of the king's ministers. Now, such an institution could not grow up all at once, nor were all the parts of its machinery instituted with a direct view to the ends which in process of time they were made to serve. Our constitution in parliament is not the creation of any one mind or the expedient of any one crisis.

There was, as we have seen, a general council and assembly of the people in Anglo-Saxon times, called the witenagemot, or meeting of the wise. It was attended by the king and the bishops and ealdormen of the shires; perhaps by the thanes of higher rank, each in a manner representing the freemen under his protection, but not either an elected nor a theoretically representative assembly. The witenagemot regulated the amount of taxation, enacted laws, heard appeals, and acted as council to the king in all measures domestic and foreign. With the Anglo-Saxon dynasty the witenagemot passed away. But the early Norman kings, well aware that none of their dependants dare lift up a finger against them, assembled a similar court every year at the great festivals, and made a show of consulting them on measures on which the apparent concurrence of the country seemed desirable, so that the notion of a great national council was never lost. As the power of the king was weakened either by personal character or by quarrels such as Henry II.'s with his family and the church, it became necessary to the monarch to gain the real as well as the apparent support of his council. True, the council was composed of his feudal dependants, but these were now becoming quickly rather united with the body of the people by sympathy and affinity than slavishly bound to a superior who always when strong enough was an oppressor. Stephen was elected king by a parliament of this sort, and compelled to grant a charter. Henry II. made use of it to pass all his great measures: the constitutions of Clarendon, the council of Northampton, in which Becket was tried, and the great parliament of Northampton of 1176, to which I have referred as passing the statutes by which the assize of novel disseisin was established. Richard I. also held parliaments at Pipewell before his crusade, and at Winchester after his return. John was elected king by a parliament to the prejudice of his nephew Arthur; and if it had not been for his subsequent cruel conduct to him, would never have been counted as a usurper. Magna Carta was forced upon him by the great council of the king, which was becoming, and soon to be, the great council of the nation.

This council, court, or parliament was composed of very different ingredients from those which we look on as necessary to a constitutional assembly. It was, for instance, but one chamber; lords and commons were not divided; nor was the representation of the commons anything like what it was shortly to become. It seems that it was little more than the assembly of the king's feudal tenants; the barons holding their estates directly from him, the bishops and abbots not appearing by virtue of their wisdom as in the Anglo-Saxon witenagemot, but as tenants in barony of the crown. But besides the barons, that is those noble landholders who held sufficient fiefs to entitle them to the baronage, there were smaller holders also, holding directly by knight service of the king. These, by the breaking up of the original great fiefs, and by subinfeudations where the principal fief had become forfeit or escheated, had become very numerous by the time of King John, so numerous that it was desirable for their own sakes that they should not be put to the expense of attending parliament, and that it was desirable for the parliament's sake that it should not be overcrowded with unwise and inexperienced countrymen. There are records extant which tend to show that these smaller tenants, holding directly of the crown, were on some occasions represented in parliament by certain elected out of their number—knights of the shire, as they were called—even as early as the reign of John; but it does not appear that their presence was thought necessary to the constitution of parliament until the forty-ninth year of Henry III., 1265. In that year the arrangement by representation, to which I have referred, became a part of the parliament; two knights were summoned from every shire to represent the body of the county. It is a matter of doubt among lawyers by whom these county members or knights of the shire were elected. Perhaps, at first, it was only by the tenants *in capite*, the lords of manors; but later, as the distinction between these and ordinary freeholders became less and less, all the freeholders joined in the election, until, in the eighth year of Henry VI., 1430, an act was passed which, reciting that elections of knights of shires have now of late been made by very great outrageous and excessive number of people dwelling within the same shires, of the which most part were people of small substance and of no value, confines the elective franchise to freeholders of lands or tenements to the value of forty shillings. There is reason to believe that before the passing of this act the county members were elected not by the freeholders only in whom the right was vested, but by all persons whatever who came to the county court.

The representation of the towns in parliament dates from the same year, 1265. Before that time there are no trustworthy traces of any such thing; but then Simon de Montfort ordered the sheriffs to return two citizens or burgesses for every city or borough contained within their shires. I have explained to you the origin of boroughs or corporations; the exaction of tallages which they were subject to from their royal masters; the promise of Magna Carta that escuages should only be taken by consent of parliament, and its silence with regard to tallages. In 1265, fifty years after the signing of Magna Carta, the principle was admitted by the summoning of the borough members, that town and country alike ought not to be taxed without their own consent.[1] These borough members were no doubt from the beginning elected properly by the burgage tenants; but the privilege easily fell into the hands of the managing body, the corporation, by whom in some cases it was retained even until the Reform Bill. But, you will ask, how came it about that this year 1265 was signalised by so great an event; and who was Simon de Montfort, who had the wisdom or policy to found so exceedingly important a part of the institutions of the country as the house of commons? To clear up this, we must return to the accession of Henry III. He came to the crown, as you know, very

---

[1] *Select Charters*, p. 415.

young : as people who come early into their property, he learned
habits of extravagance ; he had a large connection of half-brothers
and sisters. So had his wife. She was extravagant too. The
pope was sorely in want of money, for he was an extravagant pope ;
or, rather, there was a run of them, and no money to be got but out
of the English nation. In vain were the Jews forced to ransom
their teeth ; in vain were the clergy taxed to the very utmost, and
the livings of the church given away to pay the pope's debts.
Money could not be got ; and so the kingdom went on for no less
than forty years, the king begging, borrowing, and extorting all he
could get from the parliament, and spending it quicker than he got
it. The barons, who then constituted the parliament, kicked very
hard : sometimes they refused money altogether, but generally were
persuaded or forced to give in after a remonstrance that the king
ought not to undertake wars and expenses without their knowledge
and advice, and expect them to pay for them. At length, however,
things came to a head. King and pope together were too much for
English patience. In 1255 Pope Innocent IV. offered the kingdom
of Sicily to Henry's second son, Edmund. Without asking the
advice of his people the king accepted the offer, and borrowed money
of the pope to pay the expense of the war in which it involved
him. The pope had not the power to secure the kingdom of Sicily
to his nominee ; that nominee was brought forward merely to gratify
his personal dislike to the house of Frederick II. No result followed
as far as Sicily is concerned, except the spending of the 14,000 marks
for which Henry had pawned the credit of the kingdom. Judge of
the indignation with which, in this year 1257, the king was received
by the parliament when he informed them that, without advising
with them, he had pledged their honour to repay the money ; that
his son Edmund was made a king at their expense ; and that the
pope had granted him the tenths and first-fruits of all benefices in
England. The nobility of the realm were indignant to think that
one man's folly should thus bring them to ruin. It was not so
much the amount, though that was very great, as the principle that
was at stake ; grant this, and another year might see them sold to
the Jews. The barons insisted that a council of twenty-four persons
should be nominated, half by the king and half by themselves, to
reform the state of the kingdom. In consequence, a council of
state was formed, with Simon de Montfort, earl of Leicester, the
king's brother-in-law, at the head, which named the chancellor,
justiciar, and great officers, and assumed all the functions of government. The king and the prince of Wales swore to this constitution,
called the Provisions of Oxford ; but the foreign favourites, who had
been enriched by Henry's lavishness, refused, and seceded to France.

Matters remained in this uneasy state for about a year, when, in 1260, King Henry being on a visit to France, in which he sold Normandy to the French, the prince of Wales began to hire mercenaries ; De Montfort quarrelled with the other lords, and a civil war broke out. In 1261 the king repudiated the new constitution, seized the Tower, and held it with troops against the country. From the Tower next year he went to France, and on his return swore again to the Provisions of Oxford, but brought back his foreign relations, who were particularly disagreeable to the English, and in 1263 provoked another outbreak. The barons consented to an arbitration ; the king of France was to decide, and he decided that the Provisions of Oxford should be abolished, but that an amnesty should be declared, and that the people should preserve their ancient liberties. This very fair decision offended both sides, and directly after war broke out in earnest. On May 13, 1264, at the battle of Lewes the king and the prince were taken prisoners, and De Montfort became virtually the ruler in the name of Henry. The pope excommunicated the barons and all who adhered to the Provisions ; and this is the triumphant moment when De Montfort assembled the parliament on its present basis—two knights from every county, two burgesses from every city and borough. The tide of fortune soon turned. This same year De Montfort fell at the battle of Evesham. But his great work did not perish. The system he had introduced was found too effective and too strong to be dispensed with. He himself, although a foreigner, was looked on as a popular martyr ; although excommunicated, he was canonised by the national affection ; and his tomb was visited by the pious country people for ages as the scene of wonderful miraculous cures. It is remarkable that the very barons, who from their dislike to De Montfort had restored Henry to the crown, forced upon him when victorious the most important of the Provisions of Oxford. The long reign of Henry is remarkable for the fact that during its convulsions Magna Carta was suffered to last untouched, nay was confirmed by several special confirmations extorted from the king in consideration of the subsidies that he could not dispense with. The principle was firmly established that money should not be had without consent of parliament ; and parliament was founded on a reasonable principle, a lasting basis.

The reign of Edward I. saw these principles strengthened by constant trial. This king, like his father, was an extravagant prince ; unlike him, he was a faithful and honourable man. He was a great legislator, but his chief acts in that capacity do not fall within the range of our subject. He wanted, however, to reign despotically, and the country not only would not let him, but compelled him to confirm Magna Carta, with the additional clauses that no taxes whatever should be taken without consent of the realm, save the ancient aids and prisage; tallages are abolished, and the toll upon wool, which had formerly been exacted by prerogative, was released. This great confirmation—a second and more effective Magna Carta—was granted in the 25th of Edward I., 1297. It was obtained in the usual way: the king was waging war abroad, the people were oppressed with taxation at home; the barons met together and refused to serve in the war or to grant any money for it. Edward was forced to give way. The names of these great liberators are: Roger Bigod, earl of Norfolk; Humphrey Bohun, earl of Essex; and Robert Winchelsey, archbishop of Canterbury. From this moment English liberty may be considered achieved.[1]

The weak reign of Edward II. gave it time to grow; the civil war weakening the royal authority without being waged at all for purposes of liberation. Liberty profited by the quarrels of those who united might have oppressed her.

The reign of Edward III. established three great principles by bringing them into actual usage: 1. That it was illegal to raise money without consent of the nation; 2. That both lords and commons should agree before an act should become law; 3. The commons established their right of inquiring into public abuses and impeaching public counsellors. All this was done quietly, without bloodshed or an appeal to popular violence. It is impossible now to go into detail on these particulars: the brunt of the battle was already over when the country was strong enough and united enough to enter on such an issue; but those who wish to see how it was done must go to their books to find it. It is not a constitutional history, but the several steps towards liberty, that I proposed to trace in this lecture. I have done enough when we have seen the purse strings in the hands of the representatives of the people.

And now let us in conclusion ask our question again, how was English liberty won? It was not won all at once; it was not a paper constitution written out at the will of a liberal sovereign, or extorted from a needy one according to the will and pleasure of a school of theorists. It was the growth of two hundred and thirty years of labour and sorrow; it was not designed by any one master mind; it is in its best aspect a bundle of expedients devised by their authors to meet cases which they never did meet, but which in the process of time were found to answer purposes for which they were never designed. It is a work of very fallible men, a result brought out of weakness by the strength of the Wise Ruler, King

[1] *Select Charters*, p. 494.

of kings. We are proud of it, and rightly : no other nation in the world has its like to compare with it. We may be prouder still when we see how our fathers won it. There was no foreign intervention here : no foreign liberator fought our battles. The thought of invasion had and has, at any moment of our history, the effect of uniting every contending element in the realm in defence. It was not done by secret conspiracy. There is not one such to record, effectual or ineffectual, in the period I have spoken of to-night ; nor if you search our history through will you find such contrivances successful either for or against freedom. Conspiring is not an English characteristic, and we may be thankful that tyranny has never forced us to learn it. It was not won by any one man's ambition, making his countrymen believe him a liberator while on the way to make a tyrant ; step by step, line by line, it was written by men who had no personal ambition, but abundant patriotic honour and moderation. Their works abide, while the flimsy edifices of men who have had but their own aggrandisement at heart perish. It was not won by one class at the expense or to the loss of another ; the nobles and the church won it, but not for themselves only : their cause was the people's cause, and by them the people was freed. It was not won by rebellion or cemented by perjury ; it was a gradual limitation of oppression and oppressive power that was indeed in itself a usurpation, but was a discipline needed to bring strength out of weakness ; and as it was won in moderation, and unselfishly and truly, it was stained by no great crimes or excesses. The men who earned it were not likely to sully it with disgrace ; the people for whom it was earned were gradually trained for it before it came. There was nothing in the full growth of it to turn a people from despair to extravagant excesses. We thank God that it was so ; we hope and pray that as it was won and balanced, so it may be maintained, confirmed, and extended. By the light that it gives us we can read and grieve over the abortive efforts of foreign races to win what was won for us. We cannot have much hope of freedom forced upon an unwilling people, undisciplined, unprepared to receive it. We cannot hope for lasting freedom founded upon personal ambition, maintained by perjury and cruelty. We can grieve over the oppressed, but there are worse things even than oppression, things more precious even than liberty—truth and honour and honesty. By these our rights were won : when these are lost, we are slaves indeed.

> Love thou thy land, with love far-brought
> From out the storied Past, and used
> Within the Present, but transfused
> Through future time by power of thought.

True love turned round on fixèd poles,
  Love, that endures not sordid ends,
  For English natures, freemen, friends,
Thy brothers and immortal souls.

This is the land that freemen till,
  That sober-suited Freedom chose,
  The land where girt with friends or foes
A man may speak the thing he will;

A land of settled government,
  A land of just and old renown,
  Where Freedom slowly broadens down
From precedent to precedent:

Where faction seldom gathers head,
  But by degrees to fullness wrought,
  The strength of some diffusive thought
Hath time and space to work and spread.

               We are a people yet.
Though all men else their nobler dreams forget,
Confused by brainless mobs and lawless Powers;
Thank Him who isled us here and roughly set
His Briton in blown seas and storming showers,
We have a voice with which to pay the debt
Of boundless love and reverence and regret
To those great men who fought and kept it ours.

[*See Stubbs, 'Introductions to the Rolls Series,' ed. by A. Hassall;
Round, 'The Commune of London, and other Essays'; McKechnie, 'The
History of Magna Carta.'*]

XXI

THE BEGINNINGS OF THE FOREIGN POLICY
OF ENGLAND IN THE MIDDLE AGES

I FEAR that I have been too ambitious in my choice of a subject for the present lecture, and that I should have done better if I had taken a more confined period than ten centuries to discuss in an hour's desultory talk. I fear that it will be impossible for me to give more than a meagre outline of a great history, one too that is not often looked into, and stands all the more therefore in need of detail. But, as we have chosen as we have, I will try to point out the most striking points of the subject in hand, and hope that I may excite a curiosity concerning them that will not be satisfied to-night, but may lead you on to read and think for yourselves.

I have spoken of history as the memory of nations. I should like to find out where is the conscience of nations. Coleridge, in one of his most brilliant aphorisms, describes conscience as the court of equity established by God in man: at this rate the conscience of the nation ought (by simple conversion) to be found in the high court of chancery. But this, of course, refers only to the internal conduct of affairs—domestic law; and some perhaps may think that the parallel holds in the case of abuse as well as of use; for some consciences are as long and elastic as chancery suits. Perhaps the international conscience should be found in the Foreign Office—perhaps, and too likely, there is no such thing; indeed, writers on international law, starting with the principle that there should be between nation and nation the same conscientious and equitable dealing that there is between man and man in a well-ordered commonwealth, are obliged to confess that there is no such perfect standard, no such perfect code in existence between nations as the duty towards your neighbour is between a man and his fellow-men. However much we could wish it to be otherwise, we cannot in common sense expect otherwise. We cannot expect one nation to treat another as it should itself be treated in return, if it is perfectly certain that such treatment, such reciprocity, is a Utopian expectation. The expediency of the moment must be the rule in very many transactions ; but I hope you will agree with me that it should not be so in all. I think that treaties should be as sacred as the word of private honour ; that the goodness or badness of a cause should determine us as a nation as to which side our help or sympathy should be given ; that we should not look at foreign questions only from the point of view that examines which side will be the stronger friend to ourselves ; that the best of all good causes, call it what you will, liberty, civilisation, constitutional government, or what not, is not worth winning if it is to be purchased by lying words, broken treaties, bloody *coups d'état*, assassinations, conspiracies, and judicial or extra-judicial murders.

I could wish that, in looking through the history of the period that we have chosen for to-night, we could reasonably hope to see in it a proof that England, whatever share she has taken in former times in foreign politics, has always been on the right side. I wish, I say, that we could reasonably hope to find it so. But as there are two sides to every question, and as the justice or injustice of a cause is seldom apparent at the outset of the quarrel—as there are many, nay most, quarrels of which all that we can affirm is that both sides are in the wrong ; and, further, as there are many quarrels as to which it will never be seen till Doomsday which was the right side and which the wrong—we will not carry our patriotic ardour to any such extreme. We will content ourselves if we find that the foreign conduct of England has been such as to advance the cause of Christianity, civilisation, rational order, and liberty where her influence has extended, and, secondly, such that we can confidently say of our fathers that in the long run they supported the right cause in the right way, and even when they were fighting on the wrong side fought in good faith and truth and honour and honesty.

It will be convenient, for reasons which will appear as we proceed, to divide the period of our investigation into two parts—the first from the beginning of the middle ages to the year 1066, which may be called the Anglo-Saxon period ; and the second from 1066 to about 1500, when the middle ages are generally considered to end. The Anglo-Saxon period will furnish us with very considerable matter of interest as to foreign nations and affairs under the heads of—1. Ecclesiastical matters ; 2. Royal and noble connections ; and 3. Political alliances. You will remark that I have not mentioned military affairs : during the whole time comprised in our first period England was free from foreign wars. It was, in fact, a period of defence against Scandinavian invasion and internal disruption. Neither the wars with the Danes, nor the constant quarrels first among the princes of the Heptarchy and afterwards with the Welsh and Scotch, have anything to do directly with the general politics of Europe.

First, then, of ecclesiastical matters. I will remind you, for the sake of starting clearly as to chronology, that the conversion of the Anglo-Saxons began in 597, and that the church establishment was finally settled on its present basis about 680 under Archbishop Theodore. It is most pleasing to find that our forefathers had no sooner organised the church in their own country than they began to turn their attention to foreign missions. Europe was still for the most part unconverted; in France, Christianity was so curiously mixed up with statecraft that a great portion of the true spirit of it evaporated. The bishops and clergy were ambitious, venal, and immoral: the state of Italy was little better; that of Spain was still worse, for there even the form of sound doctrine was lost, and the Arian heretics had it all their own way. In Germany, heathenism practically prevailed almost everywhere: there were a few solitary churches and abbeys, but the whole of the north and centre of that vast country was as heathen as it had been in the time of Cæsar. The Anglo-Saxons saw in this last country the field for their religious labours. In the first place, the people were their kinsmen; they worshipped the same gods as those within a century they and their fathers had renounced. They had themselves not been so long away from the Fatherland as our American relations have been away rom England—only 250 years at the most; and during those years the language of the two countries, not being refined or fixed from time to time by writers of classical authority, had developed its powers under similar circumstances; there is no reason to doubt that Anglo-Saxon and German were at this period, say about 700, mutually intelligible. The Anglo-Saxon apostles did not need a miraculous gift of tongues to start them on their work. The first country to which missionaries were sent was Friesland, a country answering very much to the modern Holland. St. Wilfrid, archbishop of York, was in 678 turned out of his see, and appealed to the pope for restitution. On his way to Rome he was driven by contrary winds to Friesland; there, says Bede, he was honourably received by that barbarous people and their king, to whom he preached Christ and instructed many thousands of them in the way of salvation. He stayed only a short time, and his labours, such as they were, only paved the way for others. Egberht, afterwards the reformer of Iona, then organised a mission to Friesland, and himself set out at the head; he was, however, prevented by contrary winds from landing, and being warned, as it was said, in a vision that his work lay in another direction, withdrew from the undertaking; he sent however one of his companions, Wictberht, who preached for two years without effect to King Radbod and then returned to his monastery. Wilfrid now took up the cause again : in 693 he consecrated St. Swidberht as bishop for Friesland, and at the same time Egberht sent out a new mission under Wilbrord, who in 696 was consecrated bishop of Utrecht at Rome, and who was supported by the authority of Pepin, the duke of the Franks, who had recently subjugated King Radbod. Swidberht and Wilbrord together completed the conversion of the Frisians, and now extended their labours into North Germany among the Old Saxons. Swidberht laboured among the former ; the other mission was conducted by the two Hewalds, the white and the black, who both suffered martyrdom and were burned at Cologne. Wilbrord continued his labours until the year of his death, about 740. Long before this, however, Wessex had sent out the famous Winfrid or Boniface, the apostle of the Germans. As early as 716 he had joined the Friesland mission, and in 723 he was consecrated at Rome as a missionary bishop. He became archbishop of Mainz about 738. He did a very great work both as a reformer in the degraded Frankish church and as a missionary to the heathen ; in his old age, when he had settled the German church, he started again as a missionary and died the death of a martyr in Friesland in 755. He founded very many episcopal sees, in which he placed Englishmen as bishops. Lullus, his successor, was a scholar of Malmesbury ; Willibald, the first bishop of Eichstadt, was a Ripon man. Burkhard of Wurtzburg was a Wessex man ; and there were many others.

I have stated this matter at length as it is sufficient to show that during this age the church of England was the light of the Western world. To the present day these names are great names in Germany : at Mainz the successors of Boniface became primates and arch-chancellors of Germany ; at Munich you see a church, one of the finest in the world, ornamented with fresco pictures of his life, and on the bridge of Wurtzburg you see the statue of SS. Kilian and Burkhard, both our countrymen. Charlemagne in consolidating his great empire sought the aid of English ministers ; the great Alcuin, the light of the eighth century, was an Englishman of York ; he carried the learning and elegance of the islanders into the court of the Frank emperor. It was from England that Charlemagne sought aid in his controversy with the Eastern church about image worship, and English councillors were called into the famous council of Frankfort, at which he repudiated that practice. And here for a time the missionary effort ceased, for the Danish invasions very soon gave the church employment enough at home ; the Danes in England were converted by King Alfred, and amalgamated with the English by his successors, but as soon as this was completed the work began again. Sweden was converted 950–1000 by St. Siegfried, a priest of York, Norway by English priests under Canute 1016–1035, Iceland in the same century. Thus the whole of the north-west and centre of Europe owes its Christianity to English missions. The missionary spirit was not quenched by the Normans; down to the reign of Edward III. there are notices of missions to India and Ethiopia which are of the highest interest but unfortunately exceedingly obscure. If we like to descend still lower, we find the germ of the German Reformation sown by Wicliffe; and lest we should omit the consideration that the good influence exercised by our countrymen has not been unalloyed, we may remember that the German infidelities and unbeliefs of which we now hear so much are lineally traceable to those of David Hume, who happily for us was a Scotchman.

We will turn now to the enumeration of the foreign alliances in marriage made by our sovereigns, and these may be quickly dismissed. The wonder of them is that when our kings were among the smaller potentates of Europe and harassed with constant invasions and rebellions, they should have stood so high in esteem as to have intermarried frequently with the highest ruling houses. Ethelwulf, the second king, married into the family of Charles the Bald; one daughter of Alfred married Baldwin II., count of Flanders; of Edward the Elder's daughters, one married Hugh, count of Paris; another, Otto, king of Germany, afterwards emperor; another, a prince of Aquitaine; another, Charles the Simple, king of France. Edward the Confessor was brought up in Hungary: two of his nephews are said to have married princesses of that country and nieces of the emperor. Canute's family formed not inferior alliances: one of his daughters married the emperor Henry III. The house of Godwin also strengthened itself by German alliances: Tostig married a daughter of the count of Flanders; and Gytha, daughter of Harold, married Wladimir, son of Usewold, tsar of Muscovy. You will have inferred from these two classes of facts that it was with Germany that political affinity chiefly existed. Egberht was brought up in the court of Charlemagne, and continued a faithful ally of that monarch's house all his life; Ethelwulf the same. Louis d'Outremer, son of Charles the Simple, was brought up at the court of Athelstan, and was conducted to his kingdom by Odo, afterwards archbishop of Canterbury. Later on, towards the Conquest, a German alliance seems to have been courted by the national party. German and Lorraine prelates filled a great many of the episcopal sees at the time of the Conquest. Edward the Confessor took up arms for the only time in his life, and set himself at the head of his fleet to support the Emperor Henry III. against the count of Flanders. His ambassador, Aldred, resided a year at Cologne as minister to the same monarch. Nor was the connection repudiated when the English were in trouble.

The connection of England with the East was less, of course, during this period. Yet King Alfred sent an annual mission to India during his prosperity, and considerable knowledge of eastern countries was kept up by means of pilgrimages; for the English, both for good and evil, were great goers on pilgrimage even down to the Reformation. Archbishop Aldred just before the Conquest went to Jerusalem; innumerable nobles and persons of inferior rank went to Rome—in fact, that pilgrimage seems to have been a part of the grand tour. Some few went to Constantinople, where their countrymen emigrated in great numbers at the Conquest and took service in the Varangian Guard.

To these notices I ought to add that there are a few signs of a tolerably brisk commercial intercourse with Germany. A corporation of German traders was settled in England in 1018, for King Ethelred, who died in that year, secured by law to the natives of the countries under the rule of the emperor the same rights when they entered English ports as those that the native English possessed, in return for which they were bound to make a donation at Christmas and Easter of two pieces of grey and one of brown cloth, ten pounds of pepper, five pairs of men's gloves, and two barrels of vinegar. These enactments probably laid the foundation of that corporation of German merchants called afterwards the Hanseatic Steelyard in London, which ceased to exist only a few years ago. So much for our first period. I am conscious that we have run very cursorily over it, but I do not know that we have omitted any point of importance. Our second period requires a few introductory remarks as to the general state of Europe.

The feudal system had grown up and, if we may use the term, run to seed in the dominions of Charlemagne, which comprised nearly the whole of then civilised Europe. The system was now nearly three hundred years old, and had wrought in France and Germany its most injurious effects. You may remember the two especial dangers against which the prudence of William the Conqueror guarded when he introduced it into England: first, that which arose from the vassals of the great nobles being bound to fealty not to the lord paramount but only to their immediate superior, by which means a great noble choosing to rebel could carry with him all his vassals against his suzerain; and secondly, the danger which arose from the entrusting of large contiguous provinces to one noble. William guarded against this by giving to his largest feudal tenants holdings in different counties, so that it was never even attempted in England to elevate earldoms into independent principalities. Well, the two evils that he thus guarded against had prevailed to a very great extent in all the countries that had constituted the empire of Charlemagne. In France, for instance, the dukes of Normandy and Brittany and Aquitaine, and the counts of much smaller provinces, were independent of the crown to all intents and purposes as soon as they had received investiture, and so far as the king was not able by physical force to reduce them to obedience. And more especially was this the case in Normandy and Brittany, in which countries the native inhabitants were of a different stock from the French-Gallic people, and were rather hostile to them than otherwise. Still more was this the case in Germany. There the princes of the several districts were in many instances sprung from the blood of the old royal races that Charlemagne had conquered : the races of inhabitants were different and very far divergent branches of the Teutonic stock ; and the duchies, although nominally fiefs held under the emperor, were almost if not quite as independent as they are at the present day under the title of kingdoms. Both in France and Germany the domains belonging to the suzerain were small. Before the Caroling family ceased to be called the kings of France, their dominions had shrunk to a very small compass about the city of Laon. The family called from Hugh Capet, which succeeded the Carolingians, were richer as counts of Paris and dukes of France than they were as kings. For two hundred years and more the struggle between the royal race and the great vassals continued, but at length, partly by escheats and partly by well-adjusted marriages, the royal house gathered together all the great fiefs into itself, and the French kingdom became one of the great powers of Europe. This was about the thirteenth century. Before that time, before the age of St. Louis, many of the vassals possessed more territory than the crown, and especially the English possessions in France gave to our Plantagenet kings a power equal to the native monarch on his own soil.

In Germany matters turned out differently. There the form of the empire and its claims over Italy and the large district that lay between the then France and Germany, called Lorraine and Burgundy, were kept up ; but the empire was an elective empire, and although an elective monarchy always has a tendency to become hereditary, it so fell out that not one of the great houses to which the great trust was confided turned out to be long-lived, and at the termination of each elective dynasty a disputed and long-contested election took place. Now, under such circumstances, it was exceedingly difficult for any real German unity to exist. A weak emperor was pretty sure to fall under the influence of the pope ; a strong one was sure to have difficulties in his path constantly arising from the insubordination of the princes, his equals, who had elected him as their superior, but were not at all inclined to let him keep them in order. Then, again, the emperor's rights in Italy were always at variance with what the pope assumed to be his rights : strong emperors claimed and exercised the power of nominating the popes ; but, on the other hand, strong popes claimed, and in some cases exercised, the power of nominating the emperor. In Germany an elected monarch until he was crowned by the pope was known as king of the Romans ; and the emperors in return claimed the right of at least vetoing the election of the pope.

Now, this state of things, the contest between pope and emperor, or, as it was called in Italy, between Guelf and Ghibelline, lasted during the whole of our period, at the termination of which the house of Austria managed to make the empire completely hereditary and put an end to the Guelf and Ghibelline controversy by giving entire support to the pope against all enemies spiritual and temporal ; but during the space of about five hundred years there was a continual contest going on, a sort of triangular duel between the emperor, the pope, and the princes. You must not conceive of an emperor as of the fashion of these days : in those times there was but one in the West and one in the East of Europe, the successor of Constantine at Rome or in Germany, and the successor of Constantine at Constantinople. Nor were they merely as now the equals of kings, or differing from them only as despotic from constitutional sovereigns. An emperor was a great deal greater man than a king, and his power was of a very much more constitutional character and origin. Kings and great prelates were proud to be his ministers, and although he might be both poorer and of lower descent than many of his vassals, still his court was the first in the civilised world, and his ambassadors had precedence of all other potentates' ambassadors. He was *Imperator Cæsar semper Augustus*, as Julius and Augustus had been ; and yet he was very often only a very small proprietor in point of demesne.

To make the contrast greater between France and Germany at this period, we may add that while a good king of France was a very rare exception to the general rule, a bad emperor was as rare in German history. Whether it was that the elective system was a check upon tyranny and open vice, or that the German sovereigns represented really the better tendencies of their race, and the French the worst of theirs, I cannot say, but the result is the same. The emperors were generally righteous and honourable men ; the French kings, with the exception of St. Louis, were quite the reverse.

Germany was then divided into a great number of principalities, some of them spiritual and the great majority temporal; and of these princes, seven had by the time our period opens got the power of electing the emperor into their own hands, and were called electors, three archbishops, Mainz, Cologne, and Trier, and four imperial princes, the duke of Saxony, the margrave of Brandenburg, the count palatine of the Rhine, and the king of Bohemia. It is obvious that if one of the temporal electors chose to vote for himself, he might by the aid of the ecclesiastical electors carry the day, and so it frequently happened; in other cases, the temporal electors being equally divided, the election was entirely in the hands of the three archbishops. This fact, which might at first sight seem to give the pope a chance of coming in as umpire, had the contrary effect, as there was always in the German church and nation a strong dislike to the interference of the Italian potentate in their affairs.

The other countries of Europe may be briefly dismissed. The northern states, Sweden, Norway, and Denmark, had little to do with the general politics of Europe. Spain and Portugal were split up into little kingdoms, of no weight either singly or collectively. The south of Spain was for the most part Mahometan. Hungary was employed in Turkish and barbarian struggles. Italy, though it has a history most interesting in itself, both in its northern republics and in its southern politics, only comes across our line of vision as it is connected now and then with France, Germany, and later with Spain. It will thus be seen that there was room for a great and abiding influence in European politics, a place that neither the emperor nor the king of France could quite fill. Often enough that place was unfilled. Sometimes the king of England filled it, and at all times his alliance and influence were of importance enough to be an object of earnest desire in both France and Germany. I will, if you please, shortly detail first the connection of England with France, and then go on to the less known and more interesting branch of the subject, the early connection of England and Germany.

It is almost a misapprehension to speak of a connection between England and France under the early Norman and Plantagenet kings, for it was simply that the kings of England had also large possessions on the Continent. There was no consolidation of the nations, no attempt to bring them under the same laws and institutions. This portion of our history occupies so great a part in ordinary books of education that I shall barely skim over it. William the Conqueror and his two successors owned Normandy; Henry II. added to it Anjou, and, in right of his wife, Aquitaine, the greater part of the south of France. John lost Normandy and a good deal besides. Henry III. scarcely kept what his father left him. Edward III. reconquered that and a good deal more, strangely basing his right to the French crown on his mother's descent. Henry V. conquered nearly the whole kingdom. All was lost under Henry VI. Thus the state of things between the two neighbouring princes was a chronic state of war from 1066 to 1453, when Bordeaux, the last English possession in the south, was taken, or, if you like, until 1558, when Calais fell to the French. The effect of these French wars on the English was twofold : evil, in that they caused a constant drain of men and treasure ; good, inasmuch as every strait to which the royal power was reduced was an opportunity for the assertion of old liberties. Viewed so, our connection with France was a remote cause of good ; in all other respects it was an unmitigated evil. During this long period the English did not become Frenchified, nor did the Anglo-French provinces, however much they might be attached to the persons of particular sovereigns, become in any way Anglicised. You may trace in the architecture of their churches a resemblance to that of ours, but there is none in their institutions or laws, and no advance towards anything like a resemblance in national character or unity in national feeling. Very few French families took root in England ; no English ones took root in France : English bishops were only in very rare cases introduced into French sees ; French bishops were never translated into English ones. In case of a schism in the papacy, England recognised one pope, and France another, but it by no means followed that the same pope was recognised in England and in the English provinces in France.

Under these circumstances of chronic hostility we can hardly expect that any good influence should be exercised by England in the internal politics of France, and yet the evil influence that was from time to time apparent was that of the king rather than that of the people. Occasionally the king of England backed a rebellious vassal against the king, but if he did it was as often as not represented as a support of his own right against the intruding monarch at Paris, for, as you all know, from Edward III. to George III. our kings called themselves kings of France as well as of England. France, on the other hand, was almost always in the closest alliance with Scotland, and that kingdom was a thorn in the side of English greatness for 500 years. Whatever injury England did to France was repaid by way of Scotland, which had formerly borne to the crown of England a semi-feudal relation not unlike that by which the English kings held their continental possessions of the French crown. Into these disputes, which had very little to do with Europe generally, I shall not go.

We will now turn to Germany. The first family which maintained any lengthened hold on the imperial crown was the house of Saxony, which, founded by Henry the Fowler in 919, came to an end in Otto III. in 1002 ; he was succeeded by his cousin Henry II. from 1002 to 1024, and the whole family became extinct. I have already mentioned the marriage of Otto I. with a sister of Athelstan, and the alliance which continued between our sovereigns and the Franconian emperors.   The Franconian family under Conrad the Salic, Henry III., IV., and V., were also closely connected with England.   Canute went to Rome to the coronation of Conrad the Salic in 1026.   Henry III. married Canute's daughter Gunhilda ; Henry V. married Maud, the daughter of our Henry I., so well known as the Empress Maud.   The last two of these emperors were engaged in a lifelong and internecine quarrel with the popes ; but in spite of the connection between the two countries—or, rather, in consequence of a cessation of it in the reigns of the two Williams—the English did not support the imperialist antipope.   William the Conqueror had got a papal commission to conquer England, and his minister, Lanfranc, was an Italian.   William Rufus had no religious instincts, and swayed by intense hatred towards Anselm, who was a thorough supporter of the Italian pope, somehow or other never recognised the German one.   In the subsequent quarrels of this nature we generally find England and Germany pulling together.   The reign of Stephen was an eventful one at home, but an insignificant one in Europe. During it the imperial power was first swayed by Lothaire II. (1125–1138), and after him by Conrad III., the founder of the house of Hohenstaufen.   Lothaire has no connection with English history; he was not the founder of a dynasty ; but his daughter Gertrude was the mother of Henry the Lion, duke of Saxony and Bavaria, who married a daughter of Henry II., and was the ancestor of the house of Hanover.   Through Henry the Lion almost every reigning house in Europe traces its descent to Alfred the Great. Lothaire, who was a weak and poor prince, had during his reign the escheats of some important fiefs, which he bestowed on his son-in-law, thus raising up a powerful opposition to the house of Hohenstaufen, which had nearly defeated his election and was anxiously looking for his succession.   The Saxon-Bavarian or Guelfic house naturally took the opposition side in religious politics to their rivals, and it is from them that the papal party in Germany and Italy had the name of Guelfs.   After Lothaire's death the Hohenstaufens did come in, and tried to recover the fiefs that came to Henry the Lion.   He was expelled from his dominions and sought a refuge with his father-in-law, Henry II., who assisted him also with men and money. There is something rather striking in this position of affairs. Henry II. in England, and Frederick Barbarossa in Germany and Italy, were contending against the aggressive power of the papacy; Frederick had supported four antipopes in succession, while the strength of the papal party was in Henry the Lion, Henry's son-in-law. This seems to have had the effect of keeping our king straight; he clung to the pope whom his son-in-law supported and not to the one to whom similarity of position and principles with Barbarossa might have inclined him. In 1181 the schism ended, and a few years later the second crusade was preached, to which both Henry and Frederick bound themselves. Henry, however, never attempted to keep his vow, and Frederick, one of the noblest heroes of the age, started at the head of his forces, but perished in the river Calicadnus in Cilicia in 1190. Henry died in 1189. Richard Cœur de Lion succeeded to the crown and obligations of Henry II., and immediately went on crusade. Henry VI., the successor to Frederick Barbarossa, thought it best to stay at home, and left the command of the imperial forces in Syria to Leopold, duke of Austria. We all know how Richard and Leopold quarrelled at Acre; how Leopold took him prisoner on his return and delivered him up to the emperor, who was glad enough to be able to secure the brother-in-law of Henry the Lion in a German prison. We are accustomed to feel a good deal of righteous indignation at this, but it is impossible to overlook the fact that the hardship was provoked in some measure by the conduct of Richard, who seems to have been one of the worst specimens of his unhappy and vicious family. Leopold was an estimable prince in other respects. He was not connected at all with the present house of Austria, and is chiefly remembered as performing an unparalleled surgical operation on his own foot. Henry VI. had probably interests both in Germany and Sicily, to which his wife had a claim, that ran very counter to Richard's. It is said that the ransom of Richard was applied to the building of the walls of Vienna. Henry VI. died in 1197, and Richard I. in 1199. The heir of the house of Hohenstaufen was a child, and the Brunswick Guelfic interest was strong enough to raise Otto, the son of Henry the Lion, grandson of our Henry II. and nephew of King John, to the imperial crown. Now again matters were complicated. Otto was in close alliance with his uncle John; Otto was the pope's candidate; John was the pope's enemy. Philip Augustus, the king of France, against whom the two were allied, was also an excommunicated man. However, to make matters simpler, the pope in 1211 turned round on Otto and set up the heir of Hohenstaufen as emperor; two years after he reduced John to resign the crown of England and accept it again as a papal fief. This, however, did not break the alliance between England and the empire, and it was not until after the battle of Bouvines, in which the French king defeated the united forces of England and Germany, in 1214, that the pope and his party decidedly got the upper hand.

In 1216 John died, and his son Henry III. became king: Frederick II. succeeded quietly to the empire on the death of Otto. This Frederick, the 'wonder of the world' as his contemporaries called him, is very famous for his genius and misfortunes. One of his many wives was an English princess, a daughter of John and sister of Henry III. (1235). His name occurs very frequently in the histories of England of the time, but he had difficulties at home all his life that prevented him from rendering any aid to his brother-in-law, and Henry III. was not a man to help anybody. Indeed, the part he took in continental politics was one of sub-serviency to the pope, and a great part of his debts were incurred in the support of the papal power against his own brother-in-law. On the death of Frederick in 1250 began the long interregnum which is sometimes looked on as the termination of the empire as established by Charlemagne. One of the competitors for the vacant crown was Richard, earl of Cornwall, brother of our King Henry III., and the richest prince of the age, as his brother was the poorest. Richard was elected in 1256, and shortly afterwards was crowned king of the Romans.

Henry, although quite unable to manage his own dominions, was very anxious to fill a great place in Europe. He accepted the kingdom of Sicily, part of the spoils of the Hohenstaufen, in 1257, for his second son, Edmund, and soon saw his brother on the high way to the empire. Richard, however, never was actually emperor. He spent a good deal of money in Germany, and granted charters to some of the Rhenish cities. He also brought German miners from the Harz to work his Cornish mines; but he did not find it pay to be a king without a kingdom. He returned to England in 1259 and lived at Berkhamsted in Herts till 1271, known and recognised still as the king of the Romans and king of Germany. Three years after his death the Germans elected the celebrated Rudolf of Hapsburg, the ancestor of the present Austrian house, as emperor, and one of his first measures was to seek an English alliance. In 1276 it was proposed that Hartmann, the second son of Rudolf, should marry Joanna, daughter of Edward I. of England. The young princess was to have a dowry of 10,000 marks; Hartmann was to present her with a nuptial gift of 2,000*l*. He was also to succeed to the imperial crown, and in the meantime to be elected king of Arles, in which character his dominions would lie very near the French possessions of Edward, and he might be a useful neighbour. Somehow or other the negotiations hung fire, and the marriage was delayed from time to time until it was finally broken off by the death of Hartmann, who was drowned in the Rhine in 1281. This catastrophe did not, however, prevent the friendship of Rudolf and Edward continuing. The diplomatic intercourse was very continuous and close as long as Rudolf lived. He died in 1292. His successor, Adolf of Nassau, was also a friend of England, at least for his own purposes. Edward I. hired him as an ally in his war with France, and Adolf spent the money in the purchase of Misnia and Thuringia. The transaction is not very creditable to either side. Edward was moreover called in to arbitrate between the Flemings, the emperor, and the king of France. In this he was very unsuccessful, and the French king, as usual, got the advantage. Adolf was assassinated in 1298 by Albert of Hapsburg, who succeeded him, and was murdered by his own nephew after a reign of ten years. Henry VII., who succeeded him, was the founder of the house of Luxemburg, a very great and noble prince, but his reign was spent in a struggle with Italy, in which country he was poisoned in the sacramental cup in 1313. His successor was Lewis IV. of Bavaria, who reigned from 1315 to 1347. Lewis was the heir of the policy and principles of the Hohenstaufen, and had to maintain a lifelong struggle with the papal party and the French in conjunction : the popes were now entirely under French influence, and even lived at Avignon from 1305 to 1367. These circumstances are enough to account for his being a close ally of England, and the connection was drawn still closer by Lewis's marrying the sister of Queen Philippa, wife of Edward III. The interests of England and Germany in Flanders were of course the same—a resistance to French aggression. Flanders also was conveniently near to the French frontier, and a standing point from which Edward could make his claims on the French crown heard and felt. In 1337 Lewis and Edward formed a very close alliance. Lewis had plenty of soldiers ; Edward had very good credit, which, however, was very soon exhausted. The emperor and the Fleming democratic party under Jacob van Artevelde were to lend very efficient assistance to the English king. The latter monarch went over to Flanders in 1338, and thence into Germany, where he tried hard to reconcile the opposing powers, but only succeeded in getting further and further into debt. At Coblentz, Lewis invested Edward with full powers as the vicar of the empire—a most important position if he could have made it good, as it would have enabled him to employ all the forces of Rhenish Germany on his side in his war with France.

Unfortunately the German princes did not like to be ordered about by a foreign monarch, and Edward got very little assistance from the empire. With the best of wills Lewis had enough to do at home, where he was kept in a constant ferment by the Austrian, Luxemburg, and papal parties. We always at this period find England and Germany recognising the same pope, and France and Scotland the other.

It was during this transaction that the English navy won its first victory at Sluys in 1341. Edward's pecuniary difficulties went on increasing; he pawned his crown jewels to German merchants, but his credit was still so good that money was never wanting for military purposes. In 1346 the pope set up a new emperor against Lewis—Charles, the son of the blind king John of Bohemia, who of course took the part of France against England. Both he and his father were present at the battle of Crécy on the French side. The father was killed, but the emperor-elect fled. Lewis died the next year. Charles IV. continued to be a tool of the pope all his life; his principal aim was to aggrandise his own family, and his politics accordingly came very little in contact with the English. He was, however, the father of the good Queen Anne of Bohemia, wife of our Richard II.; and his two sons, who were emperors after him, were closely allied with us. Sigismund, who reigned in Germany from 1413 to 1437, spent a long time in England in the year 1416. He was received with great pomp, but soon became unpopular, got into difficulties, and had to be smuggled away into France. He failed in the object of his mission to England, which was to engage the king in his plan of giving peace to the church and empire at the council of Constance, but he did conclude a treaty offensive and defensive with Henry V. He was faithful to his engagements, and the friendship between the two kings was ardently sincere. Sigismund was present at the treaty of Troyes, which ended for the time the war of Henry with France, and the king in his will characterised him as the most faithful defender of the church and faith, and left him a magnificent sword. The death of Henry V. did not put an end to the alliance; in 1427 Cardinal Beaufort led an army into Bohemia against the Hussites. Soon, however, the troubles of England and France, followed by the Wars of the Roses, kept the people at home; and the death of Sigismund in 1437, in whom the house of Luxemburg came to an end, prevented any assistance reaching us from that side. The Austrian family which followed was in its earlier years sufficiently occupied in keeping its own footing, and it was not until the accession of Charles V. that any great and active cordiality between England and Germany prevailed.

This brings us to the end of our period. I am afraid that you will think such a mere skeleton catalogue of names and dates in the highest degree uninteresting. The very brief notice that we can give to them is really the cause; they might *in extenso* give you some very curious and interesting details ; as it is, I can only use them as premisses to the conclusions towards which I hope to carry you. I have not, as you will see, made any mention of the crusades : both those earlier ones in which the English under Robert of Normandy, Richard I., and Edward I. made so great a figure ; nor the later ones under the Teutonic knights in Prussia and Poland, and under the Knights Hospitallers of Rhodes and Malta in the south. In both of these the English were among the foremost champions. Henry IV., when earl of Derby, fought several campaigns in Prussia, and the English Knights Hospitallers were so numerous as to constitute a separate langue or division of the order. But these were private adventures, and do not touch the main interest of our subject, to which I have felt bound to keep as close as possible. I might also have noticed the literary intercourse between England and the Continent, the connection of the universities and schools of learning, which seems at one time to have been very close ; but we must stick to politics, and that field of observation restricts itself to our relations with France and Germany. No great war was waged by England but in connection with those powers. The war of the Black Prince in Spain is the only exception that I remember, and that was in a measure a French war rather than an English one.

What conclusions do we draw from these facts ? The first is, I think, that there was, by a community of interest, sympathy, and race, a friendship between England and Germany throughout the middle ages which contrasts very strongly with the inbred hostility between England and France. The friendship was not owing only to the intimate relations of the princes, to royal marriages, and such-like. It was partly a political necessity, but it was a necessity that was gladly and heartily recognised by the people. This is proved by the fact that no dynasty of emperors was without its English alliance. Saxon, Franconian, Brunswick, Hohenstaufen, Bavarian, Luxemburg, Austrian, each, however in other respects they reversed one another's policy, sought among their first objects English support. And this they did quite irrespective of the actual amount of assistance that was got from England. The English people, who grumbled at foreigners in general, were very good friends with the Germans whether soldiers or merchants : they heartily sympathised also with the imperial as opposed to the papal policy. Henry III., the only English king who set himself in earnest against this instinct of his subjects, incurring most of his debts in supporting the pope against the Hohenstaufen, found nothing that made him so unpopular and compelled him to greater shifts than the fact that he was sacrificing the German friendship to the Roman.

I am anxious not to go into ecclesiastical matters, but I must observe that there was an independence in the German and English churches that did not exist in the French and Italian, that led them alike to resist the aggressive power of the papacy, if not in concert at least in sympathy. I think, however, that we must go deeper than common enmities to find the real secret of this sympathy. The German and English alike are non-aggressive nations : order and peace are and always have been in their eyes far before conquest: both are successful in colonisation, both are strongly patriotic, both full of independent zeal for freedom. Is it necessary to go further to find a key to the continuous hostility between the two and the French people ? It may be true that up to the time of the French Revolution there can hardly be said to have been a French people; but such as that people has shown itself since it struggled into visible existence, such was the spirit of its rulers and leaders from time immemorial—aggressive, unscrupulous, false.

I have referred before to the fact that the French kings were probably the very worst set of kings that ever disgraced the name ; and that among the German emperors there are very few that were actually bad, many that were very good, and some, like Frederick Barbarossa and Henry VII., who would have shed glory and honour on any race or country. But it was more than the personal character of the emperors that made their side the right one and the French the wrong one: it was the pressure of opinion, of balancing powers and able counsellors ; it was the constant state of defence in which the aggressive power of the French on the one hand and the papacy on the other kept them ; and these characteristics they shared, if not with the English kings, at least with the English people. The English looked on the right they had to hate the French as an article of faith. You will remember Lord Nelson's three rules of faith and duty : 1. To obey commands without asking the reason why ; 2. To look on anyone who spoke ill of the king as an enemy ; 3. To hate every Frenchman as the devil. That was certainly a strong point of practical belief through these ages. The miseries which England had endured first from the oppression of the Normans, whom they looked on as a French or Frenchified race, and after the Norman times from the French wars in which their children were sacrificed and their money wasted, produced an effect on us which lasts still. In some respects the friendship of that race was looked on as worse than their hostility. The marriages between the royal families of the two countries were proverbially unlucky. Henry III. owed his difficulties, or some of them, to his Provençal marriage; the she-wolf of France murdered Edward II.; Richard II. married a French princess, and was betrayed and murdered (though in this case superstition alone could trace a connection). Henry V. survived his French marriage only a couple of years. Henry VI. owed all his troubles to Margaret of Anjou. These things were not forgotten when Charles I. made his ill-starred match, and there is not a shadow of a doubt that it was to their French predilections and connections inherited with their Scottish blood that the Stuarts owed the loss of their throne.

On the other hand, probably no war was ever so popular in England as the one in which James I. engaged in support of the king of Bohemia, his son-in-law, and we know how cheerfully our fathers endured the taxation by which the English and German races were enabled to destroy the fabric of power raised by the first Napoleon. Still, as of old, England and Germany, whether represented by Prussia or Austria, were found fighting the battles of freedom, and still successful. God send that we never see another such war; but if we do, may we find still the old allies on the same side, with the same good cause, and we need never fear for the same result.

I have now to draw my remarks to a conclusion. I have not proved that England has always been on the right side in all her foreign wars, but I have put before you facts into which, if you will search for yourselves, you will find, I think, that for the most part it has been so. I am sure you will find that in every European perturbation our country has been on the side of order and freedom. I am sure you will find that, whatever have been the mistakes and sins of her statesmen and soldiers, the strong spirit of the nation and the main current of her policy—which could not flow if it were not sustained by the strong spirit of the nation—strong in endurance as well as action, has still been so. And I think this is a thing we may be proud of. And those aims have not been sought by evil means. Englishmen may point with pride, too, to the way they have kept their treaties and supported the cause they took up. I do not say without fear and without reproach, but with a manly fear of all that is dishonest and untrue, and in spite of every reproach that envy and hatred have dictated. Our sympathies are often engaged for aims the means towards which our national conscience cannot, dare not, approve. I suppose I need not go further for proof of this than to our neutrality in the Italian and American struggles (1859–1871). *Non tali auxilio nec defensoribus istis*, we say, in spite of every accusation of cold-heartedness and interested policy. May it be so always. Such purity is the great glory of a nation, far more than victorious armaments or perfectly symmetrical institutions. 'Righteousness exalteth a nation;' and the righteousness of a nation is in this—truth and justice, honour and faithfulness.

[*Stubbs, 'Introductions to the Rolls Series,' ed. by A. Hassall; Pollock and Maitland, 'The History of the English Law before the time of Edward I.'*]

INDEX

PRINTED BY
SPOTTISWOODE AND CO. LTD., NEW-STREET SQUARE
LONDON

Printed in Great Britain
by Amazon